Shaunessy Ashdown
Marilyn Clifford-Grein

CROSSOVER

The new edition

2

Ein Lehrwerk für berufliche Gymnasien

KLASSE 12/13

Cornelsen

Crossover 2 – The new edition wurde geplant und entwickelt von der Redaktion Moderne Fremdsprachen des Cornelsen Verlags, Berlin.

Verfasser/innen:	Shaunessy Ashdown, Berlin Marilyn Clifford-Grein, Stuttgart
Berater/innen:	Philipp Fehrenbach, Nürtingen Dorothee Gräter, Schwäbisch Gmünd Gabriele Holtermann, Ludwigsburg Petra Lehmann, Kehl
Kritische Durchsicht:	Regine Ziegler, Görlitz
Projektleitung:	Jim Austin
Redaktion:	Andreas Goebel
Redaktionelle Mitarbeit:	Lauren Chexal, Oliver Gascoigne, Stefanie Heimann, Leah Holroyd, Christine House, Steve Williams Fritz Preuss (Wörterverzeichnisse)
Bildredaktion:	Christiane Grosskopf, Gertha Maly
Layout und technische Umsetzung:	Yvonne Thron, Berlin
Umschlaggestaltung:	Klein & Halm Grafikdesign, Berlin
Illustrationen:	Thomas Maria Malangeri, Shaunessy Ashdown (S. 95, 154), Carlos Borrell (Karten), Oxford Designers & Illustrators (S. 48, 108, 123)

Erhältlich sind auch:

Workbook	ISBN 978-3-06-020484-7
Vocabulary Practice Book	ISBN 978-3-06-020501-1
Audio-CDs	ISBN 978-3-06-020485-4
Handreichungen zum Unterricht mit CD-ROM	ISBN 978-3-06-020486-1

www.cornelsen.de

1. Auflage, 1. Druck 2009

Alle Drucke dieser Auflage sind inhaltlich unverändert und können im Unterricht nebeneinander verwendet werden.

Druck: CS-Druck CornelsenStürtz, Berlin

ISBN 978-3-06-020483-0

Inhalt gedruckt auf säurefreiem Papier aus nachhaltiger Forstwirtschaft.

Vorwort

Crossover 2 – The new edition ist ein Lehrwerk für die Klassen 12 und 13 an beruflichen Gymnasien. Es bereitet auf alle Teile der mündlichen und schriftlichen Abiturprüfung vor und deckt die Themenbereiche der aktuellen Lehrpläne ab. Das Buch führt zu Stufe B2 des Europäischen Referenzrahmens, vertieft die Anforderungen dieser Stufe und führt teilweise zu Stufe C1.

Crossover 2 – The new edition entfaltet in sechs Themengruppen eine Bandbreite aktueller, relevanter und beruflicher Materialien, die es der Lehrkraft leicht machen, die Abiturvorbereitung interessant und motivierend zu gestalten, die Sprachfertigkeiten systematisch zu verbessern sowie den besonderen Auftrag des beruflichen Gymnasiums zu erfüllen.

Während die Textauswahl nach lehrplanbezogenen Kriterien erfolgte, wurde bei den Fragen der Schwerpunktsetzung und Textsortenvielfalt die Gelegenheit genutzt, auch ungewöhnliche Aspekte und überraschende Perspektiven auf die jeweiligen Themenbereiche einzubringen. So findet sich unter anderem in jedem Topic ein literarischer Text – ein Gedicht, eine Short Story, ein Romanausschnitt, ein Ausschnitt aus einem Drama oder ein Song.

Ein wichtiges Element in Crossover 2 ist die Abiturvorbereitung. Die erforderlichen Fähigkeiten, insbesondere die Schreibfertigkeit, werden auf neuartige und gründliche Weise aufgebaut. Schritt für Schritt und sehr anschaulich werden gute mit weniger gelungenen Antwortbeispielen verglichen oder mögliche Lösungen analysiert. Die vielen grafischen Darstellungen von Argumentationsmustern und Textinhalten wie Mind Maps, Flowcharts oder Ursache-Wirkungs-Diagrammen sind eine wertvolle Hilfe beim Erstellen von Antworten und Texten, da sie zeigen, wie man die inhaltliche Struktur in einer handlichen Vorlage bündeln und sich somit stärker auf die Sprache konzentrieren kann.

Die Abschnitte *World of Work*, die den Abschluss jedes der sechs Topics bilden, bieten die Gelegenheit, anhand eines längeren Textes die Fertigkeit der Mediation zu üben. Hier wird nicht bloß eine Zusammenfassung des Textinhalts auf Deutsch gefordert, sondern gleichzeitig ein methodisches Fundament für Mediationen gelegt.

Wichtig für die erfolgreiche Bearbeitung der Aufgaben ist der Anhang, auf den in der Randspalte verwiesen wird:
- Der Buchstabe **S** verweist auf den Teil **Study Skills**, der einen handlichen Leitfaden mit Lernhilfen und wichtigen Formulierungen enthält.
- Der Buchstabe **G** verweist auf die **Grammar Summary**, in der die wesentlichen Bereiche der Grammatik übersichtlich zusammengefasst sind.

Zum Nachschlagen stehen umfangreiche Wörterverzeichnisse zur Verfügung.
In der **Unit Word List** bietet die mittlere Spalte Gelegenheit zum Lernen englischer Umschreibungen und Synonyme.

Nicht zu vergessen: die hintere **Umschlagklappe**. Im Unterricht lässt sie sich für den mündlichen Gebrauch ausklappen, die eingeklappte Seite hilft bei den Hausaufgaben.

Und nun: Viel Erfolg!

Die Autoren und der Verlag

Inhalt

TOPIC 1 The Changing Patterns of Work and Consumption

BACKGROUND INFORMATION

The Consumer Society

consumer society *Konsumgesellschaft*
Industrial Revolution *Industrielle Revolution*
consumption patterns *Konsumgewohnheiten*
population *Bevölkerung*
rural area *ländliche Gegend*
possessions *Besitztümer*
technological change technischer Wandel
social pressure *gesellschaftlicher Druck*
purchase *Kauf*
item *Stück, Artikel*
luxury goods *Luxusartikel*
services *Dienstleistungen*
earn wages *Lohn verdienen*
basic needs *Grundbedürfnisse*
trade union *Gewerkschaft*
working conditions Arbeitsbedingungen
developed country *Entwicklungsland*
standard of living *Lebensstandard*
trade *Handel*

In the period before the Industrial Revolution consumption patterns were very different from those of today. The vast majority of the population lived in rural areas and their clothing and household possessions were extremely limited by today's standards. Clothes were made by household members or by local people from the village. Fashions, technological change and social pressure did not drive people to make new purchases. Major items like winter coats were expected to last a lifetime and were often passed on from one generation to the next. A small elite, of course, often bought luxury goods and services. The Industrial Revolution meant that workers moved to the cities to work in factories. They earned wages which they spent on their basic needs. With the help of trade unions, political reformers and humanitarian groups, wages and working conditions improved and so in the course of time the consumer society as we know it today came into being. In the developed countries of the world, the economy and therefore our standard of living depends on the constant trade of goods and services between organisations and individuals.

Changes in Consumption

basic essentials *lebenswichtige Güter*
non-essential *nicht lebensnotwendig*
upmarket *exklusiv*
leisure goods *Freizeitartikel*

Over the last 50 years consumption patterns have changed greatly. The percentage spent on basic essentials such as clothes, food and housing is far lower that that spent on non-essential items. In fact, a huge amount is spent on upmarket luxury goods, such as cars, and on leisure goods and services.

The Consumers of the Future

share *Anteil*
emerging market *Schwellenland*
benefit *Vorteil, Nutzen*

A growing share of the consumer class now lives in developing countries or emerging markets. China and India alone claim 20% of the global total. Emerging markets also have the greatest potential to increase the number of consumers. In China and India the number of consumers is only 16% of the population at present, whereas in Europe it is 89% – an indication that the number of consumers in emerging markets may grow enormously. A consumer society creates many benefits, and it would be unfair to think that the advantages gained by an earlier generation of consumers should not be shared by those who come later. Nonetheless, the industrial countries remain responsible for the consumption of the bulk of the world's resources as well as for the associated global environmental degradation.

industrial country *Industriestaat*
bulk *Gros, Großteil*
degradation *Verschlechterung*

Consumerism

Nowadays people have become very critical of consumerism – the purchasing and consuming of goods and materials in excess of basic needs. Retail shops in the high streets tempt people to spend money on products they believe will enhance them personally or give them a certain status. These products often have a short life and are quickly replaced. One of the main reasons why over-consumption is criticised is that the planet clearly can no longer sustain a further growth in consumption as this will inevitably lead to dwindling resources and extreme pollution.
There is an anti-consumerism movement but until this becomes a mass movement it will have little effect. As Gandhi said: 'There is enough on earth for everybody's needs but not for everybody's greed.'

consumerism *Konsumdenken*
purchase *kaufen*
retail shop *Einzelhandelsgeschäft*
over-consumption *übermäßiger Konsum*
sustain *aushalten, tragen*
growth *Zuwachs*
dwindling resources *schwindende Ressourcen*
pollution *Umweltverschmutzung*
greed *Gier*

Advertising

Advertising is a form of communication with potential customers to inform them about products and services. Mass production and mass consumption would not be possible without advertising. Many ads are designed to generate over-consumption using brand names, brand image and brand loyalty. Advertisements can contain factual information or just a persuasive message. Advertisements can be placed anywhere where the consumer can see them. Some of the more unusual places are: on the seat of shopping trolleys, on the sides of buses or on football shirts. In Great Britain the Advertising Standards Agency watches over advertising standards and deals with complaints about sexism, brutality, indecency and dishonesty.

advertising *Werbung*
customer *Kunde/Kundin*
mass production *Massenproduktion*
brand name *Markenname*
brand image *Markenimage*
brand loyalty *Markentreue*
persuasive message *überzeugende Botschaft*
advertising standards *Werbestandards*
complaint *Beschwerde*
indecency *Anstößigkeit*
dishonesty *Unaufrichtigkeit*

Globalisation, the Consumer and the Worker

Globalisation is a deeply controversial issue. It is a process of interaction and integration among the people, companies and governments of different nations, usually for the purpose of international trade. As a result of technological advances in the past few decades there have been great increases in cross-border trade. Proponents argue that it allows poor countries and their citizens to develop economically and raise their standard of living. Critics say that the creation of an international free market has benefited multinational corporations at the expense of local enterprises, local culture and common people.

globalisation *Globalisierung*
technological advance *technischer Fortschritt*
cross-border trade *grenzüberschreitender Handel*
proponent *Befürworter/in*
citizen *Bürger/in*
economic *wirtschaftlich*
multinational corporation *multinationales Unternehmen*
local enterprise *ortsansässiger Betrieb*

TEXT 1 Shoppers and Shopaholics

WARM-UP

CD 1 Track 2

S ► Practising Listening Skills (p. 188)

1 A radio programme interviewed young people in a shopping centre in Cardiff to get their opinion about the question "Are we turning into a nation of shopaholics?".

1. Listen to the speakers and write short notes about what the speakers think.
2. Listen again. Which of the speakers can you identify with?
3. Read the following text to find out what kind of shopper you are.

CD 1 Track 3

Shopping Away the Blues

by Carol Gioia and Amber Daniels

I just can't help myself, I'm a shopaholic. I just love shopping!

Failed an exam? No problem, go buy some new shoes and you'll feel better. Didn't get the job you interviewed for? Once again, I have the answer to your problems: go shopping for a cute shirt, and you'll forget all about that awful interview. The acquisition of a new item, be it clothing, shoes, accessories, even something for the kitchen, is thrilling. What is it about shopping? It's super-addictive, and it really does lift you up when you're feeling down. Just shop those blues away, and the whole world looks a better place.

But, of course, this doesn't work for everybody. My friend, for one, hates shopping. The crowds make him feel anxious, he starts to sweat profusely and would give his life to get out of the store. Maybe it's a girl thing. Something passed on from mother to daughter. Some of my fondest memories are of going shopping with my mom. Still today, when I spend time with my mom or my girlfriends it inevitably revolves around food or shopping. When I was in university, I remember my mother actually encouraging me to go and buy something nice for myself when she thought that I was feeling a little lonely. It was as if she was trying to say: well, I can't be there in person, but I can send you some money so you can go shopping. It's the next best thing. And honestly, it was!

As for my friend, he doesn't enjoy shopping for clothes and he hates crowds. However, he'll spend hours shopping for some new gadget at the nearest Future Shop. He had a rough year and wanted to treat himself to something nice, so he went and bought a new laptop. When you're feeling down, buy something nice for yourself that you've wanted for a long time and you'll be happy! At least for a little while.

Of course, shopping the blues away only provides temporary relief. It doesn't solve the issue that was making you unhappy in the first place. Shopping is a form of distraction, it gives us a feeling of fulfillment that makes us feel very good in general. And for however long it lasts, that's worth going shopping for. So go ahead, don't feel guilty.

Apart from those people who go shopping to get rid of the blues, there are other types of shoppers. Here they are:

Compulsive shoppers
These individuals have a need to go out at regular intervals and acquire the latest fads and styles. They often have two or more of everything at home, but will continue to add to their inventory with the latest colors and fashions. Shopping is way up

5 **acquisition** the act of buying sth
6 **thrilling** exciting and enjoyable
addictive becoming a strong habit
10 **profusely** a lot
13 **inevitably** certain to happen
20 **gadget** device, utensil
25 **temporary** lasting only a short time
27 **distraction** amusement, entertainment
32 **compulsive** difficult to stop or control
33 **acquire** obtain sth by buying it
34 **fad** sth people are interested in for a short time
35 **inventory** a list of all the things in a particular room/building

there on their mental "to do" list, like brushing their teeth. It is something they must do every day.

Impulsive shoppers

They don't mean to overspend, but temptation is all around them. They seldom pre-plan, so these shoppers will wander through a store for an hour and choose nothing. On the way out, they will pick up five or six items at the checkout display, because they can't resist, and they consider it a wasted trip to go home empty-handed.

Bargain shoppers

Coupons, discounts, end-of-season sales and bargain racks all put a gleam in these shoppers' eyes. They will drive miles to save a few dollars, and spend money to have items altered that don't really fit, and they don't really need, but the sale was irresistible. They regard their purchase as a kind of trophy. They are not always up to date, but you can be sure, whatever they have, it was a good deal.

Window shoppers

These shoppers rarely buy, but spend fortunes in their fantasies, as they walk around the malls mentally buying the finest clothes and household goods. They will be gone for hours, and return refreshed and proud of not having bought anything.

(661 words)

Source: January 2008, www.helium.com

39 temptation the desire to have sth that you know is not good

43 bargain a thing bought for less than the usual price

44 rack a piece of equipment used for holding things

gleam an expression in a person's eyes which shows emotion

48 irresistible having an overpowering appeal

52 fortune a large amount of money

WORKING WITH THE TEXT

2 Match the following types of shoppers to the explanations a–d.

1 compulsive shoppers
2 impulsive shoppers
3 bargain hunters
4 window shoppers

a shoppers who only buy something if it is a good deal
b shoppers who spontaneously buy a lot of things
c shoppers who just have to have the latest fashion in everything
d shoppers who just gaze at shop windows or wander around the malls without buying anything

3 Summarise in your own words what you found out about the types of shoppers listed above.

S ▸ How to Deal with Instructions (p. 192)

MEDIATION

4 Explain to your partner in German the difference between a compulsive and an impulsive shopper.

SPEAKING

5 Read the questions on the following page and think about what kind of shopper you are. Then follow the steps below.

1 Discuss your shopping habits with a partner.
2 Exchange your ideas with another pair. One person in the group of four reports back to the class.

1 Do you sometimes go shopping and buy lots of things which you didn't intend to buy?
2 Are you a bargain hunter who can't resist buying things in the sales?
3 Is shopping one of your favourite free-time activities?
4 Does shopping help you to feel better if you are a bit down?
5 Do you carefully plan what you want to buy?
6 Can you spend hours just looking in shop windows and wandering about department stores without buying anything?
7 Is it important to you to have the latest designs in clothes and the latest gadgets?

WORKING WITH WORDS

6 Here are some questions and answers on the text. Rewrite the answers by replacing the underlined words with another expression. Sometimes you need to change the sentence structure.

Example:

Q Why did he buy himself a new laptop?
A He had a rough year and was feeling a bit down.
→ *He didn't have a good year and was feeling a little unhappy/depressed.*

1 Q Why do people always buy new things?
A The acquisition of a new item is thrilling.
2 Q What positive effect can shopping have?
A You'll forget the awful interview or the exam you failed.
3 Q Why do impulsive shoppers buy things at the checkout display?
A They consider it a wasted trip if they come home empty-handed.
4 Q Do impulsive buyers have a shopping list?
A No, they seldom pre-plan.
5 Q Describe the window shopper.
A These shoppers rarely buy anything but spend a fortune in their fantasies.
6 Q Describe one characteristic of a compulsive shopper.
A These individuals have a need to go out shopping at regular intervals.

7 a Match each group of words with a word or an expression from the box.

accessories | acquisition | bargain | clothes | have the blues | high-street shops | household goods | items | mall

1 shopping paradise, lots of shops and cafés
2 feel unhappy, sad, down
3 tie, belt, hat
4 a good deal, a good buy, reduced goods, sale
5 buying, purchase, buy
6 coffee machine, dishes, glasses
7 dress, trousers, jacket
8 goods, articles
9 outlet, chain store, department store, supermarket, post office

b Complete the text with suitable words and phrases from above. There may be more than one possibility.

Buying an unnecessary expensive …[1] can be therapeutic and often has nothing to do with the act of purchasing everyday …[2]. When you're …[3], shopping can be cheaper than a psychiatrist. Shopping is a woman's sport. Men get bored by going from one …[4] to another looking for …[5]. For women successful …[6] hunting in a …[7] is a triumph from which they get an adrenalin rush.

LOOKING AT LANGUAGE

8 **Translate these sentences (which are similar to ones in the text). Be careful with the position of adverbs.**

G ▸ Adverbs and Adjectives (p. 217)

G ▸ Word Order – Positions of Adverbs (p. 218)

1 Wenn du unglücklich über ein schlechtes Vorstellungsgespräch bist, kauf dir eine hübsche Bluse und du wirst das Gespräch schnell vergessen!
2 Wenn ich mit meiner Mutter zusammen bin, gehen wir unweigerlich einkaufen.
3 Meine Mutter sagte mir, dass ich etwas wirklich Nettes kaufen sollte.
4 Sie hat mich sogar richtig ermuntert einkaufen zu gehen.
5 Wenn mein Freund einkaufen geht, fängt er stark zu schwitzen an.
6 Einkaufen lenkt vorübergehend ab und macht für eine kurze Zeit glücklich.

ANALYSING CHARTS

9 **Look at the two pie charts and compare household spending in the UK in 1957 and 2006.**

S ▸ Interpreting Charts and Graphs (p. 200)

1 What are the greatest changes in spending since 1957?
2 Do you think the number of impulsive buyers has increased? Say why.

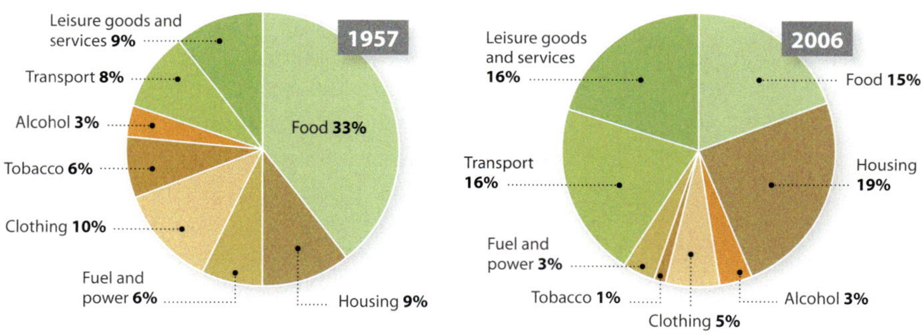

Source: Office for National Statistics

HOLDING A CLASSROOM DEBATE

HANDS-ON TASK

10 **In this unit we have heard lots of opinions about shopping. In two groups carry out a debate about shopping online. One group is made up of online shoppers and the other of those who dislike shopping on the Internet.**

S ▸ Debating (p. 203)

1 Prepare a short presentation of your arguments. Two students present these to the class.
2 Carry out the debate.
3 Vote to find out how many students find shopping on the Internet great.

Internet buyers: List all the reasons why you buy on the Internet. Think about the following points:

- compare prices more easily
- better selection if you don't live in a town
- easier
- great bargains
- find unusual items

High-street buyers: List the reasons for not shopping online. Think about the following points:

- try on clothes
- fun
- meet friends
- window shopping
- exercise
- dangers of shopping on the Internet

TEXT 2 Overcoming Consumerism

WARM-UP

1 **Study the table. What differences in lifestyles could explain these figures?**

Consumer Spending and Population, by Region, 2000		
Region	**Share of World Private Consumption Expenditures (%)**	**Share of World Population (%)**
United States and Canada	31.5	5.2
Western Europe	28.7	6.4
Latin America and the Caribbean	6.7	8.5
Eastern Europe and Central Asia	3.3	7.9
South Asia	2.0	22.4
Sub-Saharan Africa	1.2	10.9

CD 1 Track 4

Two Families Compared

The Able Family

The Able family makes a list of things which they need and not which advertising suggests they might want. If a household item breaks, it is repaired. If this is not possible or they can't find a second-hand replacement, they then research the purchase of a new item. Research means using the Internet or personal recommendations from friends. For the Ables, advertising is a sign that the item is probably of lesser quality – otherwise why spend money touting it?

Whenever possible, these researched items are purchased from small local businesses whose owners have a stake in their community. The items that the Ables buy may cost more in the short term but the pleasure they give and the durability compensate for this.

Michael Able often researches his purchases online but he never buys this way – instead he calls the vendor's 800 number or goes to the retail outlet because no matter what the website says, no matter what gimmicky security software they tout, he just doesn't trust it. Besides, he enjoys talking with people. If an 800 number is answered by people in India that work for slave wages, he hangs up and abandons the company for good.

Lorna Able's huge contribution to family economy is that she doesn't spend a lot on things for herself or to change her appearance. Eating healthy food, working in the backyard and getting enough sleep is her beauty regimen. Michael's contribution is that he doesn't buy all the macho toys that tempt most Americans such as the sports car or all-terrain pickup truck, the widescreen TV, golf clubs or other junk.

They spend less on material things than many of their neighbors and thus can actually save some money or choose to work less which gives the family more time for leisure, interaction with each other, neighbors and friends.

(306 words)

12 **tout** try to persuade people to buy sth
16 **have a stake** have a share in sth
20 **durability** the quality of lasting for a long time
23 **vendor** seller
24 **retail outlet** shop, store
26 **gimmicky** attracting attention
31 **abandon** stop doing business with
39 **regimen** a set of rules you follow to keep healthy
41 **tempt** make sb do sth even if it is wrong

And Now, the Binge Family

They watch lots of TV and lust after the endless things advertised there. Their house is a mess, full of clutter and junky products that break and then get thrown out.

These folks succumb to the latest fashions and purchase on impulse without researching prices or quality. Many of the goods they buy are made cheaply overseas and are sold in high-rent department stores with huge overhead expenses paid for by the inflated price of the merchandise sold therein. These high prices are often masked by expensive advertising campaigns which promote "sales" and "discounts" designed to tempt in consumers.

So how do we know all this about them? What's on the sidewalk in front of their house on garbage day reveals a lot.

This is the kind of family that always has the television on, even when they have visitors. And what about their community? They have absolutely no time for anything except the mall and fast-food restaurants.

Relationships with friends and neighbors must suffer in this environment because, after all, for them consumption is a form of aggressive competition. They are constantly showing off the latest knick-knack that they have bought. They literally go out of their way to drive by in their newly acquired all-terrain pickup truck or even walk up to neighbors' fences to show off the latest thing.

Mrs. Binge is a sight to behold. She buys lots and lots of beauty products. They don't necessarily improve her looks although she must think that they do. Her hair is heavy with spray, she reeks of perfume, lays the make-up on to cover up the junk-food induced acne and she stinks of cigarettes. Underneath it all, you can occasionally see traces of the young woman she used to be.

Manicures, pedicures, facials, waxing, god knows what plastic surgery, but the battle is still being lost because she doesn't get enough sleep judging from the blue flickering light coming from her bedroom window until late at night. (335 words)

Source: www.verdant.net

1 **lust after** feel a strong desire for sth

3 **clutter** untidy mass of objects

6 **succumb to** not be able to resist

12 **overhead expenses** regular costs, such as rent, electricity, etc.

40 **behold** look at

45 **reek** smell strongly and unpleasantly

46 **induce** cause

47 **underneath** under, below

WORKING WITH THE TEXT

2 Finish the following sentences with information from the text.

1. The Ables only buy a new household item if …
2. The Ables buy from small local businesses because …
3. Michael Able never buys on the Internet …
4. In order to look good, Lorna …
5. The Binges' house looks a mess because …
6. The high rents in some department stores …
7. When the Binges have bought the latest knick-knack, they …

S ▸ How to Deal with Instructions (p. 192)

3 **Compare the two families with regard to the points below. The language in the box will help you.**

whereas | while | compared to | in comparison with | in contrast to | on the one hand …, on the other hand

1 buying new items **2** advertising **3** cosmetics **4** garbage **5** showing off

WORKING WITH WORDS

4 a **Match the American English words (1–5) with their British English synonyms (a–e).**

1 garbage
2 sidewalk
3 backyard
4 closet
5 mall

a pavement
b cupboard
c rubbish
d shopping centre
e back garden

b **Complete the sentences with suitable words from above in the correct form.**

1 Americans often have barbecue parties in their …
2 … have replaced many local shops in Britain's high streets.
3 In American cities it is often difficult to walk along the streets because there aren't any …
4 In Britain the dustmen collect the … which is in black plastic bags.
5 The Able family don't have any problems with … full of junk and unnecessary clutter.

LOOKING AT LANGUAGE

G ▸ Participle Constructions (p. 220)

5 **Rewrite the following shortened participle sentences using a relative clause.**

Example: The Ables eat food grown in their own backyard.
⟶ *The Ables eat food which is grown in their own backyard.*

1 The Binges long to have things advertised on TV.
2 The Ables buy things from people involved in the local community.
3 Cheap goods bought on impulse end up in the Binges' backyard.
4 Mrs Binge's make-up covers the acne caused by junk food.
5 The blue light coming from her bedroom window means she is watching TV.
6 Advertising campaigns promote sales designed to lure customers like the Binges into shops.
7 Some families used to watching TV even leave it on when they have guests.
8 The Binges don't realise that the high rents for department stores are paid for by the high prices of goods sold there.

COMPOSITION

S ▸ Writing an Essay (p. 196)

6 **Choose one of the following tasks.**

1 The Binges and Ables are examples of extreme families. Describe an average family.
2 'Money can't buy happiness.' Give your opinion.
3 You are spending a year in the USA and your host family are the Binges – or the Ables. Describe how you feel about staying with them.

TEXT 3 The Petrol – Obesity Connection

WARM-UP

1 Look at the two cartoons and do the tasks.

S ▸ Interpreting Pictures and Cartoons (p. 199)

1. Describe the cartoons and say what they tell us about the Western way of life, especially with regard to eating habits.
2. What is the message in the speech bubble in the cartoon on the left?
3. What is the connection between the car and the obese man?

Rising Petrol Prices Could Force Obese Americans to Hit the Street

CD 1 Track 5

Leonard Doyle

For overweight Americans relief is on the way, in the form of ever-higher petrol prices. Getting into the car to drive downtown for a super-sized plate full of fatty fast food is the highlight of the day for many Americans. The result is the public health crisis with four out of ten American adults already overweight or heading that way.

After consuming mountains of chips, fried meat and baked goods all washed down with corn-sweetened soft drinks, overweight Americans then worry which best-selling diet book will help them see their toes again. It turns out that higher petrol prices can slim down more than the wallets of the overweight. The ever-rising cost of filling their cars is prompting millions of Americans to pack their own lunch and walk to the bus.

The statistics are dramatic: they show that when petrol prices have risen in the US, obesity has shown a corresponding fall of as much as 10 per cent according to a new study, *A Silver Lining? The Connection Between Gas Prices and Obesity.*

obesity the state of being fat in an unhealthy way
[1] **relief** help
[7] **corn** *(AE) BE:* maize
[10] **prompt** encourage
[14] **silver lining** good aspect (of a bad thing), as in the proverb: 'Every cloud has a silver lining'

22 **correlate** connect closely
32 **subsidy** financial help
48 **spike** sudden increase

The author of the study, Charles Courtemanche, from the University of Washington, St Louis, said his inspiration came when he was filling up his car: "I was pumping gas one day, thinking with gas prices so high I may have to take the Metro," he said. After figuring out that he would get an extra 30 minutes of exercise per day by walking to and from the Metro, he correlated statistics for obesity and petrol prices in America.

American obesity rates began to rise sharply in the early 1980s. Part of this has been blamed on an overworked population demanding convenience foods – prepared, packaged products and restaurant meals that contain more calories than home-cooked meals.

According to Marion Nestle of New York University, the arrival of the Reagan administration in 1980 brought government subsidies for farmers who grew more food. Fast-food companies reacted by serving larger portions and inventing new snacks. The calories available per capita nearly doubled to 3,000 a day and a crisis was born.

But to his shock, Mr Courtemanche found that 13 per cent of the rise in obesity between 1979 and 2004 could be attributed to the falling price of petrol. "First, if a person used public transportation, such as subways, buses, trolleys or rail services, the need to get to and from the public transport stops is likely to result in additional walking, again decreasing weight," he said.

"Second, since the cost of eating out at restaurants rises when the price of gas increases, people may substitute eating out with preparing their own meals at home, which tend to be healthier."

Now petrol prices are on the up again, reaching a record high in May 2007, and so according to the theory, obesity levels should now be falling. "The recent spike in gas prices may have the 'silver lining' of reducing obesity in the coming years," the study said. It calculated that an increase of $1 per gallon in real gasoline prices would reduce US obesity to 15% after five years. That would save 16,000 lives and $17 bn a year, according to the research. (522 words)

Source: *The Independent*, 13 September 2007

WORKING WITH THE TEXT

S ▸ Close Reading (p. 184)
S ▸ How to Deal with Instructions (p. 192)

2 Do the following tasks.

1 List the reasons why Americans lose weight when petrol prices are high.
2 Describe the effects reduced obesity would have.

3 Explain the reasons for the rise in obesity in America in the early 1980s. Before you start, structure the reasons in a chart like the following.

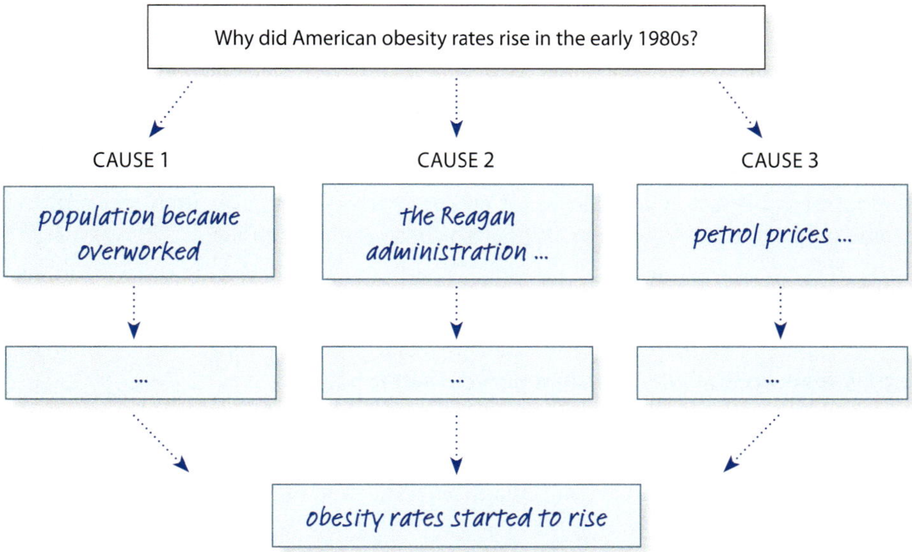

4 a **Describe the graph.**
b **Does the graph confirm the information in the text or contradict it?**

S ▸ Interpreting Charts and Graphs (p. 200)

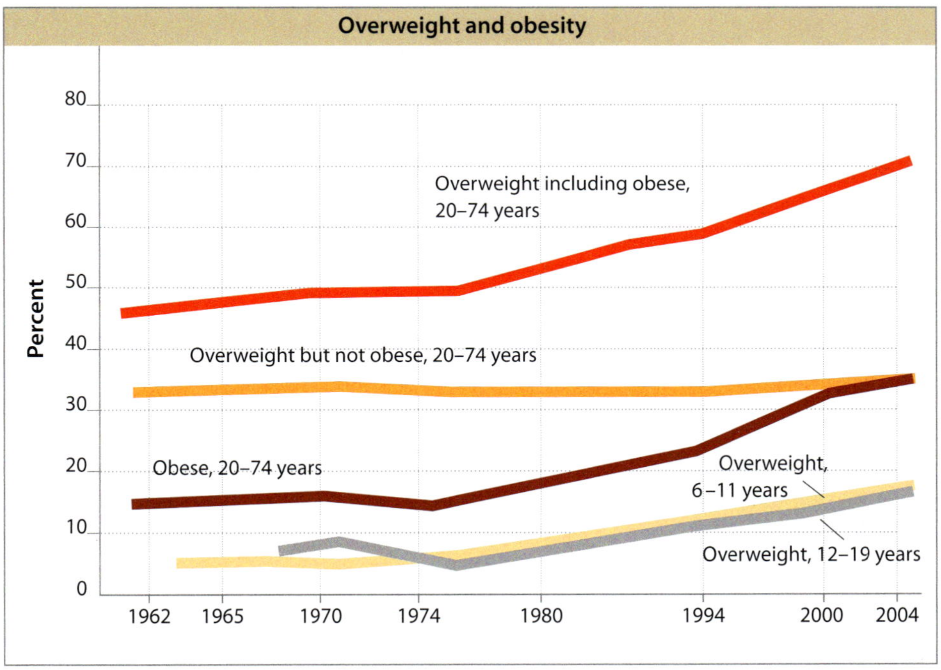

Source: National Center for Health Statistics, United States 2006, *National Health and Nutrition Examination Survey*

WORKING WITH WORDS

5 a **Combine these words with words from the box to form expressions from the text.**

1 super-… **2** ever-… **3** corn- … **4** best-… **5** fast … **6** home-…

cooked | food | rising | selling | sized | sweetened

b Complete the following text with the expressions you found.

...[1] petrol prices can influence how Americans use their cars. They will think twice about driving a hundred metres to buy ...[2] in the form of a ...[3] hamburger followed by a ...[4] soft drink. The high cost of filling their cars with gas may encourage Americans to pack their own lunch and walk to the bus stop. The result could be that obese Americans may not need the ...[5] diet book to help them see their toes again. People may eat out less and eat ...[6] food which is usually healthier.

DISCUSSION

S ▸ Group Discussions (p. 203)

6 Use the above vocabulary to talk about your eating habits.

1 Ask your partner what he/she eats during the day.
2 Find out how much exercise he/she gets.
3 Decide whether your partner has a healthy diet and lifestyle. Give reasons.
4 Report back to the class.

TRANSLATION

G ▸ Gerund/Infinitive (p. 215)
S ▸ Translation (p. 204)

7 Translate the following sentences containing the gerund into German.

1 Getting into the car to drive downtown for a super-sized meal of fast food is the highlight of the day for many Americans.
2 After consuming mountains of chips and fried meat, Americans then worry which best-selling book will help them to see their toes again.
3 After figuring out that he would get an extra 30 minutes of exercise per day by walking to and from the Metro, Charles Courtemanche correlated prices for obesity and petrol prices in America.
4 Fast-food companies reacted to lower prices for food by serving larger portions and inventing new snacks.
5 Walking to public transport stops means additional exercise, again decreasing weight.
6 As the cost of eating out at restaurants rises when petrol prices rise, people may substitute eating out with preparing their own meals.

HANDS-ON TASK

WRITING A REPORT

S ▸ Improving your Writing Skills (p. 197)

8 Using the Internet, find statistics or other information about eating habits in Germany/Europe. Write a short report for your partner school's magazine.

TEXT 4 The Secret of Brand Names

WARM-UP

1 Look at the pictures and do the following tasks.

1. Name the products advertised in the photos.
2. What do the sponsors expect to achieve?
3. Do you consciously notice all the logos and brand names when you watch sport?
4. Do you prefer to buy brands? If so, why?
5. Where do you personally encounter the most advertising? Are you always happy about it?
6. In the box there are some examples of places where you find advertising. With a partner, add a few more to the list.

commercial TV | newspapers | posters | flyers

The Brand Name Bandwagon

By Jo Robinson

CD 1 Track 6

Industry experts predict that half of all the fresh meat products in the supermarket will carry a brand name in the near future. The reason for branding is simple: merely adding a name to a package can increase sales by thirty percent or more.

Why do brand names carry such clout? Part of the answer is "word association". The right words can trick customers into believing that meat that comes from a confined, medicated, and hormone impregnated steer is the most wholesome product they can buy.

Here's how it works. Imagine that you're the owner of a large feedlot operation in Iowa, and you're wondering if jumping onto the branded meat bandwagon will boost your sales. To find out, you hire a team of marketing consultants. The consultants inform you that adding a brand name can be very effective as long as you follow their advice. First, they say, your brand name should include the name of a specific farm or person. If you call your meat "Marvin's Beef", for example,

4 **clout** power and influence
5 **confined** not free to move around
6 **steer** bull
wholesome good for your health
8 **feedlot operation** area where thousands of cows are kept on one small piece of ground
9 **jump onto the bandwagon** join a popular trend to become successful
10 **boost** increase

19 **enhance** improve
20 **bucolic** connected with country life
yearn for wish for
24 **barn** farm building for storing grain
haystack a pile of hay used for storing until needed
25 **imbue** fill
27 **lure in** attract
28 **ubiquitous** all over the place
31 **prior to** before
32 **stale** unfresh
pastry a mixture of flour, fat and water that is baked
urea *Harnstoff*
34 **feds (coll.)** US federal officials
38 **quaint** old-fashioned, charming
40 **conjure up** bring to mind
lush growing thickly and healthily
43 **pasture** land covered with grass, suitable for feeding animals
49 **manure** dung, animal droppings

customers are going to assume there's a Marvin somewhere who cares about his reputation and, therefore, his beef. (Of course, the fact that Marvin doesn't exist and that the name was selected by your consultants remains your little secret.)

You will boost sales even more, they tell you, if you add "Iowa" to your label. Most people have a positive association with where they live.

To further enhance your brand name, your consultants point out, it would be wise to add a bucolic term or two. Most consumers yearn for anything that suggests country living. How about "Farmer Marvin's Iowa Beef", you ask? They explain this is an excellent choice of words because "Farmer Marvin" evokes the past as well as the countryside. You give your graphic artists the go-ahead to design a logo with a red barn and haystack to reinforce this link with the past.

Great. With just four carefully chosen words, you've managed to imbue your feedlot meat with integrity, local pride, wholesome country living, and the nostalgic past. But has your brand name lured in the "green" consumers yet? Not really. So, say your consultants, it's time to reach for some of those ubiquitous words linked with health, nature, and wholesomeness. Luckily, the USDA* allows you to add the words "fresh" and "natural" to any unfrozen animal product that has not been altered after slaughter. Prior to slaughter, of course, your animals may have been stressed, implanted with hormones, fattened on stale pastry and urea, and fed a steady diet of sub-therapeutic antibiotics. Nonetheless, once they are butchered they become "fresh and natural" in the eyes of the feds.

So, now you have: "Farmer Marvin's Fresh 'n Natural Iowa Beef". (Note how that "'n" adds a little extra folksy charm?) But then your advisors say that they're beginning to hear about something called "grass-fed meat". They think that this quaint concept – keeping animals home on the range – might be the new, new thing in meat products. Once again, they have the solution. Simply add the words "meadows" or "prairie" to your label. These words conjure up lush fields of grass without actually saying your animals eat any of the stuff. Image is everything.

Unfortunately, all this branding of feedlot beef is going to make life much more difficult for the hundreds of pioneering farmers who are raising their beef on pasture without the use of hormones or antibiotics.

I have some advice for shoppers. Call the meat producer's 1-800 phone number and say that you want to come for a visit. This is the one arena in which factory farming cannot compete. The producers of Farmer Marvin's Fresh 'n Natural Iowa Meadow Beef will not allow you to tour their feedlots. They know full well that seeing hundreds of cattle standing around in a dusty feedlot surrounded by manure lagoons will not help sales. Money can buy the image, but it cannot buy the real thing.

(670 words)

*USDA = United States Department of Agriculture

WORKING WITH THE TEXT

2 a Here are names added to the product bit by bit. Explain why they were added.

1 Marvin **2** Iowa **3** Farmer **4** Fresh 'n Natural **5** Meadow

b Now state why some of these names are untrue.

3 ***Fresh*** **and** ***natural*** **are examples of words added to product names to create a certain impression. With a partner, find other examples of German or English products which use similar words. State why they were chosen, using the arguments from the text, and consider how truthful the names really are.**

ANALYSING A CARTOON

4 Describe the contents and message of the comic strip. In what way is the comic strip connected to the text?

S ▶ Interpreting Pictures and Cartoons (p. 199)

DISCUSSION

5 Before you start, choose a group speaker. Discuss the reasons why advertising is often criticised and the reasons why advertising is necessary. Report back to the class.

S ▶ Group Discussions (p. 203)

Here are some expressions the group speaker could use to report to the class:

I would like to present the results of my group / of group …
We had an interesting / a controversial discussion about …
On the whole, we all agreed that/about …
One or two members of the group disagreed about …
So here are our results.
First of all, I want to list / state / report on the reasons why …
Now I want to …
Finally, we all think that …

LOOKING AT LANGUAGE

6 Put in the passive of the verbs in brackets. Pay attention to the tenses.

G ▶ The Passive (p. 214)

For some time now children …[1] (name) after famous brands such as L'Oréal, Chevrolet or Armani. The trend …[2] (discovered) after social security records …[3] (survey) by psychology professor C. Evans who has studied baby names for 25 years. In the survey it …[4] (find) that car models and designer clothes were a popular source of names: 55 boys …[5] (now call) Chevy and almost 300 girls …[6] (give) the name Armani. There are even two little boys who …[7] (call) after the Sports Channel ESPN. Why …[8] (parents/impress) by brand names nowadays? Professor Evans says the names …[9] (associate) with money or exclusivity which shows the material hopes of such families. It was no different in the 19th century when children …[10] (call) Opal or Ruby.

COMPOSITION

7 **Look at the following slogans and interpret their message. Most of the slogans are old. How can you tell?**

1 More doctors smoke Camel than any other cigarette. Camel Cigarettes
2 One of the senior citizens in the Soviet state of Georgia thought Dannon was an excellent yogurt. She ought to know. She's been eating yogurt for 137 years. Dannon Yogurt
3 Aren't you glad you use Dial's? Don't you wish everybody did? Dial Soap
4 Often a bridesmaid but never a bride. For Halitosis use Listerine. Listerine Mouthwash
5 While in Europe pick up an ugly European. Volkswagen

CD 1 Track 7

LISTENING

S ► Practising Listening Skills (p. 188)

8 a **In the radio programme "Health Matters" Mike Mackintosh interviewed Diana Bevin, a campaigner against advertising to children, and Dr Thomas Hill, who carried out a study about McDonald's and brand names. Listen to the interview and answer the questions.**

1 What was the aim of the study?
2 Who was the target group?
3 How was it carried out?

b **Listen again and write down what the survey found out. Summarise the statistics in a bar chart.**

HANDS-ON TASK

ANALYSING AN ADVERTISEMENT

9 **Do the following tasks.**

1 Describe the ad.
2 What is it advertising?
3 Analyse it by using the AIDA formula: attract **attention**, arouse **interest**, create **desire**, make **action** easy. Does it fulfil all these demands?
4 Why do you think many people criticised this ad with the result that it was forbidden?
5 Choose an ad that you think is good. Explain to the class why it fulfils the demands of the AIDA formula.

TEXT 5 The Effects of Globalization

WARM-UP

1 Describe the products in the photos and then answer the following questions.

1. Where might these products have been produced?
2. List the reasons why products manufactured in developing countries are usually much cheaper than those produced in Europe.

2 With a partner, follow these steps.

1. Think about what you understand by globalization.
2. Discuss your ideas about globalization with a partner.
3. Share your ideas with two other students.
4. Choose a group speaker and report the ideas to the class.

S ▸ Group Discussions (p. 203)

3 Read the following text quickly and say in which order these aspects are discussed.

a Women Exploited
b Standardized World
c Globalization – a Force for Good or Evil?

S ▸ Skimming (p. 184)

CD 1 Track 8

The Global Impact of Globalization

Emily McMillan, Environmental Studies, Dalhousie University

We live in an era of globalization. How often have we heard this? And how often have we really thought about what it means? Most people think they know what it is, but do they really?

The term 'globalization' has taken on a life of its own. Globalization is seen as a beneficial thing, even a cosmopolitan thing, a 'hip' thing. Many people feel that globalization is a great force bringing the world closer together. There are even new cuddly phrases like 'global village' which make us feel good about globalization bringing us all closer together. Yet when we think about what globalization really is – when we look beneath this surface glamour – we can see the true meaning of the word and the true proponents of this phenomenon.

Unfortunately, globalization is not brought about by elementary school children writing to internet pen pals (as cozy as this sounds). The real agents of globalization are our friends the multinational corporations – the 'super-companies'. Globalization is nothing more than the product of the multinational corporations' search for profit. So, rather than being driven by positive things like the wish to bring the world closer together, globalization is driven by corporations seeking to maximize profits, and part of that search for profits involves the search for cheaper labor. Many companies move into less developed countries to take advantage of the lack of organization of labor there which allows these companies to pay below subsistence-level wages.

So, rather than making the world a more friendly place, globalization is leading to things such as 'Export Processing Zones' – places where millions of people – mostly women – make products which are then shipped into the more developed countries and sold for a huge profit. These zones are integral to what globalization is and does.

5 **beneficial** having a useful effect
7 **cuddly** soft, positive
10 **proponent** a person who supports an idea
12 **cozy** warm, comfortable and safe
19 **subsistence-level** having just enough food or money to stay alive
23 **integral** essential

Increasingly, globalization is also about avoiding environmental regulations. This also results in terrible working conditions for those working in these zones. So, the next time someone talks about the global community, ask yourself if this is something we really want.

The most important result of globalization is that of the global market. The same products are being sold all around the world. As a consequence, you can go anywhere in the world and buy the same things; McDonald's is everywhere.

This standardization means that life is becoming more uniform everywhere. We can see this developing in different ways:

Way of Dressing
Everyone now wears jeans or a suit and tie. This is the European way of dressing, and so local ways of dressing are disappearing.

Way of Life
It has become common for everyone to get a job; alternative lifestyles are disappearing. Conspicuous consumption is also becoming more common.

Language
Everyone speaks English these days. In Israel, people don't learn Arabic as a second language, which would make sense. Instead, their second language is English. English is now the most common second language in the world.

Media
Standardization of media can be seen on TV and the radio. CNN is everywhere. TV shows seen now around the world are mainly American TV shows. American and European music is everywhere. Often in other countries you will hear elevator music of Beatles songs rather than local music.

Clearly, what standardization really means is the standardization of the American way of life, be it TV shows, music or clothing. (554 words)

www.elements.nb.ca

38 **conspicuous** easy to see or notice
46 **elevator** *(BE) AE:* lift

WORKING WITH THE TEXT

S ▸ Answering Comprehension Questions (p. 191)

4 Answer the questions.

1 List the reasons why people think that globalization is something positive.
2 How does the author feel about globalization with regard to super-companies?
3 What are the working conditions often like in less developed countries?

S ▸ Interpreting Pictures and Cartoons (p. 199)

5 Describe the cartoon. In what way does it correspond to information in the text?

WORKING WITH WORDS

6 **Replace the underlined parts according to the instructions in brackets. Sometimes you have to change the structure of the sentence.**

Example: We live in an era of globalization. (synonym)

→ *We live in an* ***age*** *of globalization.*

1. It has become **a sort** of mystical romantic **term**. (synonyms)
2. **This results in terrible** working conditions. (noun, synonym)
3. It would **make sense** for Israelis to learn Arabic. (be + adjective)
4. **Rather than** making the world a better place, globalization is leading to export processing zones where workers, **mostly** female, **work for very little money**. (synonyms, synonymous expression)
5. The same products **are being sold** all around the world. (make active, start with "Shops …)

TRANSLATION

7 **Translate the following short text into German. Pay attention to the participles.**

S ▸ Translation (p. 204)

Globalization of Culture

One of the most controversial aspects of globalization being debated at present is the worldwide spread and dominance of American culture. Just as American goods, produced in a country widely unaffected by war, flooded the markets after World War II, US culture is now penetrating every continent through the dramatic growth of mass media, in particular music, television, films and the Internet. American companies seeking higher profits have expanded into foreign countries. From China to France to the Middle East, activists fear that global culture may become too Americanised, destroying their own cultural, economic and religious traditions.

LOOKING AT LANGUAGE

8 **Replace the participles in the following sentences with subordinate clauses.**

G ▸ Participle Constructions (p. 220)

Example: People think that globalization is a force bringing people closer together.

→ *People think that globalization is a force* ***that brings*** *people closer together.*

1. Globalization is not brought about by children writing to pen pals.
2. Globalization is driven by corporations seeking to maximise profits.
3. The people working there are mostly women working for very little money.
4. Looking beneath the surface we can see the true meaning of globalization.
5. There is a lack of organization of labor allowing companies to pay very low wages.
6. The goods produced in developing countries are sold for huge profits.

GIVING A PRESENTATION

HANDS-ON TASK

9 **Compare the working conditions in Europe to those in countries such as China. In groups research and give a presentation on your findings. Consider the following:**

S ▸ Giving a Presentation (p. 201)

- weekly/daily working hours
- holidays
- health and safety in the workplace
- women in the workforce
- child labour
- trade unions

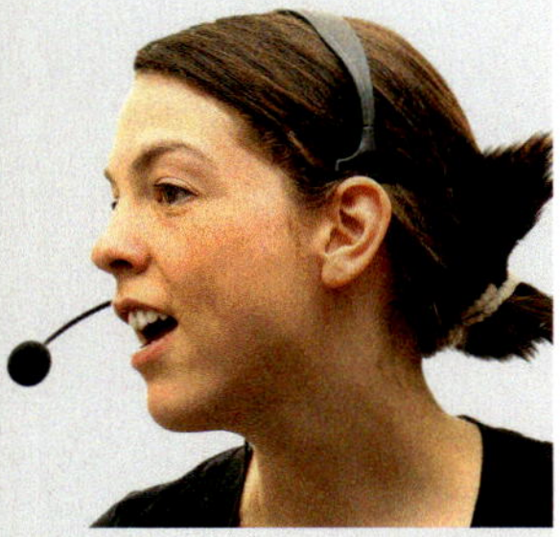

TEXT 6 Women At Work

WARM-UP

1 **Look at the cartoon and state whether it reflects the 'normal' division of work in the household nowadays. Give reasons. The words in the box will help you.**

childcare | household chores | housewife and mother | labour-saving machines

S ▶ Scanning (p. 185)

2 a **Scan the text to find out the following:**

1 whether more women work nowadays than in 2000,
2 what Bianchi found out about childcare and popular belief,
3 whether men play a greater role in childcare now than in the past.

b **Look at these expressions from the text and decide which of the meanings is correct.**

1 longer-term (line 8)
a *an expression longer than another one*
b *relating to what will happen in the future*

2 to stay out of the labor force (line 16)
a *not to work*
b *not be forced to work*

3 they turned to labor-saving machines (line 26)
a *they looked for …*
b *they started to use …*

4 to handle household work (line 27)
a *to deal with household work*
b *to do household work by hand*

5 stay-at-home mothers (line 38)
a *mothers who don't work*
b *mothers who rarely go out*

CD 1 Track 9

Women in the Workplace – Trend is Reversing

Eduardo Porter

For four decades the number of women entering the workplace grew at a rapid pace, causing a powerful cultural and economic transformation of American society. But since the mid-1990s, various studies have shown that the growth in the percentage of adult women working outside the home has come to a standstill, even dropping somewhat in the last five years, leaving it at a rate well below that of men.

2 **pace** rate, speed

While the change has been under way for a while, it was initially viewed by many specialists as simply a pause in the longer-term movement of women into the workforce. But now, social scientists are engaged in a heated debate over whether the gender revolution at work may be over.

Is this evidence for the popular notion that many mothers are again deciding that they prefer to stay at home and take care of their children?

Maybe, but many researchers are coming to a different conclusion: women are not choosing to stay out of the labor force because of a change in attitudes, they say. Rather, the broad changes in women's lives that allowed most of them to pursue jobs outside the home appear to be hitting some serious limits.

Starting in the 1960s, tens of millions of women rearranged bits of their lives, spending more and more of their time on housework and their jobs. They married later and had fewer children. To save time they turned to labor-saving machines and paid others to help handle household work; they persuaded the men in their lives to do more chores.

At the peak in 2000, some 77 percent of women between 25 and 54 were in the workforce. Since then numbers have slowly decreased. The daily challenge facing many mothers at nearly all income levels is now at a breaking point.

"What happened on the road to gender equality?" asked Suzanne Bianchi, a sociologist at the University of Maryland. "A lot of work happened."

Bianchi has concluded that, contrary to popular belief, the broad movement of women into the paid labor force did not come at the expense of their children. Not only did fathers spend more time with children, but working mothers, she found, spent an average of 12 hours a week on childcare in 2003, an hour more than stay-at-home mothers did in 1975.

Women simply worked more overall. Bianchi found that employed mothers, on average, worked at home and on the job a total of 15 hours more a week and slept 3.6 fewer hours than those who were not employed. Indeed, according to the research, women may have already reached their limits in the amount of work they can pack into a week. Since 2003 the time spent by mothers on work outside the home has fallen by almost 4 hours a week. This is having broad repercussions for the economy. (473 words)

Source: *New York Times*, 2 March 2006

[7] **initially** at the beginning
[10] **gender** the fact of being male or female
[11] **notion** idea, concept, belief
[21] **pursue** do (a job)
[28] **chores** unpleasant tasks, work
[35] **at the expense of** with negative effects on
[44] **repercussion** (negative) consequence

WORKING WITH THE TEXT

3 Answer the questions. Use your own words.

1 What major change in the role of women took place in the 1960s?
2 State the various reasons given by researchers and social scienticists to explain why fewer women are entering the workforce nowadays.

S ▸ Answering Comprehension Questions (p. 191)

S ▸ How to Deal with Instructions (p. 192)

4 Give a very brief summary of the information in the text using the following dates.

1960 to the 1990s | the mid-1990s | 2000 | 1975 and 2003 | 2003

DISCUSSION

5 With a partner, follow steps 1–4 to interpret what the author means by these expressions:

1 cultural and economic transformation of American society (line 2)
2 gender revolution (line 10)

Step 1: Make notes about what you think these expressions mean.
Step 2: Compare your ideas with your partner's.
Step 3: Compare your notes and your partner's with another pair.
Step 4: Report the main findings to the class.

WORKING WITH WORDS

6 a Copy and complete the table.

verb	noun
arrange	…
choose	…
…	conclusion
decide	…
drop	…
…	earnings
employ	…
grow	…
increase	…
marry	…
…	payment
…	persuasion

b Complete this short summary of the text with words from above in the correct form.

Beginning in the 1960s the number of working women …[1] rapidly. Since then it has begun to …[2] a little. However, in recent years women …[3] to stay at home not because they …[4] to. Social scientists are coming to the …[5] that women have reached their limits. Since the 1960s, women …[6] their lives around their jobs. …[7] took place later and with some …[8] their husbands took over chores in the household. Ms Bianchi discovered that …[9] mothers worked far more and slept less than unemployed women. Since 2003 the time women can spend at home …[10] by four hours a week.

ANALYSING CHARTS AND GRAPHS

7 a **Look at the chart and graph below. Describe the information given in them.**
b **There is no information at all in the text on p. 26/27 about one of the diagrams. Decide which one and give reasons.**

S ▸ Interpreting Graphs, Diagrams and Tables (p. 200)

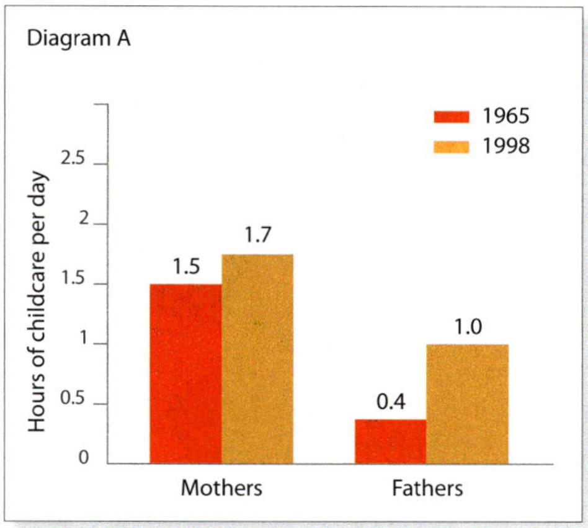

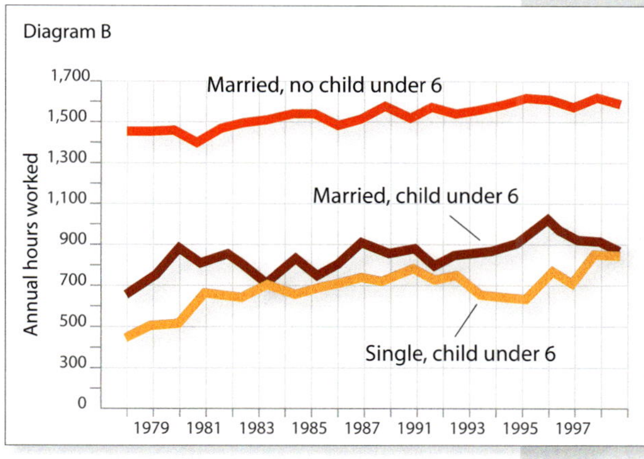

LOOKING AT LANGUAGE

8 **Complete the text with the correct form of the verbs in brackets.**

Stay-at-home Dads

When Christine Black ...[1] (date) photographer Mark Howells ten years ago, he ...[2] (tell) her that someday he ...[3] (want) to stay home to raise their kids. Christine, a lawyer, ...[4] (think) that ...[5] (be) just great. Nine years later, Christine Howells ...[6] (be) a successful partner at a San Francisco law firm, while Mark ...[7] (spend) his time at home with their 5-year-old son, Micky, and infant daughter, Sarah. The 2006 US census ...[8] (report) that there ...[9] (be) about 143,000 stay-at-home dads, a tiny number next to the 11 million stay-at-home mums. These men ...[10] (be) social entrepreneurs challenging traditional definitions of manliness by throwing over one of the key measures of masculinity: the size of the paycheck. Men ...[11] (have to) be tolerant. The solo stroller*-pushing dad ...[12] (remain) a target for unwanted advice.

* (AE) Kindersportwagen

CLASS SURVEY

HANDS-ON TASK

9 **Do a class survey to find out the following. (The survey can be done in groups who exchange information with each other.)**

1. How many girls want to have a serious career and not have children?
2. How many girls want to work for a while and then stop altogether when they marry and have children?
3. How many girls want to have a family and work at the same time?
4. How many boys want to give up work for a while to look after children?
5. How many boys want their future wives to stay at home and look after the children?

Work out the percentages and then report back to the class.

TEXT 7 Reading Poetry

WARM-UP

1 **Discuss why a supermarket is super.**

CD 1 Track 10

John Updike

John Updike

Superman

1954

I drive my car to supermarkets,
The way I take is superhigh,
A superlot is where I park it,
And Super Suds are what I buy.

Supersalesmen sell me tonic –
Super-Tone-O for Relief,
The planes I ride are supersonic,
In trains I like the Super Chief.*

Supercilious men and women
Call me superficial – me
Who superbly learned to swim in
Supercolossality.

Superphosphate-fed foods feed me:
Superservice keeps me new.
Who would dare to supersede me,
Super-super-superwho?

* the name of a luxury train travelling from Chicago to Los Angeles and famous for its gourmet meals and Hollywood clientele

2 **superhighway** *(AE) BE:* motorway
3 **superlot** a very large parking area
4 **suds** *(pl.)* foam/bubbles from soap, name for a washing powder
7 **supersonic** faster than the speed of sound
9 **supercilious** proud and arrogant
12 **colossal** very large
15 **supersede** replace

WORKING WITH THE POEM

2 **Answer the questions.**

1. Describe in your own language what Superman does in the first six lines and what he buys.
2. What other forms of transport does he use?
3. Why do people call him superficial?
4. How can the line "me / Who superbly learned to swim …" be interpreted?

3 **Divide up into small groups and interpret what John Updike wanted to express in his poem. In the box on the opposite page you will find useful information to help you understand the poem. A group speaker reports back to the class.**

Reading and Understanding a Poem

STEP 1
Read the poem once and concentrate on the meaning and then read it once again.

STEP 2
Read it aloud.

STEP 3
Try to paraphrase the individual lines, stanzas or verses.

STEP 4
Identify who is speaking.

STEP 5
Identify the setting – if there is one.

STEP 6
Notice the sounds and patterns. How do alliteration*, repetition and rhyme help you to understand the poem?

STEP 7
What figures of speech are used, e.g. imagery, alliteration, simile, metaphor? (See page 138.)

STEP 8
Does the poem reflect what *you* feel about the experiences mentioned in the poem?

*Alliteration means the repetition of a consonant at the beginning of words close together.

WORKING WITH WORDS

4 a **Look up the following adjectives in the dictionary to find out if they are formal or informal English. They all describe something great.**

awesome | magnificent | marvellous | smashing | super | superb | terrific

b **Now use these to describe in about 100 words a really good weekend/holiday/film/disco/date that you have experienced.**

INFO

Supermarkets

Shopping in supermarkets changed the American public. The fact that people in America were more mobile and could travel further from home to look for goods made them feel that they had a wider choice. Shopping in the most modern stores which were located further from home and were much larger than local shops made shopping more tiresome. And although parking lots, shopping carts and multiple check-out lines made it faster to get in and out of the store, it took longer to escape the supermarket's environment. In the late 1950s supermarkets offered more products and more amenities to keep people shopping longer. Large refrigerators and home freezers made it possible to reduce the number of shopping trips to one a week but the abundance of goods overwhelmed shoppers who spent hours there and the trips became a weekly ritual.

MEDIATION

5 **Read the info box on supermarkets and use it to write a short encyclopedia entry in German about supermarkets in the USA.**

S ▸ Mediation (p. 204)

INTERNET PROJECT

6 **Look up John Updike and his contemporaries Margaret Atwood, Joyce Carol Oates, Ray Bradbury and Philip Roth on the Internet. In groups give a short talk about one of these authors and about their most famous works. Some of their novels have been made into films. Choose one which you would like to watch in class.**

HANDS-ON TASK

S ▸ Giving a Presentation (p. 201)

World of Work

MEDIATION Work Experience

S ▸ Mediation (p. 204)

1 Do the following mediation task. Before you start, read the instruction carefully. Then follow steps a) and b) below.

Sie beraten Schülerinnen und Schüler in ihrem letzten Schuljahr über das Verfassen einer Bewerbung und eines Lebenslaufs. Sie haben den folgenden Artikel in einer englischen Zeitschrift gefunden. Sie möchten die Informationen über Praktika an Ihre Schülerinnen und Schüler weitergeben. Machen Sie Notizen auf Deutsch über folgende Aspekte des Textes:

1 Warum ist ein Praktikum nützlich?
2 Wann sollte man ein Praktikum machen?
3 Welche Arten von Praktika gibt es?

Geben Sie abschließend ein Beispiel für ein interessantes Praktikum.

a Here are some answers to point 1: why work experience is useful. Two points are incorrect. Read the text and find out which ones.

- Ein Praktikum macht die Studienzeit interessanter.
- Es kann bei Stellenbewerbungen ein Pluspunkt sein.
- Es handelt sich dabei fast ausschließlich um Teilzeitjobs.
- Es zeigt potentiellen Arbeitgebern, dass man fähig ist, Initiative zu zeigen.
- Man könnte nach dem Studium eine feste Stelle bei derselben Firma bekommen.
- Es zeigt dem zukünftigen Arbeitgeber, dass man die Arbeit zeitlich im Griff hat.
- Man sollte nur berufsrelevante Praktika bei einer späteren Stellenbewerbung erwähnen.

b Before you do the rest of the task, look at the following tips.

- Read the instructions carefully. Remember that if you write anything irrelevant, you may lose points.
- Your version should be much shorter than the original as you do not have to repeat all the information in the text.
- Leave out unnecessary examples, lists and quotations.
- This is not a translation so do not translate the whole text!

Why Do Work Experience?

'Work experience' – those two words strike fear into the hearts of most students, particularly if there's a glaring white space on their CV under that heading.

Many employers look for some kind of work experience, so think about it carefully. It could be one of the most valuable things you do whilst at university, and it is far easier and quicker to get than you think.

Work experience is neither 'cheap labour' for businesses, nor is it a 'waste of time' for students. It is becoming a very important part of an undergraduate's life and can only enhance your time as a student. Work experience encompasses a whole variety of employment possibilities: it can be short-term or long-term, full-time or part-time, paid or unpaid.

1 **strike fear into sb** make sb be afraid
2 **glaring** very bright and unpleasant
4 **valuable** very useful or important
7 **undergraduate** a university or college student who is studying for their first degree
8 **encompass** include a large number or range of things

You could try to get some work experience before you start studying, but your university years are the ideal time to gain work experience. You will probably have more free time than at any other stage in your life: free mornings or afternoons, weekends and the long summer holidays. Today, with more people than ever before going to university, a graduate needs more than just a degree to 'stand out from the crowd' and attract the attention of a potential employer.

Work experience can underline your determination to break into your chosen career, it shows great initiative and gives you the chance to showcase your work-related skills. It might even lead to full-time employment with the same employer after you finish university.

Many students have to work part-time to support themselves and pay for their studies. The jobs are often quite menial – bar work, shop work, factory work – but it is all valuable work experience. Even if the job is not in the field you hope to have a career in, it still shows future employers that you are responsible enough to hold down a part-time job alongside your studies, and that you are capable of managing your time.

Case Studies

Mark Breedon did most of his work experience during the summer holidays before his final year at university. He had a two-week placement with the BBC where he was a 'runner' on various productions. This involved him researching interviewees for programmes, making cups of tea, shopping for studio props, filing, typing, helping out in the studios and with outside broadcasts and lots more. He thoroughly enjoyed his placement and more importantly learned a lot. The BBC later invited him back to work for them again.

Emily Osmond was studying economics at Lincoln University when she got a job with the university's 'student crew', a group of students who act as guides for visitors to the university. Her job was to show prospective students and other visitors around the campus. Working for the university meant that there was no travel time and she could easily fit in her work around her studies.

There are many vacancies out there just waiting to be filled by students like you. The National Council for Work Experience is just one of the organisations which offer undergraduates work placement opportunities with leading businesses, short-term or long-term depending on your needs. These include bank work, charity work, retail work and conservation work both abroad and in the UK. The Council says, 'Whenever employers are asked what they value in graduates, they constantly refer to the benefits of any form of work experience and place it firmly at the top of their lists.'

Some areas of work and some companies are harder to get placements in than others. However, write a good covering letter explaining who you are and why you want work experience, include a polished CV written with the company in mind, and you may be surprised. Don't despair if once you're through the door all you do for the first day is make tea. Be firm but polite and ask what more you can do to help. Demonstrate your skills and act confident in your new surroundings.

Work is not the same thing as work experience, but you can turn work into work experience. This means doing more than just turning up to do the job and then going home again in the evening. It means making the most of the opportunities to develop personal and course-related or job-specific skills. Whatever you have been doing at work, however ordinary it may seem, you can and must present it as a desirable skill on your CV. (735 words)

15 **graduate** a person who has a university degree
18 **showcase** present in an attractive way
22 **menial** not skilled or important, and often boring or badly paid
24 **hold down a job** keep a job for some time
25 **capable** having the ability or qualities necessary for doing sth
29 **placement** a job, often as part of a course of study, where you get some experience of a particular kind of work
32 **thoroughly** very much, completely
39 **vacancy** a job that is available for sb to do
43 **retail** the selling of goods to the public, usually through shops/stores
conservation the protection of the natural environment
49 **polished** well-written, neat and tidy
50 **despair** stop having any hope that a situation will change or improve

JOB SKILLS Applying for a Job (1)

LISTENING

CD 1 Track 11

S ▸ Practising Listening Skills (p. 188)

2 a **Listen to two students reporting about their work experience in Great Britain. Note down what they are talking about.**

b **Listen to Andres again and answer questions 1–3 in note form.**

c **Now listen to Juliette a second time and answer questions 4–6 in note form.**

1 What kind of work is Andres doing?
2 What differences has he experienced between working in Spain and working in England?
3 What is his advice to future interns?
4 What tasks has Juliette been given?
5 In which way has she profited from her experience?
6 What is her advice to future interns?

UNDERSTANDING A CV

3 a **Here are some German words from a CV. Find the corresponding English terms in the CV on the opposite page.**

1 Praktikum	**5** Mittlere Reife
2 Schulbildung	**6** Abitur
3 Führerschein	**7** Berufliches Gymnasium
4 Fächer	**8** Geburtsdatum

b **Compare the CV with a German one. What are the main differences?**

INFO

Useful Words for Describing Your Education in a CV

The British equivalent of *Abitur* is **A levels** (plural). In Britain you do 3–4 subjects.
The British equivalent of *Mittlere Reife* is **GCSE** (**General Certificate of Secondary Education**).
There is no British equivalent of the *Realschule*, so just write **secondary school**.
A *Gesamtschule* is a **comprehensive school**. There are many of these in Britain.
A *Gymnasium* is a **grammar school**. There is no equivalent of the *berufliches Gymnasium* in Britain, but you can write 'vocational grammar school'.

c **With a partner look at Heike's CV again. You would like to know more about her and what she has done. Write down questions you would ask her if you were interviewing her.**

WRITING A CV

4 **A luxury hotel in London is looking for school leavers to do an internship of 6–8 weeks or longer. Write your CV using Heike's as a sample.**

Before you start, read the tips on the next page.

1 Always write out the month in full, e.g. 14th October 2009.
2 An employer will find out a lot about you by just glancing at your personal profile. So think about this very carefully.
3 Always explain German expressions like 'Mittlere Reife'.
4 Don't forget to mention your interests and activities outside school, e.g. helping out in a youth club, as they tell the employer something about your personality.
5 Give an e-mail address. This makes corresponding easier.
6 Mention all the skills which are important for working in an English speaking country, e.g. fluent/good/basic English, previous experience, etc.

	Heike Bülow
Address	Untere Straße 6, 70123 Hornberg, Germany
Telephone	+49 744 23456 (home) | +49 160 987654 (mobile)
E-mail	heike.bülow@t-line.de
Date of Birth	26th September 1989
Nationality	German

Personal Profile

An excellent communicator with extensive organisational skills who always works well under pressure.

Education and Qualifications

2008	*Abitur* (equivalent to A levels) in the following main subjects: Economics, English, German, French Average mark 2.1 (equivalent to B)
2005–2008	Johann-Friedrich-von-Cotta-Schule (vocational grammar school)
2005	*Mittlere Reife* (equivalent to GCSE) in 9 subjects, including Maths, English, French and German. Average mark: 2.5 (equivalent to a B–)
2000–2005	Raitelsburg Realschule (secondary school)

Work Experience

August 2007	Internship at the Schlosshotel Hornberg Main responsibilities: cleaning rooms, assisting at reception, helping foreign guests with communication problems Skills gained: communication, team work, interpersonal, problem solving
August 2006	General office work at the Schwäbische Papierfabrik (Swabian Paper Factory) in Hornberg Main responsibilities: filing, entering information into the computer system

Skills	Good knowledge of French and English, both spoken and written Excellent communication skills IT skills Ability to remain calm and friendly under pressure
Interests and Activities	Travelling, interior design, languages, cooking Active member of the church community
Additional Information	Clean driving licence
References	Available on request

TOPIC 2 Save the Planet! Save Ourselves!

BACKGROUND INFORMATION

global warming *Erderwärmung*
climate change *Klimawandel*
manmade *von Menschen verursacht*
greenhouse gas *Treibhausgas*
release *abgeben*
carbon dioxide *Kohlendioxid*
curb *aufhalten*
animal migration pattern *Tiermigrationsverhalten*
natural disaster *Naturkatastrophe*
melting of glaciers *Gletscherschmelze*
rising sea levels *steigende Meeresspiegel*
flooding *Hochwasser* **drought** *Dürre*
desertification *Wüstenbildung*
soil erosion *Bodenerosion*
depletion of the ozone layer *Abbau der Ozonschicht*
extinction of spezies *Artensterben*
impact *Auswirkung* **heatwave** *Hitzewelle*
water shortage *Wassermangel*
resettle *umsiedeln*

Global Warming

Experts are increasingly unified in the opinion that the climate change we are experiencing is, at least partly, manmade. The main cause appears to be the greenhouse gases we are releasing into the atmosphere, particularly carbon dioxide. Experts believe global warming, if it is not curbed, will lead to changing weather and animal migration patterns, an increased frequency of natural disasters, the melting of glaciers and other ice formations, rising sea levels, flooding, drought, desertification, soil erosion, depletion of the ozone layer, the extinction of species, and other problems. Most of these events are already occurring and can be directly linked to global warming. If global warming continues as predicted, it will eventually have a strong impact on human health and wellbeing. Heatwaves will claim the lives of the sick and the elderly. Water shortage will increasingly become a source of international conflict. Farmland will dry up, causing food shortages. Coastal land will disappear, forcing people to resettle inland.

water supply *Wasserversorgung*
damming *Dammbau*
chain of events *Folge von Ereignissen*
aquatic *Wasser-*
plant life *Pflanzenwelt*
shrink *schrumpfen*
sanitation *sanitäre*

Water Supply

Global warming is not the only reason why the threat to global water supply is worsening. Human actions such as massive damming also cause chains of events which include falls in river flows and rising saltiness in biologically-rich waterways, followed by a loss of fish and aquatic plant life, shrinking farmland, damage to fisheries and food insecurity. Water shortage is already a problem for billions of people who lack drinking water and proper sanitation.

climate crisis *Klimakrise* **generate** *erzeugen*
dependence *Abhängigkeit* **oil/petroleum** *Erdöl*
sustainable *tragbar, nachhaltig*
fossil fuel emission *Ausstoß fossiler Brennstoffe* **environment** *Umwelt*
peak oil production *Scheitelpunkt der Erdölproduktion*
nuclear energy *Atomenergie*
nuclear power *Atomkraft*
radioactive fallout *radioaktiver Niederschlag*
radiation *Strahlung* **conserve** *einsparen*
alternative sources of energy *alternative Energiequellen*

Energy

The climate crisis is forcing us to re-examine how we generate our energy. It has become clear that our dependence on oil/petroleum is not sustainable. Not only are fossil fuel emissions damaging the environment, but someday we will reach peak oil production. The use of nuclear energy is being reconsidered as it is clean and cheap compared to fossil fuels. However, the use of nuclear power remains controversial due to the risk of radioactive fallout and radiation. Economic opportunities are created by the search for ways to conserve energy and the search for alternative sources of energy, such as solar power and other kinds of renewable energy.

Biofuels (and **Industrial Agriculture**)

Biofuels are made from crops such as maize/corn and palm oil, and so only release as much carbon into the atmosphere as they absorb when they grow. However, the current production scheme of biofuels is blighted by the typical problems of industrial farming: the monetary and environmental cost of transportation, the depletion of soil nutrients, pollution and deforestation.

biofuel *Biotreibstoff*
industrial agriculture *industrielle Landwirtschaft*
crops *Anbaupflanzen* **maize/corn** *Mais*
palm oil *Palmöl* **carbon** *Kohlenstoff*
absorb *aufnehmen, absorbieren*
transportation *Beförderung, Transport*
depletion of soil nutrients *Erschöpfung der Bodennährstoffe*
pollution *Umweltverschmutzung*
deforestation *Entwaldung*

Deforestation

Meeting the West's demand for biofuels is a recent development in the long history of deforestation. Farmers (and others) have been clear-felling forests at an unsustainable rate for a long time. When peat bogs are clear-felled, the plant material is either burned or left to decompose, releasing tons of carbon dioxide into the atmosphere. This is one reason why deforestation causes global warming; another reason is that the forests, particularly the tropical rainforests, absorb carbon dioxide. The destruction of these ecosystems also has other catastrophic consequences: animal habitats are destroyed and humans suffer too. Forests continue to be threatened, and it is now more important than ever to protect them.

clear-fell *abholzen*
unsustainable *untragbar*
peat bog *Torfmoor*
decompose *sich zersetzen*
tropical rainforest *tropischer Regenwald*
ecosystem *Ökosystem*
habitat *Lebensraum*
threaten *bedrohen*

Pollution

There are many kinds of pollution, the main kinds being air pollution, water pollution and soil contamination. Industrial agriculture is the main source of many pollutants due to its immoderate use of pesticides, herbicides, fungicides, etc., and because it produces vast quantities of animal waste, all of which contaminate the soil and the ground water. We also produce pollutants in the form of sewage and as part of our consumption of energy: exhaust from our cars is one example of a pollutant which creates smog in cities and causes acid rain. Outside our cities, nuclear power stations produce nuclear waste. All of these pollutants are toxic/poisonous in some way.

soil contamination *Bodenverschmutzung*
pollutant *Umweltschadstoff*
pesticide *Pestizid, Schädlingsbekämpfungsmittel*
herbicide *Unkrautvernichtungsmittel*
fungicide *Schimmelbekämpfungsmittel*
animal waste *tierische Abfallstoffe*
contaminate *verseuchen, verschmutzen*
sewage *Abwasser*
exhaust *Abgase*
acid rain *saurer Regen*
nuclear power station *Atomkraftwerk*
nuclear waste *Atommüll*
toxic/poisonous *giftig*

Waste Disposal

Humans are producing more rubbish/garbage/trash than ever, and it all has to go somewhere. Some of it gets reused or recycled. Organic waste is biodegradable and can therefore be composted. Rubbish sent to a landfill, on the other hand, takes a very, very long time to break down. Another problematic disposal method is incineration, which pollutes the air.

waste disposal *Abfallentsorgung*
rubbish/garbage/trash *Müll, Abfall*
reuse *wiederverwenden* **organic waste** *Biomüll*
biodegradable *biologisch abbaubar*
landfill *Mülldeponie* **break down** *abbauen, zerfallen*
incineration *Abfallverbrennung*
pollute *verschmutzen*

TEXT 1 A Generational Mission

WARM-UP

1 a Discuss the following questions in groups.

- For what causes will your parents' and grandparents' generations be remembered? What was important to them? What were they willing to do for their causes? What were their failings?
- For what causes will your generation be remembered?

S ▸ Skimming (p. 184)

b Scan the following text. What, according to the author, could become our 'generational mission'?

CD 1 Track 12

Al Gore, Former Vice President of the United States

inconvenient troublesome, difficult
2 **issue** topic for debate
9 **virtually** almost
glacier mass of ice
10 **mound** hill
11 **prop up** support
19 **saturation** amount contained within
20 **interfere with** prevent or disturb
22 **habitat** home of an animal
extinction when every member of a species dies
25 **wreak havoc** cause chaos
27 **unprecedented** that has never been known before
30 **harness** control and make use of

An Inconvenient Truth

by Al Gore

Global warming is not just about science and it is not just a political issue. It is really a moral issue.

危
機

Crisis

What we are facing is not just a cause for alarm, it is paradoxically also a cause for hope. As many know, the Chinese expression for "crisis" consists of two characters side by side. The first is the symbol for "danger", the second the symbol for "opportunity".

The climate crisis is, indeed, extremely dangerous. In fact it is a true planetary emergency.

We are melting the North Polar ice cap and virtually all of the mountain glaciers in the world. We are destabilizing the massive mound of ice on Greenland and the equally enormous mass of ice propped up on top of islands in West Antarctica, threatening a worldwide increase in sea levels of as much as twenty feet.

The list of what is now endangered due to global warming also includes the continued stable configuration of ocean and wind currents that has been in place since before the first cities were built almost 10,000 years ago.

We are dumping so much carbon dioxide into the Earth's environment that we have literally changed the relationship between the Earth and the Sun. So much of that CO_2 is being absorbed into the oceans that if we continue at the current rate we will increase the saturation of calcium carbonate to levels that will prevent formation of corals and interfere with the making of shells by any sea creature.

Global warming, along with the cutting and burning of forests and other critical habitats, is causing the loss of living species at a level comparable to the extinction event that wiped out the dinosaurs 65 million years ago. That event was believed to have been caused by a giant asteroid. This time it is not an asteroid colliding with the Earth and wreaking havoc; it is us.

But along with the danger we face from global warming, this crisis also brings unprecedented opportunities.

What are the opportunities such a crisis also offers? They include not just new jobs and new profits, though there will be plenty of both, we can build clean engines, we can harness the Sun and the wind; we can stop wasting energy; we can use our planet's plentiful coal resources without heating the planet.

The procrastinators and deniers would have us believe this will be expensive. But in recent years, dozens of companies have cut emissions of heat-trapping gases while saving money. Some of the world's largest companies are moving aggressively to capture the enormous economic opportunities offered by a clean energy future.

But there's something even more precious to be gained if we do the right thing.

The climate crisis also offers us the chance to experience what very few generations in history have had the privilege of knowing: a generational mission; the exhilaration of a compelling moral purpose; a shared and unifying cause; the thrill of being forced by circumstances to put aside the pettiness and conflict that so often stifle the restless human need for transcendence; the opportunity to rise.

When we do rise, it will fill our spirits and bind us together. Those who are now suffocating in cynicism and despair will be able to breathe freely. Those who are now suffering from a loss of meaning in their lives will find hope.

When we rise, we will experience an epiphany as we discover that this crisis is not really about politics at all. It is a moral and spiritual challenge. (587 words)

Source: *An Inconvenient Truth: The Planetary Emergency of Global Warming and What We Can Do About It* (2006)

32 procrastinator *Zögerer, Zauderer*
denier one who denies
33 heat-trapping greenhouse
35 capture catch
36 precious valuable
38 exhilaration euphoria
39 compelling powerful
thrill excited feeling
40 pettiness concern with unimportant things
stifle inhibit, suppress
41 transcendence go beyond normal experience
43 suffocate feel trapped or oppressed (as if dying from lack of air)
45 epiphany wonderful moment when a meaning suddenly becomes clear

WORKING WITH THE TEXT

2 a Using a full sheet of paper, re-draw this incomplete diagram showing some of the causes and effects of global warming. Fill in the empty boxes with the following:

- melting of the polar ice cap and mountain glaciers
- cutting and burning of forests
- dumping of CO_2 into the environment
- interference with the formation of coral and shells
- destabilization of wind currents

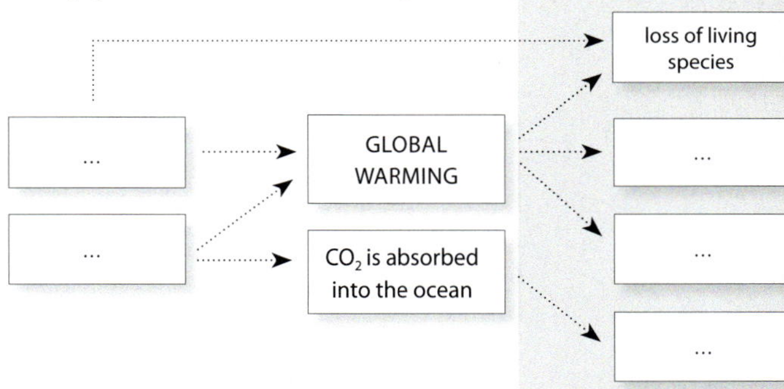

b Now use the diagram to explain the causes and effects of global warming presented in the text.

3 a Work with others in a group to make a mind map about the opportunities that global warming presents, according to the text.

S ► Mind Mapping (p. 191)

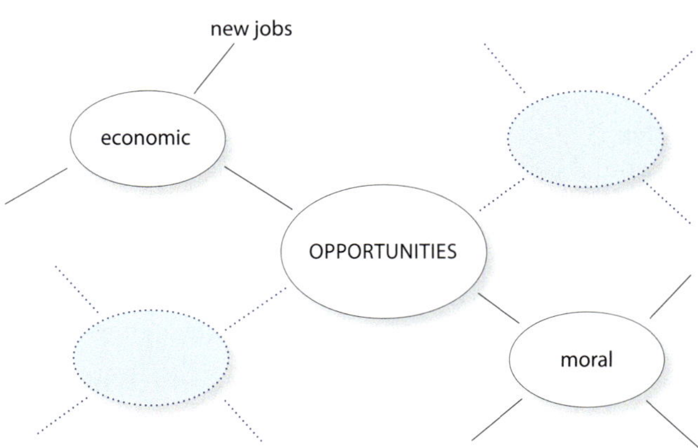

b Outline the author's views on these opportunities. Use the mind map to help you.

S ► How to Deal with Instructions (p. 192)

WORKING WITH A DICTIONARY

4 **The following words are commonly mispronounced. Use a dictionary to choose the correct phonetic transcription for each word. Look out for the position of the apostrophe ('): the main stress in a word always follows it.**

1 *moral*
a ['mɒrəl]
b [mə'rɑːl]

2 *interesting*
a [ɪnt'restɪŋ]
b ['ɪntrəstɪŋ]

3 *massive*
a ['mæsɪv]
b [mə'siːv]

4 *crisis*
a ['kraɪsɪs]
b ['kriːzɪs]

5 *aggressive*
a [ægrə'siːv]
b [ə'gresɪv]

6 *catastrophe*
a [kə'tæstrəfi]
b [kætə'strəʊfi]

7 *surface*
a [sɜ'feɪs]
b ['sɜːfɪs]

8 *comfortable*
a [kʌmfə'teɪbl]
b ['kʌmftəbl]

9 *purchase*
a [pə'tʃeɪs]
b ['pɜːtʃəs]

LOOKING AT LANGUAGE

G ▸ Verb + Object + *to* infinitive (p. 217)

5 **Translate the following sentences into English using the correct forms of the verbs in brackets with an object + *to* infinitive.**

Example: Die schmelzenden Gletscher haben zur Folge, dass der Meeresspiegel steigt. *(be causing)* ⟶ *Melting glaciers are causing the sea level to rise.*

1 Kalziumkarbonat bewirkt, dass Meerestiere Schwierigkeiten mit der Bildung von Muschelschalen haben. *(be causing)*
2 Man erwartet nicht, dass die Erderwärmung bald aufhört. *(expect)*
3 Wir würden uns sehr freuen, wenn die Erde so bleiben würde, wie sie ist. *(would love)*
4 Ich hätte gern, dass sich mehr Leute leidenschaftlich um die Umwelt kümmern. *(would like)*
5 Al Gore sagt der Regierung seit vielen Jahren, dass sie Kohlenstoff besteuern muss. *(have been telling)*
6 Er will, dass wir die Umweltkrise zur Mission unserer Generation machen. *(want)*

INTERPRETING GRAPHS

S ▸ Interpreting Graphs (p. 200)

6 **You are going to compare two ways of performing the typical exam task of analysing a graph.**

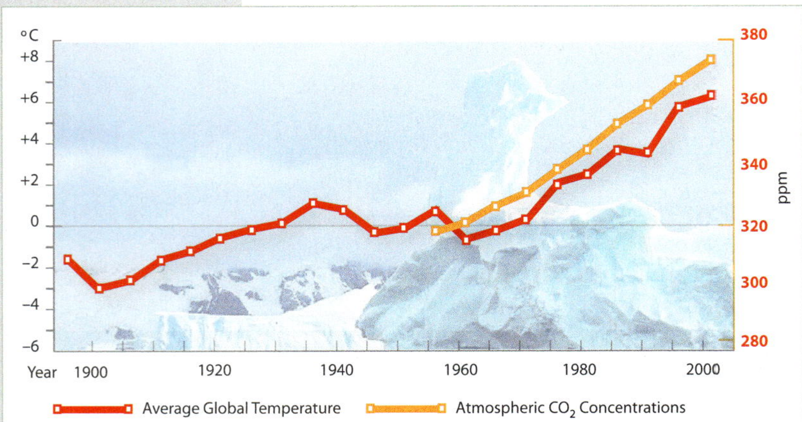

a **First read the task and look at the graph. Then go on to the next page.**

TASK: Study the graph and describe the trends. Does the information given correspond to the information given in the text 'An Inconvenient Truth' on pages 38/39? Give reasons for your answer.

b **Look at the two answers. The text on the left is grammatically correct, but it would nevertheless not get a very high mark. The text on the right is better in terms of content, organisation and language. (Don't think about the middle column yet.)**

average version | **tips** | **improved version**

average version

A line shows the temperature from the year 1900 to 2005. The line fluctuates and goes up. The temperature rose very fast after 1965. There is a second line. It shows concentrations of CO_2 from 1960 to 2005. It increased sharply. The rise in global temperature confirms the author's view that global warming exists. The rise in atmospheric CO_2 confirms the author's view that "We are dumping so much carbon dioxide into the Earth's environment". The graph does not prove that humans are the cause of the CO_2 …

tips

1

improved version

The graph shows the relationship between atmospheric CO_2 and average global temperature. A line shows the average global temperature from the year 1900 to 2005. This line fluctuates a bit, but the overall trend is clearly upwards, and the temperature rose especially fast after 1965. There is also a second line showing concentrations of atmospheric CO_2 from 1960 to 2005, which increased sharply and steadily.

The graph illustrates the information in the text in the following way. First, the rise in global temperature supports the author's claim that global warming exists. Secondly, the rise in atmospheric CO_2 confirms the author's statement that we are putting great amounts of CO_2 into the environment.

However, the graph does not prove that humans are the cause of the CO_2 …

c **Now look at the middle column and match the tips 1–8 to the arrows to find out what makes the text on the right 'excellent' in comparison with the 'mediocre' version on the left.**

1. A large and varied vocabulary is the most important feature of good writing.
2. Begin with an introductory sentence stating the general theme of the diagram or diagrams.
3. Organise your essay into more than one paragraph.
4. Do not use the author's words. Rephrase them or use synonyms.
5. Occasionally connect ideas using a participle.
6. Occasionally connect ideas using a subordinate clause.
7. Use connecting words – see 'Language for Writing' on the back flap of the book for more of these.
8. Use the language on p. 201 to describe diagrams.

COMPOSITION

7 **Do you agree with Al Gore that fighting global warming is the most important thing our generation can devote itself to, or do you think there is something else more important?**

S ▸ Writing an Essay (p. 196)

TEXT 2 People Affected by Climate Change

WARM-UP

S ▶ Group Discussions (p. 203)

1 Which of the following statements, if any, do you agree with? Discuss in small groups.

1. Global warming is a myth.
2. It's obvious that the climate is changing because of human influence.
3. I'm sceptical about humans being the cause of global warming. The earth's climate has always been changing. It has nothing to do with us.
4. I'm really concerned about what the climate will be like in the future.
5. I'll be dead and buried before the climate changes significantly.
6. Whether the climate changes or not, the earth will always be the perfect home.

2 You are going to read an article about the Alaskan island village of Shishmaref. These two photos were taken there before and after a storm. What has changed? Why do you think this happened?

Before

After

CD 1 Track 13

The End of an Island and a Way of Life

Off the coast of mainland Alaska, on little Sarichef Island, there is a small village called Shishmaref which has existed for centuries. Almost all the people there are indigenous Inupiaq Eskimos who still live, to a large extent, as they have for many thousands of years. They still feed themselves largely by fishing, by gathering, and by hunting animals like caribou, seal, and walrus. Sled dogs and sealskin kayaks are still means of transport. But the climate in Alaska is warming so rapidly that, by the time you read this, Shishmaref may no longer exist.

Shishmaref and Sarichef Island are disappearing into the sea. The rising sea level caused by melting glaciers is only one of the ways this is occurring. The snow and ice on the Alaskan land is also melting, with serious consequences. These vast, white regions reflect 70% of the sun's rays back out into space, and when they disappear, the heat is absorbed into the ground, which warms the climate even more. This vicious cycle is the reason why the climate is changing faster here than in other parts of the world. The ground itself in Alaska is mostly permafrost, some of which has been frozen for 100,000 years, but that is melting, too. Sarichef Island was once as hard as ice; now it is soft and vulnerable to weather. And what weather it is! Autumn storms have become so terrifyingly violent that the rain and waves literally

3 **indigenous** native
4 **gather** harvest wild foods
13 **vicious cycle** a recurring sequence of bad events
16 **vulnerable** able to be hurt

wash the island away. Sea ice used to protect the island from the waves, but now that doesn't form until late December. The result of all this is erosion on a grand scale. Locals estimate that the coastline recedes 3–15 metres every year. It has now reached the town's main road.

These boys will soon be moving to the mainland to attend college. After getting their degrees, they would like to return to Shishmaref ... if it still exists.

In a desperate attempt to protect the village from the waves, the US army began building a rock seawall to do the job the sea ice used to do. It is costing $6.8 million but not solving anything. Some residents' houses have had to be moved inland in order to save them from the fate of those which have already fallen into the sea.

But keeping a house anywhere has become difficult because the entire island has become a muddy bog, virtually impassable by sled or on foot. The sled dogs, snow shoes, and snow vehicles are now useless most of the year. This change in the Alaskan terrain is threatening to expose toxic and even radioactive materials which the government buried in the ground throughout the state during the time when the thawing of the ancient permafrost was still inconceivable.

Sled dogs used to be an important means of transportation. Now they are kept only for races in the winter.

Also inconceivable was what happened in 2000, when a group of Inupiaqs had to be rescued by helicopter because the ice on which they were hunting unexpectedly broke off from the shore. Since then, this has become a common occurrence throughout the Arctic region, and some hunters have even fallen through the ice to their deaths. The sea ice which the Inupiaq hunters used to know so intimately has become unpredictable and scarce; summer ice has shrunk by 15%–20% over the past 30 years. This forces the hunters to travel further and use boats which use much more fuel – another example of the cyclical nature of global warming as well as its monetary cost.

Hunting on the thinning ice

Virtually every aspect of traditional food sourcing has been affected. Drying fish has become difficult because flies and other insects which now thrive on the island lay their eggs in the hanging fish. Wild berries, another staple of the diet, are blooming too early in the year, and then frost stops the little fruits from growing.

Very soon, the 562 inhabitants of Shishmaref will have to evacuate their ancestral home and move to the mainland. Other villages will also have to resettle. Of Alaska's 213 native villages, 184 are experiencing floods and erosion. (642 words)

20 **recede** retreat, go back
34 **bog** moor
38 **expose** uncover
41 **thaw** <> freeze
49 **scarce** rare
57 **thrive** live very well
59 **staple** essential component
63 **ancestral home** place belonging to many generations

MEDIATION

S ▶ Mediation (p. 204)

3 With a partner, summarise the text in German.

Partner 1, describe to your partner in German why Shishmaref's island is disappearing into the sea.
Partner 2, tell your partner in German about some of the ways that life has changed for the inhabitants of Shishmaref.

LISTENING

CD 1 Track 14

S ▶ Practising Listening Skills (p. 188)

4 Listen to Shishmaref resident Ardith Weyioanna. What thoughts, questions and concerns does she have about the future of her island and her people? What had to happen for her to really understand what 'global warming' means? Take notes while you listen.

Thoughts, questions and concerns about the future	*1 …* *2 …* *3 …* *4 …*
How she came to understand what 'global warming' means	

WORKING WITH THE TEXTS

5 Think of the texts you have read and listened to. What will happen to Shishmaref? What will the residents do?

WORKING WITH WORDS

6 Fill in the blanks with eight of the ten words in the box, putting the verbs in their correct forms.

erode | evacuate | form | affect | indigenous | melt | muddy | occur | rapidly | vast

1. We Inupiaq are … people who survive by hunting.
2. Soon, our entire village will have to … and move inland.
3. Rain and waves are … our island, now that it has thawed.
4. Much of the ground in Alaska is permafrost, and has not … in many millennia.
5. The once frozen earth on the island has become soft and …
6. Sea ice … a barrier around the island which protects it from the waves.
7. Autumn storms are stronger and are … more frequently.
8. We are not the only Arctic community being … by global warming.

7 Choose one of the following tasks.

1. Write a description of the 'before' and 'after' photos in the warm-up using as many of the words from Exercise 6 as possible.
2. In small groups, take turns making sentences which describe the photos in this unit and tell the stories behind them. Use as many of the words from Exercise 6 as possible.

LOOKING AT LANGUAGE

8 Complete each conditional sentence by putting the verb in its correct form.

G ▸ Conditionals (p. 214)

1. Inupiaqs would lose their identity if they … *(move)* to big cities like Anchorage.
2. If the affected villages decide to build sea walls, where … *(they/get)* the money?
3. If villages built sea walls to protect the islands, there … *(be)* no guarantee that they would work.
4. If they … *(get)* enough money, they … *(build)* a new Shishmaref on the mainland.
5. It … *(require)* both state and federal funds if the Inupiaq villages are to be preserved.
6. If the Inupiaqs relocate, … *(they / still be able to)* hunt like they do now?

HOLDING A DEBATE

HANDS-ON TASK

9 You live in an Inupiaq village on the coast of Alaska, where everyone has just received this newsletter. Read the newsletter and do the task below.

S ▸ Debating (p. 203)

Shaktoolik News

Goings-on in our village

Dear fellow residents,

Aa, liqaa!

I do not need to tell you about the erosion being experienced by our village as well as by 183 others in Alaska. Now engineers from the army have come up with future cost estimates for seven affected villages, which you can see in the following table.

Army Corps of Engineers' assesment of seven communities affected by erosion

Communitiy	Cost of future erosion protection	Cost to relocate	How long do communities have?
Bethel	$ 5,000,000	N/A	>100 years
Dillingham	$ 10,000,000	N/A	>100 years
Kaktovik	$ 40,000,000	$ 20– 40 million	>100 years
Kivalina	$ 15,000,000	$ 95–125 million	10–15 years
Newtok	$ 90,000,000	$ 80–130 million	10–15 years
Shishmaref	$ 16,000,000	$ 100–200 million	10–15 years
Unalakleet	$ 30,000,000	N/A	>100 years

We know that the people of Shishmaref have already decided that they wish to relocate their entire village to a site on the mainland, yet they do not yet know how this will be financed. As far as we know, none of the other villages have reached a decision as to what they will do.

While we are still waiting for engineers to finish making cost estimates for our village, this information certainly gives us food for thought and discussion.

One thing is sure, the time will come very soon when we in Shaktoolik will have to make some very difficult decisions.

Your task is to guess what will happen to the villages which have been assessed by the army's engineers. Do not form an opinion until you have heard what the others have to say. Discuss each village individually.

Partner A, turn to File 1 on page 180. **Partner B**, turn to File 6 on page 182. **Partner C**, turn to File 10 on page 183.

If there is a fourth partner, he/she also takes role card A or B.

TEXT 3 Don't Drink the Water and Don't Breathe the Air

WARM-UP

1 a With a partner or two, take turns making sentences about this image. Your teacher will give you a time limit. Make a tick (✓) for every correct sentence you make before your time is up.

Tom Lehrer

b After you have counted the number of correct sentences your group made, turn to File 5 on page 182.

CD 1 Track 15

[4] **beware of** mind, be careful of
[8] **sewage** waste water
[10] **crud** dirt
[11] **halibut** *Heilbutt*
[12] **sturgeon** *Stör*
[13] **detergent** soap
[25] **veil** cloth which covers the face
[31] **sink** basin with water supply and drain
[33] **hunch** intuitive guess

Pollution

by Tom Lehrer

If you visit [an] American city,
You will find it very pretty.
Just two things of which you must beware:
Don't drink the water and don't breathe the air.

Pollution, pollution,
We got smog and sewage and mud.
Turn on your tap and get hot and cold running crud.

See the halibuts and the sturgeons
Being wiped out by detergents.
Fish gotta swim and birds gotta fly,
But they don't last long if they try.

Pollution, pollution,
You can use the latest toothpaste,
And then rinse your mouth with industrial waste.

Just go out for a breath of air,
And you'll be ready for Medicare.
The city streets are really quite a thrill.
If the hoods don't get you, the monoxide will.

Pollution, pollution,
Wear a gas mask and a veil.
Then you can breathe, [as] long as you don't inhale.

Lots of things there that you can drink,
But stay away from the kitchen sink.
Throw out your breakfast garbage and I've got a hunch.
That the folks downstream will drink it for lunch.

So go to the city, see the crazy people there.
Like lambs to the slaughter,
They're drinking the water
And breathing the air.

WORKING WITH THE SONG

2 a **What makes the song humorous?**

b **What forms of pollution are mentioned in the song? What other kinds of pollution exist?**

WORKING WITH WORDS

3 **Find the nouns in the song which are pictured here. The first letter has been given.**

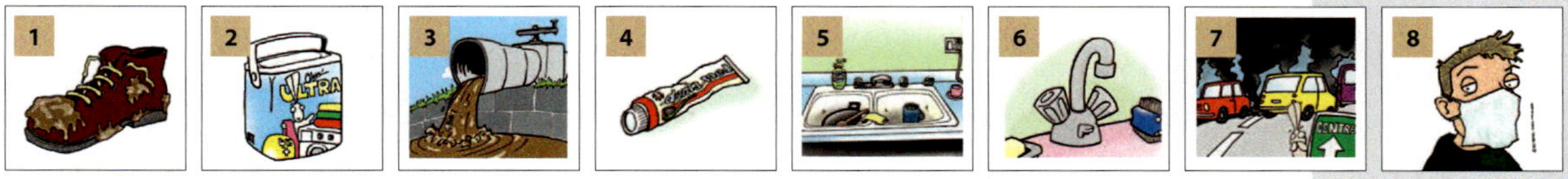

1 *m…* **2** *d…* **3** *s…* **4** *t…* **5** *s…* **6** *t…* **7** *s…* **8** *v…*

LOOKING AT LANGUAGE

4 **If a verb is needed twice in an English sentence, we can often substitute it with an auxiliary or a modal verb instead of repeating it. Complete the following sentences using a form of *be*, *do*, *have* or a suitable modal verb.**

Example:
I always think about the impact of my actions on the environment, but many people …
→ *I always think about the impact of my actions on the environment, but many people* ***don't***.

1 Don't go in that water! If the alligators don't get you, the industrial waste …
2 You may want to go to stinky Los Angeles, but I most certainly …
3 Cell phones ringing don't bother me as much as their radiation …
4 The Americans don't want to give up their precious cars. But then who …?
5 If the skyscrapers didn't impress the tour group, maybe the litter … either.
6 The American grizzly bear hasn't become extinct yet but the Mexican grizzly …
7 Holding your breath while you're in the city isn't possible, but wearing a mask …
8 Acid rain has turned the museum facade black and so … the car exhaust.

CREATIVE WRITING

HANDS-ON TASK

5 **Choose one of the following tasks.**

1 Make a funny travel brochure or poster for a city of your choice, perhaps a fictitious one, which promotes itself through its pollution in the ironic manner the song does.

2 Make a funny script for a tour guide to read while leading a bus tour through the city.

TEXT 4 Fuelling Deforestation

WARM-UP

decompose rot
release set free
carbon *Kohlenstoff*

1 **Using the diagram, complete the text with the verbs from the box in the correct form.**

absorb (2x) | burn | combine | decompose | form | release (3x) | remain

The carbon cycle

The carbon cycle works as follows. Carbon dioxide is …[1] by live plants. The carbon atoms …[2] in the plants while they grow and the oxygen gets …[3] into the atmosphere. When the plants die, the carbon they held re-…[4] with oxygen in the atmosphere to …[5] carbon dioxide, which is …[6] into the atmosphere. This happens whether the plant matter dies and …[7], is …[8], or is used to make biofuel. The advantage of biofuels over traditional fossil fuels is, therefore, that biofuels only …[9] as much carbon dioxide into the atmosphere as they …[10] from it while they were growing.

The carbon cycle

2 **Look at the map, the photo and the title of the text. What do you think it will be about?**

CD 1 Track 16

1/2 peat bog/swamp *Torfmoor*
10 roam move around without any definite direction
dome *Kuppel*
14 debris small pieces
18 clear-fell cut down all trees in a certain area

Indonesia's Carbon Catastrophe

I am standing in the heart of the world's second largest tropical peat swamp, the Kampar bog in central Sumatra, watching the swamp's water drain away along a small canal. Across the western side of the bog there are dozens more drains. The peat bog is bleeding to death before me.

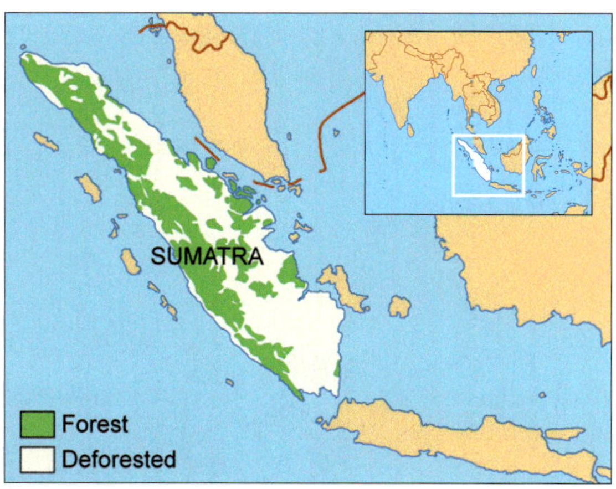

Until five years ago, Kampar was a true bog with water at the surface, and it was covered by a rich rainforest in which Sumatran tigers roamed. A huge dome of living peat, up to 15 metres deep, had built up over the past 6000 years as woody debris fell into the swamp. It contains several billion tonnes of carbon. Now this part of the Kampar bog has been clear-felled, and the canals have been installed to turn it into plantations. As water levels fall beneath the blackened and treeless wasteland, the peat is drying and decomposing, releasing more carbon dioxide into the atmosphere per square kilometre than many cities do.

I watched as workers planted acacia trees for paper and palm oil trees destined to make biofuels to help reduce Europe's CO_2 emissions. Yet draining the peat will release 30 times more CO_2 than will be saved by replacing fossil fuels with biofuels – an irony that is hard to stomach. The fact that European countries can meet their Kyoto Protocol obligations by sponsoring activities that have helped turn Indonesia, of which the giant island of Sumatra is a part, into the world's third largest emitter of greenhouse gases is a savage charge against the perverse incentives created by the protocol.

The destruction of tropical peatland forests is a disaster for many reasons, not least its global impact. Peat holds many times more carbon than the forest above it. Marcel Silvius, a tropical ecologist at Wetlands International, estimates that in south-east Asia, 130,000 square kilometres of peatland forests have already been cut down and partially drained. As a result, an average of 2 gigatonnes of CO_2 is being released each year through decomposition and burning of peat. That's equal to 8 per cent of the total annual global CO_2 emissions from fossil fuels – and 90 per cent of it comes from Indonesia alone.

Here, forests are being cut and the peat drained to make way for two crops: palm oil trees for food and biofuels, and acacia for paper. This is happening fastest on Sumatra, and most intensively of all in the central Sumatran province of Riau. Until the late 1980s, Riau was 80 per cent jungle. Today it's just 30 per cent.

Palm oil is used for cooking and as an ingredient in everything from shampoo to biscuits. Global production has been soaring and Indonesia now produces a third of the global crop. In Riau, palm oil plantations already cover more than 15,000 square kilometres – a fifth of the province – with another 5000 square kilometres planned to meet the expected demand for biofuels. Local politicians see this as boosting both industrial and rural development.

That may be true, but in climate terms, razing rainforests to grow palm oil for biofuels is madness. Clearing a hectare of tropical forest releases between 500 and 900 tonnes of CO_2. Since turning a hectare's worth of palm oil into biodiesel saves approximately 6 tonnes of fossil CO_2 emissions a year, it will take 80 to 150 years of production to offset the one-off emissions from trashing the forest. That is bad enough. If the forest is growing on a peat bog, however, the CO_2 losses are far greater and continue far longer. (594 words)

Adapted from 'Bog barons: Indonesia's carbon catastrophe' in *New Scientist*, 1 December 2007

23 **destined** intended for a purpose
26 **stomach** bear, tolerate
29 **savage** wild, cruel
charge accusation
incentive *Anreiz*
43 **ingredient** component
44 **soar** keep going up
49 **raze** tear down and destroy
53 **offset** compensate for
one-off made or happening only once
trash destroy

WORKING WITH THE TEXT

3 Complete the following summary of the text with appropriate words.

The article deals with the …1 of peat bog rainforests, which are being …2 of water in order to turn them into plantations. This is occurring on a great scale in Indonesia and having a terrible global …3. The …4 grown on the plantations include acacia trees and palm oil trees. The great irony is that the palm oil is used to …5 Europe's demand for …6, which Europe buys with the intention of reducing its CO_2 …7. But draining the forest causes the peat to die and decompose, and to …8 far greater amounts of CO_2 into the atmosphere than are saved by not using …9 fuels. This has helped turn Indonesia into the world's third largest emitter of …10 gases.

S ▸ How to Deal with Instructions (p. 192)

4 Explain how people are causing Indonesian peat bogs to release unnatural amounts of carbon dioxide into the atmosphere.

Before you start, organise your essay by making an outline. Copy the outline below into your exercise book and complete it with six of the following points. One of the points is irrelevant.

- Peat and other plant material dies
- Forests are cleared
- Palm oil to make many products
- Reduction in number of tigers
- For biofuels
- Other reason: to boost the local economy

How are people causing Indonesian peat bogs to release unnatural amounts of carbon dioxide into the atmosphere?

Paragraph **1**	Demand for agricultural products		
	1.1	…	
		1.1.1	For food products
		1.1.2	…
		1.1.3	So Europe can meet Kyoto Protocol obligations
	1.2	Acacia trees to make paper	
Paragraph **2**	…		
	2.1	Reason: to meet demand for agricultural products	
	2.2	…	
	2.3	Water is drained out	
	2.4	…	
		2.4.1	By drying
		2.4.2	By burning out
	2.5	Dying plant material releases CO_2	

COMPOSITION

S ▸ How to Deal with Instructions (p. 192)

5 Assess the impact of biofuels on the environment.

WORKING WITH WORDS

6 Rewrite each sentence, changing the underlined noun into a verb with the same root.

Example: The current system of biofuel production doesn't constitute a savings in greenhouse gases.
⟶ *The current system of biofuel production doesn't* ***save*** *greenhouse gases.*

1 We need a new system as a replacement for this one.
2 Once water is drained from the bog, decomposition of the peat takes place.
3 There has been a build-up of CO_2 in the atmosphere, which seems to be causing global warming.
4 Indonesia has very high greenhouse gas emissions.
5 Deforestation often means a short-term boost to the local economy.
6 Plants are a container for carbon.
7 Scientists' estimations are that it will take decades to undo the damage done to the atmosphere.
8 A peat bog being drained is like a body that is losing blood.

ANALYSING A GRAPH

7 Describe the graph and compare it to the information given in the text on p. 48/49.

S ▸ Interpreting Graphs (p. 200)

LOOKING AT LANGUAGE

8 Complete the text by choosing the correct adjective or adverb. Then compare the text with the graph above. Find six mistakes in the text and correct them.

S ▸ Adjectives and Adverbs (p. 217)

The graph shows the amount of forest cover in relation to the amount of palm oil production in Indonesia. Records begin in 1964 when the country had about 130 million hectares of forest. This amount increased (steady/steadily)[1] until about 2006, when records end. (Lucky/Luckily)[2], over this (42-year/42-yearly)[3] period, Indonesia lost (approximate/approximately)[4] 35% of its forested land. Palm oil production began at almost 100 million tons and fell (slow/slowly)[5] until the late 1980s, when it had a (noticeable/noticeably)[6] (sharp/sharply)[7] decrease. After a (brief/briefly)[8] dip in production in around 1997, the production of palm oil plummeted (incredible/incredibly)[9] (quick/quickly)[10] and finished off at a (massive/massively)[11] 16 million metric tons.

ANALYSING A CARTOON

9 **Explain the cartoon and compare the message it conveys with the information in the text.**
First, look at the sample answer below. Then rewrite and complete the answer, improving it and incorporating the given tips.

S ▸ Interpreting Cartoons (p. 199)

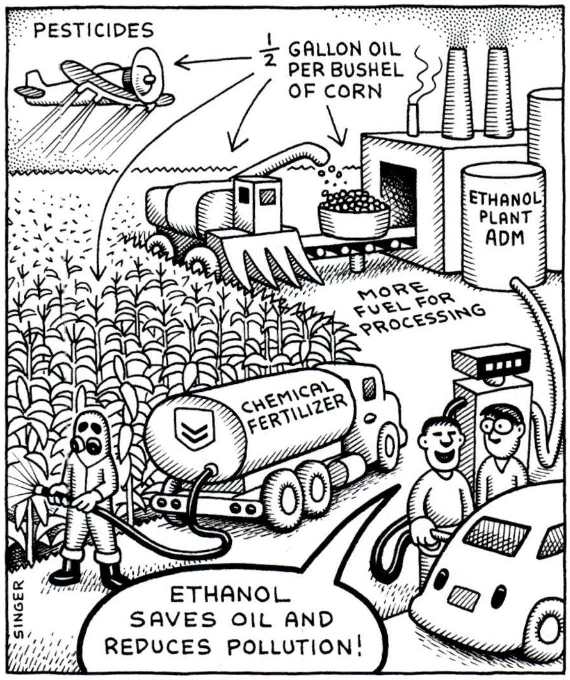

bushel *Scheffel*
corn *(AE) BE:* maize
plant factory

Average answer

Begin with an introductory sentence stating the general theme of the cartoon.

There is a man. He is spraying a corn field with chemical fertilizer. An aeroplane sprays pesticides onto the corn field from above. We can see a tractor. It is delivering the corn to be processed. Words inform us that all this requires more than half a gallon of oil per bushel of corn. ______ ______ A smiling motorist is putting petrol in his car. He is saying proudly that ethanol saves oil and decreases pollution.

The cartoonist would agree that "razing rainforests to grow palm oil for biofuels is madness".

Do not use the author's words. Rephrase them or use synonyms.

Tips for improvement

Use the present progressive to describe what is happening in the cartoon. Here the wrong tense is used.

Use connecting words – see 'Language for Writing' on the back flap of the book for more of these. Here, *finally* could be used.

Know the language for describing cartoons on p. 200.
Here, *caption* should have been used.
Here, *in the foreground* could be used.

Tips for improvement

A large and varied vocabulary is the most important feature of good writing.

Occasionally connect ideas using a participle. Here are three places where present participles could be used.

Organise your answer into four paragraphs according to the four-step description on p. 199. This essay has completely left out the second and third steps / paragraphs, and the fourth is incomplete.

TEXT 5 Controversial Forms of Activism

WARM-UP

1 **Activism which goes beyond actions such as passive demonstrations, boycotts and letter writing and which attempts to solve problems immediately is sometimes called *direct action*. Direct action can involve breaking the law or putting people in harm's way.**

a **The following table shows examples of direct action. Copy the table into your exercise book and complete columns 2 and 3.**

Action	Would take part under certain circumstances (y/n)	Would give support under certain circumstances (y/n)
go on strike	...	...
hold a sit-in	...	...
graffiti a political message on a building	...	...
block traffic	...	...
spend a month up a tree to keep it from being cut down	...	...
break into a building	...	...
sabotage or destroy a facility	...	...
put yourself in front of a moving vehicle	...	...

b **Tell your partner which actions you would take part in or support and explain under which circumstances you would do so.**

I would hold a sit-in if a law needed to be changed.

I would graffiti a building if I didn't have any other options.

c **Which of the following criteria would you use to measure the effectiveness of an action?**

1. how impressive the personal risk to activists is, i.e. going to jail or getting hurt
2. how much immediate damage is done to adversaries, so that it is difficult for them to continue doing what they're doing
3. whether or not the action brings about legislation change
4. how many people participate in the action
5. how much publicity, good or bad, the action gets
6. how the action is evaluated by the public
7. how well the activists are able to express their anger

CD 1 Track 17

1 **vigilante** sb who enforces the law without authority to do so
3 **greedy** selfishly wanting more of sth.
4 **coercive** by force
5 **ram** strike with force
vessel boat, ship
7 **violation** breaking or going against
9 **outrage** anger, offend
15 **law enforcement** making sure that people obey the laws
25 **unyielding** stubborn
27 **bend the truth** distort the truth
28 **recklessness** carelessness
29 **loathing** hate
34 **butyric acid** *Buttersäure*
37 **prop-fouler** a material used to damage ship propellers
coil rope
38 **get entangled** become caught up, knotted up
40 **drain** channel through which liquid is carried away
47 **foremost** most prominent

Neptune's Navy: Paul Watson's Wild Crusade to Save the Oceans

The Sea Shepherd Conservation Society is a vigilante organization founded by Paul Watson thirty years ago to protect the world's marine life from the destructive habits and the greedy appetites of humankind. Watson believes in coercive conservation, and for several decades he has been using his private navy to ram whaling and fishing vessels on the high seas.

When Watson is separated from land, he tends to behave like Captain Nemo, which is to say that he does what he thinks is right, even if it involves a violation of custom or the destruction of property. There are a number of rules belonging to civilization that outrage his sense of morality. If such rules interfere with his agenda, then, as far as he is concerned, rules be damned. This is particularly true when whales are at issue. Watson believes that whales are more intelligent than people, and that their slaughter is equivalent to murder. (He once compared their extermination to the Holocaust.)

He calls his fleet Neptune's Navy, and he regards it as a law-enforcement agency. Moments before ramming a vessel, Watson will radio its captain and say something that sounds very official, such as "Please remove yourselves from these waters. You are in violation of international conservation regulations." At times, he loses his cool. "We're no protest ship," he once told an unyielding captain. "Now, get out of here." His sense of urgency, his impressive ego, his argumentativeness, his love of theatrics, his tendency to bend the truth, his willingness to risk lives or injury for his beliefs (or for publicity), and his courage (or recklessness) have earned him both loathing and admiration from those who are familiar with his activism.

One stormy day last winter in the Ross Sea, Watson's ship the Hunter challenged the more than 400-foot-long whaling ship Nisshin Maru. The Japanese vessel blasted its horns and turned on its water cannons, which sent powerful jets overboard. On the Hunter's deck, crew members dressed in black uniforms, their faces covered by masks, began throwing canisters of butyric acid – a relatively harmless substance that smells like rancid butter – and smoke bombs onto the Nisshin Maru's deck. At the waterline, Watson's small, motorized boats called Zodiacs surrounded the whaler. Their crews carried cameras and prop-foulers – long knotted coils of polypropylene – which they hoped would get entangled in the Nisshin Maru's propellers. Other Zodiac crews were equipped with nail guns. They drew their boats beside the Nisshin Maru and nailed shut drains through which whale blood was released into the ocean. After a long and dangerous conflict, the Nisshin Maru eventually escaped into the Antarctic storm.

Watson's celebrity supporters, some of whom he has come to know personally, include Mick Jagger, Pierce Brosnan, Sean Penn, Aidan Quinn, William Shatner, Edward Norton, Orlando Bloom, and Uma Thurman. Sea Shepherd's board of advisers includes Elizabeth May, the leader of Canada's Green Party, and Roger Payne, one of the world's foremost experts on whales. The Dalai Lama has given him a written endorsement. Within the animal-rights community, Watson is treated like a demigod.

Those who speak badly of Watson are just as firm in their opinions. Officials in Iceland, Denmark, Norway, Japan, Canada, and Costa Rica have denounced him; some have even called him a terrorist. Watson has made enemies of other conservationists, too. For decades, Greenpeace has wanted nothing to do with him – a criticism that is particularly stinging because he was a founder of the organization. He has been barred from I.W.C. meetings since 1986, when Sea Shepherd sank two whaling ships in Reykjavik's harbor – an act of sabotage that many conservationists believe helped turn Icelandic public opinion against the cause of saving whales. Sidney Holt, one of the principal architects of the whaling moratorium, told me, "I think his involvement in all this is an absolute disaster. Almost everything he has been doing has had blowback for those who want to see an end to whaling. In too many cases, playing piracy on the ocean, and creating danger for other ships, is simply not liked." (676 words)

Adapted from *The New Yorker*, November 5, 2007 by Raffi Khatchadourian

48 **endorsement** support
49 **demigod** half-god
51 **denounce** declare to be wrong or evil
55 **stinging** painful
64 **blowback** unintended negative consequences

WORKING WITH THE TEXT

2 **How is Paul Watson described in the text?**

3 **What tactics does Paul Watson use to stop whaling?**

S ▸ Answering Comprehension Questions (p. 191)

WORKING WITH WORDS

4 **Rewrite each sentence so that it contains the word in brackets and has the same meaning.**

1 Paul Watson has been participating in conservation for decades. (involved)
2 He often makes enemies. (tendency)
3 Sometimes, he loses his cool. (upset)
4 He has a sense that everything must be accomplished very quickly. (urgency)
5 Many famous people have a very high opinion of him. (admire)
6 His crews carry cameras and tools to damage whaling ships. (equipped)
7 He is not afraid to destroy what doesn't belong to him. (property)
8 He spends most of his life in a boat with water all around him. (surrounded)
9 What he aims to do is clear. (agenda)
10 He wants to preserve life in the sea and stop whaling. (marine)

5 **Match each adjective (1–6) with its opposite (a–f).**

1 greedy	**4** urgent	**a** creative	**d** admirable
2 reckless	**5** shameful	**b** generous	**e** average
3 destructive	**6** impressive	**c** careful	**f** unimportant

LOOKING AT LANGUAGE

S ▸ Word Order – Positions of Adverbs (p. 218)

6 Rewrite the sentences putting the adverbs in brackets in the correct positions. Sometimes more than one answer is possible.

1 Our chairman is good at the art of public protest. (incredibly)
2 However, he loses his cool when debating. (sometimes)
3 He forgets to summarise after presenting a lot of important information. (always)
4 A demonstration march takes place. (usually, at 10 a.m.)
5 There is a sit-in taking place. (right now, at the town hall)
6 We prepare for the action. (often, at my place, in the evenings)
7 We break the law. (hardly ever)
8 We take risks. (never) We make sure no one gets hurt. (always)

COMPOSITION

S ▸ Writing a Comment (p. 195)

7 Choose a form of activism and comment on its effectiveness.

LISTENING

CD 1 Track 18

S ▸ Practising Listening Skills (p. 188)

8 a Listen to the CD. What means of protest are mentioned?

b Look at the 'Language for Discussion' on the back cover flap of your book. Listen again to the activists and note which phrases they use.

HANDS-ON TASK

DISCUSSION

S ▸ Group Discussions (p. 203)

9 Follow these steps.

1 Choose between one of the following causes to support.
   a Save the whales!
   b Save the rainforests! Stop the clear-felling of trees!
   c Save the Mediterranean ecosystem! No more overfishing!
   d Save the national park! No new motorway!
   e Save future generations! No more nuclear power stations!
2 Get into a group with others who support the same cause.
3 Go to File 4 on page 181 and read the information relevant to your group.
4 Elect a 'language secretary'.
5 Take a few minutes to brainstorm as many ideas as you can for ways to protest and to solve the problem.
6 Discuss and evaluate the ideas. Throughout the discussion, the language secretary gives a point each time someone uses a phrase from 'Language for Discussion', and takes a point away any time someone speaks a language other than English.

TEXT 6 Finding Solutions

WARM-UP

1 Look at these technologies. What do they all have in common?

- solar cells
- wind turbines
- recycling
- biofuels
- hybrid cars
- organic farming practices
- building insulation
- energy-efficient light bulbs

2 Race your partner! Look at the following three texts and – as fast as you can – formulate a sentence describing what they're about.

S ▸ Skimming (p. 184)

Emerging Environmental Technologies

CD 1 Track 19

I Bury the Bad Stuff – Carbon Sequestration

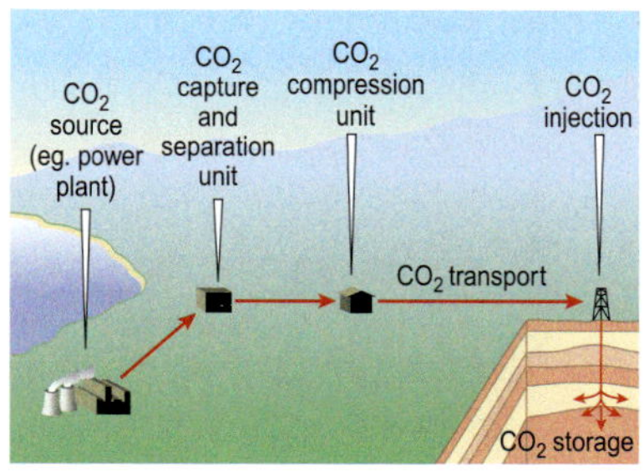

Carbon dioxide is the most prominent greenhouse gas contributing to global warming. According to the Energy Information Administration, by the year 2030 we will be emitting close to 8,000 million metric tons of CO_2, up from 5,890 million in 2006. Some experts say it's impossible to curb the emission of CO_2 into the atmosphere and that we just have to find ways to dispose of the gas. One suggested method is to inject it into the ground before it gets a chance to reach the atmosphere. After the CO_2 is separated from other emission gases, it can be buried in abandoned oil wells, saline reservoirs, and rocks. While this sounds great, scientists are not sure whether the injected gas will stay underground and what the long-term effects will be, and the costs of separation and burying are still far too high to consider this technology as a practical short-term solution. (150 words)

carbon sequestration removal and storage of CO_2 from the atmosphere
8 **dispose of** get rid of
10 **abandon** stop using
oil well hole in the ground from which oil is obtained
saline reservoir underground place which holds salt water

II Let Plants and Microbes Clean Up After Us

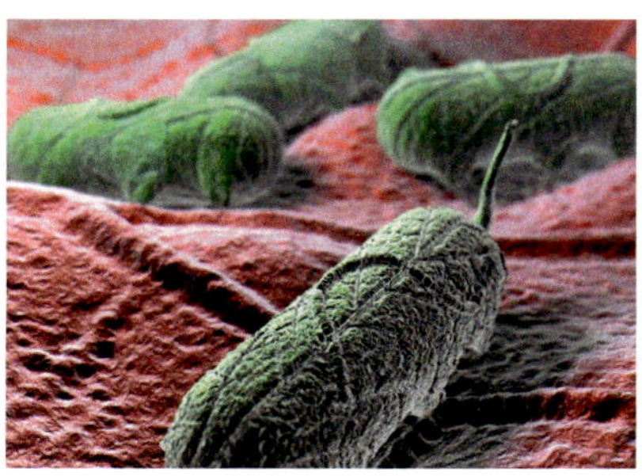

Bioremediation uses microbes and plants to clean up contamination. Examples include the clean-up of nitrates in contaminated water with the help of microbes, and using plants to take up arsenic from contaminated soil, in a process known as phytoremediation. The U.S. Environmental Protection Agency has used it to clean up several sites. Often, native plant species can be used for a site clean-up, which are advantageous because in most cases they don't require pesticides or watering. In other cases, scientists are trying to genetically modify the plants to take up contaminants in their roots and transport them all the way to the leaves for easy harvesting. The plants can then be incinerated or dried and shrunk for storage. (116 words)

15 **bioremediation** decontamination using plants and microbes
16 **contamination** impurity
19 **arsenic** a poisonous chemical element (As)
20 **soil** earth, dirt
phytoremediation decontamination using plants
26 **incinerate** burn
shrink reduce in size

29 **abundance** an amount that is more than is needed

30 **obstacle** obstruction, block

36 **buoy** an anchored object which floats on the surface

37 **swell** regular movement of the sea (waves)

III Harness Waves and Tides

The oceans cover more than 70 percent of the Earth's surface. Waves contain an abundance of energy that could be directed to turbines, which then turn this mechanical power into electricity. The obstacle to using this energy source has been the difficulty in harnessing it. Sometimes the waves are too small to generate sufficient power. The trick is to be able to store the energy when enough mechanical power is generated. New York City's East River is now in the process of becoming the test bed for six tide-powered turbines, and Portugal's reliance on waves in a new project is expected to produce enough power for more than 1,500 homes. One of the methods used to harness this form of energy is a buoy system capable of capturing the ocean's power in the form of offshore swells. (135 words)

Adapted from *Top Ten Emerging Environmental Technologies,* www.livescience.com

WORKING WITH THE TEXT

3 Which technology or technologies does each of the following statements refer to?

1 We could get electricity this way.
2 With this technology, we let nature do the work for us.
3 Before we can use this, we have to figure out how to store the energy.
4 This could slow the manmade factors contributing to global warming.
5 This is too expensive right now.
6 This might help us to burn more oil without environmental consequences.
7 This would help us to burn less oil.
8 We don't know whether this could lead to a future disaster.

S ► How to Deal with Instructions (p. 192)

4 Outline the advantages and disadvantages of each technology. Before you start, copy and complete the following table.

Technology	advantages/benefits	disadvantages/obstacles/risks
Carbon sequestration	…	…
Decontamination with plants and microbes	…	…
Energy from waves and tides	…	…

WORKING WITH WORDS

5 Complete the sentences with the past participles of these verbs. One verb does not fit.

abandon | bury | contaminate | contain | dispose | generate | modify | rely | shrink

Someday …
1 carbon emissions may be … under ground.
2 we may heat our houses with the energy … in waste products.
3 energy consumption will hopefully have … a great deal.
4 the current ways of doing things will have been … for better ways.
5 sites we have … with poisons will be clean again.
6 we will know what the long-term effects are of genetically … plants.
7 the oil we have … on for energy will be all gone.
8 more electrical power will probably be … using energy from the sun.

TRANSLATION

6 With one partner or two, translate one of the texts on pages 57/58.
When you have finished, exchange papers with another group that has translated the same text. Correct any mistakes you find.

S ▸ Translation (p. 204)

LOOKING AT LANGUAGE

7 Join the two columns by making the endings a–h into relative clauses, using *who(m)*, *whose*, or *which*.

G ▸ Relative Clauses (p. 219)

1 Monsanto is the company	**a** it is used to dispose of carbon dioxide
2 Dr Austin is the scientist	**b** he has developed a way to get energy from animal waste
3 I am the one	**c** they have a garden on their roof
4 The Spratlings are the family	**d** my company makes biodegradable packaging
5 Aren't you the person	**e** it is the leading producer of genetically modified seed
6 Harry told me about his new job	**f** we may pay for it dearly in the future
7 Carbon sequestration is a technology	**g** I spoke to you on the phone yesterday
8 Wasting energy is a luxury	**h** it will allow him to work at home

LISTENING

CD 1 Track 20

S ▸ Practising Listening Skills (p. 188)

8 a Listen to the head of a technology company pitch her technology to a potential investor at an environmental technology fair. Which of the technologies in the box is she pitching?

biodegradable plastics and packaging | geothermal energy | hydrogen fuel cells | making drinking water from salt water | no-flush toilets | ocean thermal energy conservation | rooftop gardens | solar energy | wind energy

b Listen again and complete the following phrases used by the representative.

1. That's why we think that our technology will be very important …
2. Well, it's completely waterless. It lets nature … by composting the waste.
3. So we increase the surface area of the waste so that it can dry. And … system of fans which push the air out through a vent.
4. Yes, of course. … to get the waste to decompose very quickly.
5. At the moment … ways to get that in an environmentally friendly way as well.
6. Soon … for public utilities …

MINI-PRESENTATIONS

HANDS-ON TASK

9 Prepare a short presentation and use it to convince your classmates of a new technology.
Do further research on one of the technologies described in this unit or choose another environmentally beneficial technology to research. Some suggestions are listed above in the listening task. You are going to play the role of the head of a 'green technology' company and pitch your technology to your classmates to try and get them to invest in your technology. You may wish to have a drawing to show.

World of Work

MEDIATION Renewable Energies

S ▸ Mediation (p. 204)

1 Do the following mediation task.

Ihre Firma überlegt, in neue Energie zu investieren. Sie werden gebeten, dem Vorstand die Chancen einer solchen Investition zu erläutern. Zu diesem Zweck stellen Sie eine Tischvorlage zusammen, auf der Sie stichpunktartig die Entwicklung dieses Industriezweigs zusammenfassen und die klimatischen Rahmenbedingungen umreißen.

The first section (up to 'The Power of Wind') has been done for you below, but there are four bullet points too many here. Use only those which are needed to complete the task.

- Die meisten Firmen, die heute der Umweltindustrie zugeordnet werden, galten vor ein paar Jahren noch als chancenlose Startups.
  - Ihre Gründer wurden allenfalls müde belächelt.
  - Sie hatten aus Sicht gestandener Industrieller nichts als Flausen im Kopf.
- Prognostizierter Umsatz im Jahr 2030:
  - Umweltindustrie: 1000 Milliarden
  - Vergleich mit Autoindustrie: 570 Milliarden
- 500.000 Jobs sollen in den nächsten 25 Jahren entstehen.
- Roland-Berger-Berater Torsten Henzelmann sagt: „Die grüne Industrie ist ein Jobmotor, der allmählich auf Hochtouren läuft."
- Gewinner des Klimawandels:
  - Elektrotechnik-Unternehmen wie Miele – verbrauchsarme und langlebige Waschmaschinen
    – Miele macht damit schon ewig Werbung.
  - Heizungsbauer – Umstellung von Öl- und Gasheizungen auf erneuerbare Energie
  - Hersteller erneuerbarer Energiesysteme

fuel increase sth, make sth stronger
1 **turnover** the total amount of goods or services sold by a company
6 **start-up** a company that is just beginning to operate
7 **established** (officially) recognised due to long-standing existence
11 **reckon** to think sth or have an opinion about sth
fledgling a new or inexperienced organisation

Green Energy Fuels the German Economy

Germany's environment industry will soon have a higher turnover than that of its auto manufacturers. The pioneers in the field were once considered idealistic crazies. Today many of them are world industry leaders. We've found the green angels that are fighting climate change … and earning considerable sums.

Just a few years ago, most of the companies that are today classified as belonging to the environment industry were considered hopeless start-ups. From the point of view of the established industrialists, the minds behind these companies were filled with nonsense. Now, however, it's predicted that Germany's environment industry will soon be making a higher turnover than its famous auto manufacturing and mechanical engineering *(Maschinenbau)* industries. That's what Roland Berger consultant Torsten Henzelmann reckons: the fledgling industry could reach a turnover of 1,000 billion euros in 2030, while auto manufacturing is predicted to reach only 570 billion euros in the same year. This trend will also be noticeable in the German job market. More than a half a million jobs are expected to be created in the next 25 years alone through renewable energy. 'The green industry is a job motor that's gradually reaching full speed,' says Henzelmann. It's the biggest profiteer of climate change.

Among the winners are electrotechnology companies like Miele, whose washing machines are efficient and long lasting – and who have been advertising them that way for ages. It's possible that today's customers, in these times of climate change, don't mind paying a couple of hundred euros more. Another company to profit is Heizungsbauer, which is converting more and more old oil and gas heaters to run on renewable energy. And of course the manufacturers of renewable energy systems are also among the winners.

The Power of Wind

Enercon waited for a long time for the winds of prosperity to blow their way. When Stefan Lütkemeyer began work at the wind energy company in 1996, he was one of two employees, and the company was already 12 years old. At that time it was part of the system engineers' jobs to do battle with citizens and lawyers when Enercon wanted to put up a wind turbine on a village hill. But at the end of the 90s wind energy became politically desirable and laws were put in place to promote it. That put wind under the wings of Enercon. Today Lütkemeyer, 41, is in charge of 100 employees who sell wind turbines all over the world. They have erected more than 11,000 units, and that's just the beginning: 'We're active in a gigantic market,' says Lütkemeyer. 'The demand is simply far greater than the supply.'

Success with Solar

Even if they don't get laughed at anymore, the environment industry often sees the same type of entrepreneur: the optimistic visionary with the courage to take risks, go-getting, determined and often quite idealistic. Bernhard Beck once had to watch while the harvest on his father's farm dried up. In his search for a way to help his father, he got the idea of using empty fields as solar power plants, and went to work on developing it. That was eight years ago, when Beck was 21. Today he's the business manager of Beck Energy and is building solar power plants all over Europe. He has built 22 plants in southern Germany, one in Spain, and he has Italy, Portugal and Greece in his sights. He employs 85 people, and that number is expected to grow to 100 in a couple of months.

The German farmers on whose fields Beck has built solar power plants used to wait anxiously for the weather reports. 'Today they can sit back and relax,' says Beck. 'The income from the power input always compensates for crop failure in dry summers.'

Doing Business with the Climate

Climate change will cost money. Storms will become much worse and so dikes, for example, will have to be better reinforced against the wind and waves. Meteorologists agree that temperatures on the planet will be a couples of degrees higher in the coming years. German beaches will profit, but winter tourism will suffer. The German weather service expanded it's work long ago from just predicting the weather to producing detailed climate analyses and giving consultations to cities and businesses on how the changes will affect them. The German environment industry is already exploiting the business potential of climate change. (721 words)

16 gradually slowly and steadily

22 convert change or make sth change from one form, purpose, system, etc. to another

26 prosperity the state of being successful, especially in making money

33 erect to set up or establish sth

35 demand the desire or need of customers for goods or services

supply an amount of sth provided or available for use

38 entrepreneur a person who makes money by starting or running businesses

39 go-getting determined to succeed

determined having a mind that is not easily distracted or altered

40 harvest the time of year when the crops are gathered in on a farm

48 anxious feeling worried or nervous

52 dike a long thick wall built to stop water flooding onto a low area of land

53 reinforce make a structure or material stronger

JOB SKILLS Applying for a Job (2)

CD 1 Track 21

LISTENING

2 **Listen to the human resources director of a German company talk about what she thinks makes a good job application. Make notes on the following questions.**

- What mistake do young or inexperienced applicants often make?
- What is important for an applicant to do?
- What information from job advertisements should an applicant address in their application?

READING A COVERING LETTER

3 a **Read the info box and say where the essential parts occur in the standard covering letter below.**

INFO

Essential parts of a standard covering letter

a how you heard about the company
b salutation (to a specific person if possible)
c reference to enclosed CV (AE: résumé)
d formal close
e how your experience relates to the job (usually with the present perfect tense, but simple past for one-time events)
f explanation of interest
g suggestion of an interview or a telephone call

b **How would you express the phrases in bold in German?**

Dear Human Resources Director, / Dear Sir or Madam,

I am writing in response to your advertisement on jobslist.com for an intern in your technical department. **Enclosed is my CV for your review.**

I am presently attending school in Heidelberg, Germany and **am seeking** a summer internship working with the technical aspects of renewable energies. I have chosen to write to you because **I am** especially **interested in** biofuels. I have learned about biofuels in school and have read quite a bit on the subject. Ever since I took a tour of an ethanol plant, I have been sure that I want to pursue this as a career. I am also able to prioritise and to juggle many tasks at once, **as your advertisement specifies.**

I would appreciate the opportunity to talk to you on the telephone to further discuss how
I can be an asset to your company.

Yours faithfully,

WRITING A COVERING LETTER

4 **You find the following advertisement for a summer internship in Green Earth magazine and find it very interesting. In a small group, brainstorm things you could say in a covering letter to this company. Then write your letter.**

THE CALIFORNIA CENTER
FOR SUSTAINABLE ENERGY

Position: Climate Change Intern Location: San Diego, CA

CCSE seeks a college-level intern to assist CCSE's Climate Change program manager with research, analysis and writing related to energy and climate change.

The intern will work closely on a variety of issues related to the goal of achieving a low-carbon energy economy. The intern may contribute to future editions of the Energy Connection Newsletter, energy-related CCSE reports and CCSE's news service. The Climate Change Intern may also attend relevant meetings and events in and around San Diego and report on these to CCSE staff.

Qualifications: The successful applicant will be knowledgeable in the fields of energy, renewable energy technologies and anthropogenic climate change. Excellent research, writing and communication skills are a must.
Please send your résumé to The Human Resources Director.

INTERVIEWING FOR A JOB

5 a **You are going to role-play an interview for the above internship. Read this list of common interview questions and come up with some good answers to them.**

- *Why do you feel you would be suitable for this job?*
- *What exactly are your responsibilities in your current job? (or: What exactly are you currently studying?)*
- *What have been your biggest successes? What is your greatest strength/weakness?*
- *Do you have any questions for me?*

INFO

'Power verbs' you can use to describe achievements

- **I created** a system for getting energy from ocean waves.
- **I organised** publicity events for the company.
- **I improved** the way the office was run.
- **I carried out** research on genetic engineering.

b **Now prepare some questions the interviewee could ask, e.g.:**

- *How do you produce/do your …?*
- *What are your plans for the future of the company?*
- *When will you be making a decision?*

c **Decide who will play the interviewer and who will play the candidate. Role-play the job interview. Then swap roles.**

TOPIC 3 Technology and Society

BACKGROUND INFORMATION

technological advances *technische Fortschritte*
benefit *Vorteil, Nutzen*
humanity *Menschheit*
unethical purposes *unmoralische Zwecke*

To say that technology is changing daily is an understatement. In the last 100 years technological advances have not only been a benefit to humanity, they have also been used for destruction und unethical purposes.

The Computer, Work and Interaction

communication technology *Kommunikationstechnologie*
outsource *ausgliedern, -lagern*
downside *Kehrseite*
compromise *beeinträchtigen*
security *Sicherheit*
privacy *Privatsphäre*
human race *Menschheit*
identity theft *Identitätsdiebstahl*

For the most part, our material quality of life has improved thanks to advances in technology. Nowadays, machines do a lot of the hard physical work, more is produced in agriculture, and advances in communication technology allow people all over the world to be contacted in seconds. The computer and the Internet mean that certain jobs can be outsourced from one country, for example the US, to another country, such as India, on the other side of the world. The downside is that computers have compromised the security and privacy of the human race. Anything can be found out about an individual on the Internet. Identity theft takes place in online banking, e-mails and online shopping.

Biotechnology

biotechnology *Biotechnologie*
tranfer of genes *Gentransfer*
unrelated species *nicht verwandte Arten*
novel *neuartig*
genetically engineered *gentechnisch manipuliert*
domesticated animal *Haustier*
impact *Auswirkung*
survive *überstehen*
drought *Dürre*
pest *Schädling*
application *Anwendung*
genetic engineering *Gentechnik*
controversial *umstritten*

Scientists are experimenting with the transfer of genes between unrelated species to create novel life forms which could then be cloned. In the coming century it is expected that genetically engineered organisms will be set free into the environment. In recent years genetically engineered cotton, soya and corn have been planted on millions of acres of US farmland. Genetically engineered insects, fish and domesticated animals have also been introduced. It is very difficult to assess the potential impacts that a genetically engineered organism might have on the earth.
Supporters of biotechnology believe that world hunger can be reduced by using plants which can survive droughts or pests, for example. However, some applications of genetic engineering remain very controversial.

Technology and Medicine

life expectancy *Lebenserwartung*
health care *Gesundheitsfürsorge*
transplant *Transplantation*
bone marrow *Knochenmark*
stem cell *Stammzelle*
umbilical cord *Nabelschnur*

While genetic engineering could possibly raise the average life expectancy, ever-improving health care and medicine can also help us to live longer. Increasing progress in transplants is helping to save lives, for example leukemia can be cured through bone marrow transplants. Stem cells obtained from the umbilical cord of newly born babies, normally a

waste product, are used to treat the same diseases as bone marrow transplants and are less likely to be rejected than stem cells taken from bone marrow. Scientists hope that organs taken from genetically modified pigs can be used to replace sick organs in humans. It is hoped that stem cell treatment during which a patient is injected with his or her own processed stem cell will help to cure the effects of a stroke, Alzheimer's and Parkinson's disease as well as diabetes, eye disease and heart disease.
The number of successful organ transplants is rising every year. The main problem is organ shortage, and many people die while waiting. Artificial body parts such as hearts and replacement limbs are becoming more sophisticated. There are hopes that 'spare parts' for the body can be produced from stem cells.
Robotic surgeons may play a role in operations in the future, thus reducing the risk of human error.

waste product *Abfallprodukt*
treat *behandeln*
disease *Krankheit*
reject *abstoßen*
organ *Organ*
genetically modified *genmanipuliert*
replace *ersetzen*
treatment *Behandlung*
inject *injizieren*
process *behandeln, bearbeiten*
cure *heilen*
stroke *Schlaganfall*
shortage *Mangel*
replacement limbs *Ersatzgliedmaßen*
spare part *Ersatzteil*
robotic surgeon *Operationsroboter*
human error *menschliches Versagen*

Terrorism, Defence and Surveillance

Since September 11, 2001, projects to improve surveillance have been on a fast track. So far, however, surveillance technology in the form of cameras and satellite observation has helped to find the criminals but not to prevent terrorist attacks. Technology is improving in such a way that it is hoped that 'artificial noses' will be able to sniff out explosives in endangered areas or on people who have been in contact with explosives. Sensors in reservoirs may soon be able to detect a deadly microbe and so prevent an attack with biological weapons.
DNA tests have already helped to solve many murder cases. Electronic tagging helps to track the inventory in stores and prevent theft. These and many other forms of surveillance may be more effective, but the cost could be greater intrusion into individual privacy, creating a society not even George Orwell could have imagined. People, such as prospective employers and insurers, may be able to find out far more about us than is necessary.

defence *Verteidigung, Schutz*
surveillance *Überwachung*
fast track *Überholspur*
satellite observation *Satellitenüberwachung*
prevent *verhindern*
sniff out *aufspüren*
explosive *Sprengstoff*
sensor *Sensor*
reservoir *Speicherkammer*
deadly *giftig, tödlich*
microbe *Mikroorganismus, Mikrobe*
biological weapon *biologische Waffe*
electronic tagging *elektronische Warensicherung*
track *verfolgen, aufspüren*
intrusion *Eindringen*
privacy ['prɪvəsi] *Privatsphäre*
prospective employer *potentieller Arbeitgeber*
insurer *Versicherer*

Technology, a Force for Good and Evil

Man powered by his imagination and the quest for truth has made many scientific discoveries. It is not always clear whether they are a benefit to humanity. Quite clearly the advances in medicine have benefited humanity enormously. In the field of genetic engineering, however, the fear of genetically modified plants seems to be greater than the hope that they will benefit mankind. Likewise, opinions about computers and communication are divided. The advantages are enormous – fast source of information, quick means of communication – but the threats to our privacy and the danger of misuse are alarming.

power *antreiben*
quest *Suche*
scientific discovery *wissenschaftliche Entdeckung*
mankind *Menschheit*

TEXT 1 Social Effects of Technological Progress

WARM-UP

1 a **Look at the pictures and describe the ways in which people can be controlled nowadays.**
b **When do you think this is necessary?**

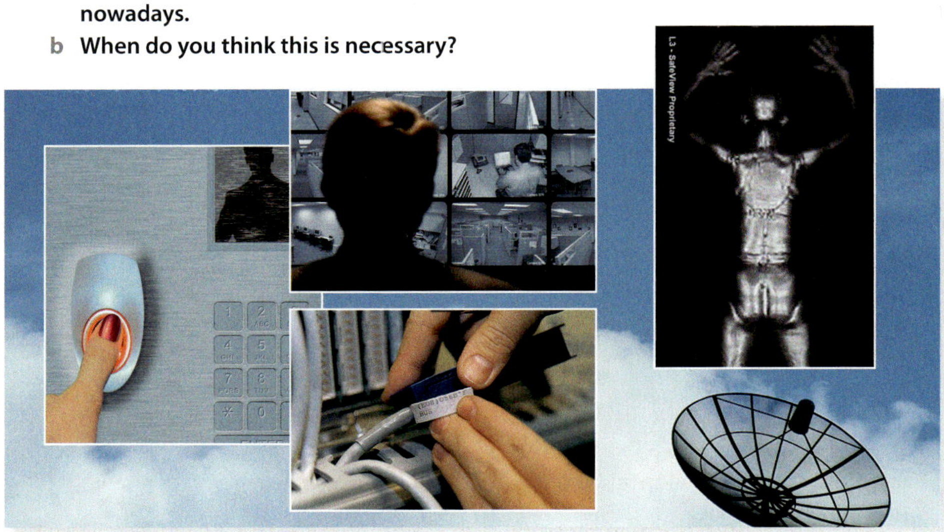

CD 1 Track 22

The Social Impact of Technology

Technological developments, especially in the field of communication, have brought about a new era. But how are they changing society? Read on to find out more.

The Social Impact of Technology on the Economy

The Internet in its current form was developed as a free exchange of information, unregulated by any one government or owned by any one person or company. It heralded a new era and was a technological revolution. This free flow of information has brought about technological advances at an unprecedented rate. It has made many rich and brought companies which failed to adapt to a standstill.

In what other ways will this technological revolution impact on our society? If the Industrial Revolution is anything to go by, there will be winners and losers in this technological revolution.

If we look at business, e-commerce has made direct trade possible, i.e. in effect making the middleman redundant. Efficiency may mean lower prices for the consumer, but that very same efficiency brings about greater wealth for shareholders, directors and owners. E-commerce creates efficiencies that effectively remove the need for a long supply chain, but at the expense of social relationships.

E-commerce and the Internet are having an impact on almost every society on earth. The barriers of trade between individuals in different countries are already more or less non-existent. Nowadays trade can take place between any two individuals anywhere. The Internet dissolves national boundaries, and people are reduced to consumers and suppliers.

The Social Impact of Technology on our Daily Lives

With technology helping to make life easier, we've become more concerned with streamlining our lives and need to find replacements for activities that used to

impact powerful effect
7 **impact on** affect sth powerfully
12 **shareholder** owner of shares in a company's business
14 **supply chain** the series of processes involved in the production and supply of goods
18 **boundary** a dividing line
22 **streamline** make sth work better

consume our time. Now we make time to play computer games, watch television, or find ways to make more money. With this lack of mental stimulation, our population is becoming increasingly dependent on antidepressants and anti-anxiety medications. Being bullied into a belief that faster is better and that if you can't keep up, you're left behind, has led many of us down a very bumpy road.

Technology and Population Control

Will the social impact of the Internet and computers challenge the status quo or will it lead to greater population control? The latter is probably more likely. For example, digital TV is being promoted as a technological innovation which offers the consumer 'better quality'. But the real difference is that this new technology enables those who own or run the systems to track what you watch, when you watch it, whether or not you switch off an ad, and perhaps even whether that pizza ad makes you pick up the phone and call for a pizza. Knowledge is power, and with people out there who can tap your phone lines, read your emails and credit card statements and know by GPS where you are by tracking your mobile phone, it would be a scary world if all that knowledge and power were to be used to oppress and control.

The Upsides and Downsides of Technology

On the upside, technology has made the developed world a richer place. Machines have allowed people to move away from physical work, so that now in Australia, for example, there are 100,000 accountants and 85,000 farmers. Perhaps technology has gone too far and there are more people counting beans than growing them!

On the other hand, the same technologies that provide so much benefit also have their downsides. Inconsiderate mobile phone users, for example, have become a common occurrence – in the underground, at the theatre, etc. The ease with which emails and text messages can be sent means that our 'conversations' with others are often more fleeting and shallow. It's also very easy to write things that probably wouldn't be said in person and, because there are no contextual clues with emails and text messages, such as vocal intonation or facial expressions, it's easy to misinterpret what has been 'said'. On the Internet, individuals can take on personalities that are completely disassociated from their personalities in real life.

A recent study found that despite the fact that we are more connected than ever before, we are becoming more isolated than ever. Obviously technology is not the only contributor to this trend, but perhaps the very tools which make communication so easy are also failing us by encouraging and promoting less meaningful communication. (733 words)

26 bully put pressure on sb, force
27 bumpy uncomfortable, difficult
36 tap listen in on (a telephone conversation) secretly
37 scary frightening
42 accountant sb who checks or keeps financial accounts
51 fleeting lasting only a short time
shallow superficial, not serious
54 clue information to help you understand sth
58 disassociated from not be connected to
62 contributor sb who helps to cause sth to happen
63 fail disappoint

WORKING WITH THE TEXT

2 **Explain the following four statements from the text.**

1. E-commerce creates efficiencies that effectively remove the need for a long supply chain.
2. We need to find replacements for activities that used to consume our time.

3 The social impact of the Internet and computers will lead to greater population control.
4 Despite the fact that we are more connected than ever before, we are becoming more isolated than ever.

S ▸ How to Deal with Instructions (p. 192)

3 The text is critical of the technological revolution but also lists some benefits. Contrast the criticism with the benefits. Before you start, sort them in two lists.

DISCUSSION

S ▸ Group Discussions (p. 203)

4 Follow these steps.

1 Think about which technological gadgets, for example mobile phones, have become part of your life. Rank them in order of importance for you.
2 With your partner, exchange ideas about why you need them.

WORKING WITH WORDS

5 a Look at the prefixes in the box. Find as many words as you can with them, e.g. *multimillionaire*. Then match the prefixes with their meanings (a–g).

anti | inter | multi | non | over | pre | under

a too little **c** between **e** too much **g** not
b many **d** against **f** before

b Use the correct prefix in the following sentences.

1 Barriers to ...national trade are almost ...-existent.
2 ...national corporations have no difficulty communicating with each other all over the world.
3 According to experts, spending hours playing games alone on the computer is ...social behaviour.
4 When buying goods on the Internet ...payment is often required.
5 In ...developed countries computer literacy is especially important.
6 Some say that the health risk of using mobile phones should not be ...rated.

TRANSLATION

S ▸ Translation (p. 204)

6 a Translate the following sentences using forms of 'sollen' when necessary.

1 New technology was meant to bring benefits to the world.
2 If knowledge were to be used to oppress and control, it would be a frightening world.
3 Technology was supposed to make life easier for everyone.
4 If you want to start your own company, you had better learn all about computers.
5 He had to contact the supplier about the delivery.
6 You should have done a course before buying your computer.
7 We no longer need to search for, or even cook, food.
8 Young children are not supposed to spend hours in front of the computer.

b **Now translate the following sentences. Use *to be supposed to, should, to be to* and *to be said to*. First, read the box below.**

1. Studenten sollten nicht alle Informationen im Internet suchen. Sie sollten auch in die Bibliothek gehen.
2. Schüler sollen das Internet ausschließlich benutzen, um Informationen zu finden, aber sie benutzen es oft zum Spielen.
3. Der Lehrer sagte, dass die Schüler ihre Ergebnisse bald abgeben sollten.
4. Internet, Computerspiele und Videos sollen das Verhalten junger Leute negativ beeinflussen.
5. Die Kommunikationstechnik sollte viele Vorteile bringen, aber viele Leute sind sehr kritisch geworden.

„Sollen" – ein Wort im Deutschen, viele Ausdrücke im Englischen

should: für Ratschläge, Empfehlungen und Verpflichtungen
to be supposed to: für Verpflichtungen und Erwartungen
to not be supposed to: für Verbote
to be to: für Termine und Pläne, die von anderen gemacht wurden
to be meant to: für Notwendigkeit, Absicht und generelle Auffassungen
to be said to: für die Weitergabe von Informationen z. B. aus den Medien sowie für Gerüchte und Annahmen

COMPOSITION

7 **Comment on the following quotation taken from an Internet blog.**

S ▸ Writing a Comment (p. 195)

"Future technology will enable us to communicate with our family far more personally than by text or mail, for example by video calling. Travelling long distances will no longer be required – we could all meet up in a virtual living room."

LISTENING

CD 1 Track 23

8 **a** **Listen to four people talking about surveillance and crime and decide which of the speakers feels positive about surveillance technology.**

b **Listen again and write down the positive and negative arguments in a table.**

S ▸ Practising Listening Skills (p. 188)

HOLDING A CLASSROOM DEBATE

HANDS-ON TASK

9 **Follow the steps below to hold a debate on the following statement:**

'The state has the right in certain circumstances to tap peoples' phones, to obtain information about bank accounts and credit card use and to look at emails.'

S ▸ Debating (p. 203)

1. Two students prepare arguments to be presented beforehand, one for and one against the motion (the subject). The students should present arguments opposed to their beliefs.
2. The students have a few minutes each to present their opposing arguments.
3. At the end of the presentations each student has time for rebuttals (replies to the arguments made by the other speaker).
4. The class asks questions.
5. Hold a vote in class to find out who agrees or disagrees with the statement. This shows which student was more convincing in their argument.

TEXT 2 Cosmetic and Reconstructive Surgery

WARM-UP

1 a Here are some Before and After pictures. Describe the changes. Some of the expressions in the box will help you.

breast augmentation | cleft lip | ears pinned back | eyelid surgery | face lift | liposuction | rhinoplasty | tummy tuck

b Suggest possible reasons for cosmetic surgery.

CD 1 Track 24

Face Transplants

It's long been the theme of science fiction, a dream of plastic surgeons and of people suffering from severe traumatic facial injury. In 2005 it became reality when doctors in France performed the first ever partial face transplant on Isabelle Dinoire, who had been attacked by her dog.
In a recently published study, Cleveland Clinic Foundation researchers used cadavers to determine the steps necessary for a full face transplant.
Many doctors in the USA say they expect to see such operations performed in the United States in the near future. Here are some of their opinions.

Dr Ablaza
"The worst injuries we see are the after-effects of a burn on the face. When the muscles are damaged people can't animate any more, can't smile, can't open their mouths to eat, can't keep liquid from dribbling out and they can't kiss. The idea that doctors can do something to help is incredible. It's one thing to have a disfigurement on your body which you can cover up with clothing, but no one covers their face. People become socially ostracized because they look frightening, and it's hard to cope with all the stares. People end up staying in and becoming shut-ins. Doctors really can't really help as there's only so much skin grafts can do. Face transplants may really be the much-needed breakthrough."

Dr Asken
"The French procedure wasn't really a face transplant going from the forehead all the way down to the chin. That didn't happen. Part of a face was transplanted onto part of the face of an injured patient.

1 **plastic surgeon** *Schönheitschirurg/in*
11 **animate** show feelings etc.
13 **disfigurement** when one's natural appearance has been spoiled
15 **ostracize** not be accepted by society
16 **stare** the act of looking at sb for a long time
17 **skin graft** piece of skin used to cover burnt skin

A full face transplant is a different story altogether because it involves denuding the skin on a cadaver and putting it on the face of the patient who has suffered trauma. The partial face transplant will be possible in the USA in the near future, but the full-face transplant is another story. In addition to the technical difficulties, such an operation would also involve ethical problems."

Dr. Edwin A. Cortez, M.D.

"The technical part of doing this operation is not really the difficult part. Really, the difficulty comes with problems like the immune system. Patients, at this point, are doomed to taking anti-rejection drugs for the rest of their life, and these drugs, of course, also have side effects.

Isabelle Dinoire

Once they get to a point – and eventually they will get to the point – where they don't have to worry about the rejection phenomenon, a lot of surgeons will consider doing this, especially those who do a lot of reconstructive work.

If we can find the right immunosuppressive drugs that don't cause a lot of secondary problems, then it would be more reasonable to consider face transplants for cosmetic reasons, not just as life-saving operations."

Ethical problems

Reconstruction is justifiable, but are cosmetic face transplants a legitimate use of modern medical technologies?

Dr Ablaza

"I'm not sure how this would work because you would need a catalogue of donors to be able to choose what they want to look like as otherwise it's a random event. Someone who didn't like their face would have to take chances on what's next available from a donor, and the donor might not be as attractive as the patient.

Also there would be a major shortage of donors.

I'm afraid there will be fugitives or criminals who will go to any extent to change their faces, including a face transplant.

The FBI takes protected witnesses and transforms their faces surgically, but no one would want a complete face transplant because there are other ways of achieving the same goals with a nose job, facelift, chin or cheek implants. A face transplant would be really extreme." (599 words)

Abridged from: *Cosmetic Surgery Times*, 1 June 2006

23 denude remove
31 doomed certain to suffer, damned
39 immunosuppressive ensuring that implanted organs are not rejected
46 donor a person who gives sth to help sb
47 random chance, uncontrolled
51 fugitive sb who is trying not to be caught by the police
53 witness sb who sees a crime and can describe what happened

WORKING WITH THE TEXT

2 Only one of the following statements is true. Find it and correct the false statements.

S ▸ Close Reading (p. 185)

1. Dr Asken thinks that a full face transplant will be available in the USA in the near future.
2. Up until now people with burns could not be given any help apart from skin grafts.
3. Dr Cortez says that you can consider carrying out transplants because the rejection problem has been solved.
4. Dr Ablaza thinks there would be no difficulty finding donors.
5. The FBI already uses face transplants to protect witnesses.
6. You can choose an attractive face for your transplant from a catalogue.

3 Summarise in German what the following people say.

1 Dr Ablaza about burn patients and donors
2 Dr Asken about the French procedure
3 Dr Cortez about drug rejection

S ▸ How to Deal with Instructions (p. 192)

4 Discuss the ethical problems of face transplants and other forms of cosmetic surgery. Think about patients' excpectations, profit-making, risks and benefits.

WORKING WITH WORDS

S ▸ Translation (p. 204)

5 Translate the following sentences using six of the words in the box. Be careful of 'false friends'!

actual | brochure | eventually | high school | not hear | possibly | overhear | prospect | sensible | sensitive | college | up to date

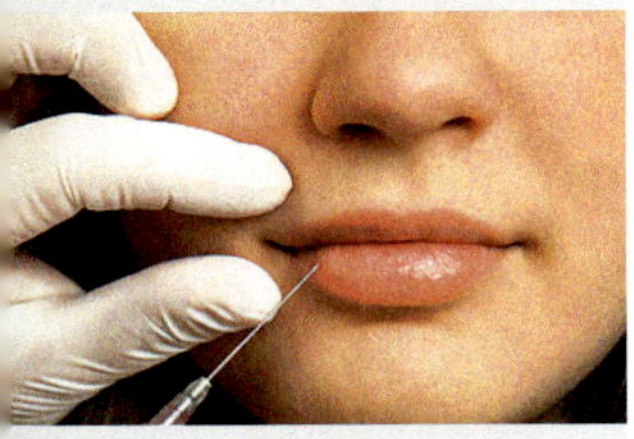

1 Seit dem Unfall ist sie sehr sensibel.
2 Zum Glück überhörte er die Bemerkung über sein hässliches Gesicht.
3 An den Hochschulen für Medizin werden Lösungen für Gesichtstransplantationen gesucht.
4 Die Prospekte über kosmetische Chirurgie versprechen Wunder *(miracles)*.
5 Die Informationen in dem Prospekt über Botox sind nicht mehr aktuell.
6 Er wird eventuell Probleme mit seinem Immunsystem bekommen.

LOOKING AT LANGUAGE

G ▸ Reported Speech (p. 211)

6 Which doctor says what? Put what they say into reported speech.

Example:
People become socially ostracized because they look frightening.
⟶ *Dr Ablaza said that people became socially ostracized because they looked frightening.*

1 The French transplant was not really a full face transplant.
2 There will be fugitives or criminals who will go to any extent to change their faces.
3 A lot of surgeons will consider doing a transplant if there are no problems with rejection.
4 People with disfigurements end up staying in.
5 At present, patients are doomed to take anti-rejection drugs for the rest of their lives.
6 In addition to technical difficulties, there are ethical problems involved.

HANDS-ON TASK

DOING A ROLE-PLAY

S ▸ Group Discussions (p. 203)

7 Work in groups of three. You are going to role-play a discussion between a doctor, a teenager and his/her mother or father about a cosmetic operation.

Doctor: Go to File 3 on page 180.
Mother/Father: Go to File 7 on page 182.
Son/Daughter: Go to File 9 on page 183.

TEXT 3 Right to Life

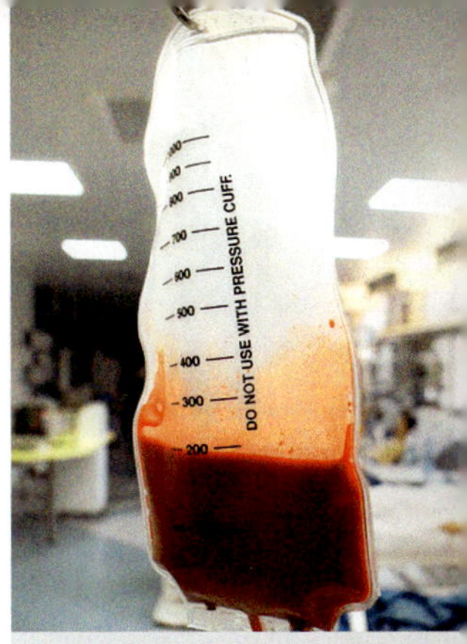

WARM-UP

1 **The following help to save lives. With a partner, match the sentences below to the three headings. Sometimes more than one solution is possible.**

Stem cell therapy | Bone marrow transplants | Blood donations

a Donors are desperately needed.
b This is important after an accident and during operations.
c Millions of donors are registered.
d People have been giving these for decades.
e The material can be taken from embryos which are only a few days old or from the umbilical cord of newly born babies.
f The patients are often babies and young people.
g This treatment is used to help patients suffering from leukemia.
h This has been developed in recent years.

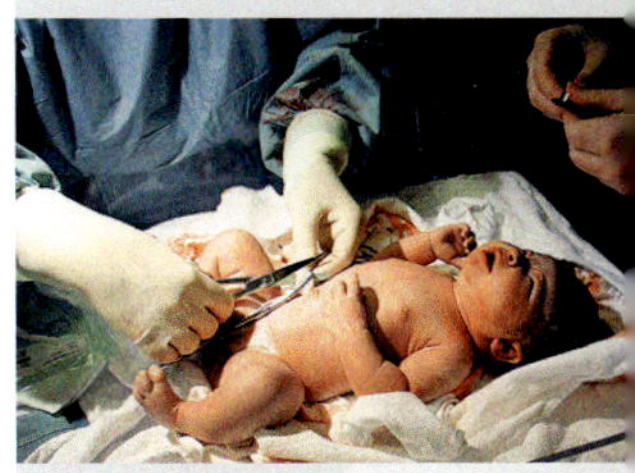

umbilical cord a long piece of tissue connecting the baby to its mother

2 **Would you be prepared to register yourself as a bone marrow donor or to give blood regularly?**

CD 1 Track 25

Grisly Trade in Baby Body Parts and Cells Uncovered in Ukraine

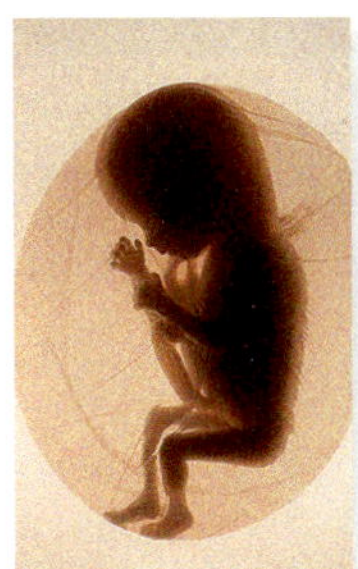

A shocking trade in body parts and stem cells taken from both aborted babies and babies stolen at birth is being uncovered in Ukraine. Ukraine has become an international supplier of embryonic stem cells used in medical research, according to the *Daily Mail*.

Irina Bogomolova of the Kiev chief prosecutor's office said she was fired for insisting on a wide-ranging investigation into the grisly practice. "I demanded an investigation into all maternity wings in hospitals across Ukraine and I was relieved of duty after making that demand," she told the *Sunday Telegraph*. "A trade in stem cells exists here and the people behind it have good connections to the authorities. I suspect there is a lot of bribery going on, up to the highest levels."

Bogomolova said that women are told by their doctors that their babies were stillborn, when actually they are taken away and butchered for their body parts. "Pregnant women, especially from rural areas, are very vulnerable targets as they will obviously believe whatever the doctors tell them," she told the *Telegraph*. "It's easy to take their babies from them and tell them they died or were born dead."

Ukrainian women have begun to speak out about their traumatic and confusing experiences. Olena Stulnev delivered what she thought was a healthy girl at Maternity Hospital Number Six in Kharkiv. "She was crying and moving her hands and legs," Stulnev told the *Daily Mail*. "I was shown the baby. After that the girl was taken away." The next day hospital officials told her the baby was dead, but gave her several inconsistent reasons why. Stulnev contacted Tatyana Zhakarova of the Ukrainian group Federation of Families with Many Children, who discovered that other women had similar sad stories.

grisly extremely horrible
2 **abort** give birth to a baby before it can survive
6 **chief prosecutor** *Oberstaatsanwalt/-anwältin*
8 **maternity wing** the part of a hospital where babies are born
9 **relieve of duty** dismiss sb from a job
12 **bribery** corruption
13 **stillborn** born dead
23 **inconsistent** differing, conflicting

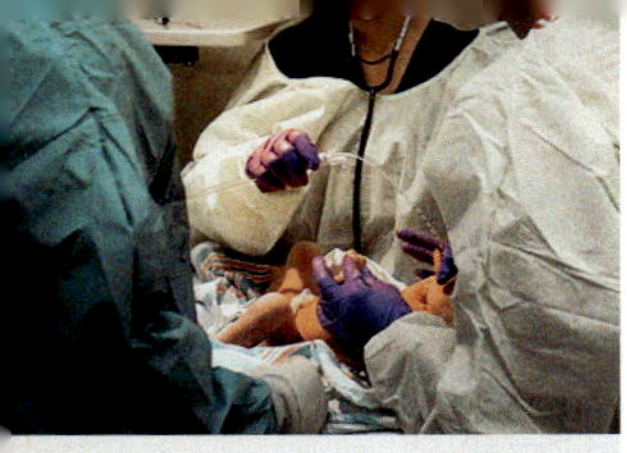

26 **postmortem examination** examination of a dead body
29 **full term** fully developed
30 **dismember** cut into pieces
jigsaw *Puzzle*
32 **harvest** collect
bone marrow *Knochenmark*
40 **remediation** cure
41 **tissue** the material forming animal or plant cells
42 **fetal** related to a foetus
45 **re-launch** start again in a different way

Zhakarova told the *Daily Mail* that she persuaded the authorities to conduct postmortem examinations on 30 babies who died at Maternity Hospital Number Six. The video she made of the examinations showed that the babies' bodies – some of them full term – had organs and brains missing. "Another body shown in the video is so badly dismembered it has to be put together piece by piece, like a jigsaw," wrote Matthew Hill in the *Daily Mail*. "Dismemberment is not standard autopsy practice and could, according to experts, indicate stem cells had been harvested from bone marrow."

"I first thought the babies were stolen for illegal adoption," Zhakarova told the *Telegraph*, "but after the bio-waste disposal ground was exhumed, I feared the worst – that they were stolen and used for medical products, or some sort of cosmetic-treatment products."

Hill investigated a clinic in Barbados that injects patients with stem cells it claims are harvested from "babies aborted between seven and ten weeks old", he wrote in the *Daily Mail*. The "treatments" are meant for the "remediation of diseases resulting from tissue damage and/or the effects of aging", according to the clinic's website, although there is absolutely no scientific evidence to show that fetal stem cells can help people look younger.

The clinic buys the cells from the Institute of Cryobiology in Kharkiv, Ukraine. The Council of Europe plans to re-launch an investigation into the Ukranian trade in babies' body parts and stem cells, the *Telegraph* reported. A 2004 investigation was halted for lack of evidence, but the work of people like Zhakarova and Bogomolova has brought the issue to international attention. (558 words)

From *Today's News & Views*, 4 January 2007

WORKING WITH THE TEXT

3 a **Explain who the following people are and what they do.**

a Irina Bogolomova **b** Olena Stulnev **c** Matthew Hill **d** Tatyana Zhakarova

b **Who said what? Match the sentences below with the correct name.**

1. I am sure that babies are being stolen as part of an illegal business in stem cells. This has to be investigated.
2. Women from the countryside usually believe what doctors tell them when they are informed that their babies died at birth.
3. Once I realised that more than one mother had lost her baby, I contacted the authorities and convinced them of the need for postmortem examinations.
4. What I saw in the film looked like parts of a puzzle, not a baby's body.
5. I found out that a clinic in Barbados was using stem cells from the Ukraine for cosmetic treatment.
6. I filmed these examinations, so I had proof of what had happened to the babies.
7. I am sure that many people, especially those at the top, are being bribed so this illegal business can flourish.
8. My daughter was alive when she was born – I saw her.
9. My research confirmed that this is not what normally happens during a postmortem.

c **Put the sentences in the order that they appear in the text.**

4 **List the evidence showing that the babies were probably killed for their stem cells.**

WORKING WITH WORDS

5 a **Match the words in the box with words a–h to form compound nouns and collocations.**

body | full | illegal | postmortem | scientific | standard | stem | stillborn

a abortion	**c** cells	**e** examinations	**g** practice
b babies	**d** evidence	**f** parts	**h** term

b **Use the word pairs from above to fill in the gaps below.**

It is suspected that because rich people in Barbados believe that …[1] can make them look younger, the number of …[2] has increased in the Ukraine. Some doctors even falsely claim that mothers, especially from rural areas, had …[3]. The babies are often dismembered and the …[4] are used to harvest stem cells. This was discovered after …[5] showed that …[6] baby bodies had brains and organs missing. Dismemberment is not …[7] during an autopsy. There is no …[8] that stem cells can help you look younger.

LOOKING AT LANGUAGE

6 a **Translate the following passive sentences into German.**

G ▸ The Passive (p. 214)

1. A shocking trade in baby parts is being uncovered in the Ukraine.
2. Irina Bogolomova was fired for insisting on an investigation.
3. Women are told by their doctors that their babies are stillborn.
4. Olena was shown her baby and then it was taken away.
5. According to the report, many babies have been stolen and used for medical products.
6. A 2004 investigation was halted for lack of evidence.
7. Stem cells are harvested from bone marrow.
8. The public will be shocked if we find evidence that babies and fetuses are being killed for any sort of treatment.

b **Complete the text below with the correct form of the verbs in brackets. Some of the sentences are in the passive.**

Destination Moscow: The Cellulite Clinic

Last year hundreds of women …[1] *(go)* to Moscow to get anti-ageing treatment for slack skin on their bodies. The cells …[2] *(obtain)* from aborted fetuses and …[3] *(inject)* into thighs, stomachs and buttocks. Moscow …[4] *(become)* the global capital of cosmetic stem cell therapy in recent years. For the past 15 years the Ukraine, home to Emcell, the largest clinic for stem cell therapy, …[5] *(openly experiment)* with stem cells. The fact that Ukraine and Russia …[6] *(now be)* at the top of the abortion league is, according to the Federation of Families with Many Children, due to their need for stem cells. Young women …[7] *(frequently persuade)* to carry babies for 8–12 weeks and then to abort them. The stem cells …[8] *(sell)* to beauty clinics.

COMPOSITION

7 **'Scientists are only interested in the financial gains to be made and do not think about the consequences.' Write a comment on this statement and illustrate it with examples.**

S ▸ Writing a Comment (p. 195)

TEXT 4 Technological Innovations in the US

WARM-UP

1 a **Overconsumption of energy in very hot or very cold periods often leads to blackouts in the USA. Discuss in groups the effects that a blackout lasting several days could have.**

S ▸ Group Discussions (p. 203)

b **Have you ever experienced a blackout?**

CD 2 Track 2

Technology to Help Cities Manage Booming USA

Blackouts in cities such as New York, Cleveland and Detroit in recent years raise questions about what will happen when aging electrical grids can't send enough power to heat and cool more people. Planners looking at the boomtowns spreading across the Southwestern desert are asking: Where's the water going to come from?

The USA is growing more rapidly than any other developed nation and is projected to gain another 100 million people by 2040. That will put new pressure on a public infrastructure that's already stretched thin. As scientists, engineers, builders and public officials grapple with how to accommodate the nation's unprecedented growth, small steps being taken today could reduce the challenge. The focus: technology that could revolutionize how power is generated and transmitted and water is recycled.

Based on current energy use, the country will need to build more than 500 medium-sized power plants to generate the extra electricity the USA will use by 2030, according to the Energy Information Administration, the statistical arm of the Department of Energy.

If the USA's per-capita water use for home, industry and agriculture remains at 1,500 gallons a day, it will need another 150 billion gallons each day – about three times what California now consumes.

Some innovations are underway.

Improving the Power Grid

The two-acre Roosevelt Park in Anaheim looks like any other Southern California neighborhood playground: plentiful trees and lush lawns, barbecue stations and winding walkways.

1 **blackout** total darkness as a result of electricity failure
2 **electrical grid** a system for sending power over a large area
5 **project** estimate
7 **stretched thin** be pushed/strained to the limit
8 **grapple with** try hard to find a solution
16 **per-capita** for each person

Under the feet of frolicking children, however, hums a high-voltage power substation encased in concrete and filled with fans and electrical converters. Ten cables stretch 23 miles underground from the invisible facility – the first of its kind in the USA – distributing enough electricity to serve more than 25,000 homes.

Using older technology, Anaheim Public Utilities would have had to build a substation 5 miles away, consume 70% more space and extend cables to neighborhoods where residents need electricity but vehemently object to power lines above their heads. The $20 million underground facility distributes electricity without eating up valuable real estate.

The 2003 blackout in parts of the Northeast and Midwest – the worst in U.S. history – affected about 40 million people in eight states and intensified concerns about the nation's aging electrical grids, particularly in densely populated areas.

Private companies, including Siemens, are working with the Long Island Lighting Authority to build a 65-mile underground cable, part of which would run underwater in New York Harbor, that will enable Long Island to tap in to electricity generated in Pennsylvania, New Jersey and Maryland.

Stretching Water Supplies

The West Basin Municipal Water District in Carson, California, south of Los Angeles, did not recycle water in 1995. Today, it recycles 35 million gallons a day – enough water for 78,000 households – and the amount is projected to double by 2020. That would reduce by half the amount of water the agency imports from northern California and the Colorado River.

"It's the new technology that really allows higher levels of water to be produced and used," says Paul Shoenberger, the district's assistant general manager. "We're reducing the amount of energy needed to produce water, we're recycling sewage effluent, we're treating it, and we resell it to industries. It just makes sense to use water more than once." Half the water the district supplies to the city of El Segundo's school yards, ball parks, golf courses, refineries and other industries is recycled.

"For water," says Daniels of the University of Pennsylvania, "the mantra is reduce, reuse and recycle. When you see new houses built, you're going to see two sets of pipes: one for gray (recycled) water to water your lawn and wash your car and one for drinking water."

Another key water issue is desalination. That's because about 97% of the Earth's water is in oceans. This method is used widely in the Middle East even though it costs up to four times as much as other water recycling methods. U.S. coastal communities are increasing their investments in desalination plants, and costs are coming down.

(667 words)

Abridged from *USA Today*, 24 April 2007

24 **frolic** play in a lively, happy way
25 **encased** covered completely
concrete material made by mixing cement and water
27 **facility** building/service provided for a specific purpose
33 **object to** oppose sth
36 **real estate** property in the form of land or houses
44 **tap in to** make use of
59 **effluent** liquid waste
61 **mantra** a phrase repeated again and again, especially in prayer
65 **desalination** the process of removing salt from sea water

WORKING WITH THE TEXT

S ▶ How to Deal with Instructions (p. 192)

2 a **Explain the advantages of underground power stations.**
b **Describe the two methods of obtaining water mentioned in the text.**

3 a **Match the sentence halves below to make a short summary of the text.**

1 There will be a great increase in the population of the USA by 2040
2 Enormous amounts of energy will be required
3 150 billion gallons of water a day more will be needed
4 New technologies are being developed
5 In Anaheim, an energy facility has been built underground
6 Carson recycles a lot of water
7 Houses in the future will have two sets of pipes
8 Desalination is a key water issue

a which supply recycled water or drinking water.
b from which 78,000 households can be supplied.
c which will improve energy supply and provide more water.
d although it is still much more expensive than other recycling methods.
e so that 500 medium-sized power plants would have to be built.
f if water usage stays as it is now.
g which will put pressure on the infrastructure.
h so that valuable real estate has not been used up and energy plants have been built.

b **Now write out the sentences again, adding connecting phrases where possible. (Check 'Language for Writing' on the back cover flap of your book.)**

Example:
There will be a great increase in …
***As a result,** enormous amounts …*
***What is more,** 150 billion …*

ANALYSING CHARTS

S ▶ Interpreting Graphs, Diagrams and Tables (p. 200)

4 a **Summarise the information given in the pie and bar charts.**
b **Does the information in the bar chart correspond with the information given in the text?**

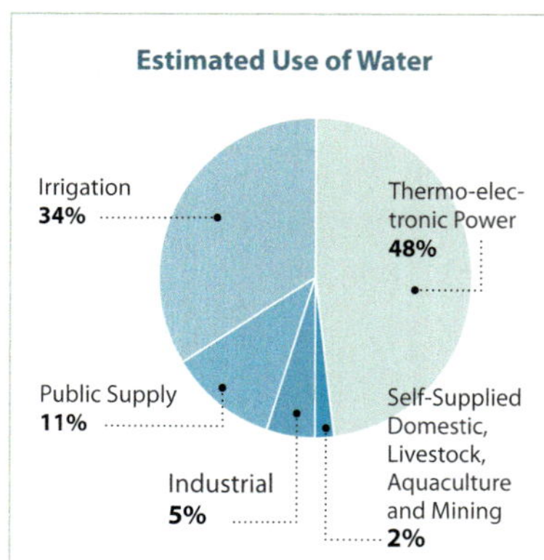

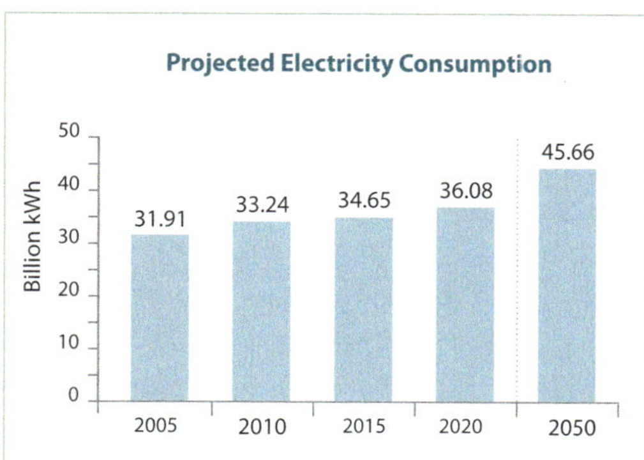

LOOKING AT LANGUAGE

G ▸ Modal Verbs (p. 210)

5 a **Complete the sentences below using the correct form of 'have to'.**
b **In which sentences can you use 'must'?**

1 To avoid blackouts in the future cities in the USA ... find solutions for ageing grids.
2 In the past, after a blackout, people ... do without electricity for hours.
3 If further solutions are not found, people ... start reducing energy consumption.
4 If Anaheim had used older technology, it ... build a substation five miles away on valuable real estate.
5 50 years ago scientists ... (not) think about solutions for saving water.
6 Schoeneberger thinks that water ... be used more than once.
7 Saltwater is widely available and it ... be used more in the future.

DISCUSSION

6 **In groups rank these activities according to the amount of water they use. Start with activities which use the most. Compare your results with the other groups.**

S ▸ Group Discussions (p. 203)

- shower
- bath
- dishwasher
- washing the car
- cooking and drinking
- washing clothes
- washing dishes by hand
- flushing the toilet

LISTENING

CD 2 Track 3

7 **You are going to listen to a radio programme about transport and congestion. Taking part in the programme are city planning expert Bob Shallow and two journalists, Mary Harding and Jack Faulkner. Follow the steps below.**

S ▸ Practising Listening Skills (p. 188)

1 Listen once and find out roughly what is being talked about.
2 Listen a second time and take notes about the steps Pomplona, Houston and Salt Lake City are taking to make public transport more attractive.
3 If necessary listen again, then list further reasons why people may want to use public transport more in the future.

GIVING A PRESENTATION

HANDS-ON TASK

8 **Choose one of the topics below. Research information on the Internet and present your findings to the class.**

S ▸ Giving a Presentation (p. 201)

S ▸ Doing Research on the Internet (p. 189)

Topic 1: Research different road charging systems, e.g. the motorway toll for lorries in Germany, the motorway toll in France or the congestion charge in London. Compare the different toll systems and discuss whether a toll system should be introduced for cars in Germany.

Topic 2: Find information about desalination and give a presentation with the title 'Desalination – advantages and disadvantages'.

TEXT 5 Biotechnology and Food

WARM-UP

1 a Read these (potential) benefits of biotechnology and put them in order from 'most helpful to mankind' to 'least helpful to mankind'.

a rice with built-in Vitamin A that can help prevent blindness in children suffering from Vitamin A deficiency
b potatoes that absorb less fat when fried, changing the ever-popular French fries from junk food into a more nutritional food
c coffee with a lower caffeine content
d cabbage that is resistant to caterpillars
e melons that have a longer shelf life
f sunflowers that produce oil with fewer saturated fats
g cereals that are resistant to drought
h crops which can grow on salty land

deficiency the state of not having enough of sth essential
caterpillar a small creature like a worm that develops into a butterfly
saturated fat type of fat that encourages the development of cholesterol
cereal grains used for flour or bread
drought long period with little or no rain
crops plants grown in large quantities, especially for food

b Now follow these steps.

1. Compare your list with that of your partner. Explain the reasons for your choices.
2. Now compare your list with another pair.
3. Report to the class.

CD 2 Track 4

GM Food

The Benefits: One Side of the Debate

Economic Benefits

GM supporters tell farmers that they stand to reap enormous profits from growing GM crops. Initially GM crops are more expensive for farmers than traditional crops, but money is saved on pesticides. With GM crops, farmers are told, it takes a shorter time to produce the desired product, they are more precise and there are no unwanted genes.

Herbicide and Pesticide-Resistant Crops

What other advantages do GM crops offer farmers? Farmers need fewer herbicides in GM fields since GM crops can be produced to be herbicide-resistant. This means that farmers could spray these crops with cheaper, 'non-selective' herbicide and kill

[2] **reap** get, obtain
[7] **herbicide** a substance which kills weeds

the weeds, without affecting the crop. In effect, the amount of herbicide used in one season would be reduced, with a subsequent reduction in costs for farmers and consumers. However, there have been no independent studies to support this claim.

There are also claims that growing GM crops reduces the need for pesticides. For example, pest resistance was built into Ingard cotton, thus reducing and even removing the need for pesticides, which are not only expensive but, more importantly, harmful to the environment.

Biotechnology companies are even experimenting with crops that can be genetically modified to be drought and salt tolerant, or less reliant on fertilizer, opening up new areas to be farmed and leading to increased productivity.

Better Quality Foods

Even animals can be genetically modified to be leaner, grow faster and need less food. They could be modified to have special characteristics, such as greater milk production in cows. These modifications again lead to improved productivity for farmers and ultimately lower costs for the consumer. Modified cattle could perhaps prevent outbreaks of diseases, such as foot and mouth, which have devastated many farmers and local economies in recent years.

No products from genetically modified animals have been released onto the market to date; however, some are under consideration. For example, GM salmon, capable of growing almost 30 times faster than natural salmon, may soon be approved by the FDA (Food and Drug Administration) in the U.S. for release into open waters without a single study of the impact this could have on human health or the environment.

The Risks: The Other Side of the Debate

Environmental Damage

The problem with GM crops is that little is known about what effect they will have in, say, 20 years' time. The genetic structure of any living organism is complex and GM crop tests focus on short-term effects.

There is always the possibility that we may not be able to destroy GM crops once they spread into the environment. In Europe, for example, a strain of sugar beet that was genetically modified to be resistant to a particular herbicide has inadvertently acquired the genes to resist another herbicide. When farmers attempted to destroy the crop in Britain, France and the Netherlands, where it was being tested, 0.5% of the crop survived. More noxious herbicides had to be used to remove the remainder of the plantation. What will happen if this herbicide resistance has passed on to weeds?

Risk to Food Web

A further complication is that the pesticide or herbicide produced in the crop may unintentionally harm creatures. In Britain, a native farm bird, the skylark, was indirectly affected by the introduction of GM sugar beets designed to resist herbicides. In growing this crop, the weeds were reduced substantially. However, since the birds rely on the seeds of this weed in autumn and winter, researchers expect that up to 80% of the skylark population will have to find other sources of food.

Disease

Another concern is disease. Since some crops are modified using the DNA from viruses and bacteria, will we see new diseases emerge? Will these antibiotic-resistant genes be transferred to microorganisms that cause disease? We already have a problem with ineffective antibiotics. How can we develop new drugs to fight these new bugs? (684 words)

American Institute of Biological Sciences, 2005

11 weed a wild plant growing where it is not wanted
12 subsequent following, later
14 claim a statement saying sth is true
16 pest insect which destroys plants and food
20 reliant on dependent on
23 lean thin
27 outbreak the sudden start of a disease
devastate destroy completely
30 salmon *Lachs*
31 approve officially agree to
40 strain type
41 inadvertent by accident
44 noxious poisonous, harmful
remainder the rest
49 skylark *(Feld-)Lerche*
59 bug any small insect

WORKING WITH THE TEXT

S ▸ How to Deal with Instructions (p. 192)

2 **Contrast the benefits and risks of GM foods. Before you start, summarise the text in a mind map using the headings and subheadings of the text to structure the individual aspects.**

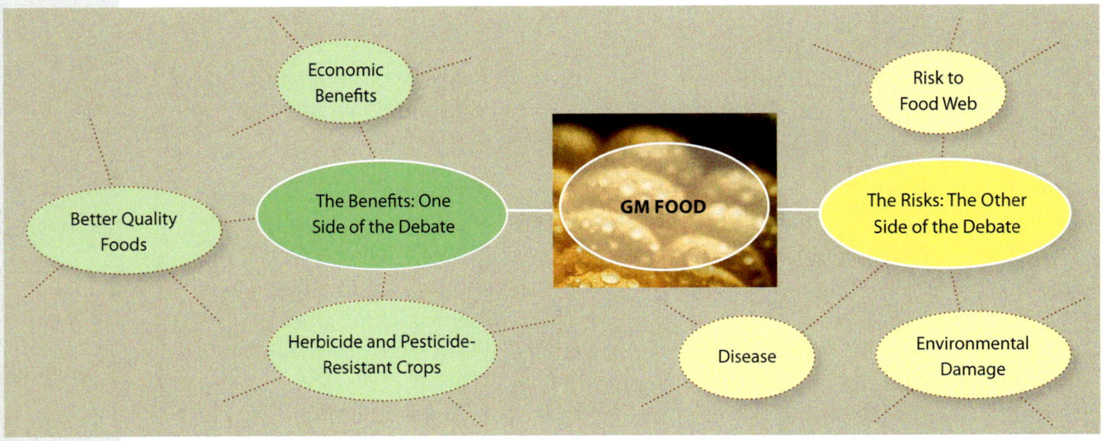

3 **Here are three arguments for GM food. In your own words, respond to these statements using critical arguments from the text. Try to use expressions such as *however, on the other hand, but,* etc.**

1. Herbicide-resistant crops mean that fewer herbicides are needed, which saves money.
2. Pesticide-resistant plants, such as cotton, no longer have to be treated with pesticides, and this is safer for the environment.
3. The farming of GM animals is more efficient and reduces costs.

ANALYSING A CARTOON

S ▸ Interpreting Pictures and Cartoons (p. 199)

4 **Describe the cartoon and explain how it is linked to the text.**

Here are some words which will help you with your description: *barbed-wire fence, insect-eating plants, prison yard.*

WORKING WITH WORDS

5 a **Combine the words 1–8 with a–g to make compound adjectives.**

1 herbicide-	**5** short-	**a** growing	**e** known
2 self-	**6** well-	**b** resistant	**f** reliant
3 built-	**7** fast-	**c** tolerant (x2)	**g** in
4 drought-	**8** salt-	**d** term	

b Now use some of the adjectives to complete this short summary of the benefits of GM food.

> Farmers in poor countries will be especially happy to use …[1] crops in order to save money on herbicides. The …[2] company Montsanto has been producing such crops for years. They are also developing crops for dry countries which are …[3]. Furthermore, in countries which are often flooded by sea water …[4] crops are being developed. Farmers are told that their crops will be …[5] so that they can harvest them more quickly.

LOOKING AT LANGUAGE

6 Translate the following sentences into English using passive forms of the modal verbs *could, might* and *must/need not*.

G ▸ The Passive (p. 214)

1. In die Entwicklung genetisch veränderter Produkte muss viel Geld investiert werden.
2. Krankheiten wie Maul- und Klauenseuche könnten verhindert werden.
3. Feldfrüchte müssen mit Pestiziden gesprüht werden.
4. Genetische veränderte Pflanzen müssen nicht gespritzt werden.
5. Es könnten Tiere mit besonderen Merkmalen entwickelt werden.
6. Sogar Kühe könnten vielleicht genetisch verändert werden, um mageres Fleisch zu liefern.

LISTENING

CD 2 Track 5

7 a Listen to Per Pinstrup-Andersen, professor of food, nutrition and public policy, talk about the advantages of genetically modified plants. In which order is he talking about the following?

S ▸ Practising Listening Skills (p. 188)

- agriculture and research
- the problem of deforestation.
- the situation of children in some countries

b Listen again and make notes on what he says about:

- deforestation
- problems of rural areas in Africa
- children in Africa
- scientific solutions

RESEARCHING VIDEOS

HANDS-ON TASK

8 On video-sharing websites like YouTube, you can find videos on the subjects below. Write a short report on the contents of one these online videos.

- ethical concerns with genetic engineering
- designer babies
- the future of genetic engineering

TEXT 6 Short Story: Ray Bradbury, 'The Pedestrian'

Ray Bradbury

CD 2 Track 6

WARM-UP

1 **You are going to read a short story. Look at the illustration of the 'The Pedestrian' from when it was first published. What do you think the story is about?**

Ray Bradbury

The Pedestrian

1953

To enter out into that silence that was the city at eight o'clock on a misty evening in November, to put your feet upon that buckling concrete walk, to step over grassy seams and make your way, hands in pockets, through the silences, that was what Mr Leonard Mead most dearly loved to do. He would stand upon the corner of an intersection and peer down long moonlit avenues of sidewalk in four directions, deciding which way to go, but it really made no difference; he was alone in this world of 2053 A.D., or as good as alone, and with a final decision made, a path selected, he would stride off, sending patterns of frosty air before him like the smoke of a cigar.

Sometimes he would walk for hours and miles and return only at midnight to his house. And on his way he would see the cottages and homes with their dark windows, and it was not unequal to walking through a graveyard where only the faintest glimmers of firefly light appeared in flickers behind the windows. Sudden gray phantoms seemed to manifest upon inner room walls where a curtain was still undrawn against the night, or there were whisperings and murmurs where a window in a tomb-like building was still open.

Mr Leonard Mead would pause, cock his head, listen, look, and march on, his feet making no noise on the lumpy walk. For long ago he had wisely changed to sneakers when strolling at night, because the dogs in intermittent squads would parallel his journey with barkings if he wore hard heels, and lights might click on and faces appear and an entire street be startled by the passing of a lone figure, himself, in the early November evening.

On this particular evening he began his journey in a westerly direction, toward the hidden sea. There was a good crystal frost in the air; it cut the nose and made the lungs blaze like a Christmas tree inside; you could feel the cold light going on and off, all the branches filled with invisible snow. He listened to the faint push of his soft shoes through autumn leaves with satisfaction, and whistled a cold quiet whistle between his teeth, occasionally picking up a leaf as he passed, examining its skeletal pattern in the infrequent lamplights as he went on, smelling its rusty smell.

2 **buckling** bent, curved outwards
3 **seam** a line where two edges meet
5 **intersection** crossroads
peer look carefully and closely
8 **stride off** walk in long steps
12 **graveyard** the place where dead people are buried
13 **firefly** a flying insect that lights in the dark
16 **tomb** a large grave, especially one built of stone
17 **cock** raise (the head) until it is at an angle
19 **intermittent** stopping and starting
squad group
21 **startle** surprise suddenly in a frightening way
25 **blaze** burn

'Hello, in there,' he whispered to every house on every side as he moved. 'What's up tonight on Channel 4, Channel 7, Channel 9? Where are the cowboys rushing, and do I see the United States Cavalry over the next hill to the rescue?'

The street was silent and long and empty, with only his shadow moving like the shadow of a hawk in mid-country. If he closed his eyes and stood very still, frozen, he could imagine himself upon the center of a plain, a wintry, windless Arizona desert with no house in a thousand miles, and only dry river beds, the street, for company.

'What is it now?' he asked the houses, noticing his wrist watch. Eight-thirty P.M.? Time for a dozen assorted murders? A quiz? A revue? A comedian falling off the stage?'

Was that a murmur of laughter from within a moon-white house? He hesitated, but went on when nothing more happened. He stumbled over a particularly uneven section of sidewalk. The cement was vanishing under flowers and grass. In ten years of walking by night or day, for thousands of miles, he had never met another person walking, not one in all that time.

He came to a cloverleaf intersection which stood silent where two main highways crossed the town. During the day it was a thunderous surge of cars, the gas stations open, a great insect rustling and a ceaseless jockeying for position as the scarab-beetles, a faint incense puttering from their exhausts, skimmed homeward to the far directions. But now these highways, too, were like streams in a dry season, all stone and bed and moon radiance.

He turned back on a side street, circling around toward his home. He was within a block of his destination when the lone car turned a corner quite suddenly and flashed a fierce white cone of light upon him. He stood entranced, not unlike a night moth, stunned by the illumination, and then drawn toward it.

A metallic voice called to him:

'Stand still. Stay where you are! Don't move!'

He halted.

'Put up your hands!'

'But –' he said.

'Your hands up! Or we'll shoot!'

The police, of course, but what a rare, incredible thing; in a city of three million, there was only one police car left, wasn't that correct? Ever since a year ago, 2052, the election year, the force had been cut down from three cars to one. Crime was ebbing; there was no need now for the police, save for this one lone car wandering and wandering the empty streets.

'Your name?' said the police car in a metallic whisper. He couldn't see the men in it for the bright light in his eyes.

'Leonard Mead,' he said.

'Speak up!'

'Leonard Mead!'

'Business or profession?'

'I guess you'd call me a writer.'

'No profession,' said the police car, as if talking to itself. The light held him fixed, like a museum specimen, needle thrust through chest.

'You might say that,' said Mr Mead.

He hadn't written in years. Magazines and books didn't sell anymore. Everything went on in the tomb-like houses at night now, he thought, continuing his fancy. The tombs, ill-lit by television light, where the people sat like the dead, the gray or multi-colored lights touching their faces, but never really touching them.

34 **hawk** *Habicht*
39 **assorted** different, various
43 **vanish** disappear
46 **cloverleaf intersection** a place where a number of main roads meet, with curved sections which form the pattern of a four-leaf clover
47 **surge** a sudden increase in the number of
48 **ceaseless** not stopping
scarab-beetle *Skarabäus, Mistkäfer*
49 **incense** *Weihrauch*
54 **cone** a shape that is round at one end and slopes to a point
entranced in a trance
55 **stunned** shocked
65 **save for** except for
75 **specimen** a single example of sth, especially of animals or plants
thrust push

81 **hiss** make a sound like a long 's'

123 **riveted** fastened with metal pins

127 **whirring** a low sound like parts of a machine moving

128 **punch-slotted card** card with holes that gives instructions to computers

129 **regressive** going back to a less advanced state

130 **thud** a sound made when a heavy object hits sth else

'No profession,' said the phonograph voice, hissing. 'What are you doing out?'

'Walking,' said Leonard Mead.

'Walking!'

'Just walking,' he said simply, but his face felt cold.

'Walking, just walking, walking?'

'Yes, sir.'

'Walking where? For what?'

'Walking for air. Walking to see.'

'Your address!'

'Eleven South Saint James Street.'

'And there is air in your house, you have an air conditioner, Mr Mead?'

'Yes.'

'And you have a viewing screen in your house to see with?'

'No.'

'No?' There was a crackling quiet that in itself was an accusation.

'Are you married, Mr Mead?'

'No.'

'Not married,' said the police voice behind the fiery beam. The moon was high and dear among the stars and the houses were gray and silent.

'Nobody wanted me,' said Leonard Mead with a smile.

'Don't speak unless you're spoken to!'

Leonard Mead waited in the cold night.

'Just walking, Mr Mead?'

'Yes.'

'But you haven't explained for what purpose.'

'I explained; for air, and to see, and just to walk.'

'Have you done this often?'

'Every night for years.'

The police car sat in the center of the street with its radio throat faintly humming.

'Well, Mr Mead,' it said.

'Is that all?' he asked politely.

'Yes,' said the voice. 'Here.' There was a sigh, a pop. The back door of the police car sprang wide. 'Get in.'

'Wait a minute, I haven't done anything!'

'Get in.'

'I protest!'

'Mr Mead.'

He walked like a man suddenly drunk. As he passed the front window of the car, he looked in. As he had expected, there was no one in the front seat, no one in the car at all.

'Get in.'

He put his hand to the door and peered into the back seat, which was a little cell, a little black jail with bars. It smelled of riveted steel. It smelled of harsh antiseptic; it smelled too clean and hard and metallic. There was nothing soft there.

'Now if you had a wife to give you an alibi,' said the iron voice. 'But –'

'Where are you taking me?'

The car hesitated, or rather gave a faint whirring click, as if information, somewhere, was dropping card by punch-slotted card under electric eyes. 'To the Psychiatric Center for Research on Regressive Tendencies.'

He got in. The door shut with a soft thud. The police car rolled through the night avenues, flashing its dim lights ahead.

They passed one house on one street a moment later, one house in an entire city of houses that were dark, but this one particular house had all of its electric lights brightly lit, every window a loud yellow illumination, square and warm in the cool darkness.

'That's my house,' said Leonard Mead.

No one answered him.

The car moved down the empty riverbed streets and off away, leaving the empty streets with the empty sidewalks, and no sound and no motion all the rest of the chill November night. (1444 words)

WORKING WITH THE TEXT

2 **Follow these steps to interpret the story. The information in the box below will help you.**

S ▸ Close Reading (p. 185)

1. Present evidence from the text to show that this is a short story.
2. Describe the setting.
3. Say how Leonard is different from the world around him and identify the imagery used to mark the contrasts. (Tip: some of the images deal with light, noise or temperature.)
4. At one point in the story, the light of the police car holds Leonard fixed 'like a museum specimen, needle thrust through chest' (lines 74/75). Explain the metaphor.

Analysing a Short Story

short story: A short story is a ficticious narrative in prose, shorter and less complex than a novel. It centres around one incident or turning point in the lives of a limited number of characters. A short story is often confined to one setting and it covers only a short period of time.

setting: The setting of a short story is the time, place and circumstances in which the action takes place. (Time: When does the action take place? At what time of year and day? Does it take place during the day or at night? Place: Where does the action take place? Indoors or outdoors? What is the landscape like? Circumstances: What is the weather like? The light conditions and temperature?)

character: A short story deals with a limited number of characters. Main characters are complex and have very individual features while minor characters are simpler and characterised by only one or two traits. A character is defined by his or her outward appearance (facial expression, posture, clothing) and feeling, mood or state of mind (e.g. happy, ill-tempered, thoughtful).

COMPOSITION

3 **Summarise the general theme of the story and explain its message.**

S ▸ Improving Your Writing Skills (p. 197)

DISCUSSION

4 **The story was written in 1953 when television was becoming increasingly popular. With regard to technological advances in the field of communication, do you think that the world is moving in the direction depicted in the story?**

S ▸ Group Discussions (p. 203)

World of Work

MEDIATION Business and Communication

S ▸ Mediation (p. 204)

1 Do the following mediation task.

Sie wollen einen Artikel für Ihre Firmenzeitschrift mit dem Titel „E-Mail als geschäftliches Kommunikationsmittel" schreiben. Der folgende Artikel dient Ihnen als Grundlage.

1 Nennen Sie die Vorteile und Nachteile von E-Mails im Geschäft.
2 Geben Sie Ratschläge zum Schreiben von geschäftlichen E-Mails.

Before you start, follow these steps.

a Look at this list of advantages for point 1. How can it be improved?

E-Mails sind nützlich:
- wenn es darum geht, schnelle Antworten zu bekommen;
- wenn man den richtigen Ansprechpartner sucht;
- um Informationen weiterzugeben.

b Before you do the rest of the task, read the following tips for point 2. Which of them is not in the text?

- Benutzen Sie das Telefon, wenn eine Frage zu kompliziert ist.
- Lesen Sie die E-Mail sorgfältig durch, bevor Sie sie absenden.
- Eine E-Mail ohne Bilder ist oft besser, da Bilder wie Werbung aussehen könnten.

Using E-Mail Effectively

There is little doubt that e-mails have revolutionised the way businesses now communicate. The e-mail is the most frequently used daily communication tool for most businesses. Yet only a few years ago many businesses didn't have an e-mail address. Today a business could not survive without one.

Most business e-mails document the activities of the company and are therefore often confidential and/or critical to the company's success. Not so long ago, e-mails were generally considered informal and were a good way of communicating information with people you knew. Nowadays the reality is that e-mails fly thick and fast between people who know each other well and complete strangers alike. In business, many things have to be decided and done quickly, and e-mails are simply the fastest way of transferring information between two or more parties.

E-mail certainly is an effective means of communication for both business and personal use, but it is not without disadvantages.

Here are some advantages of e-mail:
- It is an effective means of getting and giving quick answers to yes-or-no type questions, e.g. 'Do you deliver abroad?'
- It can help you to find the right person in the organisation to answer your questions.

6 **confidential** meant to be kept secret and not to be shared with other people
critical extremely important because a future situation will be affected by it
8 **thick and fast** quickly and in large quantities
9 **alike** equally
16 **deliver** take goods, letters, etc. to the person or people they have been sent to

- It is a good way for busy people to make appointments.
- Information can be distributed quickly to many people at the same time.

The disadvantages include the following:

- Answering complicated questions via e-mail can be time consuming. The telephone is much better for providing detailed answers.
- Misunderstandings can arise because of cultural differences in the interpretation of certain words.
- The security of an organisation can be compromised when sensitive information is distributed accidentally or deliberately to the wrong person.
- It can quickly become too impersonal.
- Employees may spend too much time on personal e-mails, resulting in a loss of productivity.

Managing the E-mail Burden

Most business people these days receive more e-mails than they can easily digest. In business it is important that e-mails do not become so burdensome that more time is spent answering them than working on key tasks.

Choosing an accurate subject line helps the recipient to prioritise your e-mail. Because many recipients only skim e-mails, make sure that the major point in your e-mail is the first one you mention. If you need to deal with several subjects, it may be best to send several e-mails with different subject lines, to make sure that no important points are missed by the recipient. This also makes your e-mails easier and quicker to reply to.

E-mail Security

Do not open an attachment or click on a link in an e-mail from someone you don't know. If the content of the e-mail looks suspicious but it is from someone you know, don't open it until you have clarified it with the sender first. Trust your intuition or you may end up with a computer virus.

Use of Mailing Lists

E-mail is a highly effective medium of communication, but remember to treat the recipient as a person, not a number on a mailing list. An e-mail needs to be easily identifiable or else it may be regarded as spam (junk e-mail) and sent off to the recycling bin or blocked by the recipient.
Be selective in your choice of recipients for each e-mail. Just because a person joins your mailing list does not mean that he or she wants to be bombarded with irrelevant information.

Marketing e-mails can look really impressive if a brochure format is adopted but, unless the pictures are there for a reason and the e-mail engages the reader by providing useful information, it is often better to send a text-based e-mail. If you need to display products, then a link to your website where the product is displayed is a better option. By providing such a link, you give the recipient the choice as to whether or not to view your product. Remember: informative e-mail is inviting; e-mail that resembles advertising is pushy.

E-mail needs to be personal yet business-like. It is a way of building up good customer relationships, and good relationships are the key to successful business. (680 words)

20 distribute give things to a large number of people
24 arise happen; start to exist
26 sensitive must be treated with great care because it may offend people
compromise bring into danger
27 deliberately done in a way that was planned, not by chance
33 burdensome causing worry, difficulty or hard work
43 suspicious making you feel that sth is wrong, illegal or dishonest, without having any proof
54 adopt use a particular method
60 pushy trying hard to get what you want, often in a way that seems rude

JOB SKILLS Writing E-mails

INFO

E-mail Tips

- Always greet the customer by name and end the e-mail with your name. Not using a recipient's name creates the impression that you can't be bothered to address them properly.
- Be polite. Use expressions like 'I would like to …', 'Could you please …'.
- Make sure your contact details are clearly displayed at the end of every e-mail. These should include your full name and company name, your business phone number, fax number, website address, mobile phone number and business address.
- Terms like 'Regards' or 'Kind regards' are formal but friendly.
- When sending out newsletters, make sure they are personal. Imagine that you are the recipient. Treat your customer like a person, not a number on a mailing list.
- Do not use capital letters as it looks as if you are shouting.
- Do not use subject lines like 'Newletter number 42' or 'Company X's weekly newsletter'. Make sure that the subject line makes the recipient want to read the e-mail. The large volume of e-mail received by the average person means that the subject needs to stand out in order to be noticed.
- Always read your e-mail through carefully before you click 'send'. E-mails containing mistakes reflect badly on you and the products or services you are offering.

WRITING E-MAILS

2 Read the info box above and rewrite the following e-mail.

Subject: Re:

Hello,
I want to meet your sales representative, Mr Braun. Make an appointment with him for me SOON.
I have time next week when I am in Germany.

Robert Palmer

LISTENING

CD 2 Track 7

S ► Practising Listening Skills (p. 188)

3 Listen to the conversation and then complete the e-mail confirmation. Some gaps may need more than one word.

Subject: Re: Your …[1] with Aruna Singh on …[2]

Dear Mr Steffens,
I would …[3] your appointment with Ms Singh on …[4] at …[5] which we made yesterday. This is …[5] for Ms Singh who will be pleased to …[6] you then to discuss a new …[7].

Kind regards,
Dilip Khan
Assistant Manager

Sunshine Industries
3 Queen Victoria Street
Bangalore, India
E-mail: dilip.khan@sunshine-industries.in
Tel. (office): 0091 80 243121
Mobile: 0732 5679568

ROLE-PLAY

4 With a partner, follow the steps below.

1. Play the roles of Dilip and Mark as in the listening text.
2. Think of a situation in which you want to make arrangements.
3. Sit back to back and role-play a phone call using the vocabulary for making arrangements and appointments. Try to use some of the following words:

appointment | arrangement | arrive | confirm | be convenient | meet | schedule

QUESTIONNAIRE

5 Do the following questionnaire to find out your electronic mail quotient (EMQ). Then check your score on page 182 and compare your answers in class.

1 When you receive an e-mail message that requires a response, when is it appropriate to reply?
a Immediately – I hate to keep people waiting! **b** Within a week. **c** Do I have to reply?

2 How often do you forward e-mails?
a Only if it's an important message like a computer virus warning.
b Sometimes – there are some pretty funny jokes out there.
c All day long – I love all those chain e-mails going around!

3 Suppose you receive a 'joke' e-mail that you think is funny. How many people might you forward it to?
a 1 person. **b** 5–10 people. **c** Everyone I know.

4 Have you ever been guilty of spamming?
a No. **b** Yes. **c** What is spamming?

5 When you send e-mails, do you usually use a subject line?
a Yes, of course, I label all of my e-mails. **b** No. Why should I? **c** What is a subject line?

6 How often do you check your e-mail?
a Every five minutes – I can't wait any longer!
b Once or twice per day.
c Never – do I even have e-mail?

7 When you compose e-mails, do you usually greet the recipient by name, e.g. 'Hello, Kathy'?
a Yes. **b** It depends. **c** No. They know who they are.

8 Do you spell-check your e-mails?
a Yes. **b** No. **c** Is that possible?

9 How do you sign, or close, your e-mails?
a With my full name or initials.
b With my nickname from college.
c I don't sign my e-mails. People know who the sender is!

10 Is it acceptable to use e-mail for more personal business correspondence, such as thanking someone for a gift or sending out company party invitations?
a Yes, of course.
b Sometimes. It depends on the particular situation.
c Never. E-mail is not the right communication channel.

TOPIC 4

The March Towards Equality

BACKGROUND INFORMATION

Great Britain – Coming to Terms with Multiculturalism

come to terms with *bewältigen*
multiculturalism *Multikulturalismus*
immigrant *Einwanderer/in*
Commonwealth *Gemeinschaft der Länder des ehemaligen Britischen Weltreichs*
colony *Kolonie*
citizenship *Staatsbürgerschaft*
origin *Herkunft*
West Indies *die Westindischen Inseln*
pass *verabschieden*
combat *bekämpfen*
racism *Rassismus*
overrun *überschwemmen*
immigrate *einwandern*
urban *städtisch*
expand *sich erweitern*
employment rules *Einstellungsregularien*
labour shortage *Mangel an Arbeitskräften*

Until 1962 immigrants from Commonwealth countries – former colonies – were allowed to live in Britain and obtain British citizenship. The most common origins were India, Pakistan, Bangladesh and the West Indies. Many laws were passed in order to combat racism, incidents of which had become more frequent as Britons felt their country had become overrun with immigrants. In 1983 laws were passed which made it more difficult to immigrate to Great Britain.

About 7.5% of people living in Britain today were born abroad, and most of them live in London or other large cities, making urban Britain very multicultural indeed.

Since the European Union expanded in 2004 to include several Eastern European states, workers from these countries have been moving to Britain, perhaps more than to any other EU country. This is attributed to the liberal employment rules for EU citizens Britain introduced in order to fill labour shortages.

The United States – a Nation Built by Immigrants

ethnic diversity *ethnische Vielfalt*
equality *Gleichberechtigung*
tribe *Stamm* **Indian** *Indianer/in*
native American *amerikanische/r Ureinwohner/in*
settler *Siedler/in*
slave *Sklave/in*
force *zwingen*
negotiate *aushandeln*
reservation *Reservat*
slavery *Sklaverei*
mistreatment *schlechte Behandlung*

Like Great Britain, the history of the USA has been one of increasing ethnic diversity and equality for all members of society.
The USA was ethnically diverse from the very beginning. The land was originally home to several tribes of what we now call Indians or native Americans. In the 17th century, settlers came from various Northern European countries. As their numbers grew, they brought in slaves from Africa and forced (or negotiated with) the natives to give up their land and move to reservations. Slavery and the mistreatment of the Indians are sources of bitterness and shame in the USA even today.

The Melting Pot

melting pot *Schmelztiegel*
persecute *verfolgen*

Ever since its founding in 1776, the US has received wave upon wave of immigrants from all over the world, each one feared and persecuted by those which came before it.
In their hearts, however, Americans know that their country is a nation of immigrants, and the USA welcomes them like no other.

The African-American Struggle

Slavery was finally abolished in 1863, but the struggle of black Americans was long from over. They continued to suffer greatly, particularly in the South, where segregation laws violated their rights using the bogus justification that they were being kept 'separate but equal'. It wasn't until 1964 that these laws were struck down as a result of the Civil Rights Movement.

struggle *Kampf*
abolish *abschaffen*
segregation laws *Rassentrennungsgesetze*
violate *verletzen*
bogus justification *falsche Rechtfertigung*
strike down *aufheben*
Civil Rights Movement *Bürgerrechtsbewegung*

The Current Situation in the US

Hispanics recently surpassed African-Americans as the largest minority, and they are also the fastest growing minority. They often face prejudice and many Americans are calling for stricter immigration control because they feel immigrants – especially Mexicans – are taking jobs away from blue-collar Americans.

Hispanic *Hispano-Amerikaner/in*
minority *Minderheit*
prejudice *Vorurteil*
immigration control *Grenzkontrolle*
blue-collar *in Arbeiterberufen*

Even today, it is the white Americans who make up most of the upper class, but members of other races are demonstrably moving up in society. The most notable example is the new US president Barack Obama.

upper class *Oberschicht*
move up in society *in der Gesellschaft aufsteigen*

The US has extreme wealth and extreme poverty. The social class system is crass but, in comparison to Great Britain, it is not reflected as much in the language, and a poor American is considered to have a strong possibility of social mobility.

wealth *Reichtum*
poverty *Armut*
social mobility *soziale Mobilität zwischen den Schichten*

Non-ethnic Minorities

Minority groups which are protected in Britain and the USA are the mentally and physically disabled. The situation for homosexuals has seen improvement in recent decades. Prior to the 1960s, these groups were practically invisible – many people did not even know they existed. Because homosexuals are often not honest about their sexual preference, it is difficult to estimate their numbers, but it could be as high as 10% of all people. Successes of the international Gay Rights Movement include state-recognised civil partnerships in Britain. There is scientific evidence that homosexuality may be inborn, yet many people still reject it on moral grounds.

protect *schützen*
mentally disabled *geistig behindert*
physically disabled *körperbehindert*
homosexual *Homosexuelle/r*
invisible *unsichtbar*
sexual preference *sexuelle Neigung*
Gay Rights Movement *Schwulenbewegung*
civil partnership *Lebenspartnerschaft*
inborn *angeboren*
reject *ablehnen, zurückweisen*
on moral grounds *aus moralischen Gründen*

Affirmative Action

Policies which are intended to promote access to education or employment for minority groups usually involve quotas. These very controversial measures, known as affirmative action, are sometimes taken by individual companies or schools, or even by governments, especially in the US.

affirmative action *Förderung von Minderheiten*
access to education *Zugang zu Bildung*
quota *Sollvorgabe, Quote*
controversial measure *umstrittene Maßnahme*

TEXT 1 How Social Class Determines Speech in England

WARM-UP

1 **Read the following and do the task below.**

Social classes exist in every society, but in England there is an especially great degree of class consciousness. Whether they admit it or not, the English easily identify their fellow countrymen's social class by noticing their clothes, their interests, their education, what they eat and drink, and especially the way they speak.

Summarise the above text in German in one sentence. Then say how you can tell what social class a person belongs to. The photos will help you.

CD 2 Track 8

Linguistic Class Codes

An English person cannot talk without immediately revealing his or her social class. As George Bernard Shaw wrote in 1916, 'It is impossible for an Englishman to open his mouth without making some other Englishman hate him or despise him'. We may like to think that we have become less class-obsessed in recent times, but Shaw's observation is as pertinent now as it ever was. All English people, whether they admit it or not, are fitted with a sort of social Global Positioning Satellite computer that tells us a person's position on the class map as soon as he or she begins to speak.

Pronunciation

One class indicator concerns which type of letter you favour in your pronunciation – or rather, which type you fail to pronounce. Those at the top of the social scale like to think that their way of speaking is 'correct', while lower-class speech is 'incorrect', a 'lazy' way of talking. Exhibit A in this argument is the lower-class failure to pronounce consonants, in particular the glottal stop – the omission (swallowing, dropping) of 't's – and the dropping of 'h's. But this is a case of the pot calling the kettle (or ke'le, if you prefer) black. The lower ranks may drop their consonants, but the upper class are equally guilty of dropping their vowels. If you ask them the time, for example, the lower classes may tell you it is 'alf past ten' but the upper class will say 'hpstn'. A handkerchief in working-class speech is 'ankercheef', but in upper-class pronunciation becomes 'hnkrchf'.

Lower classes often pronounce 'th' as 'f' ('teeth' becomes 'teef', 'thing' becomes 'fing') or sometimes as 'v' ('that' becomes 'vat', 'Worthing' is 'Worving'). Final 'g's can become 'k's, as in 'somefink' and 'nuffink'. Pronunciation of vowels is also a helpful class indicator. Lower-class 'a's are often pronounced as long 'i's – Dive for Dave, Tricey for Tracey. Working-class 'i's, in turn, may be pronounced 'oi', while some very upper-class 'o's become 'or's, as in 'naff orf'.

3 **despise** consider to be worthless or disgusting
5 **pertinent** relevant
6 **fit sb or sth with** provide with sth by fixing it on the body or thing
14 **glottal stop** a consonant formed by the audible release of the airstream
swallow cause to disappear
15 **the pot calling the kettle black** hypocrisy
16 **rank** position within a hierarchy
26 **Naff off!** Get lost!

Terminology

There are words that the English uppers and upper-middles regard as infallible class indicators. Utter any one of these in their presence, and their on-board class-radar devices will start bleeping and flashing.

Pardon

This word is the most notorious pet hate of the upper and upper-middle classes. Some even refer to lower-middle-class suburbs as 'Pardonia'.

Toilet

'Toilet' is another word that makes the higher classes flinch. The upper-middle/upper term is 'loo' or 'lavatory' (pronounced lavuhtry, with the accent on the first syllable). The working classes all say 'toilet', as do most lower-middles and middle-middles, the only difference being the working-class omission of the final 't'.

Serviette

A 'serviette' is what the inhabitants of Pardonia call a napkin.

Dinner

There is nothing wrong with the word 'dinner' in itself: it is only a working-class hallmark if you use it to refer to the midday meal, which should be called 'lunch'. Calling your evening meal 'tea' is also a working-class indicator: the higher echelons call this meal 'dinner' or 'supper'. (521 words)

Adapted from *Watching the English: The Hidden Rules of English Behaviour* by Kate Fox

28 infallible never wrong
29 utter say or make a sound
30 bleep a high-pitched noise
37 flinch a quick movement as a result of fear or pain
45 hallmark a distinctive feature
46 echelon position within a hierarchy

INFO

Is it Wrong to Say 'Pardon'?

No! The text tells us that the words *pardon*, *toilet*, and *serviette* are disliked only by the upper class, which is a very small and exclusive segment of society. Chances are that when you go to England the vast majority of people you talk to will not be upper class and will consider these words perfectly normal. If you prefer an alternative to *pardon*, you can say *sorry* or *excuse me*.

vast very large

WORKING WITH THE TEXT

2 **Say whether the following statements are true or false according to the text.**

1. Social classes do not exist in modern England.
2. Shaw said that an Englishman is hated as soon as he speaks and the reason for this is that his speech reveals his social class.
3. 'Dropping' a vowel or consonant means leaving it out.
4. The upper classes pronounce 'Dave' [deɪv] and the lower classes tend to pronounce the name [daɪv].
5. The upper classes pronounce 'eye' [aɪ] and the lower classes tend to pronounce the word [ɔɪ].
6. You should never say 'pardon', 'toilet', 'serviette' or 'dinner'.

3 **What are 'linguistic class codes'? What aspects of language do they involve? Give examples from the text. Use your own words.**

S ▸ Answering Comprehension Questions (p. 191)

WORKING WITH WORDS

4 **Complete the sentences with the correct form of the words in brackets. The first one has been done for you.**

Example: It is practically impossible for an English person to speak without ... his or her social class. (revelation) → *It is practically impossible for an English person to speak without **revealing** his or her social class.*

1 We learn languages by ... and practice. (observe)
2 The family next door seems to be ... with moving up the social scale. (obsession)
3 As far as I'm ..., a person's social class is of very little importance. (concern)
4 Did I ... your name correctly? (pronunciation)
5 The classes ... not only in their speech but also in their politics. (difference)
6 Another English millionaire has been found ... of not paying taxes. (guilt)
7 Just because we're ... of a working-class neighbourhood doesn't mean we speak in a vulgar way. (inhabit)
8 Increased security in rich communities is one ... of the ... of tension between the classes. (indicate, present)
9 A serious ... in the anthropological study is the researcher's ... to account for the effects of social class. (omit, fail)
10 The Janssens moved from the city to the ... because they think their children will get a better ... there. (suburban, educate)

WORKING WITH A DICTIONARY

5 **Complete the phonetic transcription with the correct diphthong** [aɪ], [eɪ] **or** [ɔɪ].

1 indicator ['ɪndɪk...tə]
2 toilet ['t...lət]
3 society [sə's...əti]
4 failure ['f...ljə]
5 education [ˌedʒu'k...ʃn]
6 higher ['h...ə]
7 identify [...'dentɪf...]
8 employer [ɪm'pl...ə]

LOOKING AT LANGUAGE

G ▸ The Gerund (p. 215)

6 **Rewrite the sentences replacing each noun phrase in italics with one of the phrases containing a gerund in the box. Sometimes the meaning of the sentence will change slightly.**

being overly concerned about | buying expensive land | having a lot of money | hearing from you | making another person | hate us | reading *The Times* | the pot calling the kettle black | travelling to foreign countries

1 Nowadays, *obsession with* social class is considered bad taste.
2 In England, we can't open our mouths without *a hostile result.*
3 I look forward to *your letter.*
4 *This highbrow newspaper* is associated with educated classes.
5 Does a *big bank account* move a person up the social ladder?
6 If I had a lot of money, I would spend it on *a journey around the world.*
7 *The purchase of one's own island* distinguishes one as belonging to the super-rich.
8 This is a case of *hypocrisy.*

SPEAKING

7 **With a partner, practise using the following forms to talk about social classes.**

Reading *Bild* Acting macho Buying a lot of junk Drinking champagne Going to university etc.	is associated with the	working lower middle upper educated	classes	in Germany in England etc.

LISTENING

CD 2 Track 9

8 a **Describe the cartoon.**

b **Copy the names below into your exercise book. Then listen to the radio show parody 'Know your class indicators!' and note to which social class each character belongs: lower/working class, middle class or upper class.**

S ► Practising Listening Skills (p. 188)

Phoebe: *middle class*
Man at door (Andrew): …
Suitor 1 (Philip): …
Suitor 2 (Steve): …
Suitor 3 (Roger): …

suitor *Verehrer*

c **Compare the parody to real life. Do people, either consciously or subconsciously, really look for lovers and spouses who belong to their own social class? Is this just being obsessed with class or are there good reasons for seeking out a partner from the same 'background'?**

COMPOSITION

9 **Write an essay about social classes.**

S ► Writing an Essay (p. 196)

Shaw made the statement that an Englishman 'hates' the other Englishmen who don't belong to his social class. This may be an exaggeration in most cases, yet in every society the existence of tension between the classes is undeniable. Explain some causes of this tension between the social classes.
Here is one way you could structure such an essay.

I	Introduction: describe the phenomenon of inter-class tension, perhaps giving an example.
II	Why the upper classes dislike the lower classes
III	Why the lower classes dislike the upper classes
IV	Give your own view on the subject, perhaps suggesting a way to deal with the problem.

TEXT 2 Generational Challenges of Muslim Britons

WARM-UP

1 Are the following normally considered features of Muslim culture or Western culture or both? Discuss with a partner.

- freedom
- obedience
- romantic love
- respect and care for the elderly
- longing for the past
- crime
- drug addiction

CD 2 Track 10

5 unleash set free
7 restrain hold back
9 obedience doing what someone orders
14 misguided showing faulty judgment or reasoning
15 delude persuade sb to believe sth incorrect
22 obligation duty, requirement
25 exert one's pull use one's influence
31 toss throw

"You're Muslim – You'll Never Be English"

I imagine that my parents arrived in Britain with a mixture of fear and hope. What they wanted was to progress economically but remain rooted culturally; they feared freedom. But once unleashed, progress, like freedom, is frustratingly difficult to restrain.

I was raised to believe that happiness came from obedience to Islam and acceptance of the wisdom of elders. In British society, parents believe they are there to make their children happy; in my culture, the exact opposite is the case. The first priority of children is to make their parents happy. A successful life was about being a good Muslim in secure employment, married to someone selected by your parents. To reach for a career that might be fulfilling in ways other than financial was misguided. To believe that marriage might be based upon love was deluded. Religion was applied to support the arguments of my parents. If I was spending too much time with English friends, or watching too much television, my father would say, "You're Muslim, remember; you'll never be English."

I had already been corrupted. The books I read and the songs I heard had released my imagination and conjured worlds grander than anything I had known. They revealed other ways of seeing and other things to see.

And so I chose personal freedom over family obligations, rationality over religion. I did not fast during Ramadan, or have an arranged marriage, or become a doctor. Today, I am a 31-year-old journalist who lives the liberal metropolitan life, and who only rarely thinks about his religion. And yet the old values still exert their pull. If, for example, I don't visit my family at least once every three weeks, I am overcome by guilt and convinced that I am a terrible son. My white friends think nothing of seeing their parents half a dozen times a year, but Islam teaches that "heaven lies under the feet of one's mother".

Islam offers absolute truths and explicit instructions on how to live life. Without them, one feels sometimes like the man who has tossed the road map out of the car window and now does not know where he is travelling to or how he is going to get there. The modern world offers only shades of grey; at times, we all long to return to a time when everything was black and white. Some of the generation that follows me have concluded that freedom for freedom's sake is worthless. They have adopted a clearer Islamic identity – teenage girls volunteer to take up the hijab, young men speak of an international jihad – which those looking from the outside observe with fear and suspicion.

But for every young Muslim absorbing the Koran, others are in prison for robbery, rape and worse. My best friend's mother was robbed of her gold chain by a teenage Pakistani who was probably going to sell it to fund his drug habit. When I heard about it, my first reaction was: "How could a Muslim have done that?"

The challenge for my generation is to ensure that the next generation get the benefits of being British without forgetting their heritage. It was the old values that stopped me mugging old women for gold chains. They make the idea of placing my mother in an old people's home unthinkable. Will those who follow still hold on to those values? Do they have a map? I look to the future with a mixture of hope and fear. (580 words)

Adapted from *The Guardian*, 19 June 2002

37 hijab headscarf or other female Muslim dress
jihad holy war (can also mean a personal moral struggle, e.g. to stop drinking alcohol)
39 suspicion not trusting
48 mug attack and rob in a public place

WORKING WITH THE TEXT

2 a Find the statement which, according to the author, is false.

1 The author's parents' generation ...
a are afraid of freedom and are clinging to old values.
b do not consider themselves British.
c wanted their children to integrate into British society.
d are pragmatic.

2 The author's generation ...
a have embraced freedom and chosen a rational, non-religious life.
b have been 'corrupted' by the West.
c have the task of helping the younger generation get the best of both worlds.
d have rejected their parents and the old family values.

3 The next generation ...
a are rejecting freedom and longing for clear instructions on how to live.
b have no choices about their future.
c are often criminal.
d are often religious by choice.

b Re-write each false statement to make it true.

3 Bearing in mind the qualities attributed to each generation, explain the different systems of values discussed in the text.

S ▸ How to Deal with Instructions (p. 192)

WORKING WITH WORDS

4 Match each adjective in the box to a noun to make a common collocation used in the text. Then write a sentence with the collocation.

arranged | explicit | fulfilling | secure

1 marriage **2** career **3** instructions **4** employment

5 **a** **Copy the table. Use a dictionary to fill in the missing forms of the words.**

Verb	Adjective	Adverb	Noun
…	…	…	fear
—	…	…	guilt
…	hopeful	…	…
…	imaginative	…	…
…	obedient	…	…
…	…	oppressively	…
—	happy	…	…
…	progressive	…	progress
—	…	suspiciously	…

b **Complete the sentences with suitable forms from the table.**

1 Sarfraz's parents were … that they would be able to advance economically in Britain.
2 Unfortunately, not all immigration stories end …
3 When I was a child, we had to … our parents unconditionally.
4 I couldn't … making a life in a foreign country. It must be very challenging.
5 Please don't be … of me just because I speak with a foreign accent.
6 If I don't call my parents every week or so, I feel really …
7 Unfortunately, religion is often used to … people.
8 Some say that Europe won't be able to … economically if it remains … of immigration.

TRANSLATION

S ▸ Translation (p. 204)

6 **a** **Match the English verbs from the text with their German translations. Be careful: two of the German verbs do not fit.**

1 to adopt
2 to corrupt
3 to hold on to
4 to observe
5 to overcome
6 to spend

a annehmen
b beobachten
c festhalten an
d herüberkommen
e spendieren
f überwinden
g verbringen
h *(jemanden)* verderben

b **Now translate the following text into English using the verbs from Part a.**

Einige Leute nehmen ganz neue Identitäten an, wenn sie einwandern, wobei andere an ihren alten Lebensweisen festhalten. Nachdem meine Familie im Jahr 2000 nach Deutschland gezogen war, beobachteten meine Eltern erfreut, dass ich Deutsch lernte und mich mit Deutschen anfreundete. Wir kennen aber Immigranten, die ihre Angst vor der westlichen Kultur nicht überwinden können. Sie verbringen ihre ganze Zeit zu Hause oder mit anderen Immigranten. Sie haben Angst, dass ihre Kinder vom westlichen Materialismus verdorben werden oder dass sie in die Drogenszene geraten. Natürlich ist es nicht immer so leicht für uns, sich mit Deutschen anzufreunden, aber man muss sich trotzdem bemühen!

LISTENING

CD 2 Track 11

7

a **Read the info box. With a partner, make a list of arguments for and against wearing hijab.**

INFO

Hijab

The Muslim practice of wearing a headscarf is controversial in many countries, and Britain is no exception. *Hijab*, meaning 'curtain', is the Arabic word for this modest way of dressing which includes a headscarf.

A schoolgirl wearing hijab

b **Listen to a dialogue between a British mother and her teenage daughter. One of them thinks wearing hijab is a good idea, the other one is against it. How many of the arguments in your lists were mentioned in the conversation?**

S ▸ Practising Listening Skills (p. 188)

c **Listen again and answer the questions in German.**

1 Wer von den beiden argumentiert für das Kopftuch, wer dagegen?
2 Was für schlechte Erfahrungen hat die Mutter gemacht, und mit wem – mit Muslimen, mit Weißen oder mit beiden Gruppen?
3 Welchen Aspekt britischer Kultur sieht die Tochter kritisch und worin besteht ihre Kritik?

COMPOSITION

8

Comment on the importance of values. Before you write, follow these steps.

S ▸ Writing a Comment (p. 195)

1 Consider which values you think are important. First, make a list of the values mentioned in the unit with a partner.

2 Use a dictionary to translate the words below. You may write about some of them or choose others which are more important to you.

- commitment
- compassion/empathy
- creativity
- faith
- forgiveness
- friendship
- generosity
- honesty
- humility
- independence
- integrity
- justice
- kindness
- loyalty
- patience
- peace

TEXT 3 An Era When Dreams Took Centre Stage

WARM-UP

1 **Use the following dates and illustrations to help you put the following historical events in the American Civil Rights movement (a–g) in the right order.**

a The Civil Rights Movement reaches its climax with a massive march on Washington, D.C. to protest racial discrimination and promote civil rights legislation. Martin Luther King gives his emotionally uplifting and prophetic speech, *I Have a Dream.*

b During this period, a series of racist 'Jim Crow' laws are passed in the South, stating that minorities should be 'separate but equal'. The laws segregate whites and 'persons of color' first in public transportation and schools, later in parks, cemeteries, theaters and restaurants.

c Disobeying Jim Crow, seamstress Rosa Parks refuses to give up her seat to a white man on a public bus. The Civil Rights Movement begins as a result of her arrest by police.

d The movement finally experiences its greatest victory when the federal government passes the Civil Rights Act, forbidding discrimination in public accommodations and threatening to withhold federal funds from communities that continued to maintain segregated schools.

e The first of many sit-ins is held in the South when blacks refuse to leave a 'white' lunch counter and are arrested for doing so. Such peaceful protests prove extremely effective in the Civil Rights Movement.

f The Supreme Court declares segregation in schools unconstitutional, forcing some 'white' schools to accept black students. Similar Jim Crow laws would be struck down in the years which followed. However, the federal government in Washington does not have the political power in the South to enforce the legislation there.

g Slavery is officially outlawed.

5 **uplifting** morally or spiritually elevating
7 **Jim Crow** the name given to segregation laws
13 **seamstress** woman who sews for a living
21 **withhold** keep, deny sb
23 **sit-in** occupying a place as a form of protest

2 Read the info box. Then match each description of a character in the play *A Raisin in the Sun* (1–5) to an actor in the photo.

INFO

A Raisin in the Sun

The play *A Raisin in the Sun* was written by Lorraine Hansberry at the dawn of the Civil Rights Movement in the US. In 1959 it became the first play by a black woman to be produced on Broadway, one of the many 'firsts' for African-Americans at the time.

The title of the play is from the opening lines of 'Harlem', a poem by Langston Hughes: 'What happens to a dream deferred? / Does it dry up / like a raisin in the sun?'

1 **Lena Younger**, who at the beginning of the play receives a life insurance payment of $10,000 due to the recent death of her husband. With part of the money she makes a down payment on a house, taking the first step to fulfilling her life's dream of getting out of the ghetto.
2 Her son **Walter**, whose dream is to lead the family and provide a decent life for them.
3 **Travis**, Walter's and Ruth's son.
4 **Ruth**, Walter's wife and Travis' mother, who shares her mother-in-law's dream of owning a house so that her son will have a yard to play in as well as his own bedroom. He currently has to sleep on the sofa in the living room.
5 Lena's intellectual daughter **Beneatha***, who seeks her identity in Africa and through education. She dreams of becoming a doctor.

defer put off until later
down payment first payment
yard *(AE) BE:* garden

* bə'ni:θə

3 Look at the photos from recent productions of *A Raisin in the Sun* and describe them using the words in the box below.

Talking about Plays (1)

to be set in: to take place (at a certain time or in a certain place)
setting: where the action of the play takes place
set: the collection of scenery, furniture and props used to create a particular environment on stage
props: small objects used on stage
stage: the part of the theatre where the play is shown, often a raised platform
costumes: what the actors wear
part or **character:** a role played by an actor

CD 2 Track 12

A Raisin in the Sun *(Act II, Scene 3)*

MAN Uh – how do you do, miss. I am looking for a Mrs. Lena Younger?

BENEATHA *(Smoothing her hair with slight embarrassment)* Oh – yes, that's my mother. Excuse me. *(She closes the door and turns to quiet the other two)* Ruth! Brother! *(Enunciating precisely but soundlessly: "There's a white man at the door!" They stop dancing, RUTH cuts off the phonograph, BENEATHA opens the door.)* Uh – come in please.

MAN Thank you.

BENEATHA My mother isn't here just now. Is it business?

MAN Yes … well, of a sort.

WALTER *(Freely, the Man of the House)* Have a seat. I'm Mrs. Younger's son. I look after most of her business matters. *(RUTH and BENEATHA exchange amused glances)*

MAN *(Sitting, his briefcase and hat on his knees)* Well – My name is Karl Lindner –

WALTER *(Stretching out his hand)* Walter Younger. This is my wife – *(RUTH nods politely)* – and my sister.

LINDNER How do you do?

WALTER *(Amiably, as he sits, leaning forward on his knees with interest)* What can we do for you, Mr. Lindner!

LINDNER Well – I am a representative of the Clybourne Park Improvement Association and we have had it brought to our attention at the last meeting that you people – or at least your mother – has bought a piece of residential property at four o six Clybourne Street …

WALTER That's right. Care for something to drink? Ruth, get Mr. Lindner a beer.

LINDNER *(Upset for some reason)* Oh – no, really. I mean thank you very much, but no thank you.

RUTH *(Innocently)* Some coffee?

LINDNER Thank you, nothing at all. *(BENEATHA is watching the man carefully)*

LINDNER Well, I don't know how much you folks know about our organization. *(He is a gentle man; thoughtful and somewhat labored in his manner)* It is one of these community organizations set up to look after – oh, you know, things like block upkeep and special projects and we also have what we call our New Neighbors Orientation Committee …

BENEATHA *(Dryly)* Yes – and what do they do?

LINDNER Well – it's what you might call a sort of welcoming committee, I guess. I mean they, we – I'm the chairman of the committee – go around and see the new people who move into the neighborhood and sort of give them the lowdown on the way we do things out in Clybourne Park.

BENEATHA *(With appreciation of the two meanings, which escape RUTH and WALTER)* Uh-huh.

LINDNER And we also have the category of what the association calls – uh – special community problems –

BENEATHA Yes – and what are some of those?

WALTER Girl, let the man talk.

LINDNER *(With understated relief)* Thank you. I would sort of like to explain this thing in my own way. I mean I want to explain to you in a certain way.

RUTH *(Still innocently)* Would you like another chair – you don't look comfortable.

LINDNER *(More frustrated than annoyed)* No, thank you very much. Please. Well – to get right to the point I – *(A great breath, and he is off at last)* I am sure you people must be aware of some of the incidents which have happened in various parts of the city when colored people have moved into certain areas. Well – because we have what I think is going to be a unique type of organization in American community life – not only do we deplore that kind of thing – but we are trying to do something about it. We feel – *(gaining confidence in his mission because of the interest in the faces of the people he is talking to)* – we feel that most of the trouble in this world, when you come right down to it – *(He hits his knee for emphasis)* – most of the trouble exists because people just don't sit down and talk to each other.

---

3 **enunciate** articulate clearly with the mouth
15 **amiable** friendly
19 **residential property** house or land where sb can live
29 **upkeep** maintenance
34 **give sb the lowdown on** *(coll.)* inform sb of the current situation
36 **appreciation** understanding
46 **incident** event
49 **deplore** strongly disapprove of
52 **emphasis** special importance, stress

RUTH You can say that again, mister.

LINDNER *(More encouraged by such affirmation)* That we don't try hard enough in this world to understand the other fellow's problem. The other guy's point of view.

RUTH Now that's right.

LINDNER Yes – that's the way we feel out in Clybourne Park. And that's why I was elected to come here this afternoon and talk to you people. Friendly like, you know, the way people should talk to each other and see if we couldn't find some way to work this thing out. As I say, the whole business is a matter of caring about the other fellow. Anybody can see that you are a nice family of folks, hard working and honest I'm sure. Today everybody knows what it means to be on the outside of something. And of course, there is always somebody who is out to take advantage of people who don't always understand.

WALTER What do you mean?

LINDNER Well – you see our community is made up of people who've worked hard for years to build up that little community. They're not rich and fancy people; just hard-working, honest people who don't really have much but those little homes and a dream of the kind of community they want to raise their children in. Now, I don't say we are perfect and there is a lot wrong in some of the things they want. But you've got to admit that a man, right or wrong, has the right to want to have the neighborhood he lives in a certain kind of way. And at the moment the overwhelming majority of our people out there feel that people get along better, take more of a common interest in the life of the community, when they share a common background. I want you to believe me when I tell you that race prejudice simply doesn't enter into it. It is a matter of the people of Clybourne Park believing, rightly or wrongly, as I say, that for the happiness of all concerned that our Negro families are happier when they live in their own communities.

BENEATHA *(With a grand and bitter gesture)* This, friends, is the Welcoming Committee!

WALTER *(Dumbfounded)* Is this what you came marching all the way over here to tell us?

LINDNER Well, now we've been having a fine conversation. I hope you'll hear me all the way through.

WALTER *(Tightly)* Go ahead, man.

LINDNER You see – in the face of all the things I have said, we are prepared to make your family a very generous offer … *(Drawing a form out of his briefcase)* Our association is prepared, through the collective effort of our people, to buy the house from you at a financial gain to your family.

RUTH Lord have mercy, ain't this the living gall!

WALTER All right, you through?

LINDNER Well, I want to give you the exact terms of the financial arrangement.

WALTER We don't want to hear them. You got any more to say 'bout how people ought to sit down and talk to each other? … Get out of my house, man.

LINDNER Well – I don't understand why you people are reacting this way. What do you think you are going to gain by moving into a neighborhood where you just aren't wanted and where some elements – well – people can get awful worked up when they feel that their whole way of life and everything they've ever worked for is threatened. You just can't force people to change their hearts, son. *(He puts his card on a table and exits.)* (1183 words)

64 take advantage of use sb in an unethical way
68 fancy upper-class
81 dumbfounded extremely surprised
89 the living gall *(informal AE)* arrogance, shamelessness
98 threatened in danger

WORKING WITH THE TEXT

4 Do the task and answer the questions.

S ▸ Answering Comprehension Questions (p. 191)

1. Describe in three sentences what happens in this scene.
2. Who is Mr Lindner and what does he want?
3. Which of the Youngers' dreams 'dries up like a raisin in the sun' in this scene? Has it really been lost or can it be rescued?
4. What kind of 'incidents' do you think Mr Lindner is referring to in line 46?

S ▸ Improving Your Writing Skills (p. 197)

5 **Describe the dilemma the Youngers find themselves in after this scene has taken place.**

Before writing, make a list of the reasons for and against choosing each course of action. Be sure to take into account both practical and moral arguments.

WORKING WITH WORDS

6 a **Match each of the rather informal expressions from the scene with their more formal equivalents.**

1 Have a seat.
2 Care for …?
3 give someone the lowdown on something
4 You can say that again!
5 You through?
6 Ain't this the living gall!

a inform someone of the situation
b That's really quite impertinent.
c I thoroughly agree with you.
d Please sit down, won't you?
e Would you like …?
f Have you finished?

b **Complete the sentences with a suitable expression in the correct form.**

1 Hey, I've got some candy. … a piece?
2 … The doctor will be with you in a moment.
3 Cool! I've just got one more math problem and then … with my homework.
4 In the event of an emergency: stay calm, locate a telephone and … immediately.
5 … ! I couldn't have said it better myself, Dad.
6 … Please don't speak to me that way again or I shall complain to your employer.

7 **Make sure you understand the following adverbs of manner in the stage directions used in the scene on p. 104–05.**

a *precisely* (line 4)
b *soundlessly* (line 4)
c *politely* (line 12)
d *amiably* (line 15)
e *innocently* (line 24)
f *carefully* (line 25)
g *dryly* (line 31)
h *tightly* (line 84)

With a partner, take turns saying the following lines from the play. Do not say them as they were said in the play, but in the manner of one of the above adverbs. Your partner must guess which adverb you're demonstrating.

Partner A: 'Care for something to drink?'
Partner B: 'This, friends, is the welcoming committee.'

LITERARY ANALYSIS

8 a **Read the box below then match the lines from the play with their subtext.**

Talking about Plays (2)

lines: the text the playwright has written for the actors to speak
subtext: the term in literature for the hidden meaning beneath what a character says. Subtext is very important in plays, and actors must clearly communicate it to the audience.

1 **LINDNER** We don't try hard enough in this world to understand the other fellow's problem. The other guy's point of view.
2 **LINDNER** People get along better, take more of a common interest in the life of the community, when they share a common background.
3 **BENEATHA** This, friends, is the welcoming committee!
4 **WALTER** You got any more to say 'bout how people ought to sit down and talk to each other?
5 **LINDNER** People can get awful worked up when they feel that their whole way of life and everything they've ever worked for is threatened.

a I knew it all along. What he's really saying is that we're not wanted. We're being discriminated against like always.
b Understand *my* point of view.
c What you said earlier about people communicating with each other was deception.
d If you move into our neighborhood, you will be in danger of being attacked by the other residents.
e If blacks start moving into our neighborhood, they won't get along with the whites. It's better to live racially segregated.

b **Here are some 'lines' people might say during a visit. Write a possible subtext for each of them.**

HOST What a surprise to see you!
GUEST I'm afraid dogs don't like me very much.
HOST There's not much time for housework these days, is there?
GUEST Well, it has an interesting taste.
HOST My goodness, you do get a lot of calls on that mobile, don't you?
GUEST Oh, you've got *Harry Potter* number seven! I've just been dying to read this!
HOST Your kids are really bundles of energy, aren't they?
GUEST I guess I should have put on warmer clothes before I came here.
HOST Oh dear, look at the time!

c **With a partner, take turns reading the subtext you've written. Your partner has to guess which line you wrote each subtext for.**

CREATIVE WRITING

9 **Write the next scene of the play in which Lena comes home and finds out from Walter, Ruth, and Beneatha what has happened.**

DISCUSSION

10 **What do you think the Youngers should do – take the money or move to Clybourne Park?**

S ▸ Group Discussions (p. 203)

COMPOSITION

11 **Describe the situation for blacks in the United States today. First, discuss the subject in a group and make notes.**

S ▸ Improving Your Writing Skills (p. 197)

TEXT 4 It All Depends On Where You Were Born: Hispanics in North America

WARM-UP

1 It is estimated that about six million Mexicans are living illegally in the United States. Match each statement about this phenomenon with the person who made it.

1 'I need to work in the States so that I can support my family back in Mexico.'
2 'We rely on migrant workers from Mexico to fill our labor needs.'
3 'It's our job to catch "illegals" sneaking into the United States and send them back to Mexico.'
4 'These illegal aliens are taking all the jobs from us Americans.'

a a US-American Border Patrol guard
b an unemployed US-American worker
c a US-American employer of unskilled laborers
d one of the Mexicans living illegally in the United States

CD 2 Track 13

Our Wall

Fences may make good neighbors, but the barriers dividing the U.S. and Mexico are proving much more complicated.

At various spots along the dusty U.S.-Mexican border, many miles of fences, walls, and vehicle barriers have been constructed since the 1990s to slow illegal immigration. In Arizona, the state most overrun with illegal crossings, 65 miles (105 kilometers) of barriers have been constructed already. Depending on the direction of the ongoing U.S. immigration debate, there may soon be hundreds more miles of walls.

The 800 or so residents of Naco, Arizona have been living in the shadow of a 14-foot-high (four meters) steel wall for the past decade. The 4.6-mile (7.4-kilometer) barrier is now being extended 25 miles (40 kilometers) deeper into the desert.

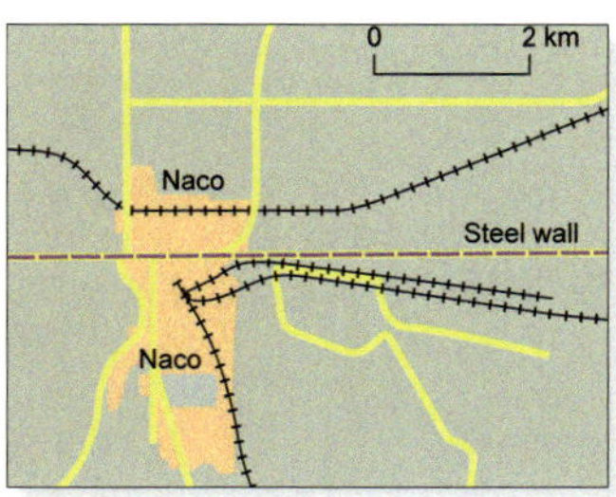

Naco used to be overrun by immigrants on their way north. At night, dozens, sometimes hundreds, of immigrants would crowd into motel rooms and storage rental sheds along the highway. Naco residents found their homes broken into by desperate migrants. Then came the wall in 1996, and the flow of people spread into the high desert outside the town.

Dan Duley, 50, is a native of the Naco area. He was living in Germany after serving in the Air Force when the Berlin Wall came down, and he thought that was a fine thing. But here he figures something has to be done. "We need help," he says. "We're being invaded. They've taken away our jobs, our security. I'm just a blue-collar man living in a small town. And I just wish the government cared about a man who was blue."

18 **storage rental shed** a small building hired for the purpose of keeping things in it
20 **desperate** having great need for sth
25 **figure** think, consider
26 **blue-collar** working-class

There is an iron law on this border: the closer one gets to the line, the more rational the talk becomes because everyone has personal ties to people on the other side. Even those who have let passing illegal immigrants use their phones or given them a ride say the exodus has to stop. And even those sick of finding trash in their yards understand why the immigrants keep coming.

A border wall seems to violate a deep sense of identity most Americans cherish. We see ourselves as a nation of immigrants. We are embarrassed by walls because they say something unpleasant about the neighbors – and us.

Rodolfo Santos Esquer puts out a weekly newspaper in Naco, Sonora, on the Mexican side of the metal wall that slashes the two communities. He finds the wall hateful. "It looks like the Berlin Wall. It is horrible. It is ugly. You feel more racism now. It is a racist wall. If people get close to the wall, the Border Patrol calls the Mexican police, and they go and question people."

And then he says all that has changed is that the "coyotes," or people smugglers, now drive to the end of the wall before crossing. And as the wall grows in length, the coyotes raise their rates. Santos figures half the town is living off migrants going north.

The border is haunted by ghosts – the hundreds who die each year from heat and cold, the ones killed in car wrecks as the packed vans of migrants flee the Border Patrol, and the increasing violence between smugglers and the agents of Homeland Security. Whenever security is increased at one part of the border, the migration simply moves to another part. The border walls built in southern California drove immigrants into the Arizona desert and, in some cases, to their deaths.

Everyone realizes the wall is a police solution to an economic problem: that jobs must be created in Mexico. Of the millions of illegal immigrants living in the United States, few would have come if there wasn't a job waiting for them. Simply crossing the border instantly raises a person's income tenfold. (630 words)

Adapted from *National Geographic*, May 2007

34 cherish protect and care for lovingly
35 embarrassed feeling awkward or ashamed
38 slash cut through violently
46 haunt often be at a place

WORKING WITH THE TEXT

2 Find the correct ending. (The sentences do not necessarily follow the order of the text.)

1 Naco, Arizona …
- **a** is overrun with migrants heading north.
- **b** is no longer overrun with migrants heading north.

2 Naco, Sonora …
- **a** still sees many migrants heading north.
- **b** sees few migrants heading north.

3 Unemployment is a problem …
- **a** in both the US and Mexico.
- **b** in Mexico, so Mexicans go to the US where there are plenty of jobs.

4 The wall is …
- **a** stopping illegal immigration.
- **b** making illegal immigration more difficult and dangerous.

5 More barriers …
- **a** will be built by the US. **b** may be built by the US.

S ▸ How to Deal with Instructions (p. 192)

3 Choose one of the following tasks.

1 Discuss the advantages and disadvantages of the US-Mexico border wall. Before you start, make lists of as many pros and cons of the wall as you can find.

pros	cons
slows illegal immigration	*not effective*
...	...

2 Assess the impact of the US-Mexico border wall. Before you start, list the people or groups affected by the wall and the effects it has had on each of them.

person/group	effects
Naco, Arizona residents	*no longer 'overrun' by Mexicans coming north*
Americans	...
...	...

WORKING WITH WORDS

4 Complete the summary of the text with eight of the adjectives in the box.

blue-collar | desperate | embarrassing | illegal | instant | past | rental | secure | sudden | unpleasant

The twin cities of Naco, Arizona and Naco, Sonora have been separated by a wall for the ...1 decade. The wall is supposed to slow ...2 immigration, which is often blamed for taking jobs away from American ...3 workers. While Naco experienced an ...4 reduction in the flow of migrants after the wall went up, it is said that people are simply entering the US at other places along the border. Getting across is very ...5 and even dangerous. Many migrants must be ...6 or they would not dare to make the journey. The wall makes some Americans feel more ...7 but it is also ...8 for a country which prides itself on being a nation of immigrants.

LOOKING AT LANGUAGE

G ▸ The Passive (p. 214)

5 a Write what has happened using the present perfect and one of the verbs in the box. Sometimes you will need the passive.

~~build~~ | immigrate | lose | raise | rise | stop

Example: There was no wall at the border. Now there's a wall.
⟶ *A wall* ***has been built*** *at the border.*

1. Mr and Mrs Hernandez were born in Mexico. Now they live in the United States.
2. There was a flow of migrants passing through Naco. Now very few pass through.
3. Mr Duley had a job. Now he's unemployed.
4. The smugglers used to charge $100 per person. Now the rate is $200.
5. In 2001 the estimated number of Mexicans living in the US illegally was three million. Now it's six million.

b Complete the sentences by putting the verb in either the present perfect or the simple past, active or passive.

G ▸ The Simple Past (p. 207), The Present Perfect (p. 208)

1 Since the 1990s, 65 miles of barriers … along the Arizona border to Mexico. (construct)
2 The wall is still being built. They … yet. (not finish)
3 In recent years the fear of illegal immigration … across the US. (spread)
4 About 250,000 Mexicans … in the US armed forces during World War II. (serve)
5 I … to Mexico but I know that unemployment is very high there. (never be)
6 Salvador … he would go back to Mexico for a short visit but then he … get back into the US. (decide, cannot)
7 The whole family … the border just a moment ago. (cross)
8 … those guys climbing over the wall? – Yes, they … by the police right away. (you see, catch)
9 I … illegal immigration until some migrants … my house. (not care about, break into)

ANALYSING A CHART

6 Work with a partner. You are going to describe a pie chart.

S ▸ Interpreting Graphs, Diagrams and Tables (p. 200)

1 First, look at the list of phrases on page 201. Make sure you understand when to use each phrase.
2 Now look at your pie chart. **Partner A**, turn to File 2 on page 180. **Partner B**, turn to File 8 on page 183.
3 Using as many of the words and phrases from page 201 as possible, describe the pie chart for your partner, who will draw it based on what you say.

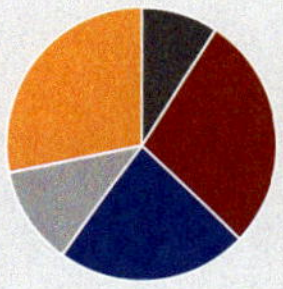

MEDIATION

7 Read the following text and use the key words in bold to summarise the text for a partner in German. Partner A: summarise the first paragraph. Partner B: summarise the second paragraph.

S ▸ Mediation (p. 204)

The Largest Minority

It is not uncommon for Mexicans to live illegally in the US for many years. Not all Mexicans in the US are illegal, though. Of the United States' 296 million citizens, 43 million are Hispanic. Hispanics recently surpassed blacks to become the **largest minority** in the US. They are also the **fastest-growing minority**. In the past five years their numbers have increased by 20% and they are expected to triple by 2050. Most of the increase doesn't come from immigration but from the **high number of births**, most Hispanics being **Catholic**.

Of course, such large numbers constitute a great economic, cultural and political force. The **purchasing power** of Hispanics has long been evident, especially in **urban areas** where advertisements and shop signs in Spanish are commonplace. Recent years have seen a great Latino wave in **pop culture**, which is gaining more and more influence in areas like music, food and fashion. Hispanic-Americans' great **voting power** has historically tended to benefit the **Democratic party**, but the Republicans have been gaining ground in recent elections, and both parties now have websites in Spanish. One of the most important political issues for Hispanics is, not surprisingly, **immigration**.

3 **surpass** *überflügeln*
5 **triple** become three times as many
8 **constitute** form, make up

CD 2 Track 14

S ► Practising Listening Skills (p. 188)

CD 2 Track 15

HANDS-ON TASK

S ► Giving a Presentation (p. 201)

S ► Doing Research on the Internet (p. 189)

LISTENING

8 a **Listen to excerpts from five presentations. The presenters can speak English very well, yet each of them makes typical mistakes in how they deliver their speeches. Describe the mistake each speaker makes.**

Example: *Speaker 1 speaks extremely fast, staccato, …*
Speaker 2 …

b **Listen to the five speakers again. This time their delivery is very good. Make notes of language that they use which is typical of presentations. You will need it in the following task.**

INTERNET RESEARCH AND PRESENTATION

9 **Research one of the following barriers and give a short presentation. Besides general information, explain what the purpose of the barrier was/is and how effective it was/is.**

The following is a suggestion for how you might structure your presentation.

Attention-getting opening line. Perhaps an impressive or a humorous fact about the barrier, a relevant quotation or a rhetorical question to get people thinking.
I. Why the barrier was built. Describe the historical situation and the problem the barrier is/was meant to solve.
II. The state of the barrier when it was at its largest or of greatest importance. If this is relevant to the barrier you choose to present, then it's your chance to impress your audience with dazzling facts and figures.
III. Any controversy surrounding the barrier. How effective was/is it? Did/Does anyone oppose it? What problems did the barrier cause / is the barrier causing?
IV. The present and/or future of the barrier.

Hadrian's Wall

The Berlin Wall

The Great Wall of China

The Maginot Line

The wall being built by Israel in the West Bank

The rabbit fences of Australia

TEXT 5 Equal Rights for Homosexuals

WARM-UP

1 Describe the different models of family pictured here and rank them from most traditional to most modern.

Redefining the Meaning of Family

CD 2 Track 16

My grandmother, then a 16-year-old Polish Jew, came to America in 1910 and never looked back. Nor did I – not, at least, on account of being Jewish. Being an American homosexual, however, is more complicated. Few of us feel or want to feel anything but American; but many of us have at one time or another looked envyingly at Europe.

Belgium, the Netherlands and Spain allow gay marriage. Seven European countries offer nationally recognized civil unions, which are almost the same as marriage, and five offer domestic-partner status. The United States, by contrast, allows same-sex couples to marry in a single, relatively small state: Massachusetts. A few other states offer civil unions or domestic-partner programs. Most states, however, ban same-sex marriage and, often, civil unions.

The federal government in Washington does not recognize same-sex couples at all. Heterosexual Americans can obtain residency for their foreign partners for the price of a $25 marriage license; countless gay Americans cannot get residency for their foreign partners at any price. To stay together, more than a few same-sex couples live in exile abroad – often in Europe.

Millions of Americans, particularly but by no means only on the religious right, continue to denounce homosexuality and campaign for public policies that do the same.

Yet, to say America is "behind" Europe on gay equality is to overlook that America's coming to terms with homosexuality is a very different kind of project than Europe's, because America is a very different kind of place. In Europe, acceptance of homosexuality is by and large an afterthought in the larger movement toward modernization and secularism. Europe is decidedly less pious than America, and homosexuality poses no conflict at all with secular modernity.

2 **on account of** because of
5 **envying** with a longing for what sb else has
13 **residency** permission to live somewhere
23 **afterthought** sth thought of or added later
24 **secularism** separation of church and state
pious devoutly religious

29 **glue** substance used for sticking objects together
31 **dissolve** break down
32 **embark on** begin
33 **reconcile** make compatible
36 **ancestry** ethnic origins
40 **abortion** intentionally ending a pregnancy
44 **contradiction in terms** a group of words making a connection between incompatible
47 **commitment** a promise to bind oneself to a person, action,or cause
48 **sluggish** slow

In much of Europe, marriage is increasingly a mere formality. Children in Denmark and Sweden, for example, are less likely than American kids to be raised by married couples, but more likely to be raised by both their parents. Something other than marriage is the glue holding these Northern European families together. In these cultures, same-sex marriage looks like a lifestyle choice, not a threat.

In short, Europe is dissolving many of the traditions that make homosexuality seem morally and socially problematic. America is not. America has embarked on a harder, perhaps more ambitious, project, which is to reconcile homosexuality with traditional moral scruples and social structures.

The United States is a country of ethnic diversity. Identity comes less from language, ancestry and birthplace than from beliefs, community and culture. Americans tend to understand who they are in terms of what they believe and who they believe it with. Millions ground themselves in the Bible, in faith communities or in generations-old unwritten norms, which is why so-called social issues like homosexuality and abortion are so central to U.S. politics.

For gay Americans, the bad news is that this reconciliation is a difficult and slow process, the work of generations. The good news is that the work is proceeding quickly, faster than I once believed possible.

Just a decade ago, same-sex marriage was a joke, a contradiction in terms. Today more than a third of Americans support it, and a majority support civil unions. Millions of Americans have come to accept the dignity and morality of homosexual love and commitment.

Where gay equality is concerned, you can call the United States the most sluggish of major secular societies, or you can call it the most progressive of great traditionalist cultures. Or, most accurately, you can say it continues to go its own way by working out how to be both at once. Whatever you call it, I would not trade it. (603 words)

Adapted from *Newsweek* Special Edition, December 2007–February 2008

WORKING WITH THE TEXT

S ▸ Answering Comprehension Questions (p. 191)

2 Answer the questions.

1 Why, according to the article, have many Americans 'looked enviously at Europe'?
2 What point is the author making about families in Denmark and Sweden?
3 Where in the world does identity come more from language, ancestry and birthplace?

S ▸ How to Deal with Instructions (p. 192)

3 Explain why it is harder for gay rights to progress in the US than in much of Europe. First, copy the diagram on the following page and complete it as instructed.

1 Complete the 'Germany' column with the following:

ancestry | birthplace | language | nationally recognised civil union | permit obtainable | smaller

2 Complete the 'US' column with the following:

beliefs | community | culture | larger | no permit | only at state level in a few states

	GERMANY	US
sources of identity	*ancestry …*	…
role of religion in society	…	…
recognition of homosexual partnership	…	…
residency for foreign partner	…	…

WORKING WITH WORDS

4 a Complete the following table with words from the text.

Verbs	Adjectives	Nouns
…	married	…
to moralize	… / immoral	… / moral / morals
–	… / …	… / traditionalism / traditionalist
…	reconciled / reconcilable	…
…	believable	…
–	…	Judaism / …
to reside	resident / residential	resident / …
to equalize	equal	…

b Choose the correct words to complete the sentences.

1 The *moral/morality* of the Frog Prince fable is that one's appearance does not define what one is.
2 Christian *moral/morality* plays a large role in the USA.
3 Some people claim that homosexuals have no *moral/morals*.
4 *Jewish/Judaism/Jew* is one of the world's great religions.
5 Bill and Dave argued a lot before they split up but now their differences are *reconciled/reconcilable*.
6 Many of the *residents/residencies* of this neighbourhood are gay.
7 She's been living separately from her American partner ever since she lost her *resident/residency* permit for the United States.
8 I know some homosexuals who have very strong religious *believes/beliefs*.

WORKING WITH A DICTIONARY

5 a **Say how many syllables the following words have.**

1 Judaism **3** married **5** reconciled
2 marriage **4** modernization **6** traditional

b **Find the words that are transcribed phonetically below.**

1 'iːkwəl **3** 'mærɪdʒ **5** rɪ'zaɪd
2 ˌhetərə'sekʃuəl **4** 'rekənsaɪl **6** 'sekjələ

c **Find the words that are transcribed phonetically below and say where the stress falls.**

1 həoməsekʃuəl **3** rekənsɪlieɪʃn **5** rezɪdənʃl
2 mədʒɜːnəti **4** rezɪdənt **6** sekjələrɪzəm

LOOKING AT LANGUAGE

G ▸ The Definite / Indefinite Article (p. 221)

6 **Complete the text by choosing the correct article.**

You may have heard of (the/–)¹ Christopher Street Day, which is celebrated once (a/the)² year in many cities on both sides of (the/–)³ Atlantic. (The/–)⁴ Christopher Street is in (the/–)⁵ New York City, and located there is (a/the)⁶ plain, little bar called the Stonewall Inn, which has considerable historical importance. On June 28, 1969 this gay bar was raided by police and (the/–)⁷ patrons were arrested for 'indecency'. This had happened many times before, but on this day (the/–)⁸ patrons got very angry and fought back against (the/–)⁹ police. (The/–)¹⁰ events that took place during the next five days have become known as the Stonewall Riots and are considered to be (the/–)¹¹ catalyst of (a/the)¹² modern Gay Rights Movement in (the/–)¹³ United States.

raid *durchsuchen, eine Razzia durchführen*
patron guest at a bar or restaurant
riot a violent disturbance of the peace by a crowd

LISTENING

CD 2 Track 17

S ▸ Practising Listening Skills (p. 188)

7 On December 21, 2005, it became legally possible in England and Wales for same-sex couples to join in civil partnerships. Sir Elton John and his partner David Furnish were one of the 700 couples who did so on that day.

a **Listen to an interviewer asking Sir Elton about his partnership, and to the singer's response. Then, share with your partner what you were able to understand. Finally, report to the class what you both understood.**

b **Read the following statements. They are all false. Now listen again and correct the statements to make them true. Remember to take notes while listening. You will hear a pause between each relevant section.**

1 Sir Elton thinks of his civil partnership with Furnish as being exactly the same as a marriage.
2 Sir Elton and Furnish chose an insignificant date to register the civil partnership because they didn't want the partnership to make a political statement.
3 Sir Elton knows many gay men who inherited vast fortunes from their partners when they died.
4 After they formed their civil partnership, Sir Elton and Furnish felt no sense of anything being different.

TEXT 6 Never Say 'Dummy' Again

WARM-UP

1 You are going to take an intelligence test. You have exactly five minutes to answer all five questions.

1 **If some wicks are slicks, and some slicks are snicks, then some wicks are definitely snicks. This statement is:**

a True
b False
c Neither true nor false

2 **Which of the figures on the right best completes the series below?**

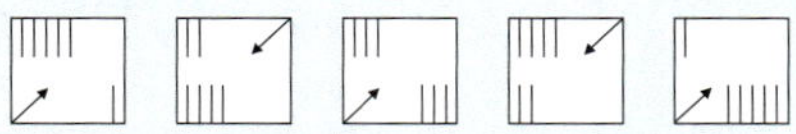

a 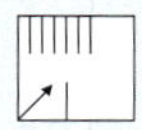
c 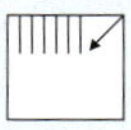
b 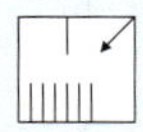
d 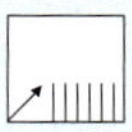

3 **Which letter comes next in this series of letters?**

C A D B E C F D G

a C
b D
c E
d F
e G

4 **Some months have 30 days, some months have 31 days. How many months have 28 days?**

5 **How many four-sided figures are in this diagram?**

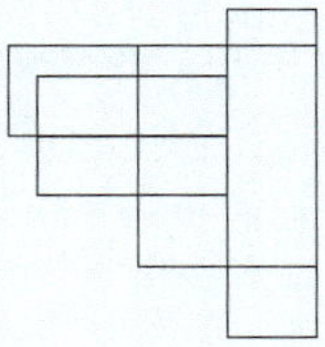

a 10
b 16
c 25
d 28

Your score:

1	correct answer	–	IQ 60	–	very low intelligence
2	correct answers	–	IQ 80	–	low intelligence
3	correct answers	–	IQ 100	–	average intelligence
4	correct answers	–	IQ 120	–	high intelligence
5	correct answers	–	IQ 140	–	very high intelligence

INFO

Intelligence tests

Intelligence tests are designed so that the results fall into a 'bell curve' pattern, meaning that the average score of 100 is achieved by the most people and the further the score is from this average, the fewer the people who achieve it.

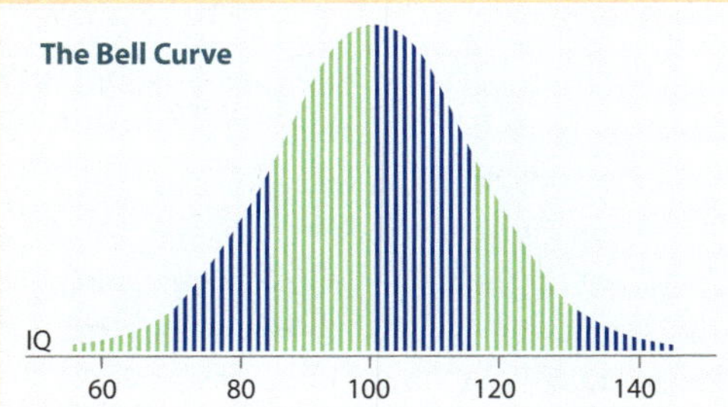

2 **Before you read, think about what qualities besides intelligence are important to society. Are any qualities more important?**

CD 2 Track 18

Prejudice Against the Stupid is Stupid

If you refuse someone a job on the basis of their skin colour, you will, in civilised countries, be in trouble. We don't enslave people on the grounds of their genetic inheritance. Such attitudes are, properly, deemed abhorrent.

Yet there is still one sort of genetic discrimination that is not only legal, it is universally applied and wholly respectable. They are the individuals who lie at the bottom of the normal range of human intelligence. I'm not talking about people with learning difficulties; these people are generally protected and helped by the state. I mean those too smart to qualify for such assistance but not clever enough to thrive easily in today's knowledge-based society.

The unfairness these people face is shocking. It is hard, for example, for someone who is illiterate to even earn a living wage in western societies. This was not always the case. A century ago in the UK, more than a million people worked in mines and millions more in agriculture – jobs which usually required no academic skills. Now most of those jobs have gone, and there is almost no way for unintelligent people to contribute to society.

How many people are we talking about? The distribution of IQ scores in a population is a bell curve, with the average roughly 100. In most western nations, 60 to 75 per cent of people score between 85 and 115. The few below about 70 can be considered to have a cognitive disability. But a significant proportion, 5 to 15 per cent, lie between 70 and 85. These people will have problems with arithmetic and language, and will likely be illiterate or close to it. In the UK alone that's between 2 and 6 million people.

Of course, many claim IQ is no more than a measure of the ability to do IQ tests. Yet while it may not measure intelligence directly, it does seem to correlate rather well with it. People with high IQs are considered to be "bright", tend to do better at school, earn more, live longer and have a greater choice of mates and careers. People with low IQs are more likely to end up on the streets or in prison.

Heritability studies suggest 50 to 75 per cent of the variability in IQ is down to our genes. Of course the right training will maximise academic potential, but everyone has their genetic limits. I can run a mile in 7 minutes; if I devoted my life to running I might knock a minute or so off this time, but I will never do it in 4 minutes. We can bring many people into the intellectual mainstream, and should do so, but some will be left behind.

You might think that a society in which people succeed based on their intelligence is fair and desirable. But the danger of a society where status is defined by merit is that the elite will feel wholly entitled to the privileges they enjoy.

Those of us lucky enough to be born higher up the IQ scale need to acknowledge that the stupid aren't bad, undeserving or inherently unable to make a useful contribution to society. Education systems that properly value vocational skills such as caring, craft or manual work would be a good start.

Throwing the unacademic on the scrap heap or pretending that they don't exist benefits no one. Instead of forcing them to waste time trying to do what they can't, let's give them the chance to do what they can. (586 words)

Michael Hanlon in *New Scientist*, 23 June 2007

4 **enslave** make sb a slave
5 **inheritance** what one receives from sb when they die
6 **deem** see as
abhorrent morally disgusting
17 **thrive** live very well
21 **illiterate** unable to read or write
38 **cognitive** related to thinking
56 **heritability** how much influence heredity has on a specific trait
61 **devote** dedicate
72 **merit** good quality
73 **be entitled to** have the right to
78 **undeserving** unworthy
inherently by nature
81 **vocational** professional
craft making sth by hand
83 **scrap heap** junk pile
84 **pretend** act as if

WORKING WITH THE TEXT

S ▶ How to Deal with Instructions (p. 192)

3 Do the following tasks.

1 List the consequences of having low intelligence.
2 Explain what makes someone intelligent or not.
3 Using the author's arguments, justify giving vocational skills such as caring and manual work higher priority in the educational system.

WORKING WITH WORDS

4 Sort the adjectives in the box into one of two categories:
a intelligent, b unintelligent.

academically challenged | academically skilled | bright | clever | daft | dumb | elite | illiterate | knowledgeable | sharp | smart | stupid | unacademic

5 Complete the sentences with the correct form of one of the following verbs.

acknowledge | contribute | deserve | leave behind | score | thrive

1 Society must learn to … the inherent value of each and every individual.
2 Don't think you're a better person just because you … over 100 on an IQ test.
3 She's not smart, but she … respect like everyone else.
4 It's a shame that so many disadvantaged kids get … by school systems.
5 Being born with intelligence is no guarantee that you will … in society, but it makes it more likely.
6 Insulting or teasing people by calling them 'stupid' only … to the problem of prejudice against the unintelligent.

LISTENING

CD 2 Track 19

S ▶ Practising Listening Skills (p. 188)

6 a Look at the description of this Internet radio show you are going to listen to. Tell your partner what you think the answers to the questions will be.

b Listen to the first part of the show and take notes on the questions.

c In the second segment, Dr Heart talks about 'self-awareness' and 'people skills'. Listen to find out what these terms mean and why they are important in the workplace.

d Now listen to the third segment. Which of the following techniques does Dr Heart use to teach people Emotional Intelligence?

- playing with animals
- meditation
- primal scream therapy
- role-playing

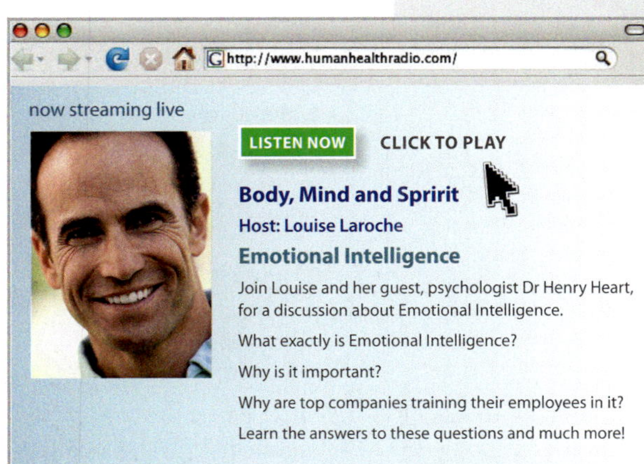

World of Work

MEDIATION Immigration to Europe

S ▸ Mediation (p. 204)

1 Do the following mediation task.

Sie arbeiten für das deutsche Bundesamt für Migration und Flüchtlinge. In dem unten aufgeführten Text werden Probleme bei der Integration beschrieben und entsprechende Maßnahmen empfohlen. Ihr Chef hat Sie gebeten, diese Probleme und Empfehlungen auf Deutsch in einem stichpunktartigen Bericht zusammenzufassen.

Before you start, do this quick quiz to make sure you know what is required.

1 True or false?
You should not translate the text exactly.

2 The length of the text you write should be:
a about one page. **b** about a third of the length of the original text.
c the same length as the original text

3 True or false?
You should not attempt to copy the style and format of the original text. The task you are given will specify the format (e.g. business letter) to use when you write your German text.

4 Which of the following things can you leave out of your text?

a lists
b quotations
c most numbers
d paragraph breaks
e your opinion
f most names

Prosperity Through Migration

Europe faces great challenges in the 21st century. Among them are an ageing population and a low rate of population growth. The situation is particularly worrying in our larger cities, where the impacts of demographic changes will be most severely felt. These changes could lead to low consumer demand, empty housing and the failure of public facilities, such as schools and hospitals, to retain sufficient users to keep them in operation. In light of this, there is an acute need for action.

It is in this context that the authors of the EU report *Prosperity through Migration* have studied the fortunes of migrants in a number of European countries: the problems they encounter and the measures that are taken to integrate them into their adopted communities.

A Valuable Labour Force

A central problem which will confront Europe in the years to come is a shortage of skilled workers – the very sector of the workforce which is critical for continued economic development. In order to meet the demand for skilled labour, many European cities will have to rely on migrant workers from outside the EU. Clearly, therefore, the successful integration of these migrants into society and employment is imperative.

prosperity state of being successful, especially in making money
5 **housing** houses, flats/apartments, etc. that people live in
facility buildings, services, etc. that are provided for a particular purpose
6 **in light of sth** after considering sth
10 **encounter** experience or discover
12 **labour force** the people who work or are available for work in a country or company
13 **shortage** situation when there is not enough of the people or things that are needed
18 **imperative** very important and needing immediate attention or action

Yet despite the forecast demographic predicament, immigration laws have actually been tightened in recent years in many European countries. For example the governments of the United Kingdom, France, Germany and Switzerland have all made it more difficult for migrants from outside the EU to obtain residency and permission to work in their countries.

A Preoccupation with Terrorism

The successful integration of migrants brings all kinds of rewards: economic, social and cultural. Unfortunately the immigration debate has increasingly been focused on a negative image of migrants and particularly on combating terrorism. This is somewhat irrational since many of Europe's terrorist attacks have been perpetrated by 'home-grown' terrorists, e.g. the London bombers of 2005 were British-born Muslims.

Unequal Treatment

Migrants from different countries are not always treated equally, and immigration practices still vary considerably throughout Europe. This leads to arbitrary selection processes and restrictive treatment of skilled migrants who do not belong to the privileged groups.

A further obstacle to migrants who want to play a full part the economic and social life of their adopted country lies in the strict and complicated requirements for obtaining citizenship. For example, in one country, applicants are required to start their own business and either invest 1 million euros in it or employ 100 citizens before they are eligible for citizenship. Often the rules are unclear and contradictory, leaving too much room for (mis)interpretation.

Lack of Recognition

Skilled migrants are often confronted with difficulties of an institutional nature when it comes to gaining recognition of qualifications from their home countries. Unclear guidelines and irregularities in this area are a major obstacle to integration.

Often individuals complete educational programmes in their home country which they believe will allow them to work in the target country, but then these qualifications prove worthless when they arrive. In most cases, access to the labour market is difficult, unstructured and full of bureaucratic hurdles.

The waiting periods during certain bureaucratic procedures, for example the work permit approval process, are often so long that the migrant's professional qualifications become outdated and this disqualifies him/her. Professional experience loses its value when it is not put to use quickly in the target country. Both the country and the migrant suffer an economic loss as a result of these delays.

Lack of Advice

There are not enough advisory services to guide migrants through steps which may be necessary to achieve employment. In many cases, migrants need language courses specifically related to their profession. They may also need supplementary higher education courses or practical training to be able to integrate into the relevant scientific and occupational system.

If migrants are given access to such services, it is much easier for them to make full use of the education they completed before migration. At the same time it speeds up the integration process, meaning that the migrant can more quickly become a productive member of the community. (735 words)

Adapted from www.bbc.co.uk

22 **residency** permission to live in a country that is not your own

24 **preoccupation** state of thinking about sth continuously

27 **combat** fight against an enemy

28 **perpetrate** commit a crime or do sth wrong or evil

33 **arbitrary** not seeming to be based on a reason, system or plan and sometimes seeming unfair

34 **restrictive** preventing people from doing what they want

40 **eligible** able to have sth because of the right qualifications

45 **obstacle** situation that makes it difficult for you to do or achieve sth

49 **hurdle** problem or difficulty that must be solved or dealt with before you can achieve sth

54 **delay** a period of time when sb/sth has to wait because of a problem that makes sth slow or late

JOB SKILLS Giving a Presentation

PREPARING SLIDES FOR A PRESENTATION

2 a Look at the two pairs of PowerPoint slides for a presentation on the integration of skilled migrants. Which pair of slides is better: 1 and 2 or 3 and 4? Why?

b In a group of three, make a list of things you should and shouldn't do when you make PowerPoint slides or other similar visuals.

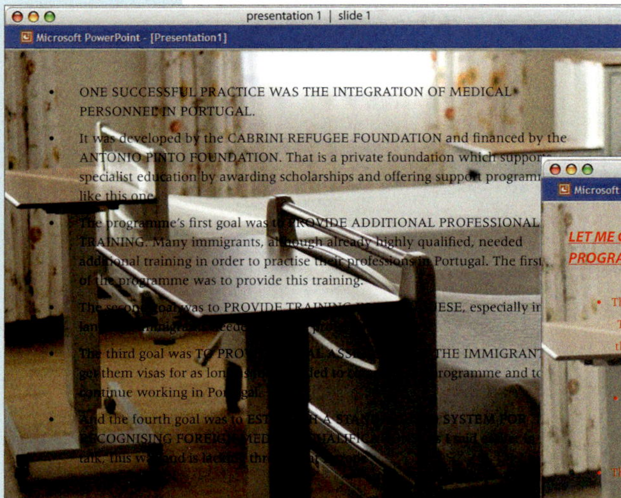

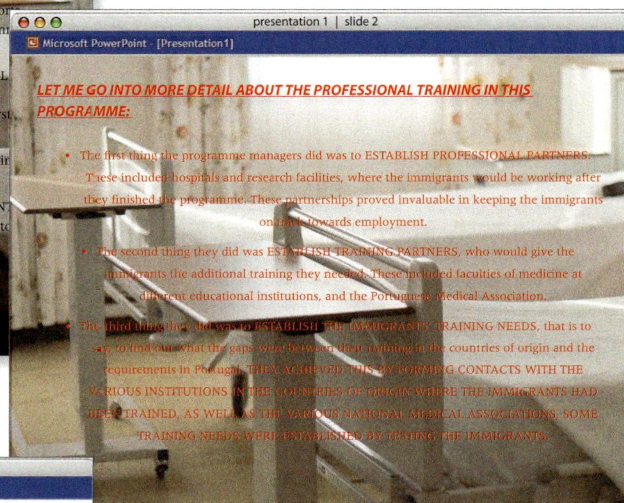

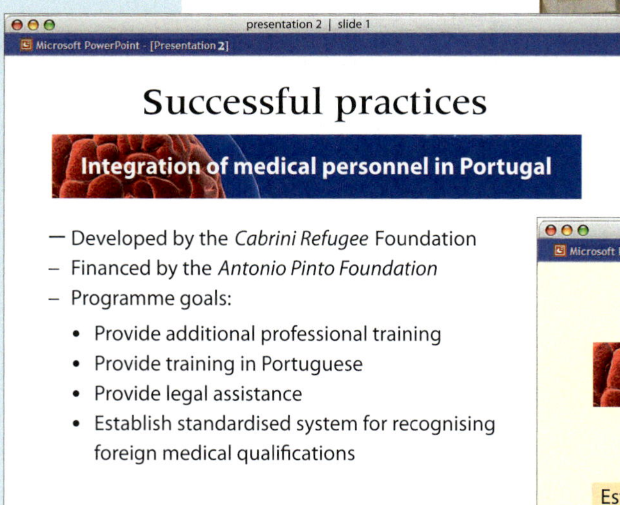

PRESENTATIONS: TYPICAL MISTAKES

3 a **Work with a partner. Match the cartoons with the typical mistakes often made during a presentation.**

- **a** Addressing a formal audience too informally
- **b** Using too many slides
- **c** Being unprepared and disorganised
- **d** Nervous body movements; making hand movements which distract the audience

b **What other things can people get wrong when they give a presentation? Make a list.**

LISTENING

CD 2 Track 20

4 The first pair of slides on p. 122 belongs to Jacques Lainez, an EU adviser. As you will hear, his slides weren't the only thing he got wrong in his presentation. Listen to him give his presentation and make notes on things he could have done better.

S ▸ Practising Listening Skills (p. 188)

CD 2 Track 21

5 The second pair of slides on p. 122 belongs to EU adviser Annika Hug, an excellent presenter. Listen to her advising Jacques on his presentation and make notes on the tips she gives him. Does she mention any of the points from your list in exercise 4?

GIVING A PRESENTATION

HANDS-ON TASK

6 Now it's your turn to prepare a presentation. It can be anything related to the world of work. Your teacher will give you a time limit.

TOPIC 5 Britain's Changing Status in Today's World

BACKGROUND INFORMATION

From Empire to Europe

establish *gründen*
colony *Kolonie*
claim *einfordern*
survive *überleben*
supply *Vorrat, Versorgung*
found *gründen*
War of Independence *Unabhängigkeitskrieg*
settlement *Siedlung*

At the beginning of the 16th century, Spain and Portugal had already established colonies in the West Indies and the Americas. During the reign of Elizabeth I, several explorers claimed land for Britain, e.g. Newfoundland (no settlers were left there) and Roanoke in North Carolina, where the settlers did not survive because of lack of supplies. Serious colonising started in the 17th century when colonies were founded in North America and on smaller Caribbean islands. The War of Independence (1776–1783) ended rule in North America, but Canada remained a British settlement. This was called the First Empire.

trade *handeln*
spice *Gewürz*
gain territory *Land hinzugewinnen*
expansion *Erweiterung*
take over rule *die Herrschaft übernehmen*
mutiny *Meuterei*

In the 17th century, a private company, the English East India Company, started trading with Asia. At first the only interest was the trade in spices, but later the East India Company became interested in gaining territory and played a role in the expansion of the Empire. The British government took over rule in India in the middle of the 19th century after an Indian mutiny in which many lives were lost.

At the end of the 19th century, the British had established colonies in Africa, among which were Nigeria, Kenya, South Africa, Rhodesia, Gambia and Ghana.

convict *Strafgefangene/r*
self-governing status *selbstverwaltender Status*

Australia was claimed by Britain in 1770 and used as a colony for convicts who had been sent to North America previously. New Zealand was claimed by the British in 1840. These colonies soon achieved self-governing status and later full independence. They still regard the Queen as Head of State, as does Canada.

extension *Ausbau, Vergrößerung*
gain control *Kontrolle gewinnen*

After World War I the last major extension of British rule took place. Britain gained control of Iraq, Palestine and the former German colonies of Tanganyika and Namibia.

The End of the British Empire

comprise *umfassen*
request *verlangen, erbitten*

Up until World War II the British Empire remained the largest the world had ever seen. It comprised about a quarter of the world's population and more than a quarter of the world's land area. After World War II Britain gave independence peacefully to any country which requested it. In 1947 the Empire lost its most valuable colony, India. In the north a Muslim state called Pakistan was created. The

Partition of India resulted in massive population exchanges and widespread violence which cost hundreds of thousands of lives. Later East Pakistan became independent and is now called Bangladesh. The last major colony of Hong Kong was handed over in 1997. A few colonies still exist, by wish of their inhabitants. One of these is Gibraltar.

partition *Teilung*
population exchange *Bevölkerungsaustausch*
inhabitant *Einwohner/in*

The Commonwealth

Most former colonies (and one former Portuguese one) are members of the Commonwealth which is a voluntary and non-political organisation aiming to promote democracy, human rights, free trade and world peace. Sixteen of these countries still recognise the Queen as Head of State. All these countries share English as their first or second language.

Commonwealth *Gemeinschaft der Länder des ehemaligen Britischen Weltreichs*
voluntary *freiwillig*
promote *fördern, vorantreiben*
democracy *Demokratie*
human rights *Menschenrechte*
free trade *freier Handel*

Their parliamentary systems and systems of law, the military, the police and the civil service are all modelled on their British equivalents, as are many universities (modelled on Oxford and Cambridge) and boarding schools. In most countries, except Canada and the USA, people drive on the left. Rugby and cricket are especially popular in Commonwealth countries. The Commonwealth Games, the second largest sporting event after the Olympic Games, take place every four years. Up until the 1960s the citizens of former colonies could enter Britain with a British passport as British Commonwealth citizens.

parliamentary system *parlamentarisches System*
system of law *Rechtssystem*
civil service *öffentlicher Dienst*
boarding school *Internat*
citizen *Bürger/in*

Britain and Europe

When Churchill made his speech about a United States of Europe after World War II he did not intend Great Britain to play a great role. At the beginning, Great Britain was not interested in joining the EEC because of its many Commonwealth links. However, in 1973 Britain became a member after France finally ended its opposition to Britain's entry. The British are still very undecided about the EU and are especially worried about losing national sovereignty and about passing political, legal and monetary matters to the EU. For most Britons an economic community would be enough. For these reasons Great Britain is divided into a land of Eurosceptics, who often seem to be in the majority, and Europhiles. Britain, like Denmark and Sweden, did not adopt the euro in 2002.

join *beitreten*
EEC *Europäische Wirtschaftsgemeinschaft*
opposition *Widerstand*
national sovereignty *nationale Souveränität*
pass to *weitergeben an*
legal *gesetzlich, rechtlich*
monetary *finanziell, Geld-*
Eurosceptic *Europaskeptiker/in*
Europhile *Europabefürworter*

Now that the euro has proved to be a success, many British politicians might consider introducing it. However, it is unlikely that the new currency would be introduced without a referendum being held first.

currency *Währung*
referendum *Volksentscheid*

TEXT 1 Reflections on Britain's Colonial Past

WARM-UP

1 **What do you know about India? Think about the following list and then exchange ideas with a partner. Share your ideas with another pair and then report to the class.**

- Bollywood
- holy cows
- religions and conflicts
- the caste system
- the IT industry
- arranged marriages

2 **Decide which of the two explanations is correct. Then scan the text below to check your answers.**

1 institutionalised
- **a** *done so long that it seems normal or monotonous*
- **b** *put in an institution*

2 rule with an iron fist
- **a** *rule with an iron sculpture of a hand*
- **b** *rule in a hard and strict way*

3 on the brink of absorption
- **a** *about to become a part of something*
- **b** *beginning to show interest in something*

4 forebears
- **a** *people who lived a long time ago*
- **b** *bears that were found hundreds of years ago*

CD 3 Track 2

An Unusual Gap Year

After working for some years, Matt Showering decided that he wanted to do some travelling and visit the former British colonies in Australia and India. This is an excerpt from his report about his experiences in India.

I chose India as my first destination, mainly because I have always been fascinated by Indian history and culture (not to mention my great love of Indian food) and because – in order to break away from my 'institutionalised' lifestyle – I felt that I needed to spend some time away from the West. I was well aware of the fact that I would be visiting the land in which my not-too-distant ancestors once ruled with an iron fist. However, I did not realise that I would be arriving in Delhi just a few weeks after the celebrations of the 60th anniversary of India's independence.

While being driven from Indira Gandhi International Airport to my hotel in New Delhi, I quickly noticed many of the expected and completely new sights associated with India: long lines of homeless people sleeping alongside the road, some knocking on the car windows to beg for money, cows freely walking through the streets, and

5 **ancestor** a person in your family who lived a long time ago

people urinating in open drains. Our tour leader repeatedly reminded us that India is a country with no welfare system, "where you always have to fight for your life".

In the small town of Chanderi, our local guide took us to the school where his children are being educated. It was midday as we watched all the schoolchildren being given their daily drill. Many Indian families cannot afford the 10 Rupees (about 15p) per month necessary to educate their children. One of my first thoughts was that some of these children – the very small ones – should not be forced to stand still for such a long time. The two songs they sung were extremely telling: first the Indian National Anthem, which is a reminder that the days are long gone when British State Schools attempted to foster respect for the Queen and Country by singing 'God save our gracious Queen …' on important occasions. This was followed by the classic protest song, 'We Shall Overcome', which recalls the struggles and sacrifices endured by people in India to achieve independence from the British. Britain today stands on the brink of absorption into a different kind of empire, the European Superstate, in which the masses believe that it is only socially acceptable for them to fly the British flag and sing the national anthem during international sports matches. Although it is true that my colonial forebears committed acts of brutality while governing the 'Jewel in the Crown', I do not think that youngsters in Britain should be discouraged from feeling proud of Britain today because of unpleasant events in the past.

It was very interesting for me to see how both Britain and India have developed since India became an independent country. This was clearly demonstrated on the platform at Varanasi station, where a beggar with a severe deformity – forcing him to walk on all fours – was asking passengers for money. I couldn't help thinking that if that man had been born in Britain, he would have been given all the medical treatment possible to try and ease his condition. He would have been given benefits for his family throughout his childhood and for himself in adulthood if he was unable to work.

It is a tragic thought that 60 years ago, Clement Attlee's Labour Government was so busy creating our beloved National Health Service and welfare state that it did not pay enough attention to the delicate matter of partitioning the soon-to-be independent India – no small contributory factor in the mass bloodshed that followed.

Since the assassination of Mahatma Gandhi in 1948, a succession of Indian leaders has vowed – and failed – to finally achieve his ultimate goal of eliminating widespread poverty. Also, there has not been any serious move towards establishing a free healthcare or a benefits system. That being said, a good starting point would seem to be the abolition of school fees for those families who cannot afford them.

(679 words)

www.britishempire.co.uk

21 **foster** encourage sth to develop
23 **sacrifice** the act of giving up sth important
endure tolerate without giving up
24 **on the brink of** on the point of
25 **absorption** the process of a smaller country becoming part of a larger country
33 **severe** extremely bad or serious
41 **partition** divide
44 **assassination** murder of an important person
succession series
45 **vow** make a serious promise
48 **abolition** the removal of a law

WORKING WITH THE TEXT

3 Answer the questions.

S ▸ Answering Comprehension (p. 191)

1. Why did Matt visit India?
2. Describe the typically Indian sights he saw on the way to the hotel.
3. Explain the 'daily drill' Matt observed at the school of the guide's children.
4. What did seeing the disabled man at Varanasi make him aware of?
5. Which goals has India not achieved since becoming an independent country?

4 What are the main differences between India and Western Europe, according to the text? Collect them in a table.

WORKING WITH WORDS

5 a **Copy and complete the table. In some cases the adjective is the same as the third form of the verb.**

Verb	Adjective	Noun
choose	...	...
arrive	–	...
associate	...	...
...	repeated	...
educate	...	...
...	achievable	...
develop	...	...
...	...	benefit
...	contributory	...

b **Complete the following summary of the text with words from the table in the correct form.**

India was my first ...[1] because I wanted to see where my ancestors had once ruled. On my ...[2] in Delhi I found out that it was a few weeks after the 60th anniversary of India's independence from Britain. There are many things which people ...[3] with India, for example lots of homeless people. Our guide told us that it costs 15p a month ...[4] their children, and lots of people cannot afford this. I wanted to see how Britain and India ...[5] since independence. Disabled people in Britain get lots of ...[6] to help them. This is just one of the ...[7] of the Labour Government 60 years ago. So far, no Indian government has made a significant ...[8] to the goal of eliminating poverty.

LOOKING AT LANGUAGE

G ▸ Participle Constructions (p. 220)

6 a **Translate the following sentences into German.**

1. While being driven from the airport to my hotel, I was not surprised by what I saw.
2. I saw many of the sights associated with India.
3. The songs being sung by the schoolchildren recalled the struggles and sacrifices endured by the people in India throughout their fight for independence.
4. While governing India, the British committed many brutal acts.
5. The beggar had a deformity, forcing him to walk on all fours.
6. India might have been different without the mismanagement leading up to the transfer of power.
7. That being said, it would be good to start by abolishing school fees.

b **Rewrite the sentences using subordinate clauses.**

Example:
On the way to the hotel, I saw long lines of homeless people sleeping alongside the road. ⟶ *On the way to the hotel, I saw long lines of homeless people* ***who were sleeping*** *alongside the road.*

INFO

Mahatma Gandhi (1869–1948)

Gandhi was a spiritual and political leader in India during the Independence Movement. He was a pioneer of the philosophy that evil should be fought through active, non-violent resistance. He led India to independence and started movements for civil rights and freedom across the world. The first occasion on which he employed civil disobedience was in South Africa where the Indian community was struggling for civil rights. On his return to India he led demonstrations of poor farmers and labourers against excessive taxation and discrimination. When he took over the leadership of the Indian National Congress, he led campaigns for the fight against poverty, for the end of discrimination against the untouchables and certain castes and, above all, for the independence of India from Britain. This aim was achieved in 1947. One of his most famous demonstrations was the salt march, in which he walked 400 kilometres to demonstrate against the salt tax imposed by the British. He practised and advocated non-violence and truth in all situations. He lived simply in an ashram* which was self-sufficient. The members of the ashram made their own clothes and produced their own vegetarian food. Gandhi often fasted for self-purification and out of protest. Gandhi was assasinated by a Hindu fanatic in 1948 who thought Gandhi was too tolerant towards the Muslims.

*a place where Hindus who wish to live apart from society live and pray together in a group

GIVING A PRESENTATION

HANDS-ON TASK

S ▸ Giving a Presentation (p. 201)

7 **Choose one of the countries listed below, which once belonged to the British Empire. Give a short presentation on its general history, culture, religion, etc. Try to use as many media sources as possible, e.g. music, pictures, excerpts from films, etc.**

- Australia
- Canada
- Tanzania
- New Zealand
- Pakistan
- Zimbabwe

TEXT 2 The Empire as Portrayed in Two Book Reviews

WARM-UP

S ▶ Scanning (p. 185)

1 **Scan this short text on the British Empire from an old encyclopedia and report what information it gives to the readers about:**

- **a** the size of the Empire
- **b** the population of the Empire
- **c** dangers for the Empire
- **d** the size and role of Britain

INFO

The British Empire

The British Empire, created from the expansion of England in the last 300 years, is the greatest of all empires so far. It comprises (with the South Pole areas) 400 million square kilometres and 460 million inhabitants, which is 27% of the earth's surface and 25% of the earth's population. Therefore, every 4th person is directly or indirectly British. In contrast to other Empires, such as the Soviet Union or China which are geographically spread out over one area, the countries of the British Empire are scattered all over the world. The Empire extends into all the cultural, climatic and economic zones of the earth.
People of different races and cultural development live in these countries, therefore it was never possible to establish cultural or racial unity. This presents an extreme danger for the Empire. The Empire is held together by the national drive and political wisdom of a small minority of 56 million people. Only 45 million of these live in Great Britain and about 11 million in the countries of the Empire.

[2] **comprise** consist of

2 **Does the text in the info box describe Britain and the Empire in a positive or negative way? Give reasons for your answer.**

S ▶ Skimming (p. 184)

3 **Skim the two texts on the following pages and decide which of the book reviews would persuade you to buy the book. Give reasons.**

The Decline and Fall of the British Empire

CD 3 Track 3

BOOK REVIEW 1: From Empire to Oblivion

Piers Brendon's The Decline and Fall of the British Empire *is a triumph of scholarship and narrative, says Robert McCrum.*

The British Empire is a five-act drama whose complex final part remains an inescapable feature of 21st-century life. Afghanistan, Burma, Iraq, Pakistan and Zimbabwe: each of these crises has its roots in the Empire. The first act took place in the West with the great American experiment. Depending on one's point of view, this experiment matured or turned sour in the closing decades of the 18th century. In a second act, British indecision and incompetence dominated the fight against the colonists for Independence. Britain surrendered its first army in Saratoga in 1777 and another one in Yorktown in 1781, leading to peace and independence for the colonists in 1783.

After that, and more spectacular than any achievement in the New World, there was the Empire of the East, from Cairo to Hong Kong: a sprawling and informal domain that consisted of about 11 million square miles and a quarter of the world's population. This third act describes what most people mean when they talk about the 'British empire'. The plot reaches its magnificent climax with the jubilee of 1897, when no fewer than 11 colonial Prime Ministers and a number of maharajahs preceded Queen Empress Victoria to a thanksgiving service in St Paul's where, it was said, only the Almighty was superior. In a darker fourth act, this empire of 'British imperialism' continued, still majestic, into the interwar years of 1919–39. In this time, despite the predictions of decline, the Empire was still a colossus. Even Adolf Hitler in *Mein Kampf* had to admit that Britain was still the greatest power on earth.

Finally, in the late 20th-century Empire there is the swift and, for its people, bewildering collapse, from India's independence (1947) to the Hong Kong handover of 1997. Like Rome, this empire is now changing smoothly from politics to culture. Thanks to technology and economics, it has done this on a scale unprecedented in human history. You could say that globalisation equals the English language plus Microsoft.

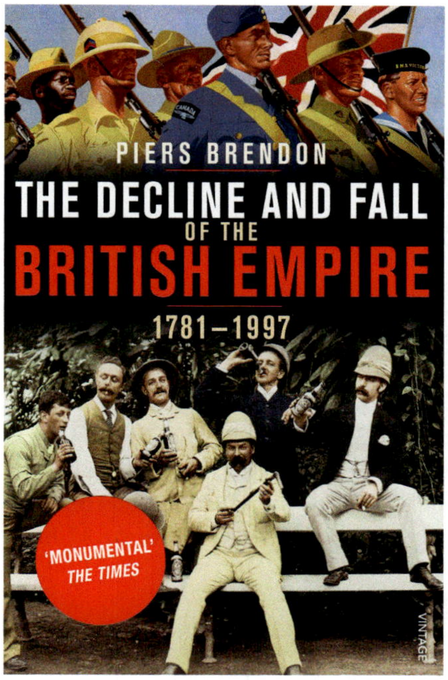

According to Brendon, the success of the Empire was made possible by the supremacy of the Royal Navy, by Britain's industrial revolution, and by the relative weakness of rival European powers in the 19th century. It was inspired by the loss of the American colonies and the rivalry with France.

If Piers Brendon has a weakness, it lies in his insufficient attention to the role of America in Britain's decline.

(421 words)

Adapted from *The Observer*, October 21, 2007

oblivion the state in which sb/sth is no longer famous
10 **mature** develop
15 **surrender** give up
22 **sprawling** covering a large area
31 **precede** go in front of sb
45 **bewildering** confusing
56 **supremacy** dominance
63 **insufficient** not enough

CD 3 Track 4

last post *Zapfenstreich*
oddball a person who behaves in a strange way
9 moustache a line of hair on the upper lip
24 boast talk with too much pride about sth
25 indulge in allow yourself to do sth, especially sth bad
vice criminal activities that involve sex or drugs
26 maverick a person who has unusual opinions and acts unusually
31 plus-fours *Knickerbocker(hose)*

BOOK REVIEW 2: Last Post for the Oddball Empire

Maja Jasanoff

Piers Brendon gives us an exciting and spectacularly detailed retelling of imperial "rise" as well as fall of the British Empire, from Yorktown to Hong Kong. Virtually every page offers up some memorable observation. For example, Brendon joyfully describes the career of that characteristic imperial accessory, the moustache. British cultivation of the hairy upper lip was inspired, he suggests, by Indian ideals of manliness, and became smaller in proportion with the decline of the empire: Harold Macmillan (Prime Minister from 1957–1963) was "the last British prime minister to have a moustache".

The Decline and Fall of the British Empire presents a glittering panorama of decadence, stupidity, farce and destruction. Brendon's characters alone could fill a pantomime stage many times over. The empire seemed to be full of British oddballs, from the notorious Richard Burton, who "liked to boast that he had indulged in every vice and indulged in every crime", to the maverick General Orde Wingate, who "would ... hold interviews while lying naked on a bed and combing his body hair with a toothbrush". Postcolonial heroes do little better. Jomo Kenyatta wore plus-fours, drank highly alcoholic gin and so satisfied his sexual appetites that he was thrown out of the church. These anecdotes make for amusing reading, but they also make it hard to take any of these figures seriously.

The real wonder, after reading this book, is how Britain ever managed to have an empire at all. (237 words)

Adapted from *The Guardian*, October 20, 2007

WORKING WITH THE TEXTS

S ▸ How to Deal with Instructions (p. 192)

4 Do the following tasks. Use your own words.

McCrum's text

1 Explain the five acts of the drama 'empire' and give each act a heading.
2 According to Brendon, what made the success of the Empire possible?
3 Does McCrum praise or criticise the book?

Maja Jasanoff's and Robert McCrum's texts

4 Compare the texts and describe how the reviews differ.
5 Comment on the headings of the reviews. What do they tell us about the authors' opinions of the book?

WORKING WITH WORDS

5 a Form the opposites of the following words using the prefix *im-* or *in-*. Most of them are in the text. Then use a dictionary, if necessary, to find the nouns.

Example: consistent – *inconsistent* – *inconsistency*

1 formal	4 decisive	7 direct
2 sufficient	5 probable	8 mature
3 dependent	6 competent	9 possible

b Complete the following sentences with suitable words from your list.

1 Brendon said that Britain was ... and ... in the fight against colonists at the end of the 18th century.

2 The service at St Paul's Cathedral in 1897 was a very … event.
3 Brendon did not pay … attention to the role of America in his book.
4 According to Brendon, the Empire would have been … if Britain had not had a strong Navy.
5 Ceylon and Burma got their … in 1948.
6 The political crises nowadays are an … result of British rule in the past.
7 Since becoming …, many countries in Africa have suffered political unrest.

COMPOSITION

6 **Comment on the statement "Great Britain has lost an empire and not yet found a role". (Acheson, a British historian)**

S ▸ Writing a Comment (p. 195)

LOOKING AT LANGUAGE

7 a **Join the following sentences by using the relative pronouns *who*, *which* or *whose*.**

Example:
The Empire was the greatest of all empires. It was formed during the expansion of England from the 17th to the 20th century. ⟶ *The Empire, which was formed …*

1 The Soviet Union was a large empire. It was spread out over one huge area.
2 Queen Victoria was Empress of India. During her reign the empire expanded most.
3 The empire was ruled by a small country. It had only 45 million inhabitants.
4 The empire could never have been a cultural unity. There were so many different cultures in it.
5 The empire is a five-act drama. Its final act continues in the 21st century.
6 The creation of the eastern Empire was a huge achievement. It stretched from Cairo to Hong Kong.

b **Translate the new sentences.**

Queen Victoria

LISTENING

CD 3 Track 5

8 a **Listen to an excerpt from a farewell speech by former Commonwealth Secretary General Don McKinnon and say in German what the speech is about.**

S ▸ Practising Listening Skills (p. 188)

b **Listen again and answer the questions. Take notes while listening.**

1 What are the main problems facing the inhabitants of some Commonwealth countries?
2 Which part of the world was economically most successful?
3 In which part of the world did economic growth decrease slightly?
4 Describe the help given by the Commonwealth.

HANDS-ON TASK

GIVING A PRESENTATION

9 **Give a presentation on one of the following subjects.**

S ▸ Giving a Presentation (p. 201)

1 Queen Victoria and her reign
2 The first British colonies in North America
3 Sir Francis Drake and the Elizabethan period

TEXT 3 The Empire in Literature

WARM-UP

S ▶ Interpreting Pictures and Cartoons (p. 199)

1
- a **Describe the cartoon in the info box.**
- b **Now read the info box and interpret the message of the cartoon.**
- c **With a partner, make a dialogue of what the two ladies and the tribesmen in the background are talking about.**

INFO

The Great Exhibition

The Great Exhibition of 1851 in London was one of the key events of the 19th century. It demonstrated the immense industrial and technological power of Britain and her Empire. It also brought together people from all around the world as interested sightseers, businessmen, financiers or even as exhibits themselves. In this cartoon, we see what is a very unflattering image of some African tribesmen. But we must remember, before we cast our modern judgements on this scene, these were exceedingly culturally homogenous days, when few Britons (inside Britain at least) would ever have seen anyone with a skin complexion different from their own.

Crystal Palace — Some Varieties Of The Human Race

S ▶ Skimming (p. 184)

2 **You are going to read an excerpt from a novel in which the visit of a British family to the 1924 British Empire Exhibition in London is described. Before you read the whole text, skim lines 57–69 and say if attitudes and reactions to black people in Britain had changed in the period between the exhibitions in 1851 and 1924.**

INFO

***Small Island* by Andrea Levy**

Andrea Levy's book *Small Island* has won several prizes, among them the Commonwealth Writer's Prize. The main part of the book, set in London in 1948, focuses on the situation of Jamaican immigrants escaping economic hardship on their own 'small island' by moving to England – the Mother Country, for which Jamaican men fought in World War II. Their reception is not warm and the opportunities not as plentiful as they hoped. In this prologue we are introduced to young Queenie Buxton and her family who go on a trip to the 1924 British Empire Exhibition in London. Later in the novel, as a grown-up, Queenie rents rooms to black immigrants who she then befriends.

Andrea Levy

Small Island

2004

CD 3 Track 6

Prologue

I thought I'd been to Africa. Told all my class I had. Early Bird, our teacher, stood me in front of the British flag – she would let no one call it the common Union Jack: 'It's the flag of Empire not a musical turn.' And I stood there as bold as brass and said, 'I went to Africa when it came to Wembley.' It was then that Early Bird informed me that Africa was a country. 'You're not usually a silly girl, Queenie Buxton,' she went on, 'but you did not go to Africa, you merely went to the British Empire Exhibition, as thousands of others did.'

It was a Butchers' Association trip. Every year there was an outing organised for the butchers, the butchers' wives and children and even the butchers' favourite workers. A day out. Mother liked to go. 'It's like a holiday,' she would say to Father.

'Bloody waste of time,' he'd grumble. But he went all the same.

Some years nearly everyone from our farm went. The inside girls who helped Mother with the pies. The outside girls who fed the pigs and poultry. (...)

The year we went to the Empire Exhibition, the Great War was not long over but nearly forgotten. Even Father agreed that the Empire Exhibition sounded like it was worth a look. The King had described it as 'the whole Empire in little'. Mother thought that meant it was a miniature, like a toy railway or model village. (...)

All the way there on the train Mother and Father chatted with other butchers and butchers' wives (...). Which left me sitting between two of our farm helpers, Emily and Graham, who spent the time giggling and flirting over my head.

(...)

Hundreds and hundreds of people were tramping in through the gates of the exhibition, past the gardens and the lake. (...) 'Over here! No, over here ... Over here's better.' The Empire in little. The palace of engineering, the palace of industry, and building after building that housed every country we British owned. Some of them were grand like castles, some had funny pointed roofs and one, I was sure, had half an onion on the top. Practically the whole world there to be looked at. (...)

There was a lot of discussion about what we should see – the whole world and only one day to see it. Mother was not interested in the different woods of Burma or the big-game trophies of Malaya. She said, 'Maybe later,' to the coffee of Jamaica. 'Ooh, no,' to the sugar of Barbados. 'What for?' to the chocolate of Grenada. And 'Where in heaven's name is that?' to Sarawak. In Canada there was a lifesize model of the Prince of Wales made in yellow butter. I had to struggle to the front to get a good look. I pressed my face close to the glass and Mother came and dragged me back. 'You hold Emily's hand,' she told me. 'I don't want you getting lost.' Then she moaned at Emily in front of the crowd (...), everyone muttering, 'Butter really? Butter? Never.' (...)

7 **as bold as brass** without showing any respect
16 **grumble** complain about sth
18 **poultry** chickens, ducks and geese
41 **moan** make a long, deep sound of unhappiness
mutter speak in a quiet voice that is difficult to understand

44 tingle feel as if sharp points are pushing into a part of the body
51 fleece all the wool cut off a sheep
53 fabric *Stoff*
56 contagious infectious
59 trail walk slowly behind sb
67 loom *Webstuhl*
68 nudge push sb gently, esp. with the elbow
74 carve make by cutting away material from wood
75 shoo sb off make sb go away
77 smudge rub sth so that it is no longer clear
sooty *rußig*
79 bulge stick out in a round shape
80 squash flatten by force
nostril the two holes in the nose
82 tease laugh and make jokes about sb
86 crimson a dark red colour

Australia smelt of apples. Ripe, green, crisp apples. A smell so sharp and sweet it made my teeth tingle. 'We'll have some of them,' Father said, as he joined the queue to buy a small brown bag of the fruit. (…)

I was promised that I would see a sheep being sheared in New Zealand but we only arrived in time to see the skinny shorn animal trotting round a pen with the fleece at the side. Hong Kong smelt of drains, and India was full of women brightly dressed in strange long colourful fabrics. And all these women had red dots in the middle of their forehead. No one could tell me what the dots were for. 'Go and ask one of them,' Emily said to me. But Mother said I shouldn't in case the dots meant they were ill – in case they were contagious.

(…)

That's when we got lost in Africa. We wandered in, following the syrupy-brown smell of chocolate. Emily trailed behind Graham only looking at me every so often to shout, 'Come on, hurry up.' I wanted one of the cups of cocoa that everyone was sipping but instead Emily pulled me by one of my pigtails and told me to keep up. Then we found ourselves in an African village with Graham looking around himself, scratching his head and telling Emily he was wanting the toilet.

We were in the jungle. Huts made out of mud with pointy stick roofs all around us. And in a hut sitting on a dirt floor was a woman with skin as black as the ink that filled the inkwell in my school desk. A shadow come to life. Sitting cross-legged, her hands weaving bright patterned cloth on a loom. 'We've got machines that do all that now,' Graham said, as Emily nudged him to be quiet. 'She can't understand what I'm saying,' Graham explained. 'They're not civilised. They only understand drums.' (…)

'Have you seen the toilet?' Graham asked her, but she didn't understand that either.

'I want to go,' I said, because there was nothing interesting to look at. But then suddenly there was a man. An African man. A black man who looked to be carved from melting chocolate. I clung to Emily but she shooed me off. He was right next to me, close enough so I could see him breathing. A monkey man sweating a smell of mothballs. Blacker than when you smudge your face with a sooty cork. The droplets of sweat on his forehead glistened and shone like jewels. His lips were brown, not pink like they should be, and they bulged with air like bicycle tyres. His hair was woolly as a black shorn sheep. His nose, squashed flat, had two nostrils big as train tunnels. And he was looking down at me.

'Would you like to kiss him?' Graham said. He nudged me, teasing, and pushed me forward, closer to this black man.

And Emily giggled. 'Go on Queenie, kiss him, kiss him.'

This man was still looking down at me. I could feel the blood rising in my face, turning me crimson, as he smiled a perfect set of pure blinding white teeth. The inside of his mouth was pink and his face was coming closer and closer to mine. He could have swallowed me up, this big nigger man. But instead he said, in clear English, 'Perhaps we could shake hands instead?'

Graham's smile fell off his face. And I shook an African man's hand. It was warm and slightly sweaty like anyone else's. I shook his hand up and down for several seconds. And he bowed his head to me and said, 'It's nice to meet you.' Then he let my hand go and stepped out of our way so we could pass. Emily was still giggling, looking at Graham and rolling her eyes. She grabbed my arm and pulled me away while Graham mumbled again that he needed the toilet. And the African man must have understood because he pointed and said, 'Over there by the tree is a rest room where I think you will find what you need.'

But Graham never found the toilet. He had to wee behind some bins while me and Emily kept a look-out.

Father said later that this African man I was made to shake hands with would have been a chief or a prince in Africa. Evidently, when they speak English you know that they have learned to be civilised – taught English by the white man, missionaries probably. (...) (1283 words)

95 **mumble** speak in a quiet way that is not clear
98 **bin** a container you put waste into

WORKING WITH THE TEXT

3 Choose three of the following tasks.

S ▸ How to Deal with Instructions (p. 192)

1. Describe the narrator.
2. List and describe briefly the other characters that appear in the prologue.
3. Describe the setting at the exhibition. First, look at the box on page 87.
4. Analyse the young people's reaction to the Africans. In what way was their impression wrong?
5. Interpret the title of the book.

WORKING WITH WORDS

4 a Complete the sentences with the verbs from the box in the correct form/tense.

arrive | go | pass | stand | step | trail | trot | wander

1. I ... in front of the class as bold as brass and said I had been to Africa.
2. Mother liked to ... on the Butchers' Association Trip.
3. When we ... in New Zealand, the sheep had already been shorn.
4. The sheep ... around the pen with the fleece at the side.
5. We ... into Africa where we could smell the chocolate.
6. In Africa Emily ... behind Graham and shouted at me to keep up.
7. The black man ... out of the way to let us ...

b The verbs on the right describe ways of speaking. They are all from the text. Using a dictionary if necessary, match them with a suitable sentence beginning.

1 "Stop tickling my feet!"	a she asked.
2 "Good morning,"	b she giggled.
3 "Has somebody seen my watch?"	c she grumbled.
4 "I'll just have to do it myself, as usual,"	d she muttered to herself.
5 "I always have to the hardest work,"	e she said.
6 "Why doesn't he stop talking,"	f she moaned.

LITERARY ANALYSIS

5 a **In order to create a certain atmosphere in her story, Andrea Levy uses several stylistic devices. Read lines 42–80 again and find examples of the stylistic devices from the box below. Explain why they are used.**

> ### Literary Terms
> **imagery:** By using imagery a writer appeals to the reader's imagination. Imagery is a term that means the use of comparisons, similes, metaphors, personification and symbols.
> **simile:** an explicit comparison; a linking of two words or things because there are similarities in parts between them. A simile says that something is like something else. Similes are used in connection with words such as "like" or "as".
> **exaggeration:** the use of a strong overstatement, i.e. when something is made bigger than in reality.
> **parallelism:** repeating similar or identical words, phrases or sentence constructions in neighbouring sentences.

b **Explain the imagery used in the following sentences.**

1 Graham's smile fell off his face. **2** He could have swallowed me up.

6 a **In the text, what do the characters associate with the following places?**

Africa | Australia | India | Jamaica | New Zealand

Example:
Queenie and her mother associate India with the rich fabrics and bright colours of the women's dresses and the country's strange religious customs.

b **What would you associate with these places?**

CREATIVE WRITING

7 **You are Queenie Buxton. Write a composition about what impressed you most at the exhibition.**

ROLE-PLAY

8 **With a partner, write and act out a dialogue about your day at the Exhibition. One of you is Queenie and the other her schoolfriend.**

The schoolfriend can ask:

- about the journey and who went
- what everyone did during the journey
- what the exhibition looked like and what was on show
- what Queenie liked best
- what impressed her in Africa
- whether she had enjoyed her day out

TEXT 4 Britain and EU Regulations

WARM-UP

1 **Look at the pictures and match the words in the box to the gaps.**

Fahrenheit | gallons | miles | pint | pound | yards

2 **Which of these is more? Use the internet to help you.**

a a pint of milk or a litre of milk
b 12 miles or 20 kilometres
c 3 feet or 3 metres
d 89° Fahrenheit or 30° Celsius
e 7 ounces or 250 grammes
f a yard or 1.2 metres

EU Gives Up On 'Metric Britain'

CD 3 Track 7

In September 2007, European Union commissioners ruled that Britain could carry on using imperial measurements such as pints, pounds and miles.

Europe's Industry Commissioner Gunter Verheugen said: "There is not now and never will be any requirement to drop imperial measurements." The decision to continue using imperial measurements did not affect law on metric measurements, but meant imperial equivalents could be used too. This decision followed years of wrangling between London and Brussels over metrication.

Pint saved

The commission had continued extending the deadline for the UK to complete the full transition to the metric system. This would have meant setting a deadline for ending the traditional delivery of pints of milk – and the sale of pints of beer in the UK's pubs. Every one of the UK's road signs would have had to be changed from miles to kilometres – a move which opponents warned would be both expensive and confusing.

But it was the move, which began in 2000, to make the UK's market traders sell their produce in kilograms rather than pounds and ounces which caused outrage among traditionalists. Sunderland grocer Steve Thoburn inspired the "metric martyr" movement with his defiance of the order to abandon imperial measurements. In 2001, he was convicted for having weighing scales which only had imperial measurements. He died unexpectedly from a heart attack three years later and, while

2 **imperial** connected with empire
5 **wrangle** argue for a long time over a complicated issue
metrication the process of changing to the metric system
7 **deadline** a point in time by which sth must be done
13 **move** step, measure
14 **produce** ['prɒdju:s] things that have been made or grown
outrage strong feeling of shock and anger
16 **defiance** refusal to obey
17 **convict** decide in court that sb is guilty

23 **display** put sth in a place where people can see it
25 **prosecution** the process of being charged with a crime in court
35 **significance** importance
46 **prolong** make sth last longer
49 **obsolete** out of date and no longer used

the campaign he founded failed to win traders the right to ignore metric weights altogether, it did bring some results.

'No problem'

Under the plans which were scrapped, even displaying the price of fruit and vegetables in pounds and ounces would have been grounds for a criminal prosecution. Mr Verheugen's role included trying to improve the EU's reputation in member states – and in an interview with the BBC, he admitted the EU had been making itself unpopular on an issue that did not really matter. "I organised a huge consultation, and the result was that industry told us there was no problem with the existing system. I want to bring to an end a bitter, bitter battle that has lasted for decades and which in my view is completely pointless. We're bringing this battle to an end."

Steve Thoburn

'Extremely misleading'

However, campaigners on both sides of the debate played down the significance of the announcement. John Gardner, director of the pro-imperial British Weights and Measures Association, said: "I've seen the European Commission statement and they have decided to allow the use of imperial measurements as additional information. We think that the European Commission statement is extremely misleading. From our point of view the situation hasn't changed and the campaign goes on. If a trader tries to conduct his business in just imperial measurements that will be illegal."

'Business as usual'

The UK Metric Association said the statement did not mean that traders could go back to weighing and pricing in imperial measures, and that it would be "business as usual". Chairman Robin Paice said: "While we regret this proposal to prolong the current muddle of metric and imperial units, it will only delay but not stop the inevitable move toward all-metric shopping. Many of the big supermarkets have already stopped giving obsolete imperial prices, and we expect this trend to continue. There is no question of going backwards."

Science and Innovation Minister Ian Pearson said he welcomed the commission's proposal. "This shows that the commission has listened to our views and recognised the strong arguments that we've made for maintaining dual metric and imperial labelling, and the right for the UK to decide on the future use of pints and miles," he said. "We know how important this is to the British people and are grateful for the commission's support for this use to continue."

The UK first put forward plans to convert to an all-metric system in 1965. That led to generations of schoolchildren being promised that they would be the last ones who would have to learn two different systems. (652 words)

news.bbc.co.uk

INFO

Imperial units or the Imperial system is a collection of units, first defined in the British Weights and Measures Act of 1824. The units were introduced in the United Kingdom and its colonies, including Commonwealth countries (most have since become officially metric, but continue to use both metric and imperial), but excluding the then already independent United States. The British currency was decimalised on 15 February 1971.

WORKING WITH THE TEXT

S ▸ How to Deal with Instructions (p. 192)

3 **a** **Explain why the metric martyr movement was founded and say what its members did to achieve their aims.**
b **Summarise the current situation and say what the situation might be like in the future with regard to metric measurements.**

4 **Describe the cartoon and explain what the message is. Compare it to the information given in the text.**

'Seven and a quarter inches of beer, please'

climbdown *Rückzieher*

WORKING WITH WORDS

5 **Use your dictionary to complete the following sentences with a phrasal verb from the box. (One of the verbs does not fit.) You may have to change the form of the verb.**

go ahead with | go along with | go back | go down | go for | go on

1. Many British people want to … using the imperial system.
2. Others would like to … to using shillings.
3. Everyone believed that the euro would … in value but it has increased greatly.
4. Many ministers … him because of his Europhile views.
5. They just could not … his favourable attitude towards the euro.

6 **Join the following sentences with a suitable expression from the box.**

because | even if | unless | when | which

1. Britain did not have to give up imperial measurements / there was a decision to allow both systems.
2. Thoburn would not have given up the imperial system / they had sent him to prison.
3. Thoburn had weighing scales / they only had imperial measurements.
4. Children have to carry on learning both systems / imperial measurements are abandoned.
5. Not everyone was happy / Mr Verheugen announced the decision

LOOKING AT LANGUAGE

7 **Change these sentences into reported speech.**

S ▸ Reported Speech (p. 211)

1. I want to bring to an end a bitter, bitter battle that has lasted for decades. *(Mr Verheugen said …)*
2. If a trader tries to conduct his business in just imperial measurements that will be illegal. *(John Gardner explained …)*
3. We think that the European Commission statement is extremely misleading and that the situation has not changed. *(Mr Gardner claimed …)*
4. Many of the big supermarkets have already stopped giving obsolete imperial prices and we expect this trend to continue. *(Robin Paice said …)*
5. This shows that the Commission has listened to our views. *(Ian Pearson said …)*
6. We know how important this is to the British people and are grateful for the commission's support for this. *(Ian Pearson pointed out …)*

TEXT 5 Britain, In or Out of Europe?

WARM-UP

1 **Test your knowledge of Britain and the EU.**

1 **After World War II, a famous politician dreamt of a United States of Europe to prevent future wars. Was it**

a Churchill? **b** Adenauer?

2 **Britain did not join the EU in the beginning because**

a it was closely associated with the Commonwealth.
b the six founding members did not want Britain to join.

3 **When Britain applied to join the EU in 1961, its membership was vetoed by**

a France.
b Italy.

4 **In 1973 Britain finally joined together with**

a Denmark and Ireland. **b** Germany.

5 **The euro was introduced in**

a 2000. **b** 2002.

6 **Which countries have not introduced the euro?**

a Britain **b** Ireland **c** Denmark

7 **Which of the following countries are not members of the EU?**

a Croatia **b** Slovenia **c** Estonia **d** Norway

CD 3 Track 8

S ▶ Practising Listening Skills (p. 188)

2 **Now listen to the recording to check your answers.**

3 **a** **Read the following excerpt from Winston Churchill's speech in 1946 and answer the questions. Churchill was Prime Minister of Britain from 1940–45 and again from 1951–55.**

1. Which of his wishes has come true?
2. Did he suggest that Britain should be a part of this United States?
3. Did his hopes about Soviet Russia come true?

b **Summarise the excerpt in German. Write one sentence for each paragraph.**

Winston Churchill

CD 3 Track 9

The Tragedy of Europe

Excerpt from Churchill's Speech on 19 September 1946 in Zurich

If Europe were once united in the sharing of its common inheritance, there would be no limit to the happiness, the prosperity, and the glory which its three or four hundred million people would enjoy. (...)

The structure of the United States of Europe will be such as to make the material strength of a single State less important. Small nations will count as much as large ones and gain their honour by a contribution to the common cause.

The ancient states and principalities of Germany, freely joined for mutual convenience in a federal system, might take their individual places among the United States of Europe. (…)

If at first all the States of Europe are not willing or able to join a union we must nevertheless proceed to assemble and combine those who will and those who can. (…)

In all this urgent work France and Germany must take the lead together. Great Britain, the British Commonwealth of Nations, mighty America, and, I trust, Soviet Russia – for then, indeed, all would be well – must be the friends and sponsors of the new Europe and must champion its right to live. (190 words)

[6] **cause** an idea that people support
[7] **principality** *Fürstentum*
convenience *hier: Nutzen, Vorteil*
[11] **proceed** continue
[16] **champion** fight for

c **Now skim the following article. Briefly compare the two different historical situations in which the two authors were writing their texts.**

S ▸ Skimming (p. 184)

Britain Should Quit EU, French Sage Says

By Colin Randall in Paris

CD 3 Track 10

France's most celebrated living intellectual – and probably its most constant Anglophile – called on Britain to leave the European Union. Maurice Druon, an author, ex-culture minister and grandee of the Académie Française, said that Britain's aversion to full integration made it unsuited to the full membership for which he campaigned more than 30 years ago. He suggested instead that it should settle for the status of "privileged partner", the much reduced level of affiliation that French opponents of Turkish EU membership believe should be offered to Ankara.

Maurice Druon

Mr Druon, 87, holder of an honorary knighthood for services to Anglo-French relations, said: "What Britain and Europe want of the EU is quite different. You want an open market, whereas the rest of us want Europe to evolve as a strong power, not just economically but diplomatically and strategically, too."

His views were aired initially in an article in *Le Figaro*. Britain, he wrote, was beginning to "go back in history – and when they are there, they stay there." Mr Druon listed the aspects of Britishness he judged incompatible with EU membership: an "umbilical" link with America; demands for special budgetary treatment; support for Turkish accession in defiance of Europe's natural boundaries; and stubborn resistance to the euro.

Britain, he said, continued to focus its policies on "the open sea". This was a reference to Churchill's remark, often quoted out of context in France since it concerned wartime events before the Common Market was even thought of: "Each time we must choose between Europe and the open sea, we shall always choose the open sea."

Mr Druon said: "Shouldn't we draw the consequences and ask whether it wouldn't be to everyone's advantage, Britain's included, for them to leave the EU's political institutions and take the status of privileged partner?" He told the *Daily Telegraph*: "I am not suggesting that Britain should be chased out of the EU. It must be Britain that takes the first step towards a modified status. You cannot stay indefinitely both in and out. If a friend cannot raise this question, who else will dare to pose it?"

(349 words)

From the *Daily Telegraph*, 17 August 2005

sage a wise person
[3] **grandee** a person of high rank and standing
[6] **affiliation** relationship
[8] **honorary** given as an honour without the person having the usual qualifications
[10] **evolve** develop gradually
[12] **air** express
[16] **stubborn** unwilling to change an attitude
[28] **dare** be brave enough to do sth

WORKING WITH THE TEXT

4 **Are these statements true or false? Correct the false statements.**

1. Maurice Druon does not like Britain.
2. 30 years ago he campaigned for the full membership of Britain.
3. Britain should be offered the same kind of partnership as Turkey.
4. Britain wants an economic partnership.
5. The rest of Europe doesn't want an economic partnership.
6. Britain does not want Turkey to become a member because of its boundaries.
7. Druon wants Britain to be chased out of the EU.

S ▸ Writing a Summary (p. 195)

5 **Summarise in your own words the reasons why Mr Druon thinks Britain should leave the EU.**

S ▸ Interpreting Pictures and Cartoons (p. 199)

6 **Do you think that Churchill would agree with Druon? Find arguments in his speech to support your opinion.**

CARTOON ANALYSIS

7 a **Describe the cartoon. What aspects of the EU are being criticised?**
b **How does the cartoon relate to the attitude of Britain towards Europe, as described in the text?**

WORKING WITH WORDS

8 **Rewrite the following sentences, replacing or changing the form of the underlined words according to the instructions. Use the given sentence beginnings.**

1. Britain's aversion to <u>full</u> <u>integration</u> made it unsuited to full membership. (adverb + verb)
   Britain did not want to be … and this made it …
2. His <u>views</u> were aired <u>initially</u> in a newspaper article. (synonyms)
   He expressed his …

3 Wouldn't it be to everyone's advantage for Britain to leave the EU's political institutions? (conditional sentence)
Wouldn't it be better for everyone if …

4 The remark concerned wartime events. (synonymous expression)
The remark referred to …

5 You can't stay indefinitely both in and out. (synonym)
It is not possible …

ANALYSING A TABLE

9 a **In groups, study the table and identify the countries. Then summarise the table in a short text using the following phrases.**

S ▸ Interpreting Graphs, Diagrams and Tables (p. 200)

The table is a survey of …
The table shows how popular/unpopular …
While people in … are happy about …, people in … believe the EU …
In most countries people's opinion about the EU did not vary a lot between 2004 and 2007 but in …

b **Does the information in the table support the information in the text about Maurice Druon?**

"Is your country's membership of the EU a good thing?" (Answer: "Yes" in %, EU 27)

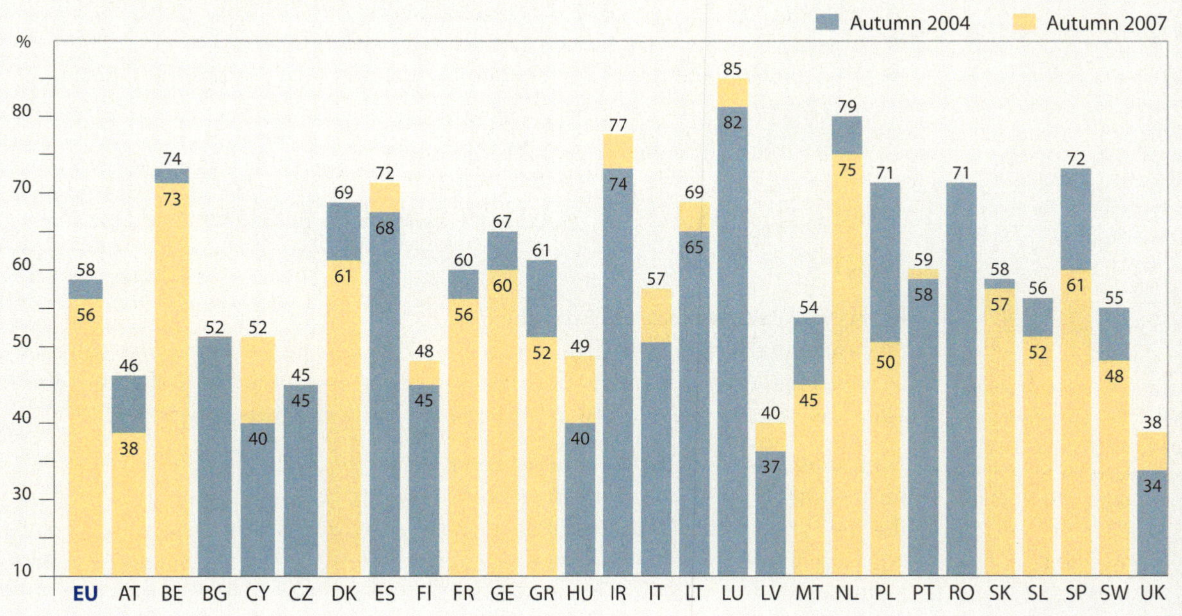

LISTENING

CD 3 Track 11

10 a **BBC's *Talking Point* asked several people the following question: "Where is Britain's place in international affairs?" Listen to the answers and say who is a Europhile or a Eurosceptic.**

S ▸ Practising Listening Skills (p. 188)

b **Listen again and make notes about the reasons given by the speakers for their attitudes.**

World of Work

MEDIATION Working with India

S ▸ Mediation (p. 204)

1 Do the following mediation task.

Ihre Firma plant, die Informatikabteilung nach Indien auszulagern und in diesem Zusammenhang regelmäßig Mitarbeiter/innen dorthin zu schicken. Sie werden beauftragt, ein Faltblatt für die Angestellten zu erstellen, um sie auf die Arbeitsgewohnheiten in Indien vorzubereiten. Sie haben die folgende Broschüre für amerikanische Geschäftsleute gefunden und entnehmen daraus Informationen für Ihr Faltblatt. Berücksichtigen Sie die folgenden Aspekte:

1 Meetings organisieren, Pünktlichkeit
2 Durchführung von Meetings
3 Treffen von Entscheidungen

Before you start, look at these notes. Which of the three aspects above do they refer to?

1. Es kommen viele Leute zu Meetings. Finden Sie heraus, wer der Leiter / die Leiterin ist.
2. Indern fällt es schwer, „Nein“ zu sagen.
3. Nicht immer werden in Meetings Entscheidungen getroffen.
4. Meetings werden nicht lange im Voraus geplant.
5. Lassen Sie sich vor Ort bestätigen, wann das Treffen stattfindet.
6. Während des Meetings kann es vorkommen, dass Ihr/e Gesprächpartner/in telefoniert.

Working with India: What To Know Before You Go

Expect true culture shock and fuzzy thinking.
Since a lot of flights to India arrive in the middle of the night, you probably won't be at your brightest the first day. Do what you can to rest up before business begins. That way you'll be relaxed and able to cope with any unexpected difficulties.

Even though we hear a lot about the 'new India', the fact is that the old India will hit you the moment you leave the airport – crowds, the intensity of everything on the street, extremes of wealth and poverty, the sheer intensity of the culture. People will stare at you, pressing in on you. There will be lots going on and everything will be just different – the temperature, the feel of the air. Your brain is not going to be functioning 100%. No matter what your usual company policy is, build in buffer time at the beginning of your trip. It will more than make up for any lost working time.

Remember to pack for business.
In an Indian business setting, men normally wear lightweight suits with ties. If the day is extraordinarily hot, you can usually dispense with the jacket, but start with it on and see how your hosts are dressed.

1 **fuzzy** confused
4 **cope with** deal successfully with sth difficult
8 **press in on** stand/walk very close to
10 **buffer time** extra time allowed for unexpected problems
14 **lightweight** made of thinner material and less heavy than usual
tie long narrow piece of cloth worn around the neck, especially by men, with a knot in front
15 **dispense with** stop using sth because you no longer need it
16 **host** person who invites guests to a meal, a party, etc.

For women, pack lightweight pant suits with sandals. Leave the short skirts at home. And, just like in a typical US setting, the air conditioning can be pretty cold – if it's working properly. So bring a shawl or a jacket.

Don't expect to start punctually.

Unlike the States, where you make appointments a month ahead of time, when you arrive in India, you need to confirm your schedule or maybe even rearrange it. Ask your host, 'Is 10 still a good time for us to meet?' You may find that the meeting times have changed.

It is not that the meeting won't happen. It will happen. But don't schedule back-to-back appointments, because often the first meeting won't start on time. It will start whenever the main person shows up. Likewise, the end will also be open.

That means you need to leave a considerable amount of time between appointments, especially if your next appointment is in another part of the city. In fact, if you're meeting with more than one service provider, don't schedule more than one meeting a day.

Don't be surprised if other people show up.

We're usually pretty concentrated in meetings in the States. We like to be very clear about when the meeting is going to be, what it is about and who is going to be there. Things are more fluid in India. Several people may show up along with the person you think you're meeting, and it won't necessarily be clear to you why they are there. These people may not be introduced, or say anything. Make sure you know who the chief person is and direct all your conversation to that person unless you have been asked to do otherwise.

Besides people walking in and out, expect phone calls and questions to the boss during the meeting. You may be sitting in a meeting with the head of a unit, and he will pick up the phone and talk while you're sitting there, or somebody will knock on the door and will just walk in to ask him a question, and he will just interrupt his conversation with you. In India, this is not considered rude so don't be upset by it.

'Yes' doesn't always mean 'Yes'.

Another problem is the Indians' aversion to saying 'No'. 'We'll try' is the diplomatic way of saying 'We really can't, but we don't want to tell you'. Americans want a direct 'Yes' or 'No'. For Indians, the tendency is to say 'Yes' and try to make it happen at all costs. That can create huge misunderstandings and variances in expectations.

Meetings are to discuss and to build relationships and to see what the issues are. But the real decision is almost always made later.

Just assume that later on you'll have a chance to sit alone with the decision maker – maybe over a meal. The topic may come up indirectly, and this decision maker may tell you either directly or indirectly that something is unrealistic. It's not likely to happen with a whole bunch of other people present.

What if you're asking questions and you see heads nod as if in assent? Don't interpret this as a 'Yes'. It really means, 'I am listening ... I understand what you are saying.'

(766 words)

Adapted from: www.cmct.net

17 **pant suit** a set of clothes for women, made up of a matching jacket and pants
19 **shawl** a large piece of cloth worn by a woman around the shoulders or head
22 **schedule** timetable
28 **considerable** significant, large
35 **fluid** likely to change, not fixed
43 **interrupt** stop sth briefly to do sth else
49 **at all costs** whatever is needed to achieve sth
55 **bunch of** a large number of things or people
56 **nod** moving the head up and down to show agreement, understanding
assent agreement to or approval of sth

JOB SKILLS Intercultural Communication (1)

CD 3 Track 12

S ▸ Practising Listening Skills (p. 188)

LISTENING

2 **If your organisation sends you to India, it will be important to know how to greet your Indian colleagues. Intercultural expert Bob Jaeger gives some tips.**

a **Listen to the recording and make notes in English about the following subjects:**

- *Namaste*
- shaking hands
- religion
- order in which to greet people
- saying goodbye

b **Now explain what the Western business people in the cartoons are doing wrong.**

CD 3 Track 13

3 **Mark Steffens is visiting Aruna Singh's firm in Bangalore to discuss a project.**

a **Listen to their conversation and number the expressions a–i in the order you hear them.**

a How are you?
b I haven't any other appointments today.
c It's nice to see you again.
d Please come in and have a seat.
e I'm sorry I'm late.
f I'm afraid Mr Khan can't come to the meeting today.
g Thank you.
h Can I plug in my laptop somewhere?
i Would you like a coffee before we start?

b **Listen again and make a note of the reply to each phrase.**

MAKING SMALL TALK

4 **You are attending a trade fair in an English-speaking country. Choose the best reply to each question. Which replies do not sound very 'English'?**

1 'Hello. How are you?'
  a 'I'm very fine indeed, thank you a lot.'
  b 'Fine, thanks. And you?'
  c 'Not so good.'
2 'This is Lukas Schmidt from Berlin.'
  a 'Pleased to meet you, Lukas.'
  b 'It's very fine to know you, Lukas.'
  c 'I went to Berlin last year.'
3 'Did you have a good flight?'
  a 'Yes, thanks. It was fine.'
  b 'Yes, of course I did.'
  c 'A good flight? You must be joking.'
4 'Would you like to come to the reception this evening?'
  a 'Yes, I will.'
  b 'No.'
  c 'Yes, I'd love to.'
5 'Do you have any dry red wine, please?'
  a 'No. Just white.'
  b 'If there isn't any on the tray, we haven't got any.'
  c 'Sorry, but may I offer you a dry white? It's very nice.'
6 'Your English is very good.'
  a 'Yes, it is.'
  b 'Thank you.'
  c 'No, it isn't.'
7 'Would you prefer tea or coffee?'
  a 'Coffee, please.'
  b 'I don't care.'
  c 'Tea.'
8 'Sorry to keep you waiting.'
  a 'That's OK.'
  b 'You're welcome.'
  c 'Forget it.'
9 'Thank you so much for your help.'
  a 'Not at all. It was my pleasure.'
  b 'It doesn't matter.'
  c 'Whatever would you do without me?'

DOING A ROLE-PLAY

HANDS-ON TASK

5 a **Brainstorm subjects which are suitable for small talk in a business context, e.g. an international trade fair or a reception for your company's international trading partners. Make a list.**

b **Role-play a conversation at an international business conference. You and your partner have just met each other for the first time. Introduce yourself (name, job, where you are from) and make small talk with your partner. Then introduce your partner to another person.**

TOPIC 6

Issues Confronting the USA

BACKGROUND INFORMATION

Ideological Beginnings

settler *Siedler/in*
economic *wirtschaftlich*
ideological *ideologisch*
pilgrim *Pilger/in*
adherence to *Festhalten an*
exert one's influence *seinen Einfluss geltend machen*

The first settlers to America came from Europe in the 17th century either for economic or ideological reasons. This latter group considered themselves religious pilgrims. Their puritan values of hard work and adherence to Biblical law shaped society then and even today continue to exert their influence.

colony *Kolonie*
rebel *rebellieren, sich erheben*
impose *verhängen, erlassen*
tax *Steuer*
colonist *Siedler/in, Kolonist/in*
violation *Verletzung*
citizen *Bürger/in*
Declaration of Independence *Unabhängigkeitserklärung*
Founding Fathers *Gründerväter*
divisive *kontrovers, Uneinigkeit stiftend*
loyalist *Loyalist/in*
Revolutionary War *Revolutionskrieg*

Thirteen British colonies established themselves on America's eastern coast. They began to rebel in the 1760s when Britain imposed a series of taxes and other laws which proved extremely unpopular. The colonists considered this a violation of their rights as British citizens because they had no voice in the British parliament. In 1776 representatives of the colonies signed the Declaration of Independence, which stated that 'all men are created equal'. The authors of this document, along with General George Washington, became known as the Founding Fathers of the United States. It was the first time that a colony had ever broken from its 'mother country', and it thrust the Americans into war with the strongest naval power on Earth. The decision was deeply divisive, and many colonists, the loyalists, fought for the British. The Americans won this Revolutionary War against all odds, and this reinforced the belief that the forming of their nation was God's plan.

manifest destiny *offenbare/selbstverständliche Bestimmung*
pioneer spirit *Pioniergeist*
Wild West *Wilder Westen*
Indian *Indianer/in*

This divine plan included manifest destiny, the belief that the United States was meant to extend from the Atlantic all the way to the Pacific. The pioneer spirit of the US was re-activated, and families settled the Wild West. The US government acquired land by warring over it with the Mexicans, by buying it from other countries, and by stealing it from the Indians.

The Civil War

Civil War *Bürgerkrieg*
secession *Abspaltung*
abolish *abschaffen*
slavery *Sklaverei*
pit *antreten lassen*
Confederacy *Konföderation, die Konföderierten Staaten von Amerika*
Union *Union, die Nordstaaten*

In 1860–61, eleven southern states declared their secession from the USA. The main reason for this was that President Abraham Lincoln wanted to abolish slavery, which was still legal and widely practised in the South, and seen by many as necessary. The terrible War Between the States raged until 1865 and often pitted 'brother against brother'. In the end, the Confederacy (the South) lost to the Union, and the slaves were freed.

World War II

The US was drawn into the Second World War in 1941 when the Japanese attacked Pearl Harbor. The US was still recovering from the Great Depression, but the entire country became mobilised in the war effort and this boosted the economy. Following the war, the US set to rebuild Europe using the Marshall Plan, which proved very successful.

Great Depression *Weltwirtschaftskrise*
boost the economy *die Wirtschaft ankurbeln*
Marshall Plan *Marshallplan*

The Superpower

Ever since the Second World War, the US has been the world's superpower, but this position has not been wholly unchallenged. The Cold War saw the US in constant competition with the Soviet Union until the fall of Communism. Despite the failure of the Vietnam War, this was a time of great prosperity for the US. The US became the leader in science, medicine, space exploration, entrepreneurship, education, film, and other areas. It also maintained the world's most powerful military.

Superpower *Supermacht*
Cold War *Kalter Krieg*
Soviet Union *Sowjetunion*
Vietnam War *Vietnamkrieg*
prosperity *Wohlstand*
space exploration *Weltraumforschung*
entrepreneurship *Unternehmertum*
military *Militär*

The 21st Century

In 2000, George W. Bush of the conservative Republican Party was elected President by a very narrow margin, and his presidency deeply divided the nation into what some call 'two Americas'. On the one side are the Conservatives, who believe in traditional 'family' values. On the other side are the Liberals, who tend to take the opposite views to those of the Conservatives and generally vote for the Democratic Party, the only other sizable party.

Republican Party *republikanische Partei*
elect sb president *jdn zum Präsidenten wählen*
narrow margin *kleiner Vorsprung*
Conservatives *Konservative*
value *Wert*
Liberals *Liberale*
Democratic Party *demokratische Partei*

On September 11, 2001 the US was attacked by terrorists in such an incredible and terrifying way that the country was filled with fear and uncertainty. President Bush and his conservative government launched what they called the 'War on Terror'. They, along with Britain and other countries, invaded Afghanistan and toppled the 'terrorist' Taliban regime there. Then, much more controversially, they invaded Iraq, claiming the government had a connection to 9/11 and possessed weapons of mass destruction. Neither of these claims turned out to be true. Many Americans protested against the war and were in turn accused of being unpatriotic and 'not supporting the troops'. The Bush presidency and the Iraq War are widely regarded as disasters, both morally and financially.

War on Terror *Kampf gegen den Terror(ismus)*
invade *einmarschieren in*
9/11 *Terroranschläge am 11. September 2001*
weapons of mass destruction *Massenvernichtungswaffen*
troops *Truppen, Armee*

In 2007 it became clear that the US was in a subprime mortgage crisis, which in 2008 led to the worst financial crisis since the Great Depression. The US is famous for reinventing itself and 'bouncing back' from crises, but in 2008 it appears possible that we may finally see it lose its superpower status.

subprime mortgage crisis *Suprime-Krise, Immobilienkrise 2007/08 in den USA*
financial crisis *Finanzkrise*

TEXT 1 Why We're Proud To Be Americans

WARM-UP

1 **Discuss these questions in class.**

1. Why do you think the United States is so patriotic?
2. What is your opinion of the United States?

CD 3 Track 14

2 shrink from be unwilling to
8 prosperity wealth
11 marvel wonder
13 beacon guiding light
17 face off get ready to fight
24 devise think up, create
eject force out
25 dither *hin und her überlegen*

'A Democracy To Be Proud Of'

by William J. Bennett

Our country is something to be proud of, something to celebrate. We should not shrink from saying so. A careful and close reading of our history demonstrates that we have provided more freedom to more people than any other nation in the history of mankind; that we have provided a greater degree of equality to more people than any other nation in the history of mankind; that we have created more prosperity and spread it more widely than any other nation in the history of mankind; that we have brought more peace and justice to the world than any other nation in the history of mankind; and that our open, tolerant, prosperous society is the marvel – and the envy – of the ages.

This is demonstrably true within our own borders. Outside those borders, we have been a beacon of freedom and opportunity to people throughout the world since the day of our creation. When people around the globe demonstrate in support of freedom and liberty, they do so with American icons and documents. I will never forget – we should never forget – how the brave Chinese students in Tiananmen Square faced off with tanks, armed with only a paper-maché Statue of Liberty and a copy of the Declaration of Independence. Harmful ideas have harmful consequences, but good and noble ideas can have good and noble consequences, too.

The noble ideas of America have led to noble consequences and noble actions on our part. For example, in the 20th century alone, as one British columnist pointed out, Americans "saved Europe from barbarism in two world wars and rebuilt the continent from ashes. They confronted and peacefully defeated Soviet Communism, the most murderous system ever devised by man. America, primarily, ejected Iraq from Kuwait and stopped the slaughter in the Balkans while the Europeans dithered."

This list could be extended tenfold and it would still be incomplete.

Put simply, America is the place people run to when, in hope or hopelessness, they are running from somewhere else. I have devised a simple test to illustrate this, the gates test, as I call it: If a nation were to have entirely free and unfettered, unchecked and unpatrolled borders, would people come in or go out? If the U.S. opened its borders, there would be streams of people trying to enter the country. Even with border patrols and immigration policies, there are people trying to get in. Many of those people – both today and in decades past – have risked life and limb to flee repressive regimes like Cuba, China, and the Soviet Union to enjoy the freedoms and opportunities unique to America.

That these freedoms and opportunities are unique to America is not merely a conservative position. Listen to what former Democratic Senator and Ambassador to the United Nations Daniel Patrick Moynihan has to say on the matter: "Am I embarrassed to speak for a less than perfect democracy? Not one bit. Find me a better one. Do I suppose that there are societies which are free of sin? No, I don't. Do I think ours is, on balance, incomparably the most hopeful set of human relations the world has? Yes, I do." (528 words)

From "A Nation Worth Defending", *USA Today Magazine*, vol. 131, November 2002

29 unfettered *frei, unbehindert*
33 risk life and limb risk one's life

WORKING WITH THE TEXT

2 Correct the following false statements to make them true.

1. The author argues that the USA is nothing to be proud of.
2. He argues this by naming the good things the US has done for Americans.
3. According to the text, some things the US has spread around the world are war, greed and bad pop music.
4. The author says that there have been a few times when the US has been responsible for 'noble actions' in other countries which were in trouble.
5. He quotes a senator from the Democratic party in order to present a conservative opinion.

3
a **Explain the author's 'gates test' in your own words.**
b **Describe the author's version of American patriotism. Before you start, list the reasons why the author is proud of the USA.**

S ▸ How to Deal with Instructions (p. 192)

LOOKING AT LANGUAGE

4 Read the info box on the following page then rewrite the spoken sentences, making them suitable for formal writing by taking out the personal pronouns and following the instructions in brackets. Try to vary the vocabulary of the original sentences wherever possible.

1. You must admit that the US has done some great things. (passive)
2. Are you going to find a better country? Impossible! (gerund: *finding*)
3. Everybody can become an American citizen (noun: *citizenship*)
4. They once considered the US to be a leader in peace promotion. (passive)
5. We know a lot about the way the government works because it's transparent. (nouns: *knowledge, transparency*)
6. In 2005, George W. Bush made a good speech about how important it is to promote freedom. (noun: *importance*)

S ▸ Improving Your Writing Skills (p. 197)

INFO

Written English vs. Spoken English

When you complete a writing task, try to avoid informal language. There are several ways of making your writing more sophisticated. Look at the following examples. The sentences on the left are typical of informal, spoken language. The sentences on the right show how the author of the text on p. 152/53 expressed the same ideas in a more formal way.

	informal	formal
vocabulary	*I have **made** a simple test **as an example**.*	*I have **devised** a simple test **to illustrate this.***
vocabulary; use of the passive	***You could add** another **ten things** to this list.*	*This list **could be extended tenfold**.*
vocabulary; use of nouns	*We have **made more people richer** than any other nation in the history of mankind.*	*We have **created more prosperity** than any other nation in the history of mankind.*
vocabulary; longer sentences, connected with a participle or gerund	*I will never forget how the brave Chinese students **fought** the tanks. **They were armed** with only a paper-maché Statue of Liberty.*	*I will never forget how the brave Chinese students **faced off** with tanks, **armed** with only a paper-maché Statue of Liberty.*

WORKING WITH WORDS

5 **Make each of the following written sentences into typical spoken sentences by using a verb from the box to replace the verb in italics. Sometimes you will also have to add or change a preposition after the verb.**

get out | give | have | leave out | let | kick out | speak for | watch

1 In the US, we are free to *express* our opinions about the government.
2 Many people have risked their lives to *flee* countries with corrupt governments.
3 Important historical facts are often *omitted* from history books.
4 The world has learned a lot by *observing* the US.
5 We mustn't *allow* a few mistakes to give the US a bad name.
6 America, for the most part, *ejected* Iraq from Kuwait.
7 There are some freedoms and opportunities which only American citizens *possess*.
8 I'm not embarrassed to *represent* a less than perfect democracy.

LISTENING

CD 3 Track 15

S ► Practising Listening Skills (p. 188)

6 a Match the beginning of each phrase with its ending to form six of the greatest moments in American history. Then match each event to a picture below.

1 Women obtaining	**a** World War II
2 The first man on	**b** the moon
3 President Abraham Lincoln declaring	**c** the Declaration of Independence
4 The signing of	**d** the right to vote
5 The end of	**e** the Bill of Rights
6 The ratification of	**f** the end of slavery

b Listen to four American historians talk about what they think the finest moment in their country's history was. Match each speaker's answer to one of the events in the pictures.

c Listen again and make notes as to why these historians are proud of the US and why they are critical.

1776

1920

1791

1945

1863

1969

SPEAKING

7 **With a partner, give some of your views on the United States using the following structure.**

The Declaration of Independence Slavery Starting the Iraq War Putting the first man on the moon Spreading prosperity Making medical advances etc.	is/was (not) something to be	proud of excited about ashamed of embarrassed about remembered	because …

HANDS-ON TASK

S ▸ Doing Research on the Internet (p. 189)

INTERNET PROJECT

8 a **Using the Internet, put the following American historical events in chronological order to match them with the American President they are associated with.**

a the Marshall Plan
b the Vietnam War
c the Revolutionary War
d the Civil War
e Lewis and Clark expedition
f the Great Depression

b **Pick one of these historical events and collect information about it on the Internet. Decribe the event to the class with the President as the protagonist or, in the case of Lewis and Clark, with them as the protagonists.**

Be sure to tell the story in a straightforward and logical order, and remember that good stories include all the information necessary for understanding the final outcome.

George Washington (President 1789–1797, military General during the war)

Thomas Jefferson (1801–1809)

Abraham Lincoln (1861–1865)

Franklin D. Roosevelt (1933–1945)

Harry S. Truman (1945–1953)

Richard Nixon (1968–1974)

TEXT 2 America: Whose Dream Is It, Anyway?

WARM-UP

1 **You are going to read a speech given by Arnold Schwarzenegger. First, look at the pictures. Who is he, where did he come from, and what has he done with his life so far?**

Arnold Schwarzenegger

The Education of an American

September 21, 2001

CD 3 Track 16

Some of the things I knew when I came to America were right on the money – and served me well. But some of the things I thought were true turned out to be terribly wrong …

The first thing I was dead right about was this: where you're from is not as important as where you're going. Take it from me: if you're too focused on where you started, you'll never get where you're headed.

Where I started was a little farm community outside the Austrian town of Graz. It was right after World War II, and the country was absolutely devastated and destroyed. We had no flushing toilet in the house. No refrigerator. No television.

Perhaps the thing I was most dead right about was this country – America.

Ever since childhood, I fantasized over the pictures of America I saw in the magazines,

17 newsreel short cinema film of news
26 embrace accept willingly
42 nurture care for
53 barrio Spanish-speaking area of a city

the movies, the newsreels. I loved the skyscrapers and the beaches – the huge cars zooming down five-lane highways. I said to myself, "I want to be there! I want to be part of it!"

Well, I came here in 1968 with $20 in my pocket. Today I stand before you – an immigrant success story.

I am the living, breathing incarnation of The American Dream.

I was dead right about it: If you have the desire and the determination – and you are willing to be a part of this country and embrace it – it will embrace you. There is nowhere like it on Earth.

Which brings me to the biggest thing I was dead wrong about: whose dream is it, anyway?

It was a great day for me in 1989, when I was called to Washington. President Bush named me Chairman of the President's Council on Physical Fitness. I traveled to all 50 states, promoting fitness and sports programs in schools.

I thought I could inspire kids with a powerful message – especially in the inner cities: "If a poor kid like me from a farm town in Europe can make it, then anyone can make it in this great country!"

This was where I got my biggest and rudest awakening.

Because as I went around from inner city to inner city, I saw first-hand that this is not the "Land of Opportunity" for those kids. Most of them don't get any of the tools that I got.

Look at everything I had in my childhood: two parents, a well-equipped school, help with homework, and safe places to do sports.

Around the clock, I had people taking care of me, encouraging and nurturing me. All this gave me a strong foundation, which gave me the confidence, which gave me the inner strength to believe in myself and know I could make it.

You know, I used to go around saying: "Everybody should pull himself up by his own bootstraps – just like I did!"

What I learned about this country is this: Not everybody has boots.

I saw it first-hand when I met the children in the inner cities. We think we're motivating them by beaming the American Dream in to them – on TV and in movies.

Wrong!

Most of them don't get the motivation. Instead, they hear: "You're a loser. You'll never make it out of the barrio or the ghetto. You'll never get out."

The more I saw, the more I realized I'd been wrong when I thought the American Dream was available to everyone. Because even though it is the Land of Opportunity for me, and the majority of Americans, millions are left behind. (588 words)

Adapted from *A Patriot's Handbook: Songs, Poems, Stories and Speeches Celebrating the Land We Love*

WORKING WITH THE TEXT

2 **Contrast the American Dream with reality and describe why the dream is not available to everyone. First, make the following lists:**

S ► How to Deal with Instructions (p. 192)

1 elements of the Dream
2 elements of reality which conform to the Dream
3 elements of reality which contrast with the Dream
4 reasons for these contrasts

WORKING WITH WORDS

3 **Connect the beginning of each sentence with its ending. The underlined phrasal verbs will help you.**

1 Sometimes problems turn …
2 In order to succeed you've got to believe …
3 Unfortunately, our school system leaves …
4 Arnold Schwarzenegger used to go …
5 It is important to focus …
6 Every day my colleague looks …
7 When will the USA finally start taking …
8 It can be fun and inspiring to learn …

a in yourself.
b around saying that everyone should just try harder.
c out to be blessings in disguise.
d a lot of kids behind.
e care of its poor people?
f about career possibilities you never considered.
g at a picture of his dream house to keep him motivated.
h on your goal and not your obstacles.

4 a **Look at these expressions from the text and say which of the two meanings is correct.**

1 be right on the money (line 1)
 a *be exactly correct*
 b *be expensive*

2 serve someone well (line 2)
 a *be what the person deserves*
 b *be useful to someone*

3 be dead right / dead wrong about something (lines 4, 24/25)
 a *be exactly right/wrong about something*
 b *be unsure about something*

4 take it from someone (line 5)
 a *take advice from someone and know that it is good*
 b *get a kiss from someone*

5 make it (line 32)
 a *star in a film*
 b *manage to succeed*

6 get a rude awakening (line 34)
 a *have an unpleasant realization*
 b *have a bad breakfast*

7 pull oneself up by one's bootstraps (line 43/44)
 a *inject heroin*
 b *help oneself without the aid of others*

8 make it out of somewhere (line 51)
 a *decorate a place*
 b *manage to leave a place*

b **Translate each expression into German.**

LOOKING AT LANGUAGE

5 a **Complete the dialogue with *anyone* or *everyone*. Before you start, take a look at the following sentence pair:**

Anyone can make it in this great country! = **Any one of the people** can succeed in this great country! (anyone = *jeder beliebige, irgendjemand*)
Everyone can make it in this great country! = **All of the people** can succeed in this great country! (everyone = *alle, jeder*)

A Who shall we appoint to be our chairperson?
B Pff! I don't know. Just pick …[1] but me.
A OK, listen up, …[2]! We need a volunteer.
C No one will volunteer. …[3] knows it's a thankless job.
A Well, I'll certainly give thanks to …[4] who does it. Come on, doesn't …[5] have a vision for our organisation?
D It's ten o'clock and the only vision …[6] has at the moment is of their bed.
A Why is …[7] being so negative? …[8] can see that our organisation has tremendous possibilities.
E Hm, it sounds like that "…[9]" might be you! What do you think, …[10]?
(…[11] except A raises their hands.)
A Very funny, …[12].

b **Translate the following sentences into German.**

Examples: Whose dream is it, **anyway**? = *Wessen Traum ist es* ***überhaupt****?*
We didn't have a refrigerator, **anyway**. = *Wir hatten* ***sowieso*** *keinen Kühlschrank.*

1 Who is this message meant for, anyway?
2 I'll never make it out of the ghetto, anyway.
3 We can't afford a car, anyway.
4 How did that happen to them, anyway?
5 What does the Chairman of the President's Council on Physical Fitness do, anyway?

HANDS-ON TASK

DOING A PROJECT

6 a **Make a dream board. This is an activity that many professional life coaches recommend to their clients.**

1 Use a variety of sources for images. Old magazines and calendars are excellent sources as well as Google Images. If possible, get a board or heavyweight paper to glue the images onto.
2 Find or draw pictures of things that represent goals that you have, or that get you thinking about what life could be like if you were in the picture.
3 Cut out the pictures neatly and stick them onto your board. Paste over any faces of the people you have cut out. This is *your* dream board!

b **Bring your dream board to class and tell a partner in English about as many of your dreams as you wish. Look up any necessary words beforehand.**

c **Write about one of your dreams. Describe the dream as vividly and in as much detail as possible.**

TEXT 3 How United is the United States?

WARM-UP

1 The motto of the United States is *'E pluribus unum'* or 'Out of many, one'. Why was this chosen as the motto in 1776?

- **a** The founders saw the United States as a pluralistic but united nation consisting of whites, blacks and Native Americans.
- **b** The founders saw the United States as a pluralistic but united nation consisting of English, Scottish, Irish, French, Dutch and Germans.
- **c** The founders, in their dislike for the English monarchy, wanted one strong leader to be elected from the people instead of a king.
- **d** The founders had many, many mottos to choose from and could not decide. The motto therefore refers to itself.

2 The following words are sometimes used to describe the United States and its people. Sort the words into negative, positive and neutral categories. Are there any words that you disagree with? Add some words of your own to each category.

racist | tolerant | bigoted | successful | individualistic | distrustful | unique | united | Calvinist | challenge-loving | proud | patriotic

bigoted ['bɪgətɪd] *bigott, fanatisch*

CD 3 Track 17

A Country and a Conundrum

Out of many, one? How in the world can that possibly work? Just watch us.

America is an improbable idea. A mongrel nation built of ever changing disparate parts, it is held together by a notion, the notion that all men are created equal, though everyone knows that most men consider themselves better than someone. It was built of bits and pieces that seem discordant, like the crazy quilts that have been one of its great folk art forms.

Out of many, one. That is the ideal.

The reality is often quite different. Many of the stories of the most pluralistic nation on earth are stories, not of tolerance, but of bigotry. Slavery and sweatshops, the burning of crosses and the ostracism of the other. Children learn in school and in the news of the lynching of blacks, the denial of rights to women, the murders of gay men. It is difficult to know how to persuade them that amid all the failures is something spectacularly successful.

This is a nation founded on a conundrum that has been characterized as "community added to individualism". These two are our defining ideals; they are also in constant conflict.

What is the point of this? What is the point of a nation in which Arab cabbies chauffeur Jewish passengers through the streets of New York – and in which Jewish cabbies chauffeur Arab passengers, too, and yet speak in theory of hatred, one for the other? What is the point of a nation in which one part seems to be always on the verge of fisticuffs with another, blacks and whites, gays and straights, left and right, Pole and Chinese and Puerto Rican and Slovenian?

Once these disparate parts were held together by a common enemy, by world wars and by communism. With the end of the cold war there was the concern that without

conundrum confusing problem
1 **mongrel** racially mixed
disparate very different
4 **discordant** unharmonious
quilt *Patchwork-, Steppdecke*
8 **bigotry** extreme prejudice
sweatshop a factory with poor working conditions
9 **ostracism** exclusion
10 **denial** refusal to give
20 **on the verge of** at the limit before something will happen
fisticuffs *(pl.)* fist-fighting

a focus for hatred and distrust, a sense of national identity would disappear, that the left side of the hyphen – African-American, Mexican-American, Irish-American – would overwhelm the right. Yet in a recent survey, the overwhelming majority agreed with this statement: "The U.S. is a unique country that stands for something special in the world."

One of the things that it stands for is this vexing notion that a great nation can consist entirely of refugees from other nations, that people of different, even warring religions and cultures can live together.

There are two behaviors that, however tenuously, support the concept of unity.

There is that Calvinist undercurrent in the American psyche that loves the difficult, the demanding, that sees mastering the impossible, whether it be prairie or subway, as a test of character, and so loves the struggle of this conundrum. And there is a fairness among the citizens of the United States that eventually leads most to admit that the new immigrants are not so different from our own parents or grandparents. Lionel Castillo, former director of the Immigration and Naturalization Service and himself the grandson of Mexican immigrants, once said proudly, "The old neighborhood Ma-Pa stores are still around. They are not Italian or Jewish or Eastern European any more. Ma and Pa are now Korean, Vietnamese, Iraqi, Jordanian, Latin American. They live in the store. They work seven days a week. Their kids are doing well in school. They're making it. Sound familiar?"

Patriotism is partly taking pride in this unlikely ability to throw all of us together in a country that across its length and breadth is as different as a dozen countries, and still be able to call it by one name. Like many improbable ideas, when it actually works, it's a wonder. (593 words)

From *Newsweek*, 27 September 2001

29 vexing annoying or worrying
30 refugee sb who is forced to flee their home
warring at war with each other
32 tenuous unsure
34 subway *(AE) BE:* underground railway
40 Ma-Pa store family-run store

WORKING WITH THE TEXT

S ▸ How to Deal with Instructions (p. 192)

3 **Discuss the divisive forces which have been present in the US and why the country stays together in spite of them.**

Before you start, copy the table below. List all of the United States' unifying aspects – those that hold its people together – and all the divisive aspects – those that threaten to divide its people – which are mentioned in the text. Some aspects will belong clearly to either the past or the present.

	unifying aspects	divisive aspects
past	– *notion that all men are created equal* – …	– *slavery* – …
present	– *notion that all men (and women!) are created equal* – …	– *violence against gays* – …

4 Why, according to the text, are the following concepts 'vexing' or 'improbable'? Answer in your own words.

1 'All men are created equal. (line 2)
2 'There is something spectacularly successful about America. (line 11/12)
3 'A nation can consist entirely of people from other diverse nations and religions. (line 29/30)

S ▸ Answering Comprehension Questions (p. 191)

WORKING WITH WORDS

5 Explain these expressions from the text using your own words.

1 What's the point of this? (line 16)
2 common enemy (line 22)
3 the left side of the hyphen ... would overwhelm the right (line 25/26)
4 overwhelming majority (line 26)

6 The author's style includes frequent use of contrasts. Match the beginning of each phrase with its ending. One beginning and one ending do not match. Complete them with a suitable opposite then check your answers in the text.

1 not of **tolerance**, ...
2 amid all the **failures** is something ...
3 **community** added to ...
4 **gays** and ...
5 **prairie** or ...

a **subway**
b and **breadth**
c but of **bigotry**
d spectacularly **successful**
e **straights**

ANALYSING A CARTOON

7 Describe the cartoon and explain its message. Compare it to the text.

S ▸ Interpreting Pictures and Cartoons (p. 199)

TEXT 4 Declaring 'War' on Terror

WARM-UP

1 **What powers does a government have in wartime that it doesn't have in times of peace?**

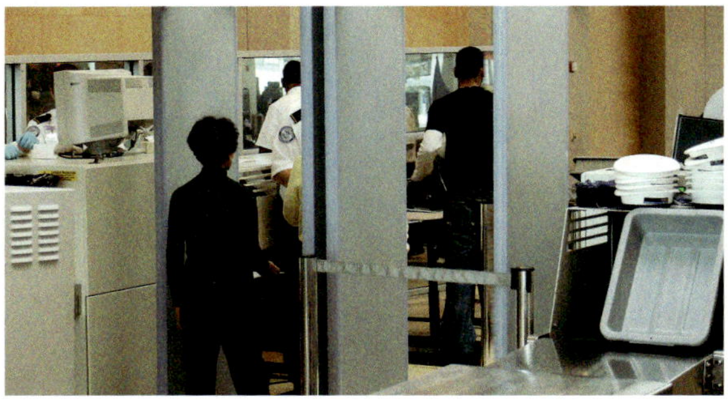

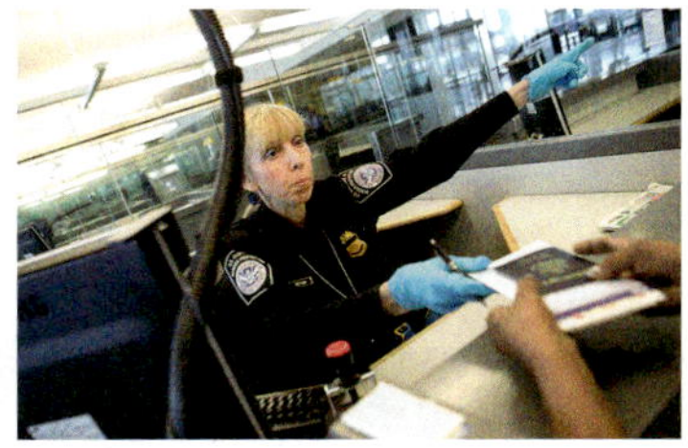

INFO

George W. Bush

George W. Bush, son of President George Bush, became president in January 2001. Eight months later, he faced the crisis of September 11, when terrorists destroyed the World Trade Center and part of the Pentagon, resulting in the loss of over 3,000 lives. A little more than two weeks after giving this speech, President Bush began his 'War on Terror' by invading Afghanistan. The invasion of Iraq would follow in 2003.

S ▸ Skimming (p. 184)

2 **President Bush uses three of the following questions as transition points in his speech. These questions have been omitted from the text below and replaced with gaps. Skim the text and decide which questions fill the gaps.**

- How will we fight and win this war?
- Will the World Trade Center be rebuilt?
- Who attacked our country?
- Why do they hate us?
- How many lives have been lost?

CD 3 Track 18

George W. Bush

Address to a Joint Session of Congress and the American People

September 20, 2001

On September 11, enemies of freedom committed an act of war against our country. Americans have known wars. But for the past 136 years they have been wars on foreign soil, except for one Sunday in 1941*. Americans have known the casualties of war. But not at the center of a great city on a peaceful morning. Americans have known surprise attacks. But never before on thousands of civilians. All of this was brought upon us in a single day. And night fell on a different world, a world where freedom itself is under attack.

4 **casualty** a killed or injured person

Americans have many questions tonight. **Americans are asking, " "**

The evidence we have gathered all points to a collection of loosely affiliated terrorist organizations known as Al Qaeda.

Al Qaeda is to terror what the Mafia is to crime. But its goal is not making money; its goal is remaking the world and imposing its radical beliefs on people everywhere.

The terrorists practice a fringe form of Islamic extremism that has been rejected by Muslim scholars and the vast majority of Muslim clerics. A fringe movement that perverts the peaceful teaching of Islam.

Our war on terror begins with Al Qaeda, but it does not end there. It will not end until every terrorist group of global reach has been found, stopped and defeated.

Americans are asking, " "

They hate our freedoms, our freedom of religion, our freedom of speech, our freedom to vote and assemble and disagree with each other. They stand against us because we stand in their way.

Americans are asking, " "

We will direct every resource at our command – every means of diplomacy, every tool of intelligence, every instrument of law enforcement, every financial influence and every necessary weapon of war – to the disruption and to the defeat of the global terror network.

Americans should not expect one battle, but a lengthy campaign unlike any other we have ever seen.

We will starve terrorists of funding, turn them against one another, drive them from place to place until there is no refuge or no rest. And we will pursue nations that provide aid or safe haven to terrorism.

Every nation in every region now has a decision to make. Either you are with us or you are with the terrorists.

And what is at stake is not just America's freedom. This is the world's fight, this is civilization's fight, this is the fight of all who believe in progress and pluralism, tolerance and freedom.

After all that has just passed, all the lives taken and all the possibilities and hopes that died with them, it is natural to wonder if America's future is one of fear. Some speak of an age of terror. I know there are struggles ahead and dangers to face.

But this country will define our times, not be defined by them. As long as the United States of America is determined and strong, this will not be an age of terror. This will be an age of liberty here and across the world.

Great harm has been done to us. We have suffered great loss. And in our grief and anger, we have found our mission and our moment. Freedom and fear are at war. The advance of human freedom, the great achievement of our time and the great hope of every time, now depends on us. (575 words)

Shortened from *A Patriot's Handbook: Songs, Poems, Stories, and Speeches Celebrating the Land We Love*

* President Bush is referring to the Japanese attack on Pearl Harbor.

9 **affiliated** connected with each other
12 **impose** force
14 **fringe** on the edge
15 **scholar** a highly educated person
24 **at one's command** available for one to use
25 **intelligence** *Geheimdienst(informationen)*
26 **disruption** interruption or disturbance
30 **starve** cut off; literally: deny food to
funding supply of money
31 **refuge** a safe place
32 **haven** a safe place
35 **be at stake** be in danger of being lost

WORKING WITH THE TEXT

3 **Paraphrase President Bush's answers to each of the three questions he says Americans are asking.**

S ▸ Writing a Comment (p. 195)

4 **Comment on President Bush's assessment of the terrorist attacks as beginning a 'war'.**

Paragraph 1: State your position as to whether or not the 'War on Terror' is really a war.
Paragraph 2: Define what a 'war' is. Explain why or why not a 'War on Terror' fits this definition.
Paragraph 3: Comment on one or more of the aspects of the 'war' as described in the speech.
Paragraph 4: Summarise and restate your opinion.

WORKING WITH WORDS

5 a **Match a pair from one group with a pair from another group to make analogies.**

Example: Al Qaeda – terror | Mafia – crime
→ *Al Qaeda is to terror what the Mafia is to crime.*

1 freedom – society
2 diplomacy – international relations
3 terrorism – politics
4 7 July 2005 London bombings – Britain
5 strategy – war

a a plot – a play
b theft – earning a living
c 9/11 – USA
d health – individual
e balance – acrobats

b **Make up three analogies of your own.**

LOOKING AT LANGUAGE

CD 3 Track 19

6 a **Listen to the seven excerpts from President Bush's speech and, for each, decide which rhetorical device is being used.**

1 a) emotional language b) exaggeration
2 a) a three-part list b) imagery
3 a) an analogy b) a rhetorical question
4 a) a three-part list b) repetition
5 a) exaggeration b) enumeration (listing)
6 a) parallelism (repeating a grammatical structure) b) an analogy
7 a) imagery b) a contrast

b **Find other instances of repetition and three-part lists in the speech.**

DISCUSSION

S ▸ Group Discussions (p. 203)

7 **In groups, discuss one of the following questions. Then compare your findings with another group that has chosen the same question.**

1 What causes terrorism?
2 How would you rid the world of terrorism? Would you use military force?
3 How would you rate the success of the War on Terror?

LISTENING TO A SONG

CD 3 Track 20

8 a **Listen to the song *Blowin' in the Wind* by the American folk musician Bob Dylan, which he released in 1963. *Rolling Stone* magazine has ranked it number 14 among the greatest songs of all time. What message or messages do you find in the song?**

Bob Dylan

Blowin' in the Wind

1962

How many roads must a man walk down
Before you call him a man?
How many seas must a white dove sail
Before she sleeps in the sand?
Yes, 'n' how many times must the cannon balls fly
Before they're forever banned?
The answer, my friend, is blowin' in the wind,
The answer is blowin' in the wind.

Yes, 'n' how many years can a mountain exist
Before it is washed to the sea?
Yes, 'n' how many years can some people exist
Before they're allowed to be free?
Yes, 'n' how many times can a man turn his head,
Pretendin' that he just doesn't see?
The answer, my friend, is blowin' in the wind,
The answer is blowin' in the wind.

Yes, 'n' how many times must a man look up
Before he can see the sky?
Yes, 'n' how many ears must one man have
Before he can hear people cry?
Yes, 'n' how many deaths will it take till he knows
That too many people have died?
The answer, my friend, is blowin' in the wind,
The answer is blowin' in the wind.

Bob Dylan

b **Write another verse of the song.**

How many … must …
Before … ?
Yes 'n' how many … must …
Before … ?
Yes 'n' how many … must …
… ?
The answer, my friend, is blowin' in the wind,
The answer is blowin' in the wind.

TEXT 5 The Role of Christian Fundamentalism

WARM-UP

1 Match the beginning of each sentence with its ending.

1. Over 75% of Americans are …
2. 36% of Americans believe that the Bible is the word of God and …
3. 59% believe the prophecies in the *Book of Revelation* …
4. 35% of all Americans say that the creation of Israel is part of a Biblical prophecy …

a is to be taken literally.
b about Jesus returning to Earth.
c Christian.
d will come true.

INFO

US Influence in the Middle East

Not long after the Second World War, Jewish settlers re-established the nation of Israel in Palestine with the help of the United Nations. Territorial wars between Israel and its Arab neighbours have been fought ever since. Israel has been able to exist under these hostile conditions largely because of help, and weapons, from the USA. Israel's actions are extremely controversial: it is repeatedly being accused of stealing more and more land from its neighbours and of violating their human rights. The one government that almost never criticises these actions is that of the USA.

So why is the government of the USA, a country that is only 2% Jewish, so firmly 'pro-Israel'? The following text will explain one major reason why.

CD 3 Track 21

bonkers crazy
2 delusion illusion
preacher religious speaker
7 deploy send into action
12 rapture *Entrückung, Verzückung*
14 devour eat up
boil *Geschwür*
sore wound
locust *Heuschrecke*
15 tribulation terrible state
16 stage organise, cause to happen

Their Beliefs Are Bonkers, But They Are At The Heart Of Power

In the United States, several million people have succumbed to an extraordinary delusion. In the 19th century, two preachers joined together a series of unrelated passages from the Bible to create the following story: Jesus will return to Earth when certain preconditions have been met. The first of these was the establishment of a state of Israel. The next involves Israel's occupation of the rest of its "biblical lands" (most of the Middle East), and the rebuilding of the Third Temple at the Temple Mount. The armies of the antichrist will then be deployed against Israel, and their war will lead to a final showdown in the valley of Armageddon. The Jews will either burn or convert to Christianity, and the Messiah will return to Earth.

What makes the story so appealing to Christian fundamentalists is that before the big battle begins, all "true believers" will be lifted out of their clothes and transported up to heaven during an event called the Rapture. Not only do the worthy get to sit at the right hand of God, but they will be able to watch, from the best seats, their political and religious opponents being devoured by boils, sores, locusts and frogs, during the seven years of Tribulation which follow.

The true believers are now seeking to bring all this about. This means staging confrontations at the old temple site (in 2000, three US Christians tried to blow up the mosques there), sponsoring Jewish settlements in Palestine, demanding ever more US support for Israel, and seeking to provoke a final battle with the Muslim world / Axis of Evil / United Nations / European Union / France or whoever the legions of the antichrist turn out to be.

By clicking on www.raptureready.com, you can discover how close you might be to flying out of your pyjamas. The infidels among us should take note that the Rapture Index currently stands at 144*. One more point and the sky will be filled with floating nudists.

"Then we who are alive and remain shall be caught up together with them in the clouds to meet the Lord in the air." (1 Thessalonians 4:17)

We can laugh at these people, but we should not dismiss them. That their beliefs are bonkers does not mean they are marginal. American pollsters believe that 15–18% of US voters belong to churches or movements which subscribe to these teachings. A survey in 1999 suggested that this figure included 33% of Republicans. The people who believe all this don't believe it just a little; for them it is a matter of eternal life and death.

And among them are some of the most powerful men in America. Among the true believers are several senators, the [former] attorney general, and the [former] House majority leader, who recently travelled to Israel to tell the parliament that "there is no middle ground, no moderate position worth taking".

So here we have a major political group in the most powerful nation on Earth, which is actively seeking to provoke a new world war. They attack the White House as soon as its support for Israel wavers: when Bush asked Israel to pull its tanks out of Jenin in 2002, he received 100,000 angry emails from Christian fundamentalists, and never mentioned the matter again.

The electoral calculation, crazy as it appears, works like this. Governments stand or fall on domestic issues. For 85% of the US electorate, the Middle East is a foreign issue, and therefore of secondary interest when they vote. For 15% of the electorate, the Middle East is not just a domestic matter, it's a personal one: if the Republicans fail to start a blaze there, their core voters don't get to sit at the right hand of God.

(601 words)

* in April 2004

Adapted from *The Guardian*, 20 April 2004

23 infidel sb who has no religion or a different religion than the majority
26 dismiss forget about
27 marginal small in number
pollster survey conductor
33 attorney general *(US-)Justizminister/in*
38 waver begin to weaken
45 blaze fire

WORKING WITH THE TEXT

2 **Find and correct one word in each statement that makes it false.**

1 Hundreds of Americans believe a quasi-Biblical prophesy that says the earth will become like hell and only 'true believers' will be saved.
2 These Christian fundamentalists want peace in the Middle East because that would fulfil the prophesy.
3 They strongly oppose the Israelis who want to occupy more of the Middle East.
4 Enough American voters believe in the Rapture to have a big influence on literature there.
5 Believers in the Rapture include some of the most powerful politicians in Israel.
6 To the minority of Americans who are not religious fundamentalists, the Middle East is not an important political issue.

S ▸ How to Deal with Instructions (p. 192)

3 a **Define the term 'Rapture'.**
b **Explain why the world should be concerned about Americans who believe in the Rapture.**

ANALYSING A CARTOON

S ▸ Interpreting Pictures and Cartoons (p. 199)

4 **Explain the cartoon and compare its message with the information given in the text.**

WORKING WITH WORDS

5 a **Some words in the text have at least two meanings. Match each word in the box with two of the definitions on the opposite page.**

passage | occupation | stage | tank | domestic

a a heavy military vehicle
b a job or profession
c a large container for liquid or gas
d a short section of a text
e a way through something
f using or having control of a place
g in a country, not foreign
h relating to the home
i to organise
j to present a performance

b **Complete the sentences with some of the words from above in the correct form.**

1 Israel is blocking the main … between Egypt and Gaza. No one can get through.
2 The Palestinians resent Israel's … of the Gaza Strip and the West Bank.
3 Last summer the church's youth group … a musical in the basement.
4 One shouldn't take a … from the Bible out of context.
5 Mr Hay's … is preacher of a church.
6 Which religious group … the demonstrations in front of the abortion clinic?

c **Write similar sentences using the remaining words from Exercise 5a and read them to your partner, who must say which definition of the word you are using.**

LISTENING

6 **a** **The senator in the cartoon is being briefed by his aide. Match each question to its answer.**

1 Who are all those people outside?
2 Don't they know that already?
3 What's on the agenda for today?
4 Are you afraid my stance on Israel is too moderate?
5 Are those Jewish Americans outside?
6 What's the Rapture?
7 What exactly do they think will happen?
8 How did these crazies come to suffer from this delusion?
9 Exactly how many of them are out there?
10 What exactly is it that they want me to do?

a It's a prophesy, sir.
b They think all the people in their religion will go to heaven and everyone else will remain on Earth and be devoured by boils, sores, locusts and frogs.
c They're protesters, sir.
d Yes, sir. You need to start talking really tough on this issue.
e No, sir. Those are fundamentalist Christians who believe in the Rapture.
f Yes, sir, they know.
g They want you to unconditionally promote the expansion of Israel and its military.
h We need to talk about Israel today, sir.
i Their clergy has been preaching it for generations, sir.
j Thousands, sir.

b **Listen to the entire conversation and answer the following questions.**

CD 3 Track 22

1 How did the senator get elected?
2 Does the senator appear to be a religious fundamentalist?
3 What does the senator decide at the end of the briefing? What convinces him?

S ▸ Practising Listening Skills (p. 188)

TEXT 6 Will the US Remain the Superpower?

WARM-UP

1 **Do the following quiz.**

1 **Match the names of the world's four most populous countries (USA, China, Indonesia, India) with their population (as of 2008).**

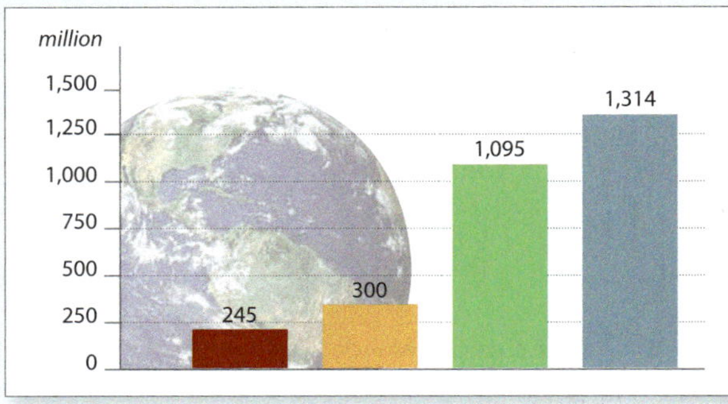

2 **Which of these countries is the world's largest economy?**

3 **Which country is set to be the largest economy in 2040?**

4 **Which country is the world's largest democracy?**

5 **Which country has 200 million Muslims, more than any other country in the world?**

6 **Which country had, in 2007, a trade deficit of $711.6 billion, the largest in the world?**

CD 3 Track 23

Make Way For the Rise of Asia

Americans shouldn't assume they'll remain on top. The world is changing, and they'd better adapt.

There's a curious paradox in America's relations with the rest of the planet these days. The United States has done more than any other country to make the world a better place. Asia especially has benefited: when Europe dominated the globe, Asia was subjugated, but when the United States took charge after World War II, Asia was liberated. The U.S. has enabled Asian economies to thrive. American universities have trained hundreds of thousands of Asian policymakers, who have in turn used U.S. practices to transform their societies. Given this historical backdrop, the United States should be reaping a global harvest of good will.

Instead, the country's reputation today stands at a record low. The U.S. intelligentsia seems to believe that this will soon pass. In fact, the problem is far more serious. The world has changed and the United States has not. The nation's relative power is declining: according to the World Bank, for example, the U.S. share of world GNI* dropped from 31 percent in 2001 to 28 percent in 2006.

To make matters worse, Washington's foreign policy has become incompetent. Take the Iraq War, one of the most disastrous American adventures in history. U.S. elites

4 **subjugate** force to play a submissive role

8 **harvest** season's yield of crops

behave as if the war was the fault of President Bush, Vice President Cheney and Defense Secretary Rumsfeld alone. Yet the reality is Congress authorized the conflict, and few American voices opposed it. Warnings, including those from the U.N. Security Council and numerous friendly governments, were ignored.

This indicates just how complacent American leaders have become. Having transformed the world, Americans today should be asking themselves whether and how they too need to adapt. Yet there are no signs that this process is taking place. Washington continues to undermine the United Nations, sacrifice trade talks to protect a few American farmers and demonstrate incredible insensitivity to Muslim sentiments around the world.

As Washington has failed, Asia has come on strong. After 9/11, when the U.S. government was distracted by Afghanistan and Iraq, China's economy grew at the fastest possible rate. And Beijing decided to share that prosperity with its neighbors. In November 2001, Chinese Prime Minister Zhu Rongji stunned the leaders of the Association of Southeast Asian Nations by offering them an unprecedented free-trade agreement (FTA). When implemented, the FTA will constitute a common market of 1.7 billion people, with a combined gross domestic product of $1.5 trillion to $2 trillion. Meanwhile, trade flows between China and other Asian states have become the fastest growing on the planet. Asia is now contributing more to the increase in global prosperity than any other region. More important, it is also experiencing a massive explosion in cultural confidence. This helps explain why countries such as China, India, South Korea and Vietnam are moving ahead so rapidly.

The big question now is what kind of role can the United States play in Asia's renewal? U.S. universities continue to churn out dynamic new Asian elites, and American businesses are taking advantage of new opportunities there. Yet even these roles are in danger. A dangerous protectionist mood is sweeping across the United States, and American politicians are once again bending to the political winds by threatening legislation against China's supposedly undervalued yuan. The problem is not the yuan; it is America's lack of competitiveness.

For too long, Americans have assumed that their nation would always remain the world's strongest and need not adapt to the rest of the globe. It's high time to abandon that belief. The United States will not always be exceptional. Indeed, in some senses, it no longer is. Its economy, like others, will have to change if it is to meet the challenges of globalization. Luckily, pragmatism is a traditional American virtue; right now the nation needs all it can get. (626 words)

Adapted from *Newsweek*, special edition 2008

* GNI = Gross National Income, formerly GNP

20 **complacent** self-satisfied, apathetic
23 **undermine** weaken
sacrifice give up
27 **distract** divert attention from something
32 **gross domestic product** *Bruttoinlandsprodukt*
40 **churn out** manufacture very quickly
43 **bend to** *sich beugen*
46 **to assume** suppose
50 **virtue** positive attribute

WORKING WITH THE TEXT

2 **Complete the following sentences with information given in the text.**

1 Because of the US, Asian countries …
2 After 2001 the US economy …
3 A major failing of US foreign policy was …
4 The country which is failing to adapt to the changing world is …
5 China's trade with other Asian countries …
6 Cultural confidence …

3 Make two lists: *a)* evidence that the US is weakening, *b)* evidence that Asia is becoming stronger.

S ▸ How to Deal with Instructions (p. 192)

4 Describe why the US needs to adapt to the current world situation.

WORKING WITH WORDS

5 Rewrite each sentence using one of the expressions in the box.

be high time | be on top | bend to the political winds | come on strong | make matters worse | make way for someone or something | reap a harvest

1 The time is definitely here for China to revalue its currency.
2 The US is going to have to allow room for rising powers like China.
3 Politicians should stop doing what they think will be popular and do what they know to be right.
4 India is another country whose economy is really doing well at the moment.
5 By 2040 it seems that China will be number one in terms of economic power.
6 China is profiting from new technologies it invested in.
7 The US is in trouble and, adding to the problem, it doesn't even realise it.

6 Find the word which does not belong to the group.

1 unskilful, unprofessional, incompetent, insensitive
2 abandon, desert, bend, throw out
3 catastrophic, devastating, reaping, disastrous
4 adjust, adapt, authorise, alter
5 unprecedented, self-satisfied, unworried, complacent
6 thrive, behave, come on strong, prosper
7 exaggerated, incomparable, exceptional, incredible
8 massive, huge, colossal, distracted

LOOKING AT LANGUAGE

7 Look at this example sentence:

The world is changing, and Americans had better adapt.
Die Welt ändert sich, und die Amerikaner sollten sich besser darauf einstellen.

Now complete sentences 1–6 with *had/'d better* and one of the verbs in the box. One verb does not fit.

authorise | develop | disturb | invest | learn | oppose | take care

1 A trade deal with India is waiting for the President's signature. He … it or we will lose the Indian market.
2 The boss is on the phone with Jakarta. We … not … her.
3 Asian factories depend on their workers. They … of them and not exploit them.
4 The US … in solar energy if it's going to gain independence from foreign oil.
5 All the *nouveau riche* in Asia want cars. We … an environmentally friendly one.
6 The Asian elite are all learning English. We … it, too!

8 **Read the section on headlines in the appendix and rewrite the following headlines as complete sentences.**

1 China to raise military spending
2 Japan's business confidence grows
3 US soldier said to have insulted Islam
4 China factory output accelerates
5 India airports strike called off
6 US recession fears on the rise
7 China-South Korea trade pact signed
8 China set to be largest economy
9 Bin Laden thought to be hiding in Afghanistan
10 US-Japan trade deficit to increase

S ▸ Understanding Headlines (p. 186)

LISTENING

CD 3 Track 24

9 **Follow these steps.**

1 Listen to a short news report from the year 2040. Which of the following stories does the programme report on?

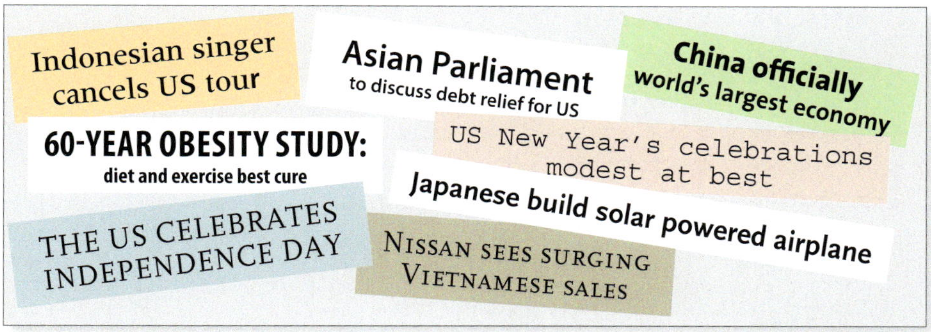

2 Listen again and make notes about the state of the USA in 2040. Compare your notes in small groups.
3 With your group, write your own news report for the year 2040. First, the group should brainstorm some possible headlines. Then, each person in the group chooses a headline on which to write a short report of two to five sentences. When you have finished, read your report to the class.

World of Work

MEDIATION American Business Culture

S ▸ Mediation (p. 204)

1 Do the following mediation task.

Ihre Firma möchte ein Team in die USA schicken, um dort drei Wochen mit ihrer amerikanischen Partnerfirma zusammenzuarbeiten. Sie werden gebeten, die Delegation Ihrer Firma über die amerikanische Geschäftskultur zu informieren. Zu diesem Zweck erstellen Sie einen Bericht, in dem Sie das Wichtigste aus dem folgenden Artikel auf Deutsch zusammenfassen.

Before you write a clean copy of your report, check your first draft using the checklist below.

MEDIATION CHECKLIST

Did you
- plan and structure your text before you wrote it?
- write the text in a way that is easily understandable?
- write the text in the proper form (in this case, a professional report)?
- mention all relevant aspects from the original?
- avoid mistakes in your German?
- leave out …
  - irrelevant and unimportant points?
  - quotations?
  - your opinion?
  - unimportant numbers, names and statistics?

If you did all these things, then you should get a good score for this part of the exam!

Success Abroad: USA

As part of our series 'Success Abroad', intercultural consultant **Staci Evans** *explains how to charm your American colleagues.*

From the lakes of Minnesota to the hills of Tennessee, America is vast and the people are as diverse as the landscape. Each region has its own ethnic and cultural make-up. And because Americans value individualism and personal freedom so much, it's impossible to make any generalisations about them without immediately being confronted with countless exceptions. When working in the USA, you can expect every American cliché you've ever heard to be shattered, and confirmed, by the people you meet.

Women and minorities still face enormous barriers in the American workplace. To give them credit, Americans don't consider everyone of colour to be 'foreign', as many Germans still do. Yet American history is so fraught with atrocities against Native Americans, black Americans, Japanese Americans, etc., that tensions between

1 **vast** extremely large in area, size
2 **diverse** very different from each other and of various kinds
3 **make-up** the different qualities that combine to form sb's character or being
6 **shatter** to destroy completely
10 **fraught** filled with sth unpleasant
atrocity cruel and violent act, especially in a war

races are markedly higher than in Germany. Therefore, it is best to just avoid referring to race as much as possible and to appear 'colour blind'.

Your American colleagues will take on a pained expression if you refer to 'that black man over there'. It's much better to say 'that man over there wearing the purple tie', for example. Do not make comments about the differences between the sexes, either, unless everyone within earshot is the same sex as you.

America was settled by Puritans, so be prepared for the Puritan work ethic. This industrious nation spends an enormous amount of time at work, often at the expense of family and health. Fifty-hour working weeks are common, as is working through weekends and holidays. Often lunch is eaten while working and dinner is a take-away. As for exercise ... what's that? The good news, I guess, is that you probably won't be expected to work as intensively as you do in Germany, and will have time to socialise at work.

Americans shake hands only upon first meeting or upon making an agreement, not every time they meet. In some industries, e.g. entertainment, you may be offered a hug by a colleague you know well, but kissing is rare. In Germany, hugging is considered more intimate than kissing; in the USA, it's just the opposite.

Business relationships, like all others, quickly become informal. Professionals introduce themselves with their full names and then use only their first names. In the US, last names are reserved for customers in a shop or on the telephone, and even then the tone service people use is bright and informal. Remember this: friendliness is a virtue in the USA. Most Americans are eager to be liked and accepted, and this is usually more important than the (German) desire to be taken seriously.

One thing you'll have to get used to is that Americans exaggerate a lot. If they say 'That will only take you like five minutes to do,' then you can bet it will take you 15 minutes. If they say 'Oh my gosh, that will take at least ten hours to do!', then you can be sure that five hours is a closer estimate. Americans just don't have quite the same degree of attention to verbal accuracy that Germans do, so try to relax about it.

Americans aren't afraid of looking silly. Humour is often used to diffuse tension when an argument is imminent. Sometimes they giggle for what seems like no reason. Smile in those moments because, in the USA, a sense of humour will get you everywhere!

You'll make friends very quickly. That's normal in the States, where families often move great distances for economic reasons and have to quickly build new social networks.

One thing that many Germans come to enjoy about working with Americans is the way they give constructive feedback. When being evaluated, you can expect to hear from others what you did well – not just what you can improve upon. The aim is to be helpful and to encourage the development of individuals and processes. This can be a refreshing change from German appraisals, which tend to be either entirely positive or entirely negative. Remember to be constructive when you give feedback, and don't be confused when you receive it.

It's business practices like this that have made the US so successful. After your experience there, you are sure to return to Germany with an impressive résumé as well as marvellous skills which you can employ in a European context. (742 words)

12 **markedly** noticeably, distinctly
17 **within earshot** near enough to be heard
18 **Puritan** member of a Protestant group in the 16th and 17th centuries who wanted to worship God in a simple way
19 **at the expense of** with loss or damage to sb/sth
24 **socialise** meet and spend time with people in a friendly way
33 **eager** wanting sth very much
41 **diffuse** break down
42 **imminent** likely to happen very soon
49 **evaluate** form an opinion of the quality of sth after thinking about it carefully
51 **encourage** make sth more likely to happen or develop
52 **appraisal** meeting in which an employee discusses with their manager how well they have been doing their job
57 **marvellous** extremely good, wonderful

JOB SKILLS Intercultural Communication (2)

WORKING WITH WORDS

2 **Complete the text with the words in the box.**

aware | consider | diversity | exceptions | inappropriate | practices | relationship | roots | tension | value

Monochronism v. Polychronism

The anthropologist Edward T. Hall came up with this very useful way of describing a culture's …[1] to time. As you can probably imagine, this has a great influence on business …[2]. Having a 'monochronic' attitude to time means that you do only one thing at a time. Having a 'polychronic' attitude to time means that you are involved in many things at once. Unfortunately, when a monochronic and a polychronic culture do business together, there can be great …[3], especially if they are not …[4] of the difference.

People from polychronic cultures can do many things simultaneously and …[5] people to be more important than schedules. For example, if two polychronic people are conversing on the street, it would be …[6] to stop the conversation abruptly in order to be on time for an appointment.

In a monochronic society, time is thought of as linear. People do only one thing at a time and the schedule is almost sacred and punctuality is a strong …[7]. Often people talk about time as if it were money – it can be 'spent', 'wasted', 'saved' or 'lost'.

The United States has its …[8] in the monochronic cultures of northern Europe, but because the US has many immigrants and great cultural …[9], you are very likely to work with people who are …[10] to this rule.

DISCUSSION

3 **Based on the description in the previous exercise, where would you place German culture on this continuum?**

monochronic ◄·········► polychronic

CD 3 Track 25

LISTENING

S ► Practising Listening Skills (p. 188)

4 a **Copy the table. Then listen to four Americans talking about their experiences working in other cultures. Complete the table with the country each speaker worked in and the context in which the incident occurred, e.g. 'at the airport'.**

	Country	Context
Speaker 1	…	…
Speaker 2	…	…
Speaker 3	…	…
Speaker 4	…	…

b Listen again and make notes about the specific details of the stories.

c Tell your partner two of the four stories.

d By talking about other cultures, people often reveal important things about their own culture. Listen again to the Americans. What does each of them unknowingly reveal about their own culture?

WRITING

5 **The following statements were made by Germans who were working abroad. Decide what each statement reveals about German culture and write it in English. The first one has been done for you.**

1 „In den USA lassen alle immer ihre Bürotüren offen."
→ *In German offices, doors are usually kept shut.*
2 „In England sind wir immer nach der Arbeit zusammen in den Pub gegangen."
3 „Wenn man in England montags im Büro telefoniert, unterhält man sich immer erst über das letzte Wochenende."
4 „Was ich in England schwierig fand, war, dass man sich alles selbst erarbeiten musste. Meist bekommt man überhaupt keine detaillierten Informationen über das, was man machen soll."
5 „In Indien brauchst du ein hartes Fell, wenn es um Preise geht. Ohne Verhandeln läuft gar nichts."
6 „Wenn du in Indien denkst, mit Geschäftspartnern redet man vor allem übers Geschäft, täuschst du dich. Die wollen alles über deine Familie wissen."
7 „Vorsicht mit Kritik in Indien! Ein Wort zu viel und die Geschäftsbeziehung kann vorbei sein."
8 „Am anstrengendsten in Italien waren die Sitzungen. Da reden immer alle gleichzeitig."
9 „In Japan musst du zwischen den Zeilen lesen können. Selbst auf sehr wichtige Fragen bekommt man oft keine direkte Antwort."
10 „Auf rein sachlicher Ebene kommt man in Polen schlecht an wichtige Informationen. Am wichtigsten sind persönliche Beziehungen."

INTERVIEWING PEOPLE

HANDS-ON TASK

6 a **Below is an unfinished questionnaire about business practices which vary from culture to culture. Complete it with five questions of your own.**

You could consider some of the following topics: small talk, greeting, shaking hands, using first names, tipping, giving presents, punctuality.

Question	Your culture	Other culture
1 How do managers dress at work?	…	…
2 Do colleagues socialise with each other outside of working hours?	…	…
3 Is it OK to criticise each other during meetings?	…	…

b **Interview someone who works in your culture and record his/her answers. Then interview someone who has worked in another culture, or who is from another culture, and record his/her answers.**

c **Did any of the answers you received surprise you?**

FILES

Topic 2, Text 2, page 45

File 1

Partner A

You generally favour relocation, when it becomes necessary, and use the following arguments:

- Before the Inupiaq began living in modern, western housing, they were a nomadic people, so the exact location is not the most important thing.
- If the villagers have to split up and go their separate ways, they will lose their identity.
- In the past, protection against erosion was ineffective (as in Shishmaref).
- Shishmaref has already decided that relocation is the best option and is setting an example for other villages.

Topic 4, Text 4, page 111

File 2

Partner A

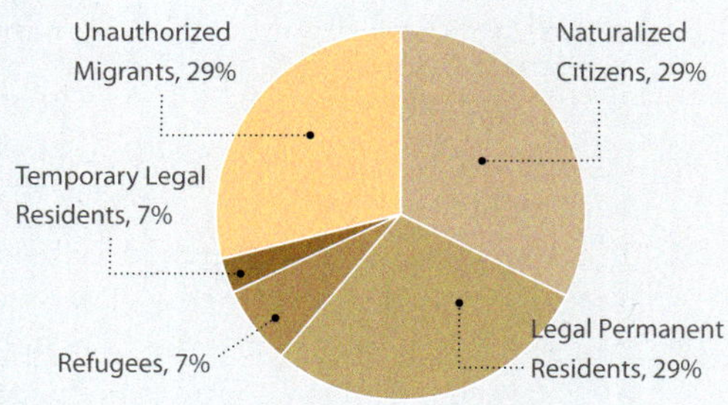

Status of foreign-born individuals living in the U.S.

Topic 3, Text 2, page 72

File 3

Doctor

He/She reminds the patient of the following things:

- It probably won't change your life.
- Teenagers are too young. The body and nose are still growing and changing.
- Mentally, speaking teenagers aren't mature enough to cope with the change.
- Surgery is stressful and risky. You may not be pleased with the result.
- Depressed teenagers normally won't feel better if they change their nose or ears. The reasons for being unhappy are usually to be found elsewhere.

Topic 2, Text 5, page 56

File 4

a Save the whales!

Whale populations are decreasing and some species may soon become extinct. Besides whaling, known environmental threats to whales include global warming, pollution, overfishing, ozone depletion, and noise from military sonar equipment. Industrial fishing threatens the whales' food supply and also puts them at risk of entanglement in fishing gear. What can be done?

b Save the rainforests! Stop the clear-felling of trees!

You read about deforestation in the last text (p. 48/49). How can you stop it when people in Brazil and Indonesia, for example, need to support their local economies? Can you convince governments there to stop clear-felling?

c Save the Mediterranean ecosystem! No more overfishing!

The Mediterranean Sea is turning into a graveyard, with many species of fish under threat. Overfishing is one of the main causes. People want to eat fish, and fishermen want to earn their living, but if overfishing continues, there may soon be none left. How can you convince governments to limit fishing and to enforce these limits?

d Save the national park! No new motorway!

Your government wants to build a four-lane motorway through one of the national parks in your country. They say it is necessary for economic growth. How can you convince them not to build it?

e Save future generations! No more nuclear power stations!

Your government has decided that nuclear energy is the way to go, but you don't agree. Despite what the nuclear industry says, building enough nuclear power stations to make a meaningful reduction in global greenhouse gas emissions would cost trillions of dollars, create tens of thousands of tons of radioactive waste, and result in a Chernobyl-scale accident once every decade. Perhaps most significantly, it would waste the resources necessary to implement really effective climate change solutions. Your government wants to build new nuclear power plants. How can you convince people that this is a mistake?

Topic 2, Text 3, page 46

File 5

Now take the same amount of time to make sentences describing *this* image. Give yourself a tick for every correct sentence again, and try to get more ticks than last time.

Topic 2, Text 2, page 45

File 6

Partner B

Although you accept that measures taken to protect against erosion have been ineffective so far, you generally favor them, wherever possible, and use the following arguments:

- Every Inupiaq has deep historical and cultural ties to the land on which they live. Some villages have existed for hundreds or even thousands of years.
- The villages have cemeteries that are very old and should not be abandoned.
- You have heard that the state of Alaska has $37 billion available which could fund erosion protection measures.

Topic 3, Text 2, page 72

File 7

Mother/Father

Wants to know:

- how much it will cost.
- if this kind of operation is covered by insurance.
- how long the daughter/son needs to recover from the operation.
- what the risks are.

Score list for the questionnaire on page 91

- If you answered **a** for 70–100% of the questions, you have a very high quotient and can communicate well using emails.
- If you answered 70–100% of the questions with options **a** or **b**, you have a high quotient and do not make too many mistakes when writing emails.
- If you answered more than 50% of the questions with option **c**, then you definitely need to work on your netiquette!

Topic 4, Text 4, page 111

File 8

Partner B

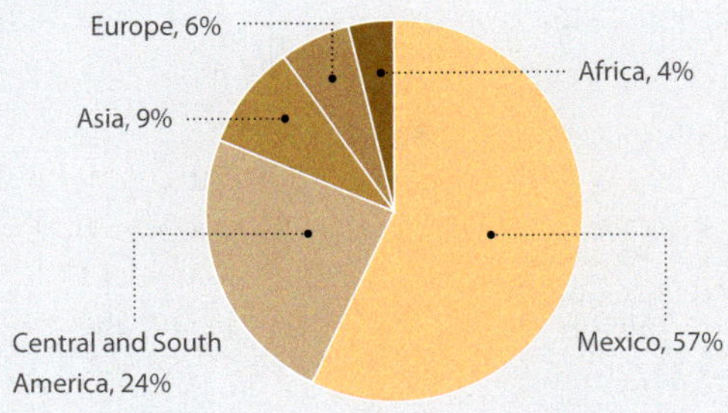

Unauthorized migrants in the U.S. by region and country

Topic 3, Text 2, page 72

File 9

Daughter/Son

Reasons for wanting the operation:

- I'll be more attractive.
- I'll feel more confident.
- My future career prospects will be better.
- I can't wait until I am older. I want the operation now.

Topic 2, Text 2, page 45

File 10

Partner C

Although you feel sad about it, you think that most villages will not be able to stay together. You know that your view is extremely unpopular, but you have the following arguments:

- Moving to cities that already exist is the practical thing to do.
- You don't think that the federal government will fund either measures to protect against erosion or relocation for the villages.
- You also think that the rest of the country will not understand why everyone can't just move to cities that already exist.
- Any money that the government has should be spent on preventing further climate change.

STUDY SKILLS

RECEPTION: READING AND LISTENING

PRODUCTION: WRITING AND SPEAKING

INTERACTION

MEDIATION

RECEPTION: READING AND LISTENING

Reading Difficult Texts

Texts are read for different reasons. Sometimes you only need to know what the text is about, so it is usually enough to just skim the text carefully. Specific information often has to be found, in which case the important thing is to pick out key words. If you want to examine a text thoroughly in order to answer questions or write an essay on it, then you have to read it thoroughly, possibly twice.

Skimming: gaining a quick overview of a text

Sometimes you will be asked to read a text quickly to get a basic understanding of the theme.

Step 1: Look for clues which give you information about the content of the text: the title and sub-headings, words in bold, pictures and their captions.

Step 2: If you are still not sure what the text is about, read the first and last sentences of each paragraph. Do not worry about individual words, difficult quotations, etc. which you do not understand.

Scanning: finding details in a text

Many questions which test your understanding of a text, or exercises like *True or false*, require you to find pieces of information quickly, rather than reading the whole text again for each question.

Step 1: Search the text for key words which will help you find the required information. If you're looking for the author's opinion on a particular subject, look out for words like *think, believe, opinion,* etc. If you're looking for information on a topic, try to think of a few key expressions which you could look out for. Sometimes it helps to imagine the key expression as a printed word and keep this image in your head as you look.

Step 2: If necessary, follow each line with your finger while you search. If you have prepared as above, the expressions you are looking for will jump out at you.

Close reading: understanding a text in detail

Do not just start reading. A few simple steps will help you to understand the text better, without getting lost in the details.

Step 1: Your first step should be to gain a basic understanding of what the text is about (see 'Skimming' above). It will be easier to understand difficult words or phrases when you understand the general context. It is helpful to quickly note down the most important points. After skimming the text 'The Social Impact of Technology' on page 66/67, for example, you could write: *The text seems to be about how computers and the Internet affect our society. It gives an overview of how technology has changed our lives and how it may change them in the future. The tone is mostly quite serious.*

Step 2: Be aware of the structure of the text. Where is the introduction? Which part contains the main information and how is it set out (sub-headings, paragraphs, etc.)? Pay attention to expressions like *only, but while, that's why, while, however,* etc., which the author uses to organise his or her arguments.

Step 3: Now read the text more carefully. Note down the key points (in the text on page 66/67, for example: *free exchange of information; technological revolution; direct trade with consumers; greater wealth for shareholders, directors and owners,* etc.). When reading a text for the first time, only look a word up in a dictionary if the meaning of the whole sentence is dependent on it. The essential meaning can often be worked out from the context.

Step 4: Make notes on the content of the text in a structured form, for instance in a mind map or a list (of themes or of advantages and disadvantages). Add phrases that will be helpful later when you write about the content of the text in your own words. Now look up the most important vocabulary.

► Note Making, p. 190
► Mind Mapping, p. 191
► Dealing with Unknown Words, p. 186

Understanding Headlines

Understanding English headlines can sometimes be challenging, but it will be necessary for you to develop the skill of understanding them quickly because there is such an immense volume of information in circulation nowadays. In headlines, there is often a lot of jargon and the absence of some words can make the grammatical structure hard to recognise. What will help you most is commanding a large and varied vocabulary. Understanding the following common structures will also help.

set + infinitive = ready, prepared, or likely
China's growth ***looks set to continue*** (= **looks like it will continue**)
Burma ***set to resume human*** *rights dialogue* (= Burma **is ready to begin** talking about human rights again)

infinitive with *to* as a future form = similar to *set* + infinitive
Washington ***to pressure*** *Beijing on currency* (= the USA **is expected to put pressure on** China regarding its currency)
Poor girl students ***to get*** *bicycles in Maharashtra* (= **it is planned that** poor female students **will receive** bicycles)

subject + *thought/said/reported* + infinitive with *to*
Bin Laden ***said to be hiding out*** *in Pakistan* (= someone **has said** that Bin Laden **is hiding out** in Pakistan)
Indonesian mosque ***thought to have helped*** *Al Qaeda* (= some people **think** an Indonesian mosque **has helped** Al Qaeda)

simple present instead of present progressive
Exports surge ***fuels*** *China growth* (= A surge in exports **is fuelling** the growth of China)

Dealing with Unknown Words

When you come across a word you don't know, always ask yourself whether it is really necessary to understand the word in order to understand the overall message of the text. Looking up words takes time and often doesn't help you to understand the most important points.

Working out the meaning from the context

- A word that you don't know could be related to another word that you already know (derivations like *aggressor* and *aggressive*, for example). Or the word may be made up of a word stem that you know and a word part that will help you to work out the meaning of the word *(formal –* ***in****formal, clockwise –* ***anti****clockwise, change – change****able****, stupid – stupid****ity****)*. Some words are also similar to German words (compare *initial* and "Initialen" or *potential* and "potenziell").
- If you are still not sure, looking at the word in the context of the sentence can give you more information. First think about what part of speech you are dealing with. Are you looking for a noun? What does the noun you are looking for represent – a building? A person? If you're looking for an adjective, is it one which describes an exact situation or someone's character?
  Look at the following sentences and try to work out the meanings of the words in bold from the context:
  Business is very bad at the moment and we don't expect it to ***rally*** *for at least a year. All the signals are very* ***inauspicious****, I'm afraid.*

Using a monolingual dictionary

Get to know your dictionary so that you understand the symbols, abbreviations and phonetic transcriptions and can use the reference sections, which are usually found at the front and back of the dictionary or on additional pages. Look at the following example of a typical entry in a dictionary.

uncountable noun

North American English = regional variant

part of speech

first meaning

reference to another entry

second meaning

countable noun

idiom = idiomatic expression

Synonym

verb/noun + 'to' infinitive = compound expression in which the verb is followed by 'to'+ infinitive

verb/noun = compound expression with verb and noun

alarm /ə'lɑːm; *NamE* ə'lɑːrm/ *noun, verb*
■ *noun* **1** [U] fear and anxiety that sb feels when sth dangerous or unpleasant might happen: *'What have you done? Ellie cried in alarm.* ◇ *I felt a growing sense of alarm when he did not return that night.* ◇ *The doctor said there was no cause for alarm.* ⇨ note at FEAR **2** [C, usually sing.] a loud noise or a signal that warns people of danger or of a problem: *She decided to* ***sound the alarm*** (= warn people that the situation was dangerous). ◇ *I hammered on all the doors to* ***raise the alarm***. – see also FALSE ALARM **3** [C] a device that warns people of a particular danger: *a* ***burglar/fire/smoke alarm.*** ◇ *The cat* ***set off the alarm*** (= made it start ringing). ◇ *A car* ***alarm went off*** *in the middle of the night* (= started ringing). **4** = ALARM CLOCK: *The* ***alarm went off*** *at 7 o'clock.* IDM **a'larm bells ring / start ringing** if you say that **alarm bells are ringing**, you mean that people are starting to feel worried and suspicious
■ *verb* **1** to make sb anxious or afraid SYN WORRY: [VN] *The captain knew there was an engine fault but didn't want to alarm the passengers.* [also VN **to** inf] ⇨ note at FRIGHTEN **2** [VN] to fit sth such as a door with a device that warns people when sb is trying to enter illegally

- Note down all the words that you want to look up and then look them all up, one after another.
- Do not read the whole entry, just look for the particular part of speech you need. For example, if you are looking for *alarm* as a verb, you can ignore the first part of the entry above. Then you must read the relevant section and the example sentences carefully, as they will help you to tell which meaning applies in which contexts.
- Look at the entries before and after your word to get an idea of the word field.
- Note down the right meaning so that you don't forget it again.

Learning new vocabulary

There are various ways of learning new words – find out which method is best for you. But whichever method you use, don't forget: words are easier to remember if you don't just write down the key word, but also expressions, synonyms, opposites, related words, examples and possibly even notes on pronunciation. Compound expressions are particularly important. These include phrasal verbs, such as *set about* and *put off*. Your notes for the word *pay*, for example, might look like this:

pay (noun)	–	Bezahlung, Gehalt, Lohn
payslip	–	Gehaltsabrechnung
pay day	–	Zahltag
pay-off	–	Abfindung
pay (verb)	–	zahlen
pay for sth	–	etw bezahlen
pay off	–	auszahlen
pay as you go (phone)	–	Prepaid(-Handy)

Of course you don't need to write out entire dictionary entries straight away. But think about which derivations of the word you have seen before, or which compound expressions you have found it in. Leave space so that you can add to your entry later – that way your entries can 'grow' as you learn more words.

Index cards: You will need index cards and an index card box divided into sections. Write the English word and any related comments on one side of the card and the meaning in German on the other side. When you think you know a word, move it from the first section to the second section. Look at the cards in the second section at intervals. Put the ones you know in the third section and look at these cards less often. If you don't know a word, put it back in the first section and look at these words as often as possible.

Vocabulary book: You can note down all the new vocabulary that you come across in lessons in a vocabulary book. Use an exercise book that has two columns on each page so that you can easily cover up one of the columns. Make learning vocabulary more interesting by choosing a page at random and learning the words on it, or by learning German-English instead of English-German from time to time.

Word families: Make lists of word families – that way you not only learn the new word, but also its derivations (*approve – approval – approving – disapprove – disapproval*).

▸ Mind Mapping, p. 191

Word fields: The best way to learn word families (groups of words related to a particular topic) is to draw mind maps (networks of words). This method is very good for learning words on a specific topic for a class test. Write the key word in the centre and the general terms for the most important aspects of the topic around it. Then write related words around each general term.

Vocabulary trainer: If you like learning on the computer, then the *Crossover* vocabulary trainer is the best solution. Go to www.phase-6.de, select 'Cornelsen' and then 'Crossover 2'. There you will find a vocabulary trainer that has been specially developed for this book. You will have to pay for it but it will be useful tool when preparing for your final exam.

Extra exercises: The 'Vocabulary Practice Book' that is available for *Crossover 2* offers the key topic vocabulary from the student's book plus a variety of exercises. Take it with you on a bus or do an exercise in the commercial break of a film – even five minutes a day is useful practice.

Practising Listening Skills

In order to understand spoken English, for example in discussions, telephone conversations, interviews, radio and television programmes, etc., you should prepare yourself well for the particular situation. Often the accents, background noises and other disturbances will make it hard to understand what is being said, so you have to concentrate on what is most important. Use the methods described below when you do the listening exercises in *Crossover 2*. This will help you to deal with difficult listening texts.

Before you listen

- Read carefully to find out exactly what you are expected to do. Make use of anything which is there to help you – pictures, headings, etc.
- If possible, write down key words, and if you have enough time, try to remember some important word fields related to the topic.

While you are listening

- Firstly listen to the entire listening text to understand what it's about. Don't make any notes during this first listening.
- Listen again, and only listen for the information which is important for the exercise. Don't concentrate on the individual words and expressions which you don't understand.
- Pay attention to expressions which make the logical train of thought clearer, such as *however, in my view, in conclusion* and so on. They will help you to follow the central theme of the text.
- Write the information down in note form, never in full sentences. A table or framework can help you to organise your notes. Here is an example framework for notes on a text about the changing roles of men and women in our society:

	changed role	reasons	consequences
men			
women			

- Use symbols, abbreviations and short forms of words to save time when making notes:

▶ Note Making, p. 190

Symbols		Abbreviations		Short forms	
=	*the same as*	e.g.	*for example*	govt	*government*
≠	*not the same as*	km	*kilometres*	impt!	*important*
+	*and*	w., w/o	*with, without*	kids	*children*

After you listen

- Write out the main points as quickly as possible using your notes – you might not be able to read all your symbols or understand your abbreviations later on.
- Try to answer every question. If there are some details that you haven't understood, then make a guess based on what you have understood.

There are plenty of useful websites where you can listen to radio broadcasts to practise your listening skills. The best place to find British English is www.bbc.co.uk where you can choose programmes from a huge radio archive. If you prefer to listen to American programmes, go to www.npr.org, the National Public Radio website, where you can get access to a similarly comprehensive radio archive.

Doing Research on the Internet

The Internet offers an enormous amount of resources to help you with your research (for an essay or a presentation, for example), but it is important to know where and how to search.

Step 1: Note down exactly what you're looking for, and think of appropriate terms you could search for. Without these guidelines (which should be as specific as possible), your search could easily turn into simply surfing the net.

Step 2: Think about where you want to begin your search. It is a good idea to build up a list of English online resources over time, such as online encyclopedias (like www.encyclopedia.com), online dictionaries (for example www.leo.org), news sites (for example www.bbc.co.uk), science and technology sites (such as www.howstuffworks.com).

Step 3: Find the best search engine and type in a search term which is as specific as possible.

Step 4: Make sure that you only use reliable sources. Generally speaking the Internet is not particularly reliable because every user is free to put whatever information they want online. Always check who is responsible for the content of a website, and don't just rely on the first information you find.

► Skimming, p. 184

Step 5: Before you read an entire article sentence by sentence, just skim through it. If only one or two sections are relevant to your topic, then just look at them and ignore the rest of the article.

► Note Making, p. 190

Step 6: Instead of copying entire sections of text into your document, note down the key points. Save the webpage in your favourites if you want to come back to it later or use material or quotations from it.

PRODUCTION: WRITING AND SPEAKING

Note Making

It is a good idea to make notes when you are reading or listening to a text. This makes it easier to remember the information later on.

When reading

At first glance it seems fairly easy to make notes when you read a text. However, many people find it difficult to make really short meaningful notes. Often people worry so much about leaving out something important that they copy out whole sentences from the original text. This not only wastes time, but also makes it harder to write about the text using your own words later on.

Here are some tips to avoid this:

- Give your notes a heading that makes the topic clear, for example *Effects of genetic engineering on the environment.*
- Go through the text and look for the most important aspects of the topic, which you can use as sub-headings. Remember to leave enough space under each heading for your notes.
- Look out for signals such as emphasis and repetition, as well as expressive adjectives like *huge, incredible, devastating,* etc. These show what the author considers important.
- Only write short notes, not full sentences.
- Make the logical development of the information clear, for example by writing certain points in a list (in a particular order), writing about each aspect in a separate section, or underlining the most important terms.
- Check that you have included all the necessary information. Don't forget that the important points are often scattered throughout the whole text.

► Scanning, p. 185

When listening

In this situation it can be difficult to make notes because you often have to write very quickly. You must concentrate on the essential points and use abbreviations so that you have more time to follow the main theme of the listening text. For tips on this, look at the section on 'Practising listening skills'.

▶ Practising Listening Skills, p. 188

Mind Mapping

A mind map is a good way to organise expressions and information clearly in a diagram with a key term in the centre. It is particularly suitable for learning vocabulary, brainstorming, collecting ideas and preparing essays or presentations.

Materials: a large sheet of paper (e.g. A3), coloured pencils

Step 1: Write the key term (if you are working on word fields) or the topic (if you are collecting ideas) in large clear letters in the centre.

Step 2: Write the most important terms around the key term. Join them to the key term with 'branches'.

Step 3: Following the same principle, add further words and ideas to each thematic section. The more specific or specialised the terms, the smaller the number of 'branches'. In other words, the route from the topic or key term leads from the general to the specific. You can add new ideas anywhere at any time.

Step 4: Use colourful markings and symbols to make important terms stand out.

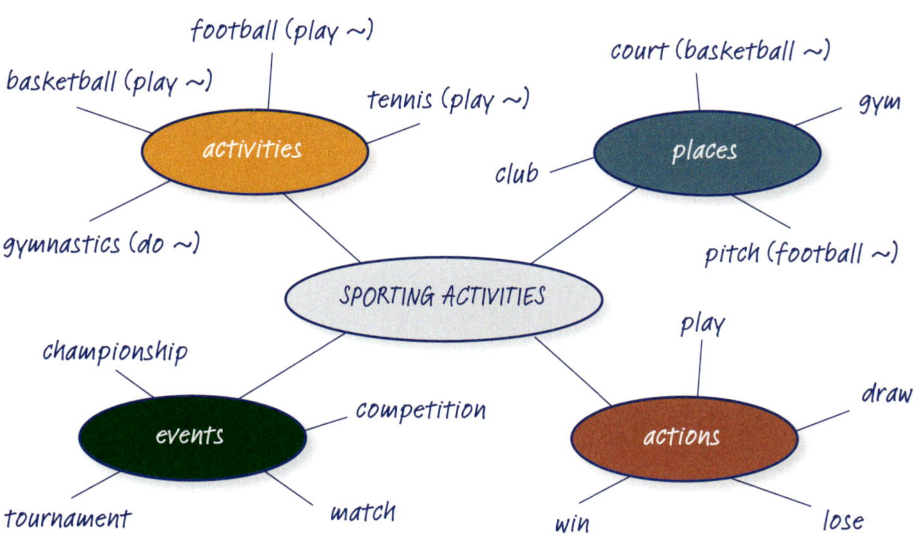

Answering Comprehension Questions

Before you start writing, make sure that you have understood the whole text. (Not every word is important – think about whether you have understood the meaning of a sentence, not every word in it.) Always read the introduction to an exercise carefully to understand exactly what sort of answer is required – a common mistake is to write something which does not answer the question properly. Also be careful not to 'waste' information in one answer which could be necessary for answering a different question.

▸ Note Making, p. 190

- If you are not allowed to mark anything in the book, make notes in the form of short points and lists, instead of writing out whole sentences from the text. In class tests and exams you should mark the most important parts of the text. It is best to mark everything that is important for one question with one colour, and then use a different colour for the next question.
- Use the same verb tense in your answer as was used in the question.
- Replace terms from the text with synonyms and rewrite sentences as much as possible, for example, *recently – in recent years; violent crime – crime involving violence; think – believe; to a great extent – greatly; when she was a child – in her childhood* and so on.
- Look for signals in the text such as emphasis and repetition, as well as meaningful adjectives or adverbs like *absolutely, unbelievably, amazing.* These show what the author considers important.
- Don't try to bring your own opinion into your answer if the question does not ask for it.

Useful phrases for writing about a text
– *According to the author, …* – *The article goes on to say that …* – *The text says that …*
– *The author makes the point that …*

Quoting from the text

If there is one particularly important statement that you would really like to take from the text in order to emphasise a point, don't simply copy the words. Instead you should show you are aware that you are quoting from the text and use language to make this clear. Do not use more than one quotation in your answer.

Building quotations into your answer
- *To quote the author, …*
- *The problem discussed in the article is that teenagers are becoming 'increasingly fixated with their weight.'*
- *Sandra Goodwin describes it as 'disappointing and frustrating' that the figures are so high.*
- *'It is disappointing,' Martin Bloomberg is quoted as saying, 'that … .'*

How to Deal with Instructions (*Operatoren*)

You will often be asked questions about the text. Sometimes, however, you will be given specific instructions that tell you what to do. These instructions are called *Operatoren*. There are many different instructions, so it is important to know what type of task they demand.

Keep the following general tips in mind when dealing with *Operatoren*:

- Always make sure you **don't mention the same aspects in different tasks**. It can be helpful to mark passages of the text in different colours, according to the tasks.
- Make sure your answers have a clear structure, not only by using phrases marking the **introduction**, the **main part** and the **conclusion**, but also by starting a new paragraph when you begin the next section.
- Always **use your own words** when you refer to the text. You can do this by using synonyms, opposites, changing word forms or using a different sentence structure.
- If you want to give examples from the text, **avoid the phrase 'and so on'**. Instead, look for other examples, or use the singular *(To give an example, …)*.

▸ Improving Your Writing Skills, p. 197

1. Instructions asking about content

The following instructions call upon you to focus on the author's main ideas.

Instruction	German	What you have to do	Tips
Summarise	*zusammenfassen*	Write the main ideas in the text in a concise, short form and in your own words. Do not include examples or illustrations or your own personal opinion.	• See the section on writing a summary. ▸ Writing a Summary, p. 195
Outline	*darstellen*	Give a description of the main facts. You can divide the outline into main points and subordinate points.	• **Before you write:** collect your ideas in a flowchart (if the question is about a development or process) or a mind map (if the text is an argumentative one). ▸ Mind mapping, p. 191
Point out	*aufzeigen*	Refer to certain significant aspects/ ideas in the text to show their importance.	• **Before you write:** highlight the passages in the text with a marker pen.
Say what the text is about	*sagen, worum es im Text geht*	Retell the contents briefly and in your own words. What you write can be shorter and less detailed than a summary.	• **Before you write:** read the text through and then write short notes about the main ideas in the text. • **When you write:** use your own words by changing the sentence structure or finding synonyms. ▸ Note Making, p. 190

The following instructions are often used to check if you have understood the text properly. They ask you to look at the text (or individual passages) and give an account of certain aspects of it.

Instruction	German	What you have to do	Tips
Describe	*beschreiben*	Say what something is like by giving details about a person, situation or object.	• **Before you write:** collect all the aspects you want to mention in a mind map. ▸ Mind Mapping, p. 191 • **When you write:** use lots of adjectives so that the reader gets a clear picture. • **Language to know:** *In the following, I shall describe …*
Define	*bestimmen, umreißen, definieren*	Describe a situation, a problem, the meaning of a term, etc. exactly.	• **When you write:** be as concise as possible. State the term to be defined and to which class or group it belongs. State the special characteristics of the term.
Say/State/ Explain why … or **State the reasons for …**	*angeben/sagen/ erklären warum* *die Gründe angeben für …*	Explain why someone did something or why something happened.	• **Before you write:** list all the reasons on a piece of paper. • **Language to know:** *To state the reasons for …, one has to look at …;* *The text gives a number of reasons why …;* *because / as a result / therefore / consequently / for this reason*
Find evidence in the text to show …	*Belege im Text finden für …*	Look for facts, objects or signs to show that something is true.	• **Before you write:** highlight all the relevant passages in the text with a marker pen.

2. Instructions to compare or structure points from the text

The following instructions are very common in exams and require a very thorough answer.

Instruction	German	What you have to do	Tips
Compare	*vergleichen*	Point out the similarities and differences between two things/concepts/systems, etc.	• **Before you write:** make a table in two columns, comparing individual aspects. • **Language to know:** *On the one hand, … On the other hand, …; The first point the author makes about … is that … However, the text goes on to say that …; both of … / neither of …*
Name the similarities and differences between …	*die Ähnlichkeiten und Unterschiede benennen*		
Contrast	*gegenüberstellen*	Point out the differences between two things/concepts/systems, etc.	
Point out	*beschreiben*	Objectively state the advantages and disadvantages of something as they are presented in the text.	
Discuss the advantages and disadvantages of …	*die Vor- und Nachteile erörtern*		

3. Instructions to analyse the text

The following instructions require you to explain the explicit ideas contained in the text, but also to 'read between the lines' and explain implicit meanings.

► Writing an Essay, p. 196

Instruction	German	What you have to do	Tips
Analyse	*analysieren*	Describe and explain certain aspects in detail.	• **Before you write:** take extra care in the structure of your essay. Make an outline to plan what you wish to say in each paragraph. • **Language to know:** *This suggests … / This seems to suggest … / This implies …*
Describe and explain	*beschreiben und erklären*		
Examine	*untersuchen*		

The following instruction asks you to explain both explicit and implicit meanings, and also to evaluate them.

Interpret	*interpretieren*	Explain the deeper meaning or 'message' of a statement, a concept, a cartoon, etc. Use your background knowledge and give your own views.	• **Language to know:** *The author wishes to communicate …; The author's thesis is that …; … can be interpreted in the following manner.*

4. Instructions to comment on or discuss a point

The following instructions call upon you to argue an opinion of your own.

Instruction	German	What you have to do	Tips
Assess	*beurteilen*	Make a judgement after thinking carefully about something, giving evidence to support your opinion.	• **When you write:** argue your case but always mention the counter-argument to show you understand it. • **Language to know:** phrases to express your opinion, e.g. *it seems to me that …; considering these arguments; I agree that …*
Evaluate	*einschätzen, bewerten*		
Comment on	*Stellung nehmen zu*		

► Writing a Comment, p. 195

The following instruction requires you to be objective.

Discuss	*erörtern*	Weigh up both sides of an issue, giving reasons for and against.	• **Before you write:** remember that *discuss* means you have to consider both sides of an issue. It is useful to structure your ideas first, e.g. in a mind map or an outline. • **Language to know:** *On the one hand, … On the other hand, …;* *While it is true that …, one can also say that …*

► Mind Mapping, p. 191
► Writing an Essay, p. 196

Writing a Comment

When you write a comment, you are expected to give your opinion on a particular topic. It is important that you justify your opinion and use examples to illustrate it.

Step 1: Make sure you know exactly what you have to write about. Read through the introduction to the exercise several times.

Step 2: Make notes. Organise your points clearly, for example in a mind map, list or table.

► Note Making, p. 190
► Mind Mapping, p. 191

Step 3: Write an introductory sentence which should refer to the question.

Step 4: Deal with each argument in one paragraph. If you are writing about arguments for and against something, then you can discuss all the arguments for and then all the arguments against. Make your line of argument clear by using structural words; look at the list on the cover flap at the back of this book *(Language for Writing)*.

Step 5: Emphasise the point of your argument with a concise concluding sentence.

Introducing a comment
- *In the following I shall deal with the the problem/subject/issue of …*
- *I would like to discuss …*
- *I intend to present arguments in favour of … and against …*

Concluding a comment
- *All in all, I think it can be said that …*
- *In conclusion, I would like to say that …*
- *I would like to conclude by saying that …*

Writing a Summary

The ability to summarise a text that you have read is not only important for fully understanding the text. It is also helpful for other situations where you need to reduce a text to its essential information. Such situations include answering comprehension questions or doing mediation exercises, for example.

Step 1: Read the text as many times as possible until you are sure that you have understood everything.

► Close Reading, p. 185

Step 2: Describe what the text is about in one or two introductory sentences, for example: *This article is about genetic modification. It deals with the advantages it could bring to farming, especially in under-developed countries.*

Step 3: Make sure you know which information from the text is important to the reader by answering *Wh*-questions: *Who? What? When? Where? Why?*, e.g.
- *Who: Hispanic immigrants in the US*
- *What: prevented from crossing the border by a wall*

▸ Note Making, p. 190

Step 4: Make notes in the form of short points.

Step 5: Write your summary, taking the following points into consideration:
- Leave out anything inessential. This includes examples, detailed lists, names, quotations, etc.
- Use your own words as far as possible.
- Don't give your own opinion on the text. Personal opinions do not generally belong in a summary.
- Try to rewrite quotations using indirect speech.
- Join the ideas, keeping to the order in the text.
- Language to know: *According to the author, ...; The author says/believes that ...*

▸ Reported Speech, p. 211

Step 6: Check your writing for mistakes and make sure that you have covered all the important aspects of the text.

Writing an Essay

Towards the end of your school life, in your final exam and also later, at university for example, you will always have to write essays on various topics. It is a good idea to adopt some rules right from the start in order to make the process itself as automatic as possible so that you can concentrate on the content of the essay. This is particularly important when there is a time limit – as in your final exam at school.

Step 1: Think clearly about the topic. Which aspects should be mentioned in your essay and which should not?

▸ Note Making, p. 190
▸ Mind Mapping, p. 191

Step 2: Brainstorm – write down all the ideas that come into your head when you think about the topic. It is important to arrange these ideas in a structured way so that you don't get lost in a desert of random scribbles. Lists or mind maps are useful for structuring ideas.

Step 3: Work out how you are going to structure your essay. You could use a mind map, for example, and number it to make the order of the ideas clear. Another possibility is to write an **outline** like this:

Should old towns be closed to private vehicles?

Introduction: Outline of the topic
Main section: Looking at the topic in detail, e.g.:

1. *Disadvantages for business*
   1.1 *Job losses*
      1.1.1 *retail trade*
      1.1.2 *fewer tourists*
         1.1.2.1 *less money for tourist attractions*
         1.1.2.2 *job losses in cafés, etc.*
   1.2 *What about town centre residents, delivery vehicles, etc.?*
2. *Advantages, positive effects on town and people*

...

Conclusion: Summary of points, summing up of argument

Step 4: Write your essay. Leave room for corrections, changes or additions. It is important that you make your line of argument clear by using words that give structure to your writing – look at the list on the cover flap at the back of the book (*Language for Writing*) and the section 'Improving Your Writing Skills' below.

Step 5: Check your draft for the following:

- **Spelling mistakes** (for example, check words that sound the same, like *there/their, meet/meat*)
- **Grammatical mistakes** (for example, make sure all the verbs are in the right tense; check that all regular adverbs end in *-ly*)
- **Choice of words** (for example, check for repetitions; check for *false friends* like "aktuell" ≠ *actual*, "eventuell" ≠ *eventual*, "spenden" ≠ *spend*)
- **Sentence structure** (for example, check that there are no incomplete answers beginning with *Because*)
- **Logical line of argument** (for example, make sure the expressions you have used are clear; make sure you have included structural expressions such as *However, On the other hand, In addition, As a result,* etc.)

Improving Your Writing Skills

Here are some ideas for improving your writing skills.

1. Connecting sentences

It is easy to write a simple English sentence and you are less likely to make mistakes. To improve your style, however, it is necessary to combine simple sentences to make more complex sentences. This can be done by using subordinate sentences.

Examples:

a Nuclear energy does not harm the environment. It is cheap to produce.
→ *Nuclear energy, which is cheap to produce, does not harm the environment.*

b He is overweight. He feels unhappy about his appearance.
→ *He is unhappy about his appearance because he is overweight.*

c He was feeling ill but he went to school.
→ *Although he was feeling ill, he went to school.*

d In the foreground we see a man. He is spraying a corn field with chemical fertiliser.
→ *In the foreground we see a man spraying a corn field with chemical fertiliser.*

2. Connecting arguments and making transitions

When you outline a new argument, start a new paragraph or conclude your composition, it is good style to use connectors.

Examples:

To list: *besides, equally important, first (second, etc.), further, furthermore, in addition, in the first place, moreover*

To give examples: *for example, for instance, in fact, to illustrate*

To compare: *likewise, similarly*

To contrast: *although, and yet, despite, even though, however, in contrast, in spite of, nevertheless, on the contrary, on the other hand*

To summarise or conclude: *all in all, in conclusion, in other words, in short, in summary, on the whole, therefore, to sum up*

To show your argument is logical: *accordingly, as a result, because, consequently, for this reason, hence, if, otherwise, since, so, then, therefore, thus*

See also *Language for Writing* on the back cover flap of the book.

3. Varying your vocabulary

▶ Learning New Vocabulary, p. 187

With a large vocabulary you will be able to express yourself in a more interesting way. Read the section 'Learning new vocabulary' for tips on how to learn new words. Here are some ideas on how to vary the vocabulary you use when you write.

a Try to use more interesting and specific verbs instead of the usual ones:

say	mention, remark, state, argue, express, claim
get	come by, come into possession of, obtain, receive
use	employ, make use of
do	carry out, perform
feel	realise, consider, experience
make	build, assemble, put together, manufacture, produce
think	believe, be of the opinion, imagine, suppose
have	possess, comprise, consist of, contain, include, be made up of
see	notice, observe, recognise, regard, understand, realise
like	be fond of (+ gerund), be keen on (+ gerund), cherish, enjoy
show	demonstrate, reveal, prove
be about (text, cartoon)	deal with, concern, have to do with, discuss, explore

b When describing things use a greater variety of adjectives:

nice	agreeable, charming, delightful, enjoyable, pleasant
beautiful	attractive, good-looking, gorgeous, lovely, stunning
not good	awful, disgusting, dreadful, horrible, terrible, unpleasant
very good	great, magnificent, outstanding, superb, wonderful
important	significant, major, essential, notable
interesting	absorbing, fascinating, gripping, engaging, thought-provoking
main	principal, major, foremost
clear	plain, explicit, evident
unclear	ambiguous, uncertain, in doubt

c Other important words that tend to be used too frequently:

part (of a text)	passage, paragraph, section
mainly	mostly, on the whole, to a large extent, predominantly
very	extremely, highly, remarkably, really
theme	topic, subject
about	approximately, around, roughly

4. Using typical English grammar

a The gerund

Try to use the gerund as often as possible. Here are some examples of words and expressions which are followed by the gerund and automatically sound good in compositions.

begin	He began working.
love	I love watching fantasy films.
hate	She hates learning vocabulary.
prefer	I prefer watching love stories.
to be fun	It's fun working in the disco.
to be worth	The film is worth seeing.
by	He improved his English by learning ten new words every day.
without	He passed his exam without working very hard.

▶ The Gerund, p. 215

See 'The Gerund' on page 215 for further examples.

b Participle constructions

English, especially written English, is full of sentences shortened by a participle. This automatically sounds more elegant. For foreign students, using the participle to shorten sentences is not always easy, but shortening relative sentences is one of the easier structures. Using the *-ing* form after *before* and *after* also improves style.

Examples:

After he saw the ad on TV, she ...	→ *After seeing the ad on TV, she ...*
Before he went to school, she ...	→ *Before going to school, she ...*
The goods which were advertised were ...	→ *The goods advertised were ...*
One ad which showed toys was ...	→ *One ad showing toys was ...*

See 'Participle constructions' on page 220.

► Participle Constructions, p. 220

Interpreting Pictures and Cartoons

It is a good idea to learn some phrases for describing and interpreting pictures and cartoons. Make sure you concentrate on the essential message of the picture rather than getting lost in the details. Keep to the following steps in order to structure your answer in a sensible way.

Step 1: **Describing the picture.** Look at all aspects of the picture but only describe the elements which are important for the picture's message.
Use the present progressive when you describe the content of the picture – unless you are using a verb that does not usually appear in this tense. For example, if you were writing about the cartoon below you could write:
The cartoon shows two men standing outside an igloo. The igloos are melting. The men are thinking about ... But be careful: the present progressive is only used for the situations and actions shown in the cartoon and not for verbs which you use to describe and interpret the picture (*The cartoon* ***shows/describes*** *... It* ***seems*** *as if climate change ...*).

► Present Progressive, p. 206

"*Now* do you believe in climate change?"

Step 2: **Interpreting the picture.** If you don't think the picture says much then you can mention this in your interpretation by referring to it as *ambiguous* or *unclear.*

Step 3: **Commenting on the picture.** Sum up the central message of the picture and/or make a comment on it, for example by saying how much of an effect you think the picture has.

Step 4: **Comparing the picture with the text** (when the task requires this). Go back to the text and look for sections which are significant in relation to the picture. State whether you think the picture supports the message of the text or contradicts it.

1. **Describing the picture**
- *The cartoon shows / appears to show …*
- *The scene depicts/shows …*
- *In the foreground/background/centre there is …*
- *The speech bubble/thought bubble/caption/label says that …*
- *On the left/right you can see …*
- *The … looks as if …*
- *The person on the left appears to … / It seems as if the person …*
- *He/She is wearing/holding …*

2. **Interpreting the picture**
- *The picture/cartoon deals with the recent discussion of …*
- *I think the cartoonist's/artist's/photographer's use of irony/exaggeration is intended to create … / is aimed at making … / conveys …*
- *The person in the centre represents/symbolises/shows …*
- *This indicates/shows/reveals that …*
- *The … represents / is in fact / stands for …*
- *The cartoonist/artist/photographer criticises / wants to say / express the idea that …*
- *Because the foreground/background is …, the impression is given that …*
- *From the way the people are depicted, it is obvious that …*
- *The point of the cartoon seems to be that …*

3. **Commenting on the picture**
- *I think the cartoon is quite right / makes a fair point.*
- *I agree with the cartoonist/artist, but …*
- *In my opinion, the cartoonist is partly right / exaggerates a little / a lot.*
- *Because of …, the picture touches me / leaves me cold.*
- *I think the … is a symbol of …*
- *The … helps to create a … atmosphere, which forces you to / has the effect of …*

4. **Comparing the picture with the text**
- *While the text says that …, the cartoon/picture shows / makes the point that …*
- *In the text we found out that …*
- *The cartoon/picture illustrates the facts/information in the text in the following way.*
- *The cartoon/picture gives a completely different opinion about the information in the text.*

Interpreting Graphs, Diagrams and Tables

As in this case of cartoons, it is useful to learn a number of set phrases for describing and interpreting graphs, diagrams and tables. Follow these steps to structure your answers well:

Step 1: **Describing the diagram.** This does not mean listing all the details but describing what the diagram shows and what sort of information is represented.

Step 2: **Summarising the trends, developments or levels shown.** What conclusions can be drawn from the data? Is it possible to give an overall summary of the results?

Step 3: **Comparing the diagram with the text** (when the task requires this). Go back to the text and look for sections which are significant in relation to the diagram. State whether you think the diagram supports the message of the text or contradicts it.

Types of diagrams

Table

	USA	UK
1995	495	105
2005	718	85

Graph, line graph

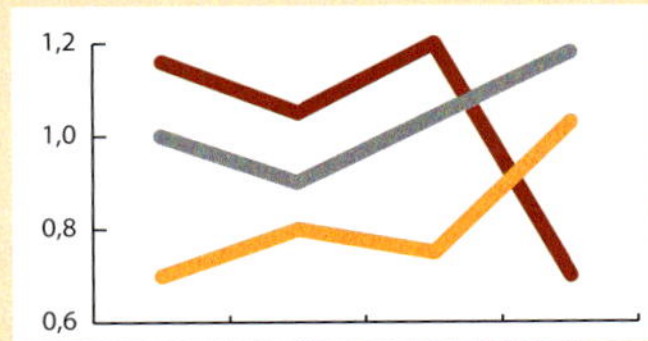

Bar chart

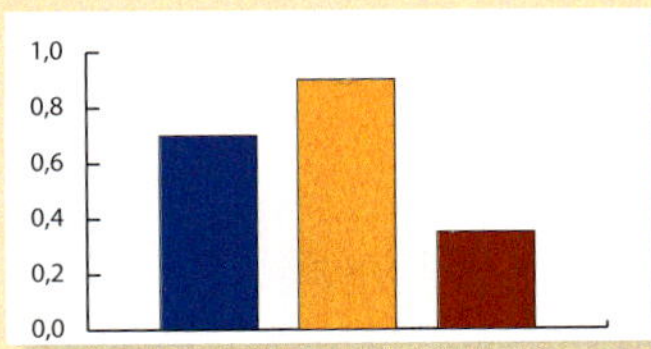

Pie chart

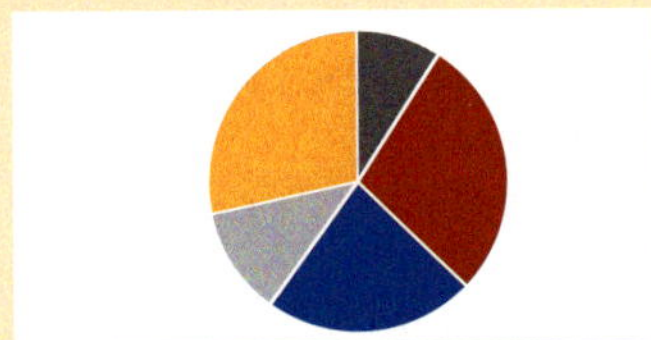

Talking about values and amounts

- *more / less than ...*
- *no less than ...*
- *eighty-five per cent (said that ...)*
- *On the other hand, almost ...*

Talking about proportions, shares and percentages

- *(over) half of ...*
- *more / less than one third / quarter of ...*
- *the (vast) majority of ...*
- *a mere third of ...*
- *to make up / comprise half of ...*

Talking about developments and trends

- *a huge/sharp increase/decrease*
- *a small / slight rise*
- *levels out, remains constant*
- *drastically, gradually, sharply, steadily*
- *rises/increases, hits a maximum*
- *drops/decreases/falls/plunges*
- *over a period of ...*
- *between 2000 and 2010*

Comparing the information in a diagram with a text

- *While the text says that ..., the diagram shows that ...*
- *The graph illustrates the facts/information in the text in the following way.*
- *The diagram gives a completely different opinion about the information in the text.*

Giving a Presentation

The ability to give a presentation effectively in front of an audience is important in the world of work and also, increasingly, at school. It is not just the content of a presentation that is important but also how clearly you present that content. This means structuring your talk so that it is easy to understand, making a varied and interesting presentation, and illustrating your points in a lively way.

Because most people in your audience *need* some visual stimulation in order to benefit from your presentation, you will most definitely want to write some key words and figures on the board. Plan how you want the board to look when your presentation is finished, and take time during your presentation to pause and write neatly. If possible, show photos related to your topic as this is sure to make an impact on your audience.

For tips on giving a presentation with multimedia equipment, see Topic 4 'World of work' on page 122/23.

Before the presentation

Step 1: Prepare your topic thoroughly and make notes in English.

Step 2: Check that your notes are correct in terms of language and that you can pronounce all the words correctly. You can find the pronunciation in a dictionary or listen to examples of how to pronounce words in online dictionaries or on dictionary CD-ROMs.

Step 3: Think about whether you could make your presentation livelier and more interesting by adding anecdotes, visual materials, audio materials, etc.

Step 4: Organise all the materials you need (OHP, flipchart, etc.).

Step 5: Practise giving the presentation, ideally in front of a small audience.

During the presentation

Step 1: Don't start analysing your topic straight away. Begin by giving a short overview of your presentation.

Step 2: Make it easier for your audience to follow the presentation. Express yourself clearly, use short sentences and speak slowly.

Step 3: The audience is more likely to stay interested if you make your presentation as varied as possible. Use visual material from time to time (OHP, flipchart, etc.) and prepare handouts. If you are using slides, keep them simple and clear, rather than overloading them with information.

Step 4: Think about your body language, face the audience, make eye contact with them, speak slowly and clearly, and use gestures to make what you are saying clearer.

Step 5: Sum up the most important points at the end of your presentation. Thank the audience for their attention and encourage them to ask questions.

Starting your presentation

Good morning/afternoon, my name is …
Today I am going to talk about …
The subject of my talk is …
If I am not speaking clearly enough, please say so.
Can you see the overhead projector/chart/ … ?

Introducing the main points

I'd like to begin by saying/showing …
I want to start by explaining … / saying something about …
As shown in the cartoon/picture/graph, …
The graph/cartoon, etc. demonstrates …
I would like to give an example …

Finishing your presentation

In conclusion, I would like to …
I would like to finish by saying …
Finally, …
Thank you very much for your attention.
If you have any questions, I would be pleased to answer them.

INTERACTION

Group Discussions

Whether you are taking part in a group discussion, a debate or a role-play, get the most out of it by thinking about the following points.

- Learn the phrases on the cover flap at the back of the book *(Language for Discussion)*. Use them in your lessons. The phrases will help you to express yourself clearly and logically.
- Think about the content of what you are going to say by preparing some bullet points related to individual aspects of the topic and noting down key terms in English.
- If there is time, prepare a few questions/answers on the topic.
- Always stay calm and think before you speak.
- Keep to the topic.
- Be responsive to your discussion partners and make eye contact.
- Join in, don't just sit back and listen. Group work is a great opportunity to speak freely.

Always indicate your wish to speak spontaneously and use plenty of expressions which show interest, surprise, scepticism, etc. This makes the discussion much livelier.

Showing that you would like to speak
- *Can I just say that …*
- *Well, if you ask me …*

Bringing someone else into the discussion
- *What do you think, Svenja?*

Expressing understanding, surprise, etc.

Ach so. / Ah ja.	*I see. / Right. / Oh, right.*
Oh je!	*Oh dear!*
Echt?	*Really?*
Gut. / Okay.	*Fine.*
Alles klar.	*OK then.*
Das ist doch wohl nicht dein Ernst!	*You're kidding!*

Debating

In a debate, two groups discuss arguments for and against a particular topic. Debates usually have a formal structure. One or two people from each group are selected to present the two different sides of the argument; then others take turns to give their views. Elect a chairperson who decides who should speak next. At the end of a debate there might be a vote to see what everyone thinks about the topic after they have heard arguments on both sides.

Debating is not only a great opportunity to practise speaking English. It also teaches you to think critically, to respect other people's opinions and to tackle interesting and sometimes controversial issues.

Stating opinions, preferences
- *I'd like to say …*
- *I think …*
- *I honestly/strongly feel that …*
- *I'm convinced that …*
- *Without a doubt, …*
- *As far as I am concerned, …*
- *The way I see it, …*

Disagreeing
- *I don't think that …*
- *Don't you think that …*
- *Shouldn't we consider …*
- *But what about …*
- *Frankly, I doubt if …*
- *Let's face it, …*
- *The truth of the matter is …*
- *The problem with your point of view is …*

Giving reasons and offering explanations
- *To start with, …*
- *The reason why …*
- *That's why …*
- *For this reason, …*
- *Allowing for the fact that …, …*
- *When you consider that …*

MEDIATION

Mediation

Written mediation means conveying the general sense of a text in another language for someone who does not understand the original. When doing a mediation exercise, the important thing is to concentrate on the essential information, rather than to translate word for word. In a mediation exercise, specific details and stylistic subtleties are only of secondary importance.

Step 1: Read exactly **in what situation** the text must be summarised and **for whom**. The particular situation usually shows what the purpose of the mediation exercise is.

▸ Reading Difficult Texts, p. 184

Step 2: Read the whole text through without concentrating on individual words. Where possible, ignore vocabulary which you don't understand – often it is not essential for understanding the meaning of the text as a whole.

Step 3: Read the instruction again to find out exactly what you are supposed to do and in what form your answer should be written. If there are several questions, use different colours to mark sections of the text that are relevant to each question.

Step 4: Summarise the main points of the text. Express yourself clearly and comprehensibly. Simplify the language of the original text by concentrating on **what** is said, not **how** it is said.

Step 5: Read your answer through again and make sure that you have expressed the content of the original in a way that is appropriate and easy to understand.

Translation

In contrast to mediation exercises, every word of the original text is important for a translation. However, a different sentence structure often has to be found in German. The following constructions are particularly tricky. Translate the example sentences into German:

- **Participle constructions**
  The jobs done by women are often badly paid.
  Some people say that feminism has been a great success pointing to the progress in the last 30 years.
- **Constructions with gerunds**
  I avoided looking at her.
  She achieved her aims by working very hard.
- **Passive constructions**
  He was offered a good job.
  He is said to be rich.

The part of speech often has to be changed as well, e.g. *There is a need to … (Es ist notwendig, zu …)* or *She used to work in France (Früher arbeitete sie in Frankreich).* A further difficulty are small particles and expressions which are often different in English and German, e.g. *after all, as, as to, as for, at all, at least, however, neither … nor, not … either, not … until, unless.*

Step 1: Read through the text once quickly.

Step 2: Now read the text word for word and look up difficult words in a dictionary. Make sure that you have fully grasped how each sentence is structured (look at the list of tricky constructions above).

Step 3: Make a first draft of your translation with double-line spacing so that you can add corrections later.

Step 4: Before you write a final version, check your draft for
Mistakes in spelling and grammar (e.g. participles, gerunds, tenses)
Expression (e.g. sentences which are too close to the original English)
Clarity (e.g. sentences which are too long or complicated)
Completeness (e.g. words or phrases that have been left out).

GRAMMAR SUMMARY

The Simple Present

1 I **go** to the disco once a week.
2 We **live** in Bavaria.
3 Mr Brown **teaches** us English every day.
4 **I don't like** chocolate.
5 **Does** he **like** chocolate?

- Man gebraucht das **simple present** für regelmäßige, sich wiederholende Ereignisse oder Handlungen (1, 3) und für Dauerzustände (2, 4, 5).
- Mit Ausnahme der 3. Person Singular (*he, she, it*) hat das **simple present** dieselbe Form wie der Infinitiv (1, 2).
  ⚠ Die **3. Person Singular** endet auf *-(e)s* (3).
- Ist **kein Hilfsverb** im Satz vorhanden, werden **Verneinung** und **Fragen** mit der entsprechenden Form von *to do* gebildet (4, 5).

Das **simple present** wird häufig mit den folgenden **Zeitangaben** benutzt:

- *always, never, often, rarely, seldom, sometimes*
- *generally, mostly, normally, regularly, usually*
- *every day/week/month/…, every morning/afternoon/…*
- *on Mondays/Tuesdays/…, on weekdays*
- *in (the) summer/winter/…*
- *at Christmas/Easter, at weekends*

The Present Progressive

1 **I'm calling** to say that Ben's ill.
2 He**'s staying** in bed today.
3 The computer **isn't working.**
4 **Are** you **sleeping?**

- Man benutzt das **present progressive** (auch **present continuous** genannt) für Vorgänge oder Handlungen, die im Moment des Sprechens oder Schreibens passieren und noch nicht abgeschlossen sind (1, 3, 4).
- Es wird auch für vorübergehende Situationen gebraucht (2).
- Das **present progressive** wird mit dem Präsens von *to be* und der *-ing*-Form des Vollverbs gebildet.

- Da beim **present progressive** immer ein Hilfsverb vorhanden ist, wird die **Verneinung** mit *not/n't* gebildet (3).
- Fragen werden durch Umstellung gebildet (4).

Das **present progressive** wird oft mit den folgenden **Zeitangaben** benutzt:

at the moment, at present, now, this week/month

⚠ Diese Verben bilden normalerweise **keine progressive-Form**:

be, believe, doubt, feel (meinen), *hate, hear, imagine, know, like/dislike, love, mean, notice, prefer, realize, recognize, remember, see* (begreifen), *seem, suppose, think* (meinen), *understand, want, wish*

The Simple Past

1 We **wanted** to go to the USA last year.
2 She **went** on a school trip to London.
3 Jasmin **did not enjoy** her holiday in Rimini last summer.
4 Where **did** you **go** last year?

- Man benutzt das **simple past**, um über Vergangenes zu berichten.
- Das **simple past** wird auch gebraucht, wenn man sagen will, **wann** etwas geschehen ist (1, 3, 4).
- Bei **regelmäßigen** Verben wird das **simple past** durch das Anhängen von *-ed* an den Infinitiv gebildet (1).
  ⚠ Die unregelmäßigen Verben haben eine Sonderform (2), die man sich merken – auswendig lernen! – muss.
- Ist **kein Hilfsverb** im Satz vorhanden, bildet man die **Verneinung** und **Fragen** mit *did/didn't* (3, 4).

► Irregular Verbs (S. 242)

Das **simple past** wird häufig mit den folgenden **Zeitangaben** benutzt:

- *yesterday, the day before yesterday, the week/month/... before last*
- *last night/week/month/summer/December/Easter/...*
- *two/three/... hours/days/years/... ago*
- *in 2005 / in the 20th century ...*
- *at that time, in those days*

The Past Progressive

1 The teacher **was talking** to Heather **during the break**.
2 The tourists **were taking** photos when a lion (suddenly) **sprang** towards them.
3 I **wasn't doing** anything particular when he **came** around.
4 **Were** you **having** breakfast when I **phoned**?

- Wenn man ausdrücken möchte, dass eine Handlung zu einem bestimmten Zeitpunkt oder während eines bestimmten Zeitraumes in der Vergangenheit **im Gange** war, benutzt man das **past progressive** (auch **past continuous** genannt) (1).
- Das **past progressive** wird auch benutzt, um zu verdeutlichen, dass eine Handlung im Gange war, als ein neues Ereignis (plötzlich) eintrat (2, 3, 4).
- Man bildet das **past progressive** mit *was/were* und der *-ing*-Form des Vollverbs (1).
- Die **Verneinung** wird mit *was not / wasn't* bzw. *were not / weren't* gebildet (3).
- **Fragen** bildet man durch Umstellung (4). ⚠ Einige Verben haben **keine progressive-Form** (siehe die Liste unter **present progressive**).

► The Present Progressive (S. 206)

The Present Perfect

1 I**'ve bought** a new car.
2 I **haven't seen** the new film yet.
3 How long **have** you **had** it?
4 We**'ve had** snow **for** two weeks.
5 She**'s had** a cold **since** December.

- Wenn man ausdrücken will, dass etwas geschehen ist, ohne dass der genaue Zeitpunkt des Ereignisses wichtig ist, wird das **present perfect** benutzt (1, 2).
- Man gebraucht das **present perfect** auch, um zu sagen, seit wann oder wie lange ein Zustand oder eine Handlung schon andauert (3–5). Dafür wird sehr oft *for* bzw. *since* verwendet. (Im Deutschen steht dafür „seit" plus Gegenwart.)
- Das **present perfect** wird mit *have/has* und der 3. Form des Vollverbs gebildet (1, 4, 5).
- Die **Verneinung** wird durch das Einfügen von *not/ n't* unmittelbar nach *have/has* gebildet (2).
  ⚠ Die unregelmäßigen Verben haben eine Sonderform (1–5), die man auswendig lernen muss.
- **Fragen** bildet man durch Umstellung (3).

▸ Irregular Verbs (S. 242)

Das **present perfect** wird oft mit den folgenden Zeitangaben benutzt:

- *already, still (not), (not) yet*
- *(not) ever, just, lately, never, recently*
- *so far this week/month/…, till/until now*

The Present Perfect Progressive

1 I**'ve been learning** English since I was 10.
2 They**'ve not been speaking** to each other lately.
3 **Has** he **been singing** in the choir for long?

- Das **present perfect progressive** (auch **present perfect continuous**) benutzt man für Handlungen und Vorgänge, die in der Vergangenheit begonnen haben und zum Zeitpunkt des Sprechens bzw. Schreibens noch nicht beendet sind.
- Das **present perfect progressive** wird mit *have/has been* und der *-ing*-Form des Vollverbs gebildet (1).
- Die **Verneinung** bildet man durch das Einfügen von *not/n't* unmittelbar nach *have/has* (2).
- **Fragen** werden durch Umstellung gebildet (3).
  ⚠ Einige Verben haben normalerweise **keine progressive-Form** (siehe die Liste unter **present progressive**, S. 125).

▸ The Present Progressive (S. 206)

The Past Perfect

1 Laura couldn't pay. She **had forgotten** her purse.
2 Nina **had** already **left** the coffee bar by the time I arrived.
3 When I visited John in hospital, he **had been** there for ten days.

- Mit Hilfe des **past perfect** drückt man aus, dass zwei Handlungen oder Vorgänge in der Vergangenheit aufeinander folgten (1, 2). Die Handlung, die zeitlich voranging, steht im **past perfect**.

- Das **past perfect** wird auch verwendet, um auszudrücken, dass ein Zustand vor einem Zeitpunkt der Vergangenheit begann und zu diesem Zeitpunkt noch andauerte (3).
  ⚠ Wenn zwei oder mehrere kurze Handlungen in der Vergangenheit direkt aufeinander folgen, wird für alle Handlungen das **simple past** verwendet:
  *The cat **ran** out when Joanne **opened** the door.*

The Past Perfect Progressive

1 Rod **had been travelling** for three months when he ran out of money.
2 When I found Mary, I could see that she **had been crying**.

- Das **past perfect progressive** wird verwendet, wenn man ausdrücken will, dass eine Handlung oder ein Vorgang vor einem Zeitpunkt in der Vergangenheit begonnen hatte und bis (oder fast bis) zu diesem Zeitpunkt andauerte.

The Future

A will

1 In the future people **will use** public transport more often.
2 We can only hope that everyone **will accept** this shift in attitudes.
3 You've forgotten your purse? Don't worry. **I'll lend** you some money.
4 Ms Smith **will not be** at the meeting this afternoon.
5 I **won't come** either.
6 **Will** he **get** the job?

- Das **will future** benutzt man, um Vorhersagen zu machen (1) oder Vermutungen über die Zukunft zu äußern (2).
- Man benutzt es auch, wenn man sich spontan zu etwas entschließt, Angebote oder Versprechen macht (3).
- Das **will future** wird mit *will* + Infinitiv des Vollverbs gebildet. Es hat für alle Personen die gleiche Form (1–3).
- Die **Verneinung** bildet man durch das Einfügen von *not* unmittelbar nach *will* (4). Im gesprochenen Englisch sagt man häufig *won't* (5).
- **Fragen** werden durch Umstellung gebildet (6).

Das **will future** kommt häufig mit den folgenden einleitenden Verben und Ausdrücken vor:

– *believe, expect, forecast, hope, imagine, suppose, think*
– *It's clear/obvious that …, There's no doubt that …*

B going to

1 Look at these clouds. It**'s going to rain** soon.
2 This time **I'm going to get** good marks in the class test.
3 Tom **isn't going to work** at the club any more.
4 When **are** you **going to take** your driving test?

- Das **going to future** benutzt man für Ereignisse und Situationen, die nach Meinung des Sprechers bald eintreten werden (weil es bereits Anzeichen dafür gibt) (1).
- Es wird auch für Pläne und Absichten gebraucht (2).
- Das **going to future** wird mit *am/is/are* + *going to* + Infinitiv gebildet (1, 2).
- Die **Verneinung** bildet man durch das Einfügen von *not/n't* unmittelbar nach *am/is/are* (3).

- **Fragen** werden durch Umstellung gebildet (4).

⚠ Der **Gebrauch des Futurs** hängt in gewissem Maße von der Absicht oder Sichtweise des Sprechers ab. Dies gilt insbesondere für das **going to future** und für zukünftige Ereignisse. Daher ist es im Zweifelsfall ratsam, das neutralere **will future** zu benutzen.

C The present progressive / the simple present

1 We**'re leaving** the house at 10.30.
2 The bus **goes** at 11 o'clock.

- Man kann das **present progressive** auch **mit einer Zeitbestimmung der Zukunft** (*at 10.30, this afternoon, on Sunday*) für bereits feststehende Pläne und Verabredungen verwenden (1).
- Genau wie im Deutschen wird auch im Englischen das **simple present mit einer Zeitangabe** benutzt, um fest terminierte Vorgänge (Fahrpläne, Stundenpläne, Programme usw.) anzugeben (2).

The Future Perfect

1 The last train **will have left** when we get to the station
2 I hope **you'll have made up** your mind by tomorrow.
3 Mike hasn't arrived yet. I expect he **will have missed** the train.

- Das future perfect wird mit *will have* + Partizip Perfekt gebildet (1–3). Meist werden die Kurzformen *'ll* und *won't* verwendet (2).
- Das **future perfect** verwendet man für Handlungen oder Vorgänge, die zu einem bestimmten Zeitpunkt in der Zukunft abgeschlossen sein werden. Der Zeitpunkt wird häufig angegeben (2).
- Mit dem **future perfect** kann man auch eine Vermutung über ein Geschehen in der Vergangenheit ausdrücken (3).

Modal Auxiliary Verbs

1 He **can speak** several languages.
3 You **must accept** your new situation.
2 We **needn't go** to work today.
4 **May** I **interrupt** you?

- Um zu sagen, was geschehen kann, muss, darf, soll usw., benutzt man ein modales Hilfsverb in Verbindung mit einem Vollverb (1–4).

⚠ Im Englischen steht ein Hilfsverb – anders als im Deutschen – nie ohne Vollverb:
– Lena kann Spanisch. ⟶ *Lena can speak Spanish.* NICHT: ~~can Spanish~~

- Modale Hilfsverben – nicht jedoch die Ersatzverben (siehe unten) – haben bei allen Personen immer die gleiche Form, einschließlich der 3. Person Singular (keine *-s*-Endung) (1, 2).
- Die **Verneinung** wird durch das Einfügen von *not/n't* unmittelbar nach dem Hilfsverb gebildet (3).
- **Fragen** bildet man durch Umstellung (4).
- Abgesehen von *could* (wenn es für eine Fähigkeit gebraucht wird) kann man modale Hilfsverben nur im Präsens und – mit einer geeigneten Zeitangabe – mit zukünftiger Bedeutung benutzen, zum Beispiel:

– *You* **can go** *home now.* (Präsens)
You **can go** *home an hour early tomorrow.* (Futur)
– *I* **must write** *these letters now.* (Präsens)
I **must write** *a long report next week.* (Futur)

⚠ Um andere Zeitformen bei modalen Hilfsverben zu bilden, z. B. die Vergangenheit, muss ein geeignetes Ersatzverb gebraucht werden:

must	*The provider* **had to block** *access to the Internet last December.*
can	*I* **couldn't start** *the car yesterday.* (Fähigkeit)
	We **weren't allowed to go** *home early last Friday.* (Erlaubnis)

Übersicht der modalen Hilfsverben nach Funktion

Funktion	Modale(s) Hilfsverb(en)	
Fähigkeit	*He* ***can*** *speak several languages.* *The first satellites* ***could*** *only transmit sound.*	
Möglichkeit	*With your qualifications you* ***could*** *work abroad.* *The boss* ***may*** *come in at any moment.* *He* ***might*** *ask you what you are doing.*	
Bitte	***Can*** *I have a word with Ms Sims, please?* ***Could*** *I speak to Ms Sims, please?* ***May*** *I interrupt you?* ***Might*** *I ask you a personal question?*	(neutral) (höflich) (betont höflich) (äußerst höflich)
Erlaubnis	*You* ***can*** *go in now.* *The boss is free. You* ***may*** *go in now.*	(neutral) (gefällig)
Verbot	*We* ***mustn't*** *be late for work tomorrow.*	
Pflicht	*You* ***must*** *wear a hard hat in the factory.*	
Wahl	*Most shop workers* ***needn't*** *work on Sundays.*	
Empfehlung	*You* ***should*** *get better qualifications.* *You* ***ought to*** *get better qualifications.* *You* ***must*** *get better qualifications.*	(neutral) (betont) (streng)

Reported Speech

A Aussagesätze

1 Some people **claim** that 'servant' robots **are putting** people out of work.
2 The speaker **reminded** his audience that there **were** some jobs robots **couldn't do**.

- Wenn man einem Dritten berichten möchte, was während eines Gespräches gesagt wurde, benutzt man die **indirekte Rede**.
- Bei Verwendung der indirekten Rede benutzt man ein einleitendes Verb wie *claim, say, remind, answer, think, mention* usw., um zu verdeutlichen, dass eine Äußerung wiedergegeben wird.
- Steht das einleitende Verb in der Vergangenheit – also *said, answered, mentioned* usw. –, dann verschieben sich die Zeiten wie folgt:

direkte Rede		indirekte Rede
simple present *she works hard*	→	**simple past** *she worked hard*
present progressive *she is working hard*	→	**past progressive** *she was working hard*
simple past *she worked hard*	→	**past perfect** *she had worked hard*
past progressive *she was working hard*	→	**past perfect progressive** *she had been working hard*
present perfect *she has worked hard*	→	**past perfect** *she had worked hard*
present perfect progressive *she has been working hard*	→	**past perfect progressive** *she had been working hard*
past perfect *she had worked hard*		(keine Verschiebung) –
past perfect progressive *she had been working hard*		(keine Verschiebung) –
will *she will work hard*	→	**would** *she would work hard*
am/is/are going to *she is going to work hard*	→	**was/were going to** *she was going to work hard*
would/might etc. *she would work hard*		(keine Verschiebung) –
would have/might have etc. *she had been working hard*		(keine Verschiebung) –

⚠ Die modalen Hilfsverben werden folgendermaßen verschoben:

Modalverb	Bedeutung	indirekte Rede
can	Fähigkeit	*could, was/were able to*
can	Erlaubnis	*was/were allowed to*
may	Möglichkeit	*might*
may	Erlaubnis	*was/were allowed to*
must	Pflicht	*had to*
mustn't	Verbot	*was/were not allowed to*
needn't	freie Wahl	*did not/didn't have to*

- Außer wenn man über ein Gespräch berichtet, das am selben Tage stattgefunden hat, müssen fast alle **Zeit-** und einige **Ortsangaben** entsprechend der folgenden Tabelle geändert werden. (Angaben, die nicht aufgeführt sind, bleiben unverändert.)

direkte Rede		indirekte Rede
today	⟶	*on that day*
tomorrow	⟶	*the next day*
yesterday	⟶	*the day before*
the day after tomorrow	⟶	*two days later*
the day before yesterday	⟶	*two days before*
next day/Friday/week/Christmas/...	⟶	*the following day/Friday/week/Christmas/...*
last Friday/week/summer/...	⟶	*the Friday/week/summer/... before*
two years/months/weeks/... ago	⟶	*two years/months/weeks/... before*
now, at present	⟶	*then*
at the moment	⟶	*at that moment*
at this time	⟶	*at that time*
here	⟶	*there*
in this place	⟶	*at that place*
this	⟶	*that*
these	⟶	*those*

B Fragesätze

1 A member of the audience **asked what had led** to the widespread use of robots in factories.
2 She **wanted to know if/whether** her job **was endangered**.

- Bei indirekten **Fragen** unterscheidet man zwischen Fragen mit Fragewort (1) und Fragen ohne Fragewort (2).
- Bei Fragen **mit Fragewort** wird das Fragewort übernommen (1).
- Bei Fragen **ohne Fragewort** benutzt man *if* bzw. *whether* (= ob), um zu verdeutlichen, dass es sich um eine Frage handelt (2).
- Alle anderen Änderungen erfolgen wie bei den Aussagesätzen (siehe **Aussagesätze** oben).

C Bitten, Aufforderungen und Befehle

1 Lucy **asked the engineer to show her** the robot.
2 He **told her not to go** too close to it.

- **Bitten** werden meist durch *asked* (= bitten) (1), **Aufforderungen** und **Befehle** durch *told* (= sagen) (2) eingeleitet.
- Bei **positiven Sätzen** erscheint das Verb als *to* + Infinitiv (1).
- Bei **negativen Sätzen** setzen wir *not* unmittelbar vor *to* (2).

⚠ Die beiden Verben *to tell* und *to ask* stehen immer mit einem Objekt, das die angesprochene Person erwähnt (1, 2). Ist dies vom Kontext her nicht erkennbar, wird einfach ein passender Begriff eingesetzt:

- *Jack said, 'Ann, can you tell Carol to give me a ring, please?'*
- *Jack* ***asked Ann*** *to tell Carol to give him a ring.*
- *Ben said, 'Don't enter the studio when the red light is on.'*
- *Ben* ***told everybody*** *not to enter the studio when the red light was on.*

The Passive

1 Measures **are being introduced** to reduce traffic pollution.
2 Pollution **is caused by** some thoughtless people.

- Ist der Verursacher einer Handlung unbekannt oder zweitrangig, benutzt man das Passiv. Im Vordergrund steht also das Ergebnis des Vorgangs (1).
- Möchte man den Verursacher doch angeben, benutzt man einen *by agent* (2).
  ⚠ Der Verursacher wird mit *by* – auf keinen mit Fall *from*! – eingeleitet.
- Das Passiv wird mit einer Zeitform von *to be* und der 3. Form des Vollverbs gebildet:

Zeit	Zeitform von *to be*	3. Form
simple present	*am/is/are*	*caused*
present progressive	*am/is/are being*	*introduced*
simple past	*was/were*	*buried*
past progressive	*was/were being*	*built*
present perfect	*has/have been*	*installed*
***will*-Futur**	*will be*	*blocked*
***going to*-Futur**	*am/is/are going to be*	*sacked*

- Beim Gebrauch von modalen Hilfsverben wird nach folgendem Muster verfahren:

bei Aussagen	Hilfsverb + *to be* + 3. Form	*must be displayed*
bei Fragen	Hilfsverb + Subjekt + *to be* + 3. Form	*Can … be persuaded?*

⚠ Das Verb *to be* bleibt im Infinitiv immer unverändert.

The impersonal passive

1 **It is said that** petrol should cost more.
2 He **is thought** to have gone to hospital.

- Das **impersonal passive** wird vor allem dann benutzt, wenn man sich objektiv bzw. unbeteiligt ausdrücken möchte. Daher kommt diese Struktur oft in Polizeiberichten, seriösen Zeitungsartikeln usw. vor.
- Bei Verben des Berichtens, Denkens usw. benutzt man häufig das Satzmuster:
  – *It is/was/…* + 3. Form des einleitenden Verbs + *that*-Satz (1).
  Hier sind weitere Beispiele dieses Musters:
  Aktiv *Some **say** that companies which cause pollution should be heavily fined.*
  Passiv ***It is said that** companies which cause pollution should be heavily fined.*
  Aktiv *Experts **recommended** that more be spent on public transport.*
  Passiv ***It was recommended** that more be spent on public transport.*
- Um das Subjekt des *that*-Satzes zu betonen, kann man folgendes Muster benutzen:
  – Subjekt + *is/was/…* + 3. Form + *to be* + andere Satzteile (2):
  Aktiv *Many **believe** that the minister is thinking of raising fuel taxes.*
  Passiv *The minister **is believed to be** thinking of raising fuel taxes.*
  ⚠ Der *by agent* wird in solchen Passivsätzen folgendermaßen verwendet:
  Aktiv *The speaker felt that the idea was too radical.*
  Passiv *The idea was felt to be too radical **by** the speaker.*

Conditionals

1 If you **drink** too much alcohol, you **get drunk.**
2 If you **heat** water to 100 degrees, it **boils.**
3 If we **invest** in new technology, a lot of people **will lose** their jobs.

4 If more people **took part** in re-training schemes, they **wouldn't have to worry** about finding new employment.
5 We **won't have** political censorship if we **don't start** to censor the Internet.
6 **Will** we soon **have** political censorship if we **start** to censor the Internet?
7 If the weather **had been** better, we **would have gone** for a walk.

- Wenn man ausdrücken will, dass **unter gleichen Bedingungen** immer wieder **die gleiche Wirkung** auftritt, steht im ***if*-Satz** und im **Hauptsatz** das **simple present** (1, 2).
- Bei **Konditionalsätzen** kommen folgende **Zeitmuster** am häufigsten vor:

Typ I	*If + simple present*	+	*will*-future (3, 5, 6)
Typ II	*If + simple past*	+	*would* + Infinitiv (4)
Typ III	*If + past perfect*	+	*would have* + 3. Form des Verbs (7)

- Ein **Konditionalsatz** besteht aus zwei Teilen: dem ***if*-Teil** und dem **Hauptteil**. Der ***if*-Teil** drückt eine **Bedingung** aus, der Hauptteil eine **Folge**.
- Je nach Sinn kann der *if*-Teil, der Hauptteil oder beide Teile des Satzes **verneint** werden (4, 5).
- Bei **Fragen** kann nur der **Hauptteil** zu einer Frage geformt werden. Dann steht dieser Teil **an erster Stelle** (6).
- *if*-Sätze werden gemäß der **Wahrscheinlichkeit** der zu erwartenden Folge eingesetzt:
  Typ I: Folge (fast) sicher.
  *If we **invest in** new technology, a lot of people **will lose** their jobs.*
  D. h. viele Leute werden (vermutlich) ihre Stellen verlieren, da wir (sehr wahrscheinlich) in die neue Technologie investieren werden.
  Typ II: Folge theoretisch möglich, aber kaum wahrscheinlich.
  *If we **invested in** new technology, a lot of people **would lose** their jobs.*
  D. h. es ist kaum zu erwarten, dass viele Leute ihre Stellen verlieren werden, da wir (wahrscheinlich) nicht in die neue Technologie investieren werden.
  Typ III: Folge unmöglich, da die Bedingung nicht erfüllt wurde und bereits in der Vergangenheit liegt.
  *If we **had invested in** new technology, a lot of people **would have lost** their jobs.*
  D. h. der Sprecher weiß schon, dass keiner den Job verloren hat, da wir in die neue Technologie nicht investiert haben.

The Gerund and Infinitive

A Gerunds in the place of noun phrases

1 **Reading** in bed is fun.
2 Do you like **books**? ⟶ Do you like **reading**?
3 I get a lot of pleasure from **books**. ⟶ I get a lot of pleasure from **reading**.
4 A person cannot live without **air**. ⟶ A person cannot live without **breathing**.
5 Laziness causes you to age faster. ⟶ **Not exercising** causes you to age faster.
6 A person cannot live without **eventually paying taxes**.
7 **Not drinking enough fluids** causes you to age faster.

- Ein Verb in der ***-ing*-Form** kann als Gerundium die **Rolle eines Substantivs** übernehmen (1–7).
- Das Gerundium kann verwendet werden als **Subjekt** (1, 5, 7), als **Objekt** (2) oder **nach Präpositionen** (3, 4, 6).
- Gerundien können **erweitert** werden, und zwar durch eine adverbiale Bestimmung (1, 6) oder ein Objekt (6, 7).
- Durch die Verwendung eines Gerundiums anstelle eines Substantivs kann der entsprechende Satzteil **länger und komplexer** werden (6, 7). Gerundien helfen Ihnen also dabei, sich differenzierter auszudrücken.

B Gerund and infinitive

1 Max **enjoys playing** football.
2 Can you **afford to buy** that DVD collection?
3 Cem and Julie **continued to meet** even though they had split up.
4 Cem and Julie **continued meeting** even though they had split up.
5 Alison **normally likes going** to parties, but **today** she would **prefer to stay** at home.

- Nach einigen Verben folgt immer die *-ing*-Form (**gerund**) (1).
  Am wichtigsten sind:

> *admit, avoid, consider, deny, enjoy, finish, imagine, mention, mind* (etwas dagegen haben), *miss, practise, risk, suggest*

- **Nach einigen Verben** folgt immer der Infinitiv (**infinitive**) (2).
  Die **wichtigsten** Verben dieser Gruppe sind:

> *afford, choose, decide, expect, hope, mean, promise, refuse, want*

⚠ Nach den Verben *begin, continue, intend* und *start* können der **Infinitiv** oder die ***-ing*-Form beliebig benutzt werden** (3, 4).

- Einige Verben werden **je nach Bedeutung** entweder mit dem **Infinitiv** oder mit der ***-ing*-Form** benutzt. Die **wichtigsten** Verben dieser Gruppe sind:

> *like, dislike, love, hate, prefer*

- Wenn von einer **allgemeingültigen Situation** die Rede ist, folgt auf diese Verben die *-ing*-**Form**. Handelt es sich aber um eine **Ausnahmesituation**, dann verwendet man den **Infinitiv** (5).

advise, allow, encourage, forbid, permit, recommend

Handelt es sich um einen **konkreten Einzelfall**, wird mit diesen Verben ein **Objekt + Infinitiv** verwendet.
*I strongly **advise you to** be more polite to people.*
Wenn es sich aber um eine **allgemeine Situation** handelt, dann steht das nachfolgende Verb in der ***-ing*-Form**.
*Most firms don't **allow smoking** in their offices.*

forget/remember

Die Struktur ***forget/remember* + *-ing*-Form** bezieht sich auf die Vergangenheit. Sie drückt etwa die Idee „Ich werde nie vergessen …“ aus.
⚠ „Vergangenheit“ bezieht sich hier nicht auf *forget/remember*, sondern auf das nachfolgende Verb.
*I still **remember getting** my first bicycle.*
*I'll never **forget going** to the Rock against Hunger concert last year.*

Die Struktur ***forget/remember* + Infinitiv** dagegen bezieht sich auf die Zukunft. Sie drückt etwa die Idee aus „Ich darf nicht vergessen, etwas zu tun“ bzw. „ich habe noch etwas zu tun, weil ich es bis jetzt vergessen habe“.
*Dad, please **remember / don't forget to pick me up** from the station.*
*Oh dear. I **forgot / didn't remember to pick Sally up** from the station.*

regret

Die Struktur ***regret* + *-ing*-Form** drückt Bedauern über eine vergangene Situation bzw. einen vergangenen Vorfall aus. Häufig geht es dabei um verpasste Chancen.

*I really **regret leaving** school without any qualifications.*
*I know they will **regret buying** such a big, expensive car.*

Die Struktur ***regret*** + **Infinitiv** – fast immer mit einem Verb des Mitteilens wie *inform, say, tell* kombiniert – drückt eine schlechte Nachricht aus.
*I **regret to say** that I can't attend the meeting tomorrow.*
*We **regret to inform** you that the vacancy has now been filled.*

stop

Bedeutet ***stop*** „aufhören, etwas zu tun", steht das nachfolgende Verb in der **-*ing*-Form**.
Bedeutet aber ***stop*** „kurz anhalten, um etwas anderes zu tun", folgt ein Verb im **Infinitiv**.
*For heaven's sake **stop shouting** at me.*
*I'm a little late because I **stopped to give** somebody a lift.*

try

Bedeutet ***try*** „etwas ausprobieren", steht das nachfolgende Verb in der **-*ing*-Form**.
Bedeutet aber ***try*** „sich anstrengen, etwas zu tun", folgt ein Verb im **Infinitiv**.
*I **tried phoning** Ellie, but she wasn't at home.*
*We**'ll try to repair** your computer by the weekend.*

Verb + Object + *to*-infinitive

1 Mr Hill **asked Kevin** to be quiet.
2 He didn't **allow the class to use** a dictionary.
3 And he **warned us not to waste** time.
4 Ms Foster **expected her pupils to work** hard.
5 She didn't **want them to get** nervous
6 She said, 'I **would like you all to get** good marks in the exam'.

- Nach bestimmten Verben kann ein **Objekt mit einem *to*-Infinitiv** stehen (1–6). Im Deutschen folgt auf das entsprechende Verb meist ein Infinitiv mit *zu*. Beispiele sind:

advise, allow, ask, encourage, force, help, invite, remind, teach, warn

- Auch bei den folgenden Verben kann ein **Objekt mit einem *to*-Infinitiv** stehen. Im Gegensatz zu den oben aufgeführten Verben steht im Deutschen jedoch kein Infinitiv, sondern ein *dass*-Satz.

cause	verursachen, dass
expect	erwarten, dass
tell	sagen, dass … soll
want	wollen, dass
would like/love	möchte(n) gern, dass

- Ist das Objekt ein **Personalpronomen**, steht dies in der **Objektform** (5).

Adjectives and Adverbs

1 John has a **new** DVD player.
2 He always buys **expensive** equipment.
3 My computer has become **very slow**.
4 That CD sounds **terrible**.
5 We can make printouts **quickly** and **cheaply**.

▸ Word Order (s.u.)

- Um **Personen** oder **Sachen** näher zu beschreiben, benutzt man **Adjektive** (1–4).
- Adjektive stehen **unmittelbar** vor Substantiven oder **unmittelbar nach** einer Form von *be* (bzw. *become* oder *seem*, die *be* ersetzen können) (3).
- **Adjektive** können mit Verben wie *feel, look* (aussehen), *sound, smell* und *taste* eine **sinnliche Wahrnehmung** ausdrücken (4).
- Um einen **Tätigkeitsverb** näher zu beschreiben, setzt man ein Adverb **unmittelbar hinter das Verb** bzw. Verb + Objekt (5).
  ⚠ Im Englischen können ein Verb und sein Objekt – anders als im Deutschen – nicht durch ein Adverb getrennt werden. Also NICHT: ~~We can make quickly printouts~~.
- Adverbien werden auch benutzt, um **Adjektive**, **andere Adverbien** und **ganze Sätze** näher zu bestimmen:
  MP3 players have become ***surprisingly cheap***. (Adverb + Adjektiv)
  My fax machine prints out ***terribly slowly***. (Adverb + Adverb)
  Luckily *Gerd left a message on my mailbox.* (Satzadverb)
- Die meisten Adverbien werden durch Anhängen von *-ly* an das Adjektiv gebildet (5). Eine kleine Anzahl von Adverbien hat dieselbe Form wie Adjektive; die häufigsten sind *fast, hard, early late, long, daily*.

Comparison of Adjectives and Adverbs

1 A hundred years ago life was **slower** and people may have been **happier**.
2 Which technological innovation is the **most/least important**?
3 Today you can copy data **more easily than** ever before.

- **Einsilbige** und **zweisilbige Adjektive**, die auf *-y* enden – zum Beispiel *easy, happy* und *lucky* –, werden mit *-(i)er/-(i)est* gesteigert (1).
- **Mehrsilbige Adjektive** und **Adverbien**, die auf *-ly* enden, werden mit *more/most* gesteigert (2, 3).
  ⚠ Die Adverbien, die dieselbe Form wie das entsprechende Adjektiv haben (*fast, hard, early* usw.), werden mit *-er/-est* gesteigert.
- Um Personen oder Sachen im Satz miteinander zu vergleichen, gibt es folgende Möglichkeiten:

– Kein Unterschied	*as good as*	genau so gut wie
– Unterschied	*not as good as*	nicht so gut wie
– Unterschied	*better than*	besser als

Word Order – Positions of Adverbs of Time, Place and Frequency

1 She goes shopping **every week**.
2 They play in a club **in Doherty Street**.
3 **Last year** we went to India for our holidays.
4 Paul and Emily went to **the USA last year**.
5 She **always finishes** school early on Fridays.
6 He **is never** at home when I call.
7 I like to stay at home **now and then**.
8 Gina acted **strangely at the party last night**.

- Zeitangaben (Wann?) und Ortsangaben (Wo?, Wohin?) stehen in der Regel am Satzende (1, 2).

- Um die Zeit eines bestimmten Ereignisses hervorheben, kann man die Zeitangabe an die erste Stelle setzen (3).
- Stehen eine Zeitangabe und eine Ortsangabe zusammen am Satzende, dann gilt die Reihenfolge Ort vor Zeit (alphabetisch merken: O vor Z!) (4).
- Besteht eine Häufigkeitsangabe aus einem Wort, z. B. *always, often, sometimes*, steht sie unmittelbar vor dem Vollverb (5).
- Lautet das Vollverb *to be*, steht das Adverb direkt dahinter (6).
- Besteht die Häufigkeitsangabe aus mehreren Wörtern, z. B. *every day, now and then*, steht sie wie eine Zeitangabe am Satzende (7).
- Adverbien der Art und Weise stehen in der Regel am Satzende. Kommen noch Zeit- oder Ortsadverbien hinzu, lautet die Reihenfolge: Art und Weise – Ort – Zeit (AOZ) (8).

Relative Clauses and Contact Clauses

1 Car manufacturers are designing cars **which/that** can use hydrogen fuel cells.
2 Wildernesses are being spoiled by tourists **who/that** want to go to 'unspoiled' places.
3 Tony filled in a Dateline questionnaire **(which/that)** he found on the Internet.
4 Fred Foley is a paparazzo **whose** photos sell for huge sums of money.
5 Call centre employees, most **of whom** come from India, work long hours.
6 Some non-GM crops are attacked by pests **against which** they have no resistance.

- Relativsätze werden benutzt, um den Hauptsatz durch zusätzliche Informationen genauer zu bestimmen.
- Für **Sachen** benutzt man das Relativpronomen *which* bzw. *that* (1) und für Personen *who* bzw. *that* (2).
- Steht das Relativpronomen für das **Objekt des Hauptsatzes**, dann kann man es weglassen (3). Solche Relativsätze heißen **contact clauses**.
- Um **Besitz** bzw. **Zugehörigkeit** anzuzeigen, gebraucht man *whose* unmittelbar vor dem **Substantiv** bei Personen und Sachen (4).
- Steht eine **Präposition** vor dem **Relativpronomen**, wird *whom* für Personen und *which* für Sachen benutzt (5, 6). In solchen Fällen ist der Gebrauch von *that* nicht möglich.

Defining and non-defining relative clauses

1 The first Europeans **who** settled in Australia came from Britain.
2 Sydney, **which** is famous for its unusually designed opera house, is situated on the south-eastern coast of Australia.

- Im **ersten Beispielsatz** ist der Sinn des Hauptsatzes *The first Europeans came from Britain* ohne den Relativsatz *who settled in Australia* offensichtlich falsch bzw. unvollständig. Relativsätze dieser Art – die wesentlich für das Verständnis des gesamten Satzes sind – nennt man **defining relative clauses** (notwendige oder bestimmende Relativsätze).
- Im **zweiten Beispielsatz** ist die Aussage des Hauptsatzes *Sydney is situated on the south-eastern coast of Australia* ohne den Relativsatz völlig verständlich, weil der Relativsatz *which is famous for its unusually designed opera house* eine zusätzliche, also nebensächliche, Information enhält. Daher werden solche Relativsätze ***non-defining relative clauses*** (nicht notwendige oder nicht bestimmende Relativsätze) genannt.
  ⚠ Notwendige Relativsätze werden immer **ohne** trennende **Kommas** benutzt. Dies signalisiert, dass sie fester Bestandteil der Hauptaussage sind.

Participle Constructions

1 Malaria, preventable with a treated bed net **costing** less than one pound, is endemic.
2 Many men believe that any work **involved** with cooking is a woman's chore.
3 **Losing** more and more people to AIDS, Africa now needs effective help more urgently than ever before.
4 **Burdened** with declining life-expectancy, large parts of Africa are caught in a poverty trap.
5 **Having fetched** water from a river for many years, some women in developing countries are now happy to be able to use the Hippo Roller.
6 **Despite facing** extreme destitution, many rural residents haven't given up hope.
7 Donors should invest in projects that help local inhabitants become self-supporting, **thereby making** sure that the money isn't wasted.
8 Poor infrastructure is a key barrier to economic growth in Nepal, **thus causing** huge additional costs to the transport of commercial goods.
9 Life is becoming hard in the developing countries, **with** many small farmers **going** out of business.
10 AIDS represents a major challenge to sub-Saharan Africa, currently **killing** more than two million people every year.

Die englische Sprache ist geprägt durch häufige Verwendung von Partizipialkonstruktionen. Diese ermöglichen einen eleganteren Sprachfluss.

- Partizipialkonstruktionen verkürzen Relativsätze; dabei kann entweder das **present participle** (1) oder das **past participle** (2) verwendet werden.
- Sie werden auch verwendet, um adverbiale Nebensätze zu verkürzen; in diesen Fällen unterscheidet man zwischen Partizipialkonstruktionen ohne Konjunktion (3–5) und solchen mit Konjunktion (6–9).
  In Sätzen ohne Konjunktion ist der Inhalt des Satzes auch ohne eine solche klar. Dagegen sind Konjunktionen nötig, um zu verhindern, dass der logische Zusammenhang des Satzes verloren geht. Zum Beispiel wird der Inhalt von Satz 6 unklar, wenn die Konjunktion *despite* ausgelassen wird.
- Wie bei der Verkürzung von Relativsätzen kommen auch bei der Verkürzung von adverbialen Nebensätzen das **present participle** (3, 6–9) und das **past participle** (4) zur Anwendung. Darüber hinaus wird hier auch noch das **perfect participle** verwendet (5), und zwar um die Vorzeitigkeit der Handlung im Nebensatz auszudrücken. (*Nachdem sie jahrelang Wasser aus dem Fluss geholt hatten, …*)
- Schließlich verknüpft man mit einer Partizipialkonstruktion zwei Hauptsätze zu einem einzigen Satz, und zwar ausnahmslos mittels **present participle** (10).

Countable and Uncountable Nouns

1 Visit our website for more **information** on our firm.	NICHT ~~informations~~
2 Have you read the paper today? The political **news** is interesting.	NICHT ~~news are~~
3 Where can I get some **advice**?	NICHT ~~an advice~~

- Einige wichtige **Substantive** sind **zählbar im Deutschen**, **nicht jedoch im Englischen**. Diese Substantive können also nicht ohne weiteres mit dem unbestimmten Artikel *a*/*an* oder mit einem Zahlwort benutzt werden.

Hier ist eine Liste solcher Wörter, die Sie auswendig lernen sollten:

advice, baggage, damage, data, equipment, evidence, furniture, garbage (Abfall), *information, knowledge, luck, luggage, machinery, news, progress, research, rubbish, work (housework, homework)*

- Um diese Substantive im Plural zu verwenden, muss *some, a bit of* bzw. *a piece of* hinzugefügt werden (3).

The Definite Article

1 **Sociologists** say that **violence** is increasing among young people.
2 Is **the current trend** partly caused by **the violent films** they watch?
3 **Most sentences** are not tough enough.
4 Nearly **half the prisoners** in **British prisons** are under 25.
5 **Spring** is my favourite season but **the spring** we're having this year is more like **winter**.
6 We had **breakfast** late this morning so we came to school **by car** instead of **by bus**.
7 They are thinking of legalizing soft drugs in **the Netherlands**.

- Hat ein Substantiv eine allgemeine, uneingeschränkte Bedeutung – also „alle ohne Ausnahme" – dann steht es ohne Artikel (1, 5).
- Ist die Bedeutung eines Substantives auf bestimmte Fälle eingeschränkt, benutzt man den Artikel (2, 5).
- Ferner wird der Artikel in den folgenden Fällen und Wendungen im Englischen – z.T. anders als im Deutschen – nicht gebraucht:
  - bei *most* in der Bedeutung „die meisten" (3),
  - bei öffentlichen Gebäuden im allgemeinen Sinn (4),
  - bei Mahlzeiten (6),
  - bei Verkehrsmitteln (6),
  - bei Straßennamen,
  - bei Tageszeiten, Wochentagen, Monaten und Jahreszeiten im allgemeinen Sinn (5).
- Der Artikel wird verwendet nach *all* und *half* (4) und mit den Pluralnamen von Staaten (7).

  ⚠ Der bestimmte Artikel steht im Englischen (viel) seltener als im Deutschen. Daher: *When in doubt, leave it out!*

UNIT WORD LIST

Dieses Wörterverzeichnis enthält alle in *Crossover 2* eingeführten, in den Texten angegebenen Vokabeln in der Reihenfolge ihres Erscheinens.

TOPIC 1 The Changing Patterns of Work and Consumption

TEXT 1 Shopping Away the Blues

page 8

acquisition [ˌækwɪ'zɪʃn]	the act of buying sth	*Erwerb, Anschaffung*
thrilling ['θrɪlɪŋ]	exciting and enjoyable	*aufregend*
addictive [ə'dɪktɪv]	becoming a strong habit	*süchtig machend*
profusely [prə'fju:sli]	a lot	*ausgiebig, stark*
inevitably [ɪn'evɪtəbli]	certain to happen	*unvermeidlich*
to revolve around [rɪ'vɒlv əˌraʊnd]	have sth as the main subject	*sich drehen um*
gadget ['gædʒɪt]	device, utensil	*(technisches) Gerät*
temporary ['temprəri]	lasting only a short time	*vorübergehend, zeitweilig*
distraction [dɪ'strækʃn]	amusement, entertainment	*Ablenkung*
compulsive [kəm'pʌlsɪv]	difficult to stop or control	*zwanghaft*
to acquire [ə'kwaɪə]	obtain sth by buying it	*erwerben*
fad [fæd]	sth people are interested for a short time	*Modeerscheinung*
inventory ['ɪnvəntri]	a list of all the things in a particular room/building	*Bestand*

page 9

temptation [temp'teɪʃn]	the desire to have sth that you know is not good	*Versuchung*
bargain ['bɑ:gɪn]	a thing bought for less than the usual price	*Sonderangebot, Schnäppchen*
rack [ræk]	a piece of equipment used for holding things	*(Kleider-)Ständer*
gleam [gli:m]	an expression in a person's eyes which shows emotion	*Glanz*
irresistible [ˌɪrɪ'zɪstəbl]	having an overpowering appeal	*unwiderstehlich*
fortune ['fɔ:tʃu:n]	a large amount of money	*Vermögen*

TEXT 2 Overcoming Consumerism

page 12

to tout [taʊt]	try to persuade people to buy sth	*werben (für), anpreisen*
to have a stake [steɪk]	have a share in sth	*teilhaben an*
durability [ˌdjʊərə'bɪləti]	the quality of lasting for a long time	*Haltbarkeit, Dauerhaftigkeit*
vendor ['vendə]	seller	*Verkäufer/in*
retail outlet ['ri:teɪl ˌaʊtlet]	shop, store	*Einzelhandel(sgeschäft)*
gimmicky ['gɪmɪki]	attracting attention	*effekthascherisch*
to abandon [ə'bændən]	stop doing business with	*aufgeben, sich abwenden von*
regimen ['redʒɪmən]	a set of rules you follow to keep healthy	*Programm, Diät*
to tempt [tempt]	make sb do sth even if it is wrong	*in Versuchung führen, verleiten*

page 13

to lust after ['lʌst ɑ:ftə]	feel a strong desire for sth	*begehren*
clutter ['klʌtə]	untidy mass of objects	*Kram*
to succumb to [sə'kʌm tə]	not be able to resist	*erliegen*
overhead expenses [ˌəʊvəhed ɪk'spensɪz]	regular costs, such as rent, electricity, etc.	*Fixkosten*
to behold [bɪ'həʊld]	look at	*betrachten*
to reek [ri:k]	smell strongly and unpleasantly	*stinken*
to induce [ɪn'dju:s]	cause	*auslösen*
underneath [ˌʌndə'ni:θ]	under, below	*(dar)unter*

TEXT 3 The Petrol–Obesity Connection

page 15

obesity [əʊ'bi:səti]	the state of being fat in an unhealthy way	*Fettleibigkeit*
relief [rɪ'li:f]	help	*Erleichterung*
corn [kɔ:n]	*(AE)* BE: maize	*Mais*
to prompt [prɒmpt]	encourage	*veranlassen*

page 16

silver lining [ˌsɪlvə 'laɪnɪŋ]	good aspect (of a bad thing), as in the proverb: 'Every cloud has a silver lining'	*gute Seite, sein Gutes*
to correlate ['kɒrəleɪt]	connect closely	*(miteinander) in Beziehung setzen*
subsidy ['sʌbsədi]	financial help	*Subvention*
spike [spaɪk]	sudden increase	*plötzlicher Anstieg*

TEXT 4 The Secret of Brand Names

page 19

clout [klaʊt]	power and influence	*Kraft/Einfluss*
confined [kən'faɪnd]	not free to move around	*eingesperrt*
steer [stentʃ]	bull	*Stier*
wholesome ['həʊlsəm]	good for your health	*gesund*
feedlot operation ['fi:dlɒt ɒpəˌreɪʃn]	area where thousands of cows are kept on one small piece of ground	*Massentierhaltung*
to jump onto the bandwagon [ˌdʒʌmp ɒn ðə 'bændwægən]	join a popular trend to become successful	*auf den Zug aufspringen*
to boost [bu:st]	increase	*steigern*

page 20

to enhance [ɪn'hɑ:ns]	improve the quality of sth	*verbessern*
bucolic [bju'kɒlɪk]	connected with country life	*ländlich, idyllisch*
to yearn for [jɜ:n]	want sth very much	*sich sehnen nach*
barn [bɑ:n]	farm building for storing grain	*Scheune*
haystack ['heɪstæk]	a pile of hay used for storing until needed	*Heuhaufen*
to imbue [ɪm'bju:]	fill	*erfüllen*
to lure in [lʊə]	attract	*anlocken*
ubiquitous [ju:'bɪkwɪtəs]	all over the place	*allgegenwärtig, unvermeidlich*
prior to ['praɪə tə]	before	*vor*
stale [steɪl]	unfresh	*alt(backen)*
pastry ['peɪstri]	a mixture of flour, fat and water that is baked	*Gebäck, Teig*
urea [jʊ'ri:ə]	a substance found in urine	*Harnstoff*
quaint [kweɪnt]	old-fashioned, charming	*kurious, altmodisch*
to conjure up [ˌkʌndʒər 'ʌp]	bring to mind	*heraufbeschwören*
lush [lʌʃ]	growing thickly and healthily	*üppig*
pasture ['pɑ:stʃə]	land covered with grass, suitable for feeding animals	*Weide(land)*
manure [mə'njʊə]	dung, animal droppings	*Dung, Gülle, Mist*

TEXT 5 The Effects of Globalization

page 23

beneficial [ˌbenɪ'fɪʃl]	having a useful effect	*nützlich, vorteilhaft*
cuddly ['kʌdli]	soft, positive	*kuschelig*
proponent [prə'pəʊnənt]	a person who supports an idea	*Befürworter/in*
cozy ['kəʊzi]	warm, comfortable and safe (*BE:* cosy)	*gemütlich*
subsistence-level [səb'sɪstəns levl]	having just enough food or money to stay alive	*am Existenzminimum*
integral ['ɪntɪgrəl]	essential	*integral, wesentlich*

page 24

conspicuous [kən'spɪkjuəs]	easy to see or notice	*auffällig*
elevator ['elɪveɪtə]	*(BE) AE:* lift	*Fahrstuhl, Aufzug*

TEXT 6 Women at Work

page 26

pace [peɪs]	rate, speed	*Tempo*

page 27

initially [ɪ'nɪʃəli]	at the beginning	*anfänglich, zuerst, zunächst*
gender ['dʒendə]	the fact of being male cr female	*Geschlecht*
notion ['nəʊʃn]	idea, concept, belief	*Vorstellung, Idee*
to pursue [pə'sju:]	do (a job)	*nachgehen*
chores [tʃɔ:z]	unpleasant tasks, work	*Haus-, Routinearbeit*
at the expense of [ɪk'spens]	with negative effects on	*auf Kosten von*
repercussion [ˌri:pə'kʌʃn]	(negative) consequence	*negative Auswirkung*

TEXT 7 Reading Poetry

page 30

superhighway ['su:pəhaɪweɪ]	*(AE) BE*: motorway	*Autobahn*
superlot ['su:pəlɒt]	a very large parking area	*Riesenparkplatz*
suds *(pl)* [sʌdz]	foam/bubbles from soap, name for a washing powder	*Seifenschaum*
supersonic [ˌsu:pə'sɒnɪk]	faster than the speed of sound	*Überschall-*
supercilious [ˌsu:pə'sɪliəs]	proud and arrogant	*hochmütig, herablassend*
colossal [kə'lɒsl]	very large	*gigantisch*
to supersede [ˌsu:pə'si:d]	replace	*ersetzen, ablösen*

TOPIC 2 Save the Planet! Save Ourselves!

TEXT 1 A Generational Mission

page 38

inconvenient [ˌɪnkən'vi:niənt]	troublesome, difficult	*unbequem*
issue ['ɪʃu:]	topic for debate	*Frage, Thema*
virtually ['vɜ:tʃuəli]	almost	*praktisch, nahezu*
glacier ['glæsiə]	mass of ice	*Gletscher*
mound [maʊnd]	hill	*Hügel*
to prop up [ˌprɒp 'ʌp]	support	*auftürmen*
saturation [ˌsætʃə'reɪʃn]	amount contained within	*Sättigung*
to interfere with [ˌɪntə'fɪə]	prevent or disturb	*stören*
habitat ['hæbɪtæt]	home of an animal	*Lebensraum*
extinction [ɪk'stɪŋkʃn]	when every member of a species dies	*Aussterben, Ausrottung*
to wreak havoc [ri:k 'hævək]	cause chaos	*verheerende Auswirkungen haben*
unprecedented [ʌn'presɪdentɪd]	that has never been known before	*beispiellos*
to harness ['hɑ:nɪs]	control and make use of	*nutzbar machen*

page 39

procrastinator [prəʊ'kræstɪneɪtə]	sb who puts off doing sth unpleasant	*Zögerer, Zauderer*
denier [dɪ'naɪə]	one who denies	*Leugner/in*
heat-trapping ['hi:t træpɪŋ]	greenhouse	*wärmespeichernd*
to capture ['kæptʃə]	catch	*ergreifen*
precious ['preʃəs]	valuable	*wertvoll, kostbar*
exhilaration [ɪgˌzɪlə'reɪʃn]	euphoria	*Hochgefühl*
compelling [kəm'pelɪŋ]	powerful	*zwingend*
thrill [θrɪl]	excited feeling	*(aufregendes) Gefühl*
pettiness ['petinəs]	concern with unimportant things	*Kleinlichkeit*
to stifle ['staɪfl]	inhibit, suppress	*ersticken, unterdrücken*
transcendence [træn'sendəns]	go beyond normal experience	*Erhabenheit*
to suffocate ['sʌfəkeɪt]	feel trapped or oppressed (as if dying from lack of air)	*ersticken*
epiphany [ɪ'pɪfəni]	wonderful moment when a meaning suddenly becomes clear	*Offenbarung*

TEXT 2 People Affected by Climate Change

page 42

indigenous [ɪn'dɪdʒənəs]	native	*eingeboren*
to gather ['gæðə]	harvest wild foods	*(Früchte) sammeln*
vicious cycle [ˌvɪʃəs 'saɪkl]	a recurring sequence of bad events	*Teufelskreis*

page 43

vulnerable ['vʌlnərəbl]	able to be hurt	*zerstörbar, verwundbar*
to recede [rɪ'si:d]	retreat, go back	*sich zurückziehen*
bog [bɒg]	moor	*Sumpf*
to expose [ɪk'spəʊz]	uncover	*freilegen, freisetzen*
thaw ['θɔ:]	<> freeze	*auftauen*
scarce [skeəs]	rare	*knapp*
to thrive [θraɪv]	live very well	*gedeihen*
staple ['steɪpl]	essential component	*Grund(nahrungsmittel)*
ancestral home [æn'sestrəl həʊm]	place belonging to many generations	*Familiensitz, angestammte Heimat*

TEXT 3 Don't Drink the Water and Don't Breathe the Air

page 46

to beware of [bɪ'weə]	mind, be careful of	*sich hüten*
sewage ['su:ɪdʒ]	waste water	*Abwasser*
crud [krʌd]	dirt	*Dreck, Brühe*
halibut ['hælɪbət]	a kind of fish	*Heilbutt*
sturgeon ['stɜ:dʒən]	a kind of fish	*Stör*
detergent [dɪ'tɜ:dʒənt]	soap	*Reinigungsmittel, Waschmittel*
veil [veɪl]	cloth which covers the face	*Schleier, Atemschutz*
sink [sɪŋk]	basin with water supply and drain	*Spüle, Ausguss*
hunch [hʌntʃ]	intuitive guess	*Verdacht*

TEXT 4 Fuelling Deforestation

page 48

to release [rɪ'li:s]	set free	*freilassen, freisetzen*
to decompose [ˌdi:kəm'pəʊz]	rot	*(sich) zersetzen*
carbon ['kɑ:bən]	a chemical element (C)	*Kohlenstoff*
peat swamp [pi:t]	a moor made up of dark, wet soil	*Torfmoor, Hochmoor*
to roam [rəʊm]	move around without any definite direction	*umherstreifen*
dome [dəʊm]	a round roof	*Kuppel*
debris ['debri:]	small pieces	*Reste, Schutt*
clear-fell [ˌklɪə 'fel]	cut down all the trees in a certain area	*roden, abholzen*

page 49

destined ['destɪnd]	intended for a purpose	*bestimmt*
to stomach ['stʌmək]	bear, tolerate	*ertragen*
savage ['sævɪdʒ]	wild, cruel	*schonungslos*
charge [tʃɑ:dʒ]	accusation	*Anklage(punkt)*
incentive [ɪn'sentɪv]	encouragement, motivation for doing sth.	*Anreiz*
ingredient [ɪn'gri:diənt]	component	*Bestandteil, Zutat*
to soar [sɔ:]	keep going up	*stark ansteigen*
to raze [reɪz]	tear down and destroy	*völlig zerstören*
to offset ['ɒfset]	compensate for	*ausgleichen*
one-off [ˌwʌn 'ɒf]	made or happening only once	*einmalig*
to trash [træʃ]	destroy	*zerstören*

page 52

bushel ['bʊʃl]	a unit of measurement	*Scheffel*
plant [plɑ:nt]	factory	*Fabrik*

TEXT 5 Controversial Forms of Activism

page 54

vigilante [ˌvɪdʒɪ'lænti]	sb who enforces the law without authority to do so	*Selbstjustizler/in*

greedy ['gri:di]	selfishly wanting more of sth	*(hab)gierig*
coercive [kəʊ'ɜ:sɪv]	by force	*Zwangs-*
to ram [ræm]	strike with force	*rammen*
vessel ['vesl]	boat, ship	*Schiff, Boot*
violation [ˌvaɪə'leɪʃn]	breaking or going against	*Übertretung*
to outrage ['aʊtreɪdʒ]	anger, offend	*verletzen, entrüsten*
law enforcement [lɔ: ɪn'fɔ:smənt]	making sure that people obey the laws	*Überwachung der Einhaltung von Gesetzen*
unyielding [ʌn'ji:ldɪŋ]	stubborn	*unnachgiebig*
to bend the truth [ˌbend ðə 'tru:θ]	distort the truth	*es mit der Wahrheit nicht so genau nehmen, die Wahrheit verbiegen*
recklessness ['rekləsnəs]	carelessness	*Rücksichtslosigkeit*
loathing ['ləʊðɪŋ]	hate	*Abscheu*
butyric acid [bjuˌtɪrɪk 'æsɪd]	a chemical compound	*Buttersäure*
prop-fouler ['prɒp faʊlə]	a material used to damage ship propellers	*Schiffsschraubenblockierer*
coil [kɔɪl]	rope	*Rolle*
to get entangled [get ɪn'tæŋgld]	become caught up, knotted up	*sich verheddern*
drain [dreɪn]	channel through which liquid is carried away	*Abfluss(rohr)*
foremost ['fɔ:məʊst]	most prominent	*oberst, führend*

page 55

endorsement [ɪn'dɔ:smənt]	support	*Unterstützung, Würdigung*
demigod ['demigɒd]	half-god	*Halbgott*
to denounce [dɪ'naʊns]	declare to be wrong or evil	*öffentlich rügen*
stinging ['stɪŋɪŋ]	painful	*verletzend*
blowback ['bləʊbæk]	unintended negative consequences	*Rückschläge*

TEXT 6 Finding Solutions

page 57

carbon sequestration [ˌkɑ:bən ˌsi:kwə'streɪʃn]	removal and storage of CO_2 from the atmosphere	*Entfernung von CO_2 aus der Atmosphäre*
to dispose of [dɪ'spəʊz]	get rid of	*beseitigen*
to abandon [ə'bændən]	to stop using	*stilllegen*
oil well ['ɔɪl wel]	hole in the ground from which oil is obtained	*Ölquelle*
saline reservoir [ˌseɪlaɪn 'rezəvwɑ:]	underground place which holds salt water	*Salzstock, -mine*
bioremediation [ˌbaɪəʊrɪˌmi:di'eɪʃn]	decontamination using plants and microbes	*biologische Reinigung*
contamination [kənˌtæmɪ'neɪʃn]	impurity	*Verschmutzung*
arsenic ['ɑ:snɪk]	a poisonous chemical element (As)	*Arsen*
soil [sɔɪl]	earth, dirt	*Erde, Erdboden*
phytoremediation [ˌfaɪtəʊrɪˌmi:di'eɪʃn	decontamination using plants	*Reinigung durch Pflanzen*
to incinerate [ɪn'sɪnəreɪt]	burn	*verbrennen*
to shrink [ʃrɪŋk]	reduce in size	*schrumpfen, verdichten*

page 58

abundance [ə'bʌndəns]	an amount that is more than is needed	*Fülle*
obstacle ['ɒbstəkl]	obstruction, block	*Hindernis*
buoy [bɔɪ]	an anchored object which floats on the surface	*Boje*
swell [swel]	regular movement of the sea (waves)	*Woge, Seegang*

TOPIC 3 Technology and Society

TEXT 1 The Social Impact of Technology

page 66

impact ['ɪmpækt]	powerful effect	*Auswirkung*
to impact on ['ɪmpækt ɒn]	affect sth powerfully	*sich auswirken auf*
shareholder ['ʃeəhəʊldə]	owner of shares in a company's business	*Aktionär/in, Anteilseigner/in*

supply chain [sə'plaɪ ˌtʃeɪn]	the series of processes involved in the production and supply of goods	*Versorgungskette*
boundary ['baʊndri]	a dividing line	*Grenze*

page 67

to streamline ['stri:mlaɪn]	make sth work better	*rationalisieren*
to bully ['bʊli]	put pressure on sb, force	*tyrannisieren, zwingen*
bumpy ['bʌmpi]	uncomfortable, difficult	*holperig*
to tap [tæp]	listen in on (a telelephone conversation) secretly	*anzapfen*
scary ['skeəri]	frightening	*furchterregend, gruselig*
accountant [ə'kaʊntənt]	sb who checks or keeps financial accounts	*Buchhalter/in, Steuerberater/in*
fleeting ['fli:tɪŋ]	lasting only a short time	*flüchtig*
shallow ['ʃæləʊ]	superficial, not serious	*seicht, flach*
clue [klu:]	information to help you understand sth	*Hinweis, Anhaltspunkt*
disassociated from [ˌdɪsə'səʊʃieɪtɪd frʌm]	not be connected to	*abgetrennt von*
contributor [kən'trɪbju:tə]	sb who helps to cause sth to happen	*Mitwirkende/r, Beteiligte/r*
to fail [feɪl]	disappoint	*enttäuschen, im Stich lassen*

TEXT 2 Cosmetic and Reconstructive Surgery

page 70

plastic surgeon [ˌplæstɪk 'sɜ:dʒən]	a doctor who performs operations to improve the patients' appearance	*Schönheitschirurg/in*
to animate ['ænɪmeɪt]	show feelings etc.	*Regungen zeigen*
disfigurement [dɪs'fɪgəmənt]	when one's natural appearance has been spoiled	*Entstellung*
to ostracize ['ɒstrəsaɪz]	not be accepted by society	*ächten, ausschließen*
stare [steə]	the act of looking at sb for a long time	*starrer Blick, Anstarren*
skin graft ['skɪn grɑ:ft]	piece of skin used to cover burnt skin	*Hauttransplantat*

page 71

to denude [dɪ'nju:d]	remove	*hier: abnehmen*
doomed [du:md]	certain to suffer, damned	*verdammt*
immunosuppressive [ˌɪmju:nəʊsə'presɪv]	ensuring that implanted organs are not rejected	*das Immunsystem unterdrückend*
donor ['dəʊnə]	a person who gives sth to help sb	*Spender/in*
random ['rændəm]	chance, uncontrolled	*Zufalls-, nach dem Zufallsprinzip*
fugitive ['fju:dʒətɪv]	sb who is trying not to be caught by the police	*Flüchtling*
witness ['wɪtnəs]	sb who sees a crime and can describe what happened	*Zeuge/Zeugin*

TEXT 3 Right to Life

page 73

umbilical cord [ʌmˌbɪlɪkl 'kɔ:d]	a long piece of tissue connecting the baby to its mother	*Nabelschnur*
grisly ['grɪzli]	extremely horrible	*grausig*
to abort [ə'bɔ:t]	give birth to a baby before it can survive	*abtreiben*
chief prosecutor [ˌtʃi:f 'prɒsɪkju:tə]	a lawyer who represents the government in a criminal prosecution	*Oberstaatsanwalt/-anwältin*
maternity wing [mə'tɜ:nəti wɪŋ]	the part of a hospital where babies are born	*Entbindungsstation*
to relieve of duty [rɪˌli:v əv 'dju:ti]	dismiss sb from a job	*des Amtes entheben, entlassen*
bribery ['braɪbəri]	corruption	*Bestechung*
stillborn ['stɪlbɔ:n]	born dead	*tot geboren*
inconsistent [ˌɪnkən'sɪstənt]	differing, conflicting	*widersprüchlich*

page 74

postmortem examination [pəʊstˌmɔ:təm ɪgzæmɪ'neɪʃn]	examination of a dead body	*Obduktion*
full term [ˌfʊl 'tɜ:m]	fully developed	*nach normaler Schwangerschaft geboren*
to dismember [dɪs'membə]	cut into pieces	*zerstückeln*
jigsaw ['dʒɪgsɔ:]	lots of small pieces cut out of cardboard which have to be fitted together again	*Puzzle*
to harvest ['hɑ:vɪst]	collect	*ernten*

bone marrow ['bəʊn mærəʊ]	a soft substance in the centre of bones	*Knochenmark*
remediation [rɪˌmi:di'eɪʃn]	cure	*Heilung*
tissue ['tɪʃu:]	the material forming animal or plant cells	*Gewebe*
fetal ['fi:tl]	related to a foetus	*fetal, fötal*
to re-launch [ˌri: 'lɔ:ntʃ]	start again in a different way	*wieder aufnehmen*

TEXT 4 Technological Innovations in the US

page 76

blackout ['blækaʊt]	total darkness as a result of electricity failure	*Stromausfall*
electrical grid [ɪˌlektrɪkl 'grɪd]	a system for sending power over a large area	*Stromnetz*
to project [prə'dʒekt]	estimate	*hochrechnen, prognostizieren*
stretched thin [stretʃd 'θɪn]	be pushed/strained to the limit	*völlig ausgelastet, an der Grenze*
to grapple with ['græpl]	try hard to find a solution	*kämpfen, sich herumschlagen mit*
per-capita [pə 'kæpɪtə]	for each person	*Pro-Kopf-*

page 77

to frolic ['frɒlɪk]	play in a lively, happy way	*(herum)tollen, toben*
encased [ɪn'keɪs]	covered completely	*eingeschlossen, ummantelt*
concrete ['kɒŋkri:t]	material made by mixing cement and water	*Beton*
facility [fə'sɪləti]	building/service provided for a specific purpose	*Einrichtung*
to object to [əb'dʒekt]	oppose sth	*Einspruch erheben, protestieren (gegen)*
real estate ['rɪəl ɪˌsteɪt]	property in the form of land or houses	*Grundstücke, Immobilien*
to tap in to [ˌtæp 'ɪn tə]	make use of	*mitbenutzen*
effluent ['efluənt]	liquid waste	*Abwasser*
mantra ['mæntrə]]	a phrase repeated again and again, especially in prayer	*Mantra, Losung, Devise*
desalination [ˌdi:ˌsælɪ'neɪʃn]	the process of removing salt from sea water	*(Meerwasser-)Entsalzung*

TEXT 5 Biotechnology and Food

page 80

deficiency [dɪ'fɪʃnsi]	the state of not having enough of sth essential	*Mangel*
caterpillar ['kætəpɪlə]	a small creature like a worm that develops into a butterfly	*Raupe*
saturated fat [ˌsætʃəreɪtɪd 'fæt]	type of fat that encourages the development of cholesterol	*gesättigte Fettsäuren*
cereal ['sɪəriəl]	grains used for flour or bread	*Getreide(art)*
drought [draʊt]	long period with little or no rain	*Dürre(periode)*
crops [krɒps]	plants grown in large quantities, especially for food	*Anbaupflanzen*
to reap [ri:p]	get, obtain	*ernten*
herbicide ['hɜ:bɪsaɪd]	a substance which kills weeds	*Unkrautvernichtungs-mittel*

page 81

weed [wi:d]	a wild plant growing where it is not wanted	*(Un-)Kraut*
subsequent ['sʌbsɪkwənt]	following, later	*(nach)folgend*
claim [kleɪm]	a statement saying sth is true	*Behauptung, Anspruch*
pest [pest]	insect which destroys plants and food	*Plage, Schädling*
reliant on [rɪ'laɪənt ɔn]	dependent on	*angewiesen auf, abhängig von*
lean [li:n]	thin	*mager, schlank*
outbreak ['aʊtbreɪk]	the sudden start of a disease	*Ausbruch*
to devastate ['devəsteɪt]	destroy completely	*zerstören, vernichten*
salmon ['sæmən]	large fish with silver skin and pink flesh	*Lachs*
to approve [ə'pru:v]	officially agree to	*genehmigen*
strain [streɪn]	type	*Art, Form*
inadvertent [ˌɪnəd'vɜ:tənt]	by accident	*unbeabsichtigt, versehentlich*
noxious ['nɒkʃəs]	poisonous, harmful	*schädlich*
remainder [rɪ'meɪndə]	the rest	*Rest(bestand)*
skylark ['skaɪlɑ:k]	a small bird that sings when it flies high into the sky	*(Feld-)Lerche*
bug [bʌg]	any small insect	*Bazillus, Insekt, Käfer*

TEXT 6 Short Story: Ray Bradbury, 'The Pedestrian'

page 84

buckling ['bʌklɪŋ]	bent, curved outwards	*holprig*
seam [si:m]	a line where two edges meet	*Naht, Aufbruch*
intersection [ˌɪntə'sekʃn]	crossroads	*Kreuzung*
to peer [pɪə]	look carefully and closely	*spähen*
to stride off [straɪd]	walk in long steps	*schreiten*
graveyard ['greɪvjɑ:d]	the place where dead people are buried	*Friedhof*
firefly ['faɪəflaɪ]	a flying insect that lights in the dark	*Leuchtkäfer*
tomb [tu:m]	a large grave, especially one built of stone	*Grab*
to cock [kɒk]	raise (the head) until it is at an angle	*(Kopf) schief legen*
intermittent [ˌɪntə'mɪtənt]	stopping and starting	*sporadisch*
squad [skwɒd]	group	*Gruppe, Meute*
to startle ['stɑ:tl]	surprise suddenly in a frightening way	*aufschrecken*
to blaze [bleɪz]	burn	*brennen*

page 85

hawk [hɔ:k]	a strong, fast bird that kills other creatures for food	*Habicht*
assorted [ə'sɔ:tɪd]	different, various	*gemischt, verschieden*
to vanish ['vænɪʃ]	disappear	*verschwinden*
cloverleaf intersection [ˌkləʊvəli:f ɪntə'sekʃn]	a place where a number of main roads meet, with curved sections which form the pattern of a four-leaf clover	*Autobahnkreuzung in Form eines Kleeblatts*
surge [sɜ:dʒ]	a sudden increase in the number of	*Flut(welle)*
ceaseless ['si:sləs]	not stopping	*unablässig*
scarab-beetle ['skærəb bi:tl]	a large black insect with a hard shell	*Skarabäus, Mistkäfer*
incense ['ɪnsens]	a substance which has a pleasant smell when you burn it	*Weihrauch*
cone [kəʊn]	a shape that is round at one end and slopes to a point	*Kegel*
entranced [ɪn'trɑ:nst]	in a trance	*benommen*
stunned [stʌnd]	shocked	*betäubt, benommen*
save for ['seɪv fə]	except for	*ausgenommen*
specimen ['spesɪmən]	a single example of sth, especially of animals or plants	*Probe, Exemplar*
to thrust [θrʌst]	push	*stoßen*

page 86

to hiss [hɪs]	make a sound like a long 's'	*zischen, fauchen*
riveted ['rɪvɪtɪd]	fastened with metal pins	*genietet*
whirring ['wɜ:rɪŋ]	a low sound like parts of a machine moving	*surrend*
punch-slotted card ['pʌntʃ slɒtɪd kɑ:d]	card with holes that gives instructions to computers	*Lochkarte*
regressive [rɪ'gresɪv]	going back to a less advanced state	*rückschrittlich*
thud [θʌd]	a sound made when a heavy objects hits sth else	*dumpfer Aufprall*

TOPIC 4 The March Towards Equality

TEXT 1 How Social Class Determines Speech in England

page 94

to despise [dɪ'spaɪz]	consider to be worthless or disgusting	*verachten*
pertinent ['pɜ:tɪnənt]	relevant	*relevant*
to fit sb or sth with [fɪt]	provide with sth by fixing it on the body or thing	*ausstatten*
glottal stop [ˌglɒtl 'stɒp]	a consonant formed by the audible release of the airstream	*Knacklaut*
to swallow ['swɒləʊ]	cause to disappear	*verschlucken*
the pot calling the kettle black [ðə pɒt ˌkɔ:lɪŋ ðə ˌketl 'blæk]	hypocrisy	*wenn man jemand anderem die eigenen Fehler vorwirft*
rank [ræŋk]	position within a hierarchy	*Rang, Schicht*
Naff off! [ˌnæf 'ɒf]	Get lost!	*Hau ab!*

page 95

infallible [ɪn'fæləbl]	never wrong	*unfehlbar*
to utter ['ʌtə]	say or make a sound	*äußern*
to bleep [bli:p]	a high-pitched noise	*piepsen*
to flinch [flɪntʃ]	a quick movement as a result of fear or pain	*zusammenzucken*

hallmark ['hɔ:lmɑ:k]	a distinctive feature	*Kenn-, Markenzeichen*
echelon ['eʃəlɒn]	position within a hierarchy	*Rang, Stufe*
vast [vɑ:st]	very large	*riesig, groß*

TEXT 2 Generational Challenges of Muslim Britons

page 98

to unleash [ʌn'li:ʃ]	set free	*entfesseln, auslösen*
to restrain [rɪ'streɪn]	hold back	*unterdrücken*
obedience [ə'bi:diəns]	doing what someone orders	*Gehorsam*
misguided [ˌmɪs'gaɪdɪd]	showing faulty judgment or reasoning	*töricht, irregeleitet*
to delude [dɪ'lu:d]	persuade sb to believe sth incorrect	*(sich oder jmdn) täuschen*
obligation [ˌɒblɪ'geɪʃn]	duty, requirement	*Verpflichtung, Zwang*
to exert one's pull [ɪgˌzɜ:t wʌnz 'pʊl]	use one's influence	*Druck ausüben*
to toss [tɒs]	throw	*werfen*

page 99

hijab [hɪ'dʒɑ:b]	headscarf or other female Muslim dress	*Kopftuch, Hidschab, Verschleierung*
jihad [dʒɪ'hɑ:d]	holy war (can also mean a personal moral struggle e.g. to stop drinking alcohol)	*Dschihad, heiliger Krieg*
suspicion [sə'spɪʃn]	not trusting	*Misstrauen*
to mug [mʌg]	attack and rob in a public place	*überfallen, ausrauben*

TEXT 3 An Era When Dreams Took Centre Stage

page 102

uplifting [ˌʌp'lɪftɪŋ]	morally or spiritually elevating	*aufbauend, erhebend*
Jim Crow [ˌdʒɪm 'krəʊ]	the name given to segregation laws	*Rassen(gesetze)*
seamstress ['si:mstrəs]	woman who sews for a living	*Näherin*
to withhold [wɪð'həʊld]	keep, deny sb	*verweigern, vorenthalten*
sit-in ['sɪt ɪn]	occupying a place as a form of protest	*Sitzstreik*

page 103

to defer [dɪ'fɜ:]	put off until later	*aufschieben, vertagen*
down payment ['daʊn peɪmənt]	first payment	*Anzahlung*
yard [jɑ:d]	*(AE) BE*: garden	*Hof, Garten*

page 104

to enunciate [ɪ'nʌnsieɪt]	articulate clearly with the mouth	*artikulieren*
amiable ['eɪmiəbl]	friendly	*freundlich, liebenswürdig*
residential property [reziˌdenʃl 'prɒpəti]	house or land where sb can live	*Wohneigentum, Wohngrundstück*
upkeep ['ʌpki:p]	maintenance	*Instandhaltung*
to give sb the lowdown on ['ləʊdaʊn]	(coll.) inform sb of the current situation	*jdm (nähere) Informationen geben über*
appreciation [əˌpri:ʃi'eɪʃn]	understanding	*Anerkennung*
incident ['ɪnsɪdənt]	event	*Ereignis, Vorgang*
to deplore [dɪ'plɔ:]	strongly disapprove of	*verurteilen, beklagen*
emphasis ['emfəsɪs]	special importance, stress	*Betonung, Nachdruck*

page 105

to take advantage of [teɪk əd'vɑ:ntɪdʒ əv]	use sb in an unethical way	*ausnutzen, übervorteilen*
fancy˘ ['fænsi]	upper-class	*vornehm*
dumbfounded [dʌm'faʊndɪd]	extremely surprised	*verblüfft, sprachlos*
the living gall [ðə ˌlɪvɪŋ 'gɔ:l]	*(informal AE)* arrogance, shamelessness	*Dreistigkeit, Unverschämtheit*
threatened ['θretnd]	in danger	*bedroht*

TEXT 4 It All Depends On Where You Were Born: Hispanics in North America

page 108

storage rental shed [ˌstɔːrɪdʒ rentl ˈʃed]	a small building hired for the purpose of keeping things in it	*Lager, Speicher*
desperate [ˈdespərət]	having great need for sth	*verzweifelt*
to figure [ˈfɪgə]	think, consider	*(sich) denken*
blue-collar [ˌbluː ˈkɒlə]	working-class	*(Fabrik-)Arbeiter-*

page 109

to cherish [ˈtʃerɪʃ]	protect and care for lovingly	*festhalten an, hegen*
to embarrass [ɪmˈbærəs]	to make sb feel ashamed	*jdn in Verlegenheit bringen*
to slash [slæʃ]	cut through violently	*zerschneiden*
to haunt [hɔːnt]	often be at a place	*heimsuchen, verfolgen*

page 111

to surpass˘ [səˈpɑːs]	be greater than	*überflügeln*
to triple [ˈtrɪpl]	become three times as many	*sich verdreifachen*
to constitute [ˈkɒnstɪtjuːt]	form, make up	*darstellen, bilden*

TEXT 5 Equal Rights for Homosexuals

page 113

on account of [ɒn əˈkaʊnt əv]	because of	*wegen*
envying [ˈenviɪŋ]	with a longing for what sb else has	*neidisch*
residency [ˈrezɪdənsi]	permission to live somewhere	*Aufenthalt(sgenehmigung)*
afterthought [ˈɑːftəθɔt]	sth thought of or added later	*nachträglicher Einfall*
secularism [ˈsekjələrɪzəm]	separation of church and state	*Säkularismus*
pious [ˈpaɪəs]	devoutly religious	*fromm*

page 114

glue [gluː]	substance used for sticking objects together	*Klebstoff, Leim*
to dissolve [dɪˈzɒlv]	break down	*auflösen*
to embark on [ɪmˈbɑːk ɒn]	begin	*einschlagen*
to reconcile [ˈrekənsaɪl]	make compatible	*versöhnen, in Einklang bringen*
ancestry [ˈænsestri]	ethnic origins	*Abstammung, Herkunft*
abortion [əˈbɔːʃn]	intentionally ending a pregnancy	*Abtreibung*
contradiction in terms [ˌkɒntrədɪkʃn ɪn ˈtɜːmz]	a group of words making a connection between incompatible concepts	*Widerspruch in sich*
commitment [kəˈmɪtmənt]	a promise to bind oneself to a person, action, or cause	*Engagement, Bindung*
sluggish [ˈslʌgɪʃ]	slow	*träge, schwerfällig*

page 116

to raid [reɪd]	enter (a building) by force to arrest people or seize illicit goods	*durchsuchen, eine Razzia durchführen*
patron [ˈpeɪtrən]	guest at a bar or restaurant	*Gast*
riot [ˈraɪət]	a violent disturbance of the peace by a crowd	*Aufstand, Krawall*

TEXT 6 Never Say 'Dummy' Again

page 118

to enslave [ɪnˈsleɪv]	make sb a slave	*versklaven*
inheritance [ɪnˈherɪtəns]	what one receives from sb when they die	*Erbe*
to deem [diːm]	see as	*ansehen, erachten*
abhorrent [əbˈhɒrənt]	morally disgusting	*abscheulich*
to thrive [θraɪv]	live very well	*gedeihen, Erfolg haben*
illiterate [ɪˈlɪtərət]	unable to read or write	*Analphabet/in*
cognitive [ˈkɒgnətɪv]	related to thinking	*kognitiv*
heritability [ˌherɪtəˈbɪləti]	how much influence heredity has on a specific trait	*Erblichkeit*
to devote [dɪˈvəʊt]	dedicate	*widmen*
merit [ˈmerɪt]	good quality	*Verdienst(e)*
to be entitled to [bi ɪnˈtaɪtld tə]	to have the right to	*berechtigt sein zu*
undeserving [ˌʌndɪˈzɜːvɪŋ]	unworthy	*unwürdig*
inherently [ɪnˈhɪərəntli]	by nature	*von Natur aus*
vocational [vəʊˈkeɪʃənl]	professional	*beruflich, Berufs-*

craft [krɑ:ft]	making sth by hand	*(Kunst-)Handwerk*
scrap heap ['skræp hi:p]	junk pile	*Schrotthaufen*
to pretend [prɪ'tend]	act as if	*vorgeben, so tun als ob*

TOPIC 5 Britain's Changing Status in Today's World

TEXT 1 Reflections on Britain's Colonial Past

page 126

ancestor ['ænsestə]	a person in your family who lived a long time ago	*Vorfahr*

page 127

to foster ['fɒstə]	encourage sth to develop	*fördern*
sacrifice ['sækrɪfaɪs]	the act of giving up sth important	*Opfer*
to endure [ɪn'djʊə]	tolerate without giving up	*erfahren, erleiden*
on the brink of [ɒn ðə 'brɪŋk əv]	on the point of	*am Rande von*
absorption [əb'sɔ:pʃn]	the process of a smaller country becoming part of a larger country	*Einverleibung*
severe [sɪ'vɪə]	extremely bad or serious	*ernst, schwer*
to partition [pɑ:'tɪʃn]	divide	*aufteilen*
assassination [ə,sæsɪ'neɪʃn]	murder of an important person	*Attentat, Ermordung*
succession [sək'seʃn]	series	*Folge, Reihe*
to vow [vaʊ]	make a serious promise	*schwören*
abolition [,æbə'lɪʃn]	the removal of a law	*Abschaffung*

TEXT 2 The Empire as Portrayed in Two Book Reviews

page 131

to comprise [kəm'praɪz]	consist of	*umfassen*
oblivion [ə'blɪviən]	the state in which sb/sth is no longer famous	*Vergessen(heit)*
to mature [mə'tʃʊə]	develop	*reifen*
to surrender [sə'rendə]	give up sth	*aufgeben*
sprawling ['sprɔ:lɪŋ]	covering a large area	*ausgedehnt*
to precede [prɪ'si:d]	go in front of sb	*vorausgehen*
bewildering [bɪ'wɪldərɪŋ]	confusing	*verwirrend*
supremacy [su:'preməsi]	dominance	*Vormacht(stellung), Überlegenheit*
insufficient [,ɪnsə'fɪʃnt]	not enough	*ungenügend*

page 132

last post [,lɑ:st 'pəʊst]	a tune played at the end of the day in military camps	*Zapfenstreich*
oddball ['ɒdbɔ:l]	a person who behaves in a strange way	*Kauz*
moustache [mə'stɑ:ʃ]	a line of hair on the upper lip	*Schnurrbart*
to boast [bəʊst]	talk with too much pride about sth	*prahlen, angeben*
to indulge in [ɪn'dʌldʒ ɪn]	allow yourself to do sth, especially sth bad	*sich gönnen*
vice [vaɪs]	criminal activities that involve sex or drugs	*Laster*
maverick ['mævərɪk]	a person who has unusual opinions and acts unusually	*Einzelgänger/in, Eigenbrötler/in*
plus-fours [,plʌs 'fɔ:z]	wide, loose trousers which end below the knee	*(weite) Knickerbocker(hose)*

TEXT 3 The Empire in Literature

page 135

as bold as brass [əz bəʊld əz 'brɑ:s]	without showing any respect	*unverfroren*
to grumble ['grʌmbl]	complain about sth	*meckern*
poultry ['pəʊltri]	chickens, ducks and geese	*Geflügel*
to moan [məʊn]	make a long, deep sound of unhappiness	*stöhnen*
to mutter ['mʌtə]	speak in a quiet voice that is difficult to understand	*raunen, murmeln*

page 136

to tingle ['tɪŋgl]	feel as if sharp points are pushing into a part of the body	*prickeln, kribbeln*
fleece [fli:s]	all the wool cut off a sheep	*Schaffell*
fabric ['fæbrɪk]	material made by weaving wool, silk etc.	*Stoff*
contagious [kən'teɪdʒəs]	infectious	*ansteckend*
to trail [treɪl]	walk slowly behind sb	*(hinterher)trotten*

loom [lu:m]	a machine for making cloth	*Webstuhl*
to nudge [nʌdʒ]	push sb gently, esp. with the elbow	*(an)stoßen*
to carve [kɑ:v]	make by cutting away material from wood	*schnitzen*
to shoo sb off [ʃu:]	make sb go away	*(weg)scheuchen*
to smudge [smʌdʒ]	rub sth so that it is no longer clear	*verschmieren*
sooty ['sʊti]	covered with soot (a black powder that is produced after wood, coal, etc. is burnt)	*verrußt, rußig*
to bulge [bʌldʒ]	stick out in a round shape	*(sich) wölben*
to squash [skwɒʃ]	flatten by force	*platt drücken*
nostril ['nɒstrəl]	the two holes in the nose	*Nasenloch*
to tease [ti:z]	laugh and make jokes about sb	*necken, ärgern*
crimson ['krɪmzn]	a dark red colour	*purpurrot*

page 137

to mumble ['mʌmbl]	speak in a quiet way that is not clear	*murmeln, nuscheln*
bin [bɪn]	a container you put waste into	*(Müll-)Tonne*

TEXT 4 Britain and EU Regulations

page 139

imperial [ɪm'pɪəriəl]	connected with empire	*imperial, aus dem Empire*
to wrangle ['ræŋgl]	to argue for a long time over a complicated issue	*streiten, zerren*
metrication [ˌmetrɪ'keɪʃn]	the process of changing to the metric system	*Umstellung auf das metrische System*
deadline ['dedlaɪn]	a point in time by which sth must be done	*Termin, Frist*
move [mu:v]	step, measure	*Schritt, Maßnahme*
produce ['prɒdju:s]	things that have been made or grown	*Produkt(e), Erzeugnis(se)*
outrage ['aʊtreɪdʒ]	strong feeling of shock and anger	*Empörung*
defiance [dɪ'faɪəns]	refusal to obey	*Missachtung, Trotz*
to convict [kən'vɪkt]	decide in court that sb is guilty	*verurteilen*

page 140

to display [dɪ'spleɪ]	put sth in a place where people can see it	*(an)zeigen, ausstellen*
prosecution [ˌprɒsɪ'kju:ʃn]	the process of being charged with a crime in court	*strafrechtliche Verfolgung*
significance [sɪg'nɪfɪkəns]	importance	*Bedeutung*
to prolong [prə'lɒŋ]	make sth last longer	*verlängern*
obsolet ['ɒbsəli:t]	out of date and no longer used	*veraltet*

TEXT 5 Britain, In or Out of Europe?

page 143

cause [kɔ:z]	an idea that people support	*Sache*
principality [ˌprɪnsɪ'pæləti]	country ruled by a prince	*Fürstentum*
convenience [kən'vi:niəns]	something that is useful, easy or suitable	*hier: Nutzen, Vorteil*
to proceed [prə'si:d]	continue	*fortfahren*
to champion ['tʃæmpiən]	fight for	*eintreten für, sich einsetzen (für)*
sage [seɪdʒ]	a wise person	*Weise/r*
grandee [græn'di:]	a person of high rank and standing	*Grande, Prominenter*
affiliation [əˌfɪli'eɪʃn]	relationship	*Angliederung*
honorary ['ɒnərəri]	given as an honour without the person having the usual qualifications	*Ehren-*
to evolve [ɪ'vɒlv]	develop gradually	*(sich) entwickeln*
to air [eə]	express	*(öffentlich) äußern*
stubborn ['stʌbən]	unwilling to change an attitude	*dickköpfig, stur*
to dare [deə]	be brave enough to do sth	*(es) wagen, sich trauen*

TOPIC 6 Issues Confronting the USA

TEXT 1 Why We're Proud To Be Americans

page 152

to shrink from ['ʃrɪŋk frəm]	be unwilling to	*zurückschrecken vor*
prosperity [prɒ'sperəti]	wealth	*Wohlstand*

marvel ['mɑːvl]	wonder	*Wunder*
beacon ['biːkən]	guiding light	*Leuchtfeuer*
to face off [ˌfeɪs 'ɒf]	get ready to fight	*entgegentreten*
to devise [dɪ'vaɪz]	think up, create	*ausdenken, entwerfen*
to eject [ɪ'dʒekt]	force out	*hinauswerfen*
to dither ['dɪðə]	not be able to decide	*hin und her überlegen*

page 153

unfettered [ʌn'fetəd]	uninhibited	*frei, unbehindert*
to risk life and limb [rɪsk ˌlaɪf ən 'lɪm]	risk one's life	*sein Leben riskieren*

TEXT 2 America: Whose Dream Is It, Anyway?

page 157

newsreel ['njuːzriːl]	short cinema film of news	*Wochenschau*

page 158

to embrace [ɪm'breɪs]	accept willingly	*umarmen, annehmen*
to nurture ['nɜːtʃə]	care for	*pflegen*
barrio ['bæriəʊ]	Spanish-speaking area of a city	*lateinamerikanisch geprägtes Stadtviertel*

TEXT 3 How United is the United States?

page 161

bigoted ['bɪgətɪd]	blindly attached to a belief or an opinion	*bigott, fanatisch*
conundrum [kə'nʌndrəm]	confusing problem	*Rätsel, Problem*
mongrel ['mʌŋgrəl]	racially mixed	*gemischtrassig*
disparate ['dɪspərət]	very different	*verschieden(artig)*
discordant [dɪs'kɔːdənt]	unharmonious	*uneinig*
quilt [kwɪlt]	blanket made up of many small pieces of fabric	*Patchwork-, Steppdecke*
bigotry ['bɪgətri]	extreme prejudice	*Bigotterie, Fanatismus*
sweatshop ['swetʃɒp]	a factory with poor working conditions	*Ausbeuterbetrieb*
ostracism ['ɒstrəsɪzəm]	exclusion	*Ächtung*
denial [dɪ'naɪəl]	refusal to give	*Verweigerung*
on the verge of [ɒn ðə 'vɜːdʒ əv]	at the limit before something will happen	*am Rande von*
fisticuffs *(pl.)* ['fɪstɪkʌfs]	fist-fighting	*Handgemenge*

page 162

vexing ['veksɪŋ]	annoying or worrying	*verzwickt*
refugee [ˌrefju'dʒiː]	sb who is forced to flee their home	*Flüchtling*
warring ['wɔːrɪŋ]	at war with each other	*Krieg führend*
tenuous ['tenjuəs]	unsure	*schwach*
subway ['sʌbweɪ]	*(AE) BE*: underground railway	*U-Bahn*
Ma-Pa store [ˌmɑː 'pɑː stɔː]	family-run store	*Tante-Emma-Laden*

TEXT 4 Declaring 'War' on Terror

page 164

casualty ['kæʒuəlti]	a killed or injured person	*Opfer, Verletzte/r, Tote/r*

page 165

affiliated [ə'fɪlieɪtɪd]	connected with each other	*miteinander verbunden*
to impose [ɪm'pəʊz]	force	*aufzwingen*
fringe [frɪndʒ]	on the edge	*Rand-*
scholar ['skɒlə]	a highly educated person	*Gelehrte/r*
at one's command [ət wʌnz kə'mɑːnd]	available for one to use	*zu jds Verfügung*
intelligence [ɪn'telɪdʒəns]	secret government information	*Geheimdienst(informationen)*
disruption [dɪs'rʌpʃn]	interruption or disturbance	*Störung, Behinderung*
to starve [stɑːv]	cut off; literally: deny food to	*sperren, blockieren; wörtlich: aushungern*
funding ['fʌndɪŋ]	supply of money	*Finanzierung*
refuge ['refjuːdʒ]	a safe place	*Schutz, Zuflucht*
haven ['heɪvn]	a safe place	*Zufluchtsort*
to be at stake [bi ət 'steɪk]	be in danger of being lost	*auf dem Spiel stehen*

TEXT 5 The Role of Christian Fundamentalism

page 168

bonkers ['bɒŋkəz]	crazy	*verrückt, wahnsinnig*
delusion [dɪ'lu:ʒn]	illusion	*Illusion, Irrglaube*
preacher ['pri:tʃə]	religious speaker	*Prediger/in*
to deploy [dɪ'plɔɪ]	send into action	*einsetzen, entsenden*
rapture ['ræptʃə]	ecstasy	*Verzückung, Entrückung*
to devour [dɪ'vaʊə]	eat up	*verschlingen*
boil [bɔɪl]	a kind of swelling on the skin	*Geschwür*
sore [sɔ:]	wound	*Wunde*
locust ['ləʊkəst]	a kind of insect	*Heuschrecke*
tribulation [ˌtrɪbju'leɪʃn]	terrible state	*Plage*
to stage [steɪdʒ]	organise, cause to happen	*inszenieren, veranstalten*

page 169

infidel ['ɪnfɪdəl]	sb who has no religion or a different religion than the majority	*Ungläubige/r*
to dismiss [dɪs'mɪs]	forget about	*abtun, hinweggehen über*
marginal ['mɑ:dʒɪnl]	small in number	*unwesentlich*
pollster ['pəʊlstə]	person who conducts a survey	*Meinungsforscher/in*
attorney general [əˌtɜ:ni 'dʒenrəl]	principle legal officer of a country	*(US-)Justizminister/in*
to waver ['weɪvə]	begin to weaken	*wanken*
blaze [bleɪz]	fire	*Glut, Flammen*

TEXT 6 Will the US Remain the Superpower?

page 172

to subjugate ['sʌbdʒugeɪt]	force to play a submissive role	*unterwerfen*
harvest ['hɑ:vɪst]	season's yield of crops	*Ernte*

page 173

complacent [kəm'pleɪsnt]	self-satisfied, apathetic	*gleichgültig, selbstzufrieden*
to undermine [ˌʌndə'maɪn]	weaken	*untergraben*
to sacrifice ['sækrɪfaɪs]	give up	*opfern, verzichten auf*
to distract [dɪ'strækt]	divert attention from something	*ablenken*
gross domestic product [ˌgrəʊs dəˌmestɪk 'prɒdʌkt]	total value of goods produced and services provided within a country in one year	*Bruttinlandsprodukt*
to churn out [ˌtʃɜ:n 'aʊt]	manufacture very quickly	*am laufenden Band produzieren*
to bend to [bend]	curve one's body	*(sich) beugen*
to assume [ə'sju:m]	suppose	*annehmen, glauben*
virtue ['vɜ:tʃu:]	positive attribute	*Tugend*

A–Z WORD LIST

Dieses Wörterverzeichnis enthält alle in *Crossover 2* eingeführten, in den Texten angegebenen Vokabeln in alphabetischer Reihenfolge.

A

to abandon 12, 57 aufgeben, sich abwenden von; stillegen
abhorrent 118 abscheulich
abolition 127 Abschaffung
to abort 73 abtreiben
abortion 114 Abtreibung
absorption 127 Einverleibung
abundance 58 Fülle
account: on account of 113 wegen
accountant 67 Buchhalter/in, Steuerberater/in
to acquire 8 erwerben
acquisition 8 Erwerb, Anschaffung
addictive 8 süchtig machend
advantage: to take advantage of 105 ausnutzen, übervorteilen
affiliated 165 miteinander verbunden
affiliation 143 Angliederung
afterthought 113 nachträglicher Einfall
to air 143 (öffentlich) äußern
amiable 104 freundlich, liebenswürdig
ancestor 126 Vorfahr
ancestral home 43 Familiensitz, angestammte Heimat
ancestry 114 Abstammung, Herkunft
to animate 70 Regungen zeigen
appreciation 104 Anerkennung
to approve 80 genehmigen
arsenic 57 Arsen
assassination 127 Attentat, Ermordung
assorted 85 gemischt, verschieden
to assume 173 annehmen, glauben
attorney general 169 (US-)Justizminister/Justizministerin

B

bargain 9 Sonderangebot, Schnäppchen
barn 20 Scheune
barrio 158 lateinamerikanisch geprägtes Stadtviertel
beacon 152 Leuchtfeuer
to behold 13 betrachten
to bend the truth 54 es mit der Wahrheit nicht so genau nehmen, die Wahrheit verbiegen
to bend to 173 (sich) beugen
beneficial 23 nützlich, vorteilhaft
to beware of 46 sich hüten
bewildering 130 verwirrend
bigoted 161 bigott, fanatisch
bigotry 161 Bigotterie, Fanatismus
bin 137 (Müll-)Tonne
bioremediation 57 biologische Reinigung
blackout 76 Stromausfall
to blaze 84 brennen
blaze 169 Glut, Flammen
to bleep 95 piepsen
blowback 55 Rückschläge
blue-collar 108 (Fabrik-)Arbeiter-
to boast 131 prahlen, angeben
bog 43 Sumpf
boil 168 Geschwür
bold: as bold as brass 135 unverfroren
bone marrow 74 Knochenmark
bonkers 168 verrückt, wahnsinnig
to boost 19 steigern
boundary 66 Grenze
bribery 73 Bestechung
brink: on the brink of 127 am Rande von
buckling 84 holprig
bucolic 20 ländlich, idyllisch
bug 80 Bazillus, Insekt, Käfer
to bulge 136 (sich) wölben
to bully 67 tyrannisieren, zwingen
bumpy 67 holperig
buoy 58 Boje
bushel 52 Scheffel
butyric acid 54 Buttersäure

C

to capture 39 ergreifen
carbon 48 Kohlenstoff
carbon sequestration 57 Entfernung von CO_2 aus der Atmosphäre
to carve 136 schnitzen
casualty 164 Opfer, Verletzte/r, Tote/r
caterpillar 79 Raupe
cause 143 Sache
ceaseless 85 unablässig
cereal 79 Getreide(art)
to champion 143 eintreten für, sich einsetzen (für)
charge 49 Anklage(punkt)
to cherish 109 festhalten an, hegen
chief prosecutor 73 Oberstaatsanwalt/-anwältin
chores 27 Haus-, Routinearbeit
to churn out 173 am laufenden Band produzieren
claim 80 Behauptung, Anspruch
clear-fell 48 roden, abholzen
clout 19 Kraft/Einfluss
cloverleaf intersection 85 Autobahnkreuzung in Form eines Kleeblatts
clue 67 Hinweis, Anhaltspunkt
clutter 13 Kram
to cock 84 (Kopf) schief legen
coercive 54 Zwangs-
cognitive 118 kognitiv
coil 54 Rolle
colossal 30 gigantisch
command: at one's command 165 zu jds Verfügung
commitment 114 Engagement, Bindung
compelling 39 zwingend
complacent 173 gleichgültig, selbstzufrieden
to comprise 127 umfassen
compulsive 8 zwanghaft
concrete 77 Beton
cone 85 Kegel
confined 19 eingesperrt
to conjure up 20 heraufbeschwören
conspicuous 24 auffällig
to constitute 111 darstellen, bilden
contagious 136 ansteckend
contamination 57 Verschmutzung
contradiction in terms 114 Widerspruch in sich
contributor 67 Mitwirkende/r, Beteiligte/r
conundrum 161 Rätsel, Problem
convenience 143 hier: Nutzen, Vorteil
to convict 139 verurteilen
corn 15 Mais
to correlate 16 (miteinander) in Beziehung setzen
cozy 23 gemütlich
craft 118 (Kunst-)Handwerk
crimson 136 purpurrot
crops 79 Anbaupflanzen
crud 46 Dreck, Brühe
cuddly 23 kuschelig

D

to dare 143 (es) wagen, sich trauen
deadline 139 Termin, Frist
debris 48 Reste, Schutt
to decompose 48 (sich) zersetzen
to deem sb sth 118 ansehen, erachten
to defer 103 aufschieben, vertagen
defiance 139 Missachtung, Trotz
deficiency 79 Mangel
to delude 98 (sich oder jmdn) täuschen
delusion 168 Illusion, Irrglaube
demigod 55 Halbgott
denial 161 Verweigerung
denier 39 Leugner/in
to denounce 55 öffentlich rügen
to denude 71 hier: abnehmen
to deplore 104 verurteilen, beklagen
to deploy 168 einsetzen, entsenden
desalination 77 (Meerwasser-)Entsalzung
desperate 108 verzweifelt
to despise 94 verachten
destined 49 bestimmt
detergent 46 Reinigungsmittel, Waschmittel
to devastate 80 zerstören, vernichten
to devise 152 ausdenken, entwerfen
to devote 118 widmen
to devour 168 verschlingen
disassociated from 67 abgetrennt von
discordant 161 uneinig
disfigurement 70 Entstellung
to dismember 74 zerstückeln
to dismiss 169 abtun, hinweggehen über
disparate 161 verschieden(artig)

subsistence-level 23 am Existenz-minimum
subway 162 *(AE)* U-Bahn
succession 127 Folge, Reihe
to succumb to 13 erliegen
suds *(pl.)* 30 Seifenschaum
to suffocate 39 ersticken
supercilious 30 hochmütig, herablassend
superhighway 27 Autobahn
superlot 30 Riesenparkplatz
to supersede 30 ersetzen, ablösen
supersonic 30 Überschall-
supply chain 66 Versorgungskette
supremacy 130 Vormacht(stellung), Überlegenheit
surge 85 Flut(welle)
to surpass 111 überflügeln
to surrender 130 aufgeben
suspicion 99 Misstrauen
to swallow 94 verschlucken
sweatshop 161 Ausbeuterbetrieb
swell 58 Woge, Seegang

T

to tap 67 anzapfen
to tap in to 77 mitbenutzen
to tease 136 necken, ärgern
temporary 8 vorübergehend, zeitweilig
to tempt 12 in Versuchung führen, verleiten
temptation 9 Versuchung
tenuous 162 schwach
to thaw 43 auftauen
threatened 105 bedroht
thrill 39 (aufregendes) Gefühl
thrilling 8 aufregend
to thrive 43 gedeihen, Erfolg haben
to thrust 85 stoßen
thud 87 dumpfer Aufprall
to tingle 136 prickeln, kribbeln
tissue 74 Gewebe
tomb 84 Grab
to toss 98 werfen
to tout 12 werben (für), anpreisen
to trail 136 (hinterher)trotten
transcendence 39 Erhabenheit
to trash 49 zerstören
tribulation 168 Plage
to triple 111 sich verdreifachen

U

ubiquitous 20 allgegenwärtig, unvermeidlich
umbilical cord 73 Nabelschnur
to undermine 173 untergraben
underneath 13 (dar)unter
undeserving 118 unwürdig
unfettered 152 frei, unbehindert
to unleash 98 entfesseln, auslösen
unprecedented 38 beispiellos
unyielding 54 unnachgiebig
upkeep 104 Instandhaltung
uplifting 102 aufbauend, erhebend
urea 20 Harnstoff
to utter 95 äußern

V

to vanish 85 verschwinden
vast 95 riesig, groß
veil 46 Schleier, Atemschutz
vendor 12 Verkäufer/in
verge: on the verge of 161 am Rande von
vessel 54 Schiff, Boot
vexing 162 verzwickt
vice 131 Laster
vicious cycle 43 Teufelskreis
vigilante 54 Selbstjustizler/in
violation 54 Übertretung
virtually 38 praktisch, nahezu
virtue 173 Tugend
vocational 118 beruflich, Berufs-
to vow 127 schwören
vulnerable 43 zerstörbar, verwundbar

W

warring 162 Krieg führend
to waver 169 wanken
weed 79 (Un-)Kraut
whirring 86 surrend
wholesome 19 gesund
to withhold 102 verweigern, vorenthalten
witness 71 Zeuge/Zeugin
to wrangle 139 streiten, zerren
to wreak havoc 38 verheerende Auswirkungen haben

X–Y–Z

yard 103 Hof, Garten
to yearn for 20 sich sehnen nach

GEOGRAPHICAL NAMES

(Great) Britain [ˌgreɪt ˈbrɪtn]	Großbritannien
(New) Delhi [njuː ˈdeli]	(Neu-)Delhi
(the) Atlantic [ði ətˈlæntɪk]	(der) Atlantik
(the) Pacific [ðə pəˈsɪfɪk]	Pazifik
Afghanistan [æfˈgænɪstɑːn]	Afghanistan
Africa [ˈæfrɪkə]	Afrika
Alaska [əˈlæskə]	Alaska
Anaheim [ˈænəhaɪm]	Anaheim
Ankara [ˈæŋkərə]	Ankara
Antarctica [æntˈɑːktɪkə]	Antarktis
Arizona [ærɪˈzəʊnə]	Arizona
Asia [ˈeɪʃə]	Asien
Australia [ɒˈstreɪliə]	Australien
Bangladesh [ˌbæŋgləˈdeʃ]	Bangladesch
Barbados [bɑːˈbeɪdɒs]	Barbados
Belgium [ˈbeldʒəm]	Belgien
Bethel [ˈbeθl]	Bethel
Burma [ˈbɜːmə]	Burma, Myanmar
Cairo [ˈkaɪrəʊ]	Kairo
California [ˌkæləˈfɔːniə]	Kalifornien
Cambridge [ˈkeɪmbrɪdʒ]	Cambridge
Canada [ˈkænədə]	Kanada
Cardiff [ˈkɑːdɪf]	Cardiff
Caribbean [ˌkærəˈbiːən]	Karibik
Carson [ˈkɑːsn]	Carson
Central Asia [ˌsentrəl ˈeɪʃə]	Zentralasien
Ceylon [sɪˈlɒn]	Ceylon
Chanderi [tʃænˈderi]	Chanderi
Chicago [ʃɪˈkɑːgəʊ]	Chikago
China [ˈtʃaɪnə]	China
Cleveland [ˈkliːvlənd]	Cleveland
Clybourne Park [ˈklaɪbɔːn pɑːk]	Clybourne Park
Clybourne Street [ˈklaɪbɔːn striːt]	*Straßenname*
Colorado River [ˌkɒləˈrɑːdəʊ rɪvə]	Colorado River
Costa Rica [ˌkɒstə ˈriːkə]	Costa Rica
Croatia [krəʊˈeɪʃə]	Kroatien
Cuba [ˈkjuːbə]	Kuba
Dalhousie [dælˈhaʊzi]	Dalhousie
Denmark [ˈdenmɑːk]	Dänemark
Detroit [dɪˈtrɔɪt]	Detroit
Dillingham [ˈdɪlɪŋəm]	Dillingham
East River [ˌiːst ˈrɪvə]	East River
Eastern Europe [ˌiːstən ˈjʊərəp]	Osteuropa
Egypt [ˈiːdʒɪpt]	Ägypten
El Segundo [el səˈgʊndəʊ]	El Segundo
England [ˈɪŋglənd]	England
Estonia [eˈstəʊniə]	Estland
Europe [ˈjʊərəp]	Europa
France [frɑːns]	Frankreich
Gambia [ˈgæmbiə]	Gambia
Gaza [ˈgɑːzə]	Gaza
Gaza Strip [ˌgɑzə ˈstrɪp]	Gazastreifen
Georgia [ˈdʒɔːdʒə]	Georgia
Germany [ˈdʒɜːməni]	Deutschland
Ghana [ˈgɑːnə]	Ghana
Gibraltar [dʒɪˈbrɔːltə]	Gibraltar
Graz [grɑːts]	Graz
Greenland [ˈgriːnlənd]	Grönland
Grenada [grɪ ˈneɪdə]	Grenada
Hong Kong [ˌhɒŋ ˈkɒŋ]	Hong Kong
Houston [ˈhjuːstən]	Houston
Iceland [ˈaɪslənd]	Island
Illinois [ˌɪləˈnɔɪ]	Illinois
India [ˈɪndiə]	Indien
Indonesia [ˌɪndəʊˈniːziə]	Indonesien
Iowa [ˈaɪəwə]	Iowa
Iraq [ɪˈrɑːk]	Irak
Ireland [ˈaɪələnd]	Irland
Israel [ˈɪzreɪl]	Israel
Italy [ˈɪtəli]	Italien
Jakarta [dʒəˈkɑːtə]	Jakarta
Jamaica [dʒəˈmeɪkə]	Jamaika
Japan [dʒəˈpæn]	Japan
Jenin [dʒəˈniːn]	Dschenin
Kaktovik [ˈkæktəvɪk]	Koaktovik
Kampar [ˈkæmpɑː]	Kampar (Moor in Sumatra)
Kenya [ˈkenjə]	Kenia
Kharkiv [ˈkɑːkɪv]	Charkiw
Kiev [ˈkiːef]	Kiew
Kivalina [ˌkɪvəˈliːnə]	Kivalina
Kuwait [kuˈweɪt]	Kuwait
Latin America [ˌlætɪn əˈmerɪkə]	Lateinamerika
London [ˈlʌndən]	London
Long Island [lɒŋ ˈaɪlənd]	Long Island
Los Angeles [lɒs ˈændʒəliːz]	Los Angeles
Malaya [məˈleɪə]	Malaya
Maryland [ˈmeərɪlənd]	Maryland
Mexico [ˈmeksɪkəʊ]	Mexiko
Middle East [ˌmɪdl ˈiːst]	Mittlerer Osten
Moscow [ˈmɒskəʊ]	Moskau
Naco [ˈnækəʊ]	Naco
Namibia [nəˈmɪbiə]	Namibia
New Jersey [njuː ˈdʒɜːzi]	New Jersey
New York [ˌnjuː ˈjɔːk]	New York
New York Harbour [ˌnjuː jɔːk ˈhɑːbə]	New York Harbour
New Zealand [ˌnjuː ˈziːlənd]	Neuseeland
Newfoundland [ˈnjuːfndlənd]	Neufundland
Newtok [ˈnjuːtɒk]	Newtok
Nigeria [naɪˈdʒɪəriə]	Nigeria
North America [ˌnɔːθ əˈmerɪkə]	Nordamerika
North Carolina [ˌnɔːθ kærəˈlaɪnə]	North Carolina
Norway [ˈnɔːweɪ]	Norwegen
Oregon [ˈɒrɪgən]	Oregon
Oxford [ˈɒksfəd]	Oxford
Pakistan [ˌpækɪˈstɑːn]	Pakistan
Palestine [ˈpæləstaɪn]	Palästina
Paris [ˈpærɪs]	Paris
Pennsylvania [ˌpenslˈveɪniə]	Pennsylvania
Pomplana [pɒmˈpleɪnə]	Pomplana
Portugal [ˈpɔːtʃʊgl]	Portugal
Reykjavik [ˈreɪkjəvɪk]	Reykjavik
Rhodesia [rəʊˈdiːʃə]	Rhodesien
Riau [riˈau]	Riau
Roanoke [ˈrəʊənəʊk]	Roanoke
Rome [rəʊm]	Rom
Roosevelt Park [ˈrəʊzəvelt pɑːk]	Roosevelt Park
Russia [ˈrʌʃə]	Russland
Salt Lake City [ˌsɔːlt leɪk ˈsɪti]	Salt Lake City
San Francisco [ˌsæn frənˈsɪskəʊ]	San Francisco
Saratoga [ˌsærəˈtəʊgə]	Saratoga
Sarawak [ˈsærəwək]	Sarawak
Sarichef Island [ˈsærɪtʃef aɪlənd]	Sarichef Insel
Shaktoolik [ʃækˈtuːlɪk]	Shaktoolik
Shishmaref [ˈʃɪʃmærəf]	Shishmaref
Slovenia [sləʊˈviːniə]	Slowenien
Sonora [səˈnɔːrə]	Sonora
South Africa [saʊθ ˈæfrɪkə]	Südafrika
South Korea [ˌsaʊθ kəˈrɪə]	Südkorea

South Pole [ˌsaʊθ 'pəʊl]	Südpol
South Saint James Street [ˌsaʊθ snt 'dʒeɪmz striːt]	*Straßenname*
south-east Asia [ˌsaʊθ iːst 'eɪʃə]	Südostasien
Southern California [ˌsʌðən ˌkælə'fɔːniə]	Südkalifornien
Soviet Union [ˌsəʊviət 'juːniən]	Sowjetunion
Spain [speɪn]	Spanien
St. Louis [sən 'luːɪs]	St. Louis
Sub-Saharan Africa [ˌsʌb sə'hɑːrən æfrɪkə]	Subsahara-Afrika
Sumatra [su'mɑːtrə]	Sumatra
Sweden ['swiːdn]	Schweden
Tanganyika [ˌtæŋgən'jiːkə]	Tanganjika
the Americas [ði ə'merɪkəz]	der amerikanische Doppelkontinent
the Balkans [ðə 'bɔːlkənz]	Balkanhalbinsel
the Midwest [ðə mɪd'west]	der Mittlere Westen
the Netherlands [ðə 'neðələndz]	die Niederlande
the Northeast [ðə ˌnɔːθ 'iːst]	der Nordwesten
the Ross Sea [ðə 'rɒs siː]	das Rossmeer
the UK = the United Kingdom [ðə ˌjuː 'keɪ, ðə juˌnaɪtɪd 'kɪŋdəm]	das Vereinigte Königreich
the West Indies [ðə ˌwest 'ɪndiz]	Westindische Inseln
Tiananmen Square [tiˌænən'men skweə]	Platz des himmlischen Friedens
Turkey ['tɜːki]	Türkei
Ukraine [ju'kreɪn]	Ukraine
Unalakleet [ˌʌnə'lækliːt]	Unalakleet
United States (of America)= USA [juˌnaɪtɪd 'steɪts əv ə'merɪkə, ˌjuː es 'eɪ]	Vereinigte Staaten (von Amerika) = USA
Vietnam [ˌviːet'næm]	Vietnam
Washington ['wɒʃɪŋtən]	Washington
Washington, D.C. ['wɒʃɪŋtən, ˌdiː 'siː]	Washington D.C.
Waukegan [wəʊ'kiːgən]	Waukegan
Wembley ['wembli]	Wembley
West Bank [ˌwest 'bæŋk]	Westjordanland
Western Europe [ˌwestən 'jʊərəp]	Westeuropa
Yorktown ['jɔːktaʊn]	Yorktown
Zimbabwe [zɪm'bɑːbwi]	Zimbabwe
Zurich ['zʊərɪk]	Zürich

IRREGULAR VERBS

be – was/were – been	*sein*
beat – beat – beaten	*schlagen, besiegen*
become – became – become	*werden*
begin – began – begun	*anfangen, beginnen*
behold – beheld – beheld	*erblicken, beobachten*
bend – bent – bent	*(sich) beugen*
bind – bound – bound	*binden*
break – broke – broken	*brechen*
build – built – built	*bauen*
burn – burnt – burnt	*(ver)brennen*
buy – bought – bought	*kaufen*
cast – cast – cast	*(seine Stimme) abgeben; werfen*
catch – caught – caught	*fangen, verstehen*
choose – chose – chosen	*(aus)wählen*
come – came – come	*kommen*
cost – cost – cost	*kosten*
creep – crept – crept	*(ein)schleichen*
cut – cut – cut	*schneiden*
do – did – done	*tun, machen*
deal – dealt – dealt	*sich befassen; handeln; austeilen*
draw – drew – drawn	*zeichnen*
dream – dreamt/dreamed – dreamt/dreamed	*träumen*
drink – drank – drunk	*trinken*
drive – drove – driven	*fahren*
dwell – dwelt/dwelled – dwelt/dwelled	*sich den Kopf zerbrechen; wohnen*
eat – ate – eaten	*essen*
fall – fell – fallen	*fallen*
feed – fed – fed	*füttern, ernähren*
feel – felt – felt	*(sich) fühlen, empfinden*
fight – fought – fought	*kämpfen*
find – found – found	*finden*
fit – fit/fitted – fit/fitted	*passen*
fly – flew – flown	*fliegen*
forget – forgot – forgotten	*vergessen*
freeze – froze – frozen	*(ge)frieren*
frolic – frolicked – frolicked	*(herum)tollen, toben*
get – got – got (AE gotten)	*bekommen*
give – gave – given	*geben*
go – went – gone	*gehen, fahren*
grow – grew – grown	*wachsen*
hang – hung – hung	*hängen*
have – had – had	*haben*
hear – heard – heard	*hören*
hide – hid – hidden	*(sich) verstecken*
hit – hit – hit	*schlagen; treffen auf*
hold – held – held	*halten, festhalten*
hurt – hurt – hurt	*verletzen, weh tun*
keep – kept – kept	*behalten*
know – knew – known	*kennen, wissen*
lay – laid – laid	*legen*
lead – led – led	*führen*
learn – learnt/learned – learnt/learned	*lernen*
leave – left – left	*abfahren, verlassen, weggehen*
let – let – let	*lassen*
lie – lay – lain	*liegen*
light – lit – lit	*anzünden, beleuchten*
lose – lost – lost	*verlieren*
make – make – make	*machen*
mean – meant – meant	*meinen, bedeuten*
meet – met – met	*treffen*
offset – offset – offset	*ausgleichen*
pay – paid – paid	*bezahlen*
put – put – put	*setzen, stellen, legen*
quit – quit/quitted – quit/quitted	*verlassen, aufhören*
read – read – read	*lesen*
ride – rode – ridden	*reiten, fahren*
rise – rose – risen	*(an)steigen*
ring – rang – rung	*läuten, klingeln*
run – ran – run	*laufen, rennen*
say – said – said	*sagen*
see – saw – seen	*sehen*
seek –sought – sought	*suchen*
sell – sold – sold	*verkaufen*
send – sent – sent	*senden, schicken*
set – set – set	*setzen, stellen*
shake – shook – shaken	*schütteln*
show – showed – shown	*zeigen*
shrink – shrank – shrunk	*schrumpfen, verdichten; zurückschrecken*
shut – shut – shut	*schließen*
sing – sang – sung	*singen*
sink – sank/sunk – sunk	*sinken*
sit – sat – sat	*sitzen*
sleep – slept – slept	*schlafen*
smell – smelt/smelled – smelt/smelled	*riechen*
speak – spoke – spoken	*sprechen*
spell – spelt/spelled – spelt/spelled	*buchstabieren*
spend – spent – spent	*ausgeben, verbringen*
spin – spun – spun	*sich drehen, herumwirbeln*
stand – stood – stood	*stehen*
steal – stole – stolen	*stehlen*
stride – strode – stridden	*schreiten*
strive – strove/strived – striven/strived	*streben (nach)*
swim – swam – swum	*schwimmen*
take – took – taken	*nehmen*
teach – taught – taught	*unterrichten, beibringen*
tell – told – told	*sagen, erzählen*
think – thought – thought	*denken*
thrive – thrived – thrived	*florieren*
throw – threw – thrown	*werfen*
thrust – thrust – thrust	*stoßen*
understand – understood – understood	*verstehen*
wake – woke/waked – woken/waked	*aufwachen, wecken*
wear – wore – worn	*tragen*
win – won – won	*gewinnen*
withhold – withheld – withheld	*verweigern, vorenthalten*
write – wrote – written	*schreiben*

QUELLENVERZEICHNIS

RF-Fotos:

Alamy: S. 66/3 J.R. Bale, S. 67 Toby Burrows, S. 78 Radius Images, S. 80/1, S. 113/1 bananastock, S. 176 Tetra Images. **Corbis:** S. 13 Bloomimage/Corbis. **Shutterstock:** S. 8/1/2, S. 9, S. 11, S. 16/2, S. 18/1/2/3, S. 23/2/3/5, S. 25, S. 26/1/2, S. 29, S. 30/3, S. 31, S. 38/1/2/3, S. 43/2, S. 56/1, S. 57, S. 66/1/2/5, S. 68, S. 69, S. 72, S. 73/1/2/3, S. 74, S. 76/2, S. 81/2, S. 94/1/2/3/4/5/6/7, S. 98/1, S. 101/2, S. 112/1/2/3, S. 113/2/3/4, S. 116, S. 119, S. 126/1/2/3/4/5, S. 129/2/3/4/5, S. 140, S. 146, S. 149, S. 152/1/3, S. 156/1, S. 157/4/5, S. 158/1, S. 161/1/2, S. 164/2, S. 178

RM-Fotos:

Alamy: S. 12 Jim West, S. 16/1 Richard Levine, S. 23/1 Robin Beckham, S. 27 Bilderbox, S. 30/1 Jeff Morgan Hay on Wye/2 Pictorial Press, S. 43/3 Bryan and Cherry Alexander, S. 46/2, S. 53/1/2 Julia Guest 3/ Sylvia Cordaiy Photo Library Ltd, S. 66/6 Ann Eriksson, S. 70/3 Echoes Archives/Redferns Agency, S. 80/1 Vanessa Miles/2 Nick Cobbing/3 McPHOTO/ KPA, S. 81/1 Sunpix Environment, S. 83/1 Stan Kujawa/2 Blaine Harrington III, S. 98/2 Marc Cator, S. 101/1 Richard Smith, S. 112/4 Photos 12/5 Paul Prescott/6 Krystyna Szulecka Photography, S. 133 Lebrecht, S. 142/1 Molly Cooper/2 Gianni Muratore, S. 143/1 David Cole, S. 152/2 Ted Foxx, S. 156/2 North Wind Picture Archives, S. 158/2 R. Krubner, S.164/3 Ted Pink/5 Dennis Brack, S. 167/1 Pictorial Press. **The Advertising Archives:** S. 23. **Corbis:** S. 23/4 Benelux, S. 32 Helen King, S. 56/2 Stephen Hird, S. 70/4 Reuters, S. 76/1 Reuters/3 Peter Turnley, S. 84 Douglas Kirkland, S. 99 Ashley Cooper, S. 102/1 Corbis/2 Bettman/3 Bettman/5 Jack Moebus /6 Bob Adelmann/7 Bettman, S. 120 Sion Touhig, S. 126/6 Arko Datta, Reuters, S. 135 Hulton-Deutsch Collection, S. 136/1/2 Hulton-Deutsch Collection, S. 152/4 Jacques Langevin, S. 155/1 Bettman/2 Bettman/5 Corbis, S. 156/3 PoodlesRock /4 Bettman/5 Bettman/6 Henri Bureau Sygma, S. 157/1 Bettmann/3 Cinema/Photo, S. 168 Corbis/Reuters, S. 172/1 Steve Raymer/2 Bob Sacha. **Fotofinder:** S. 19/1 Keystone/J. Zick, 3 Visum/A. Buellesbach, 4 U. Kraft Fotografie, S. 108 Jochen Tack Fotografie, S. 109 Jochen Tack Fotografie. **Getty:** S. 43/1 Brian Summers, S. 46/1 Michael Ochs Archives, S. 70/1/2 Topical Press Agency Kollektion, S. 155/4 Hulton Archive/6 Neil A. Armstrong, S. 157/2 Hulton Archive, S. 167/1 Pool/2 Peter Muhl, S. 167/2 Keystone. **PictureAlliance:** S. 19/2 B. Weißbrod, S. 49 R. Hessing, S. 66/4 epa TSA HO, S. 71 Chu_Amiens ASA-PICTURES, S. 167/3 Landov Xinhua. **Ullstein-Bild:** S. 54/1/2 Röhrbein, S. 55 Röhrbein, S. 102/4 Polizeifoto, S. 129/1 Ullstein Bild, S. 143/2 Roger-Viollet, S. 155/3 Granger Collection

Cartoons: S. 15/1 John Deering, Creators' Syndicate, S. 21 Mark Pett, S. 24 Matt Wuerker, S. 52 Andy Singer, S. 82 Chris Madden, S. 141 Telegraph Media Group Ltd, S. 144 Alan Irvine, S. 163 Jeff Parker

Texte:

S. 8/9: http://www.helium.com/items/683499-shopping-trips-should-confused und http://www.helium.com/items/664332-myself-shopaholic-shoppingfailed-problem; S. 12/13: http://www.verdant.net/families.htm; S. 15/16: http://www.independent.co.uk/news/world/americas/rising-petrol-prices-could-force-obese-americans-to-hit-the-street-402197.html; S. 19/20: © 2005 Jo Robinson, Eatwild.com; S. 23/24: http://www.elements.nb.ca/Theme/globalization/emily/emily.htm; S. 26/27: http://www.nytimes.com/2006/03/02/business/02work.html; S. 30: *The New Yorker*, November 12, 1955; S. 32/33: http://www.bbc.co.uk/lincolnshire/student_life/work_experience.shtml; S. 38/39: Al Gore, *An Inconvenient Truth*, Rodale 2006; S. 46: *Too Many Songs by Tom Lehrer*, Pantheon Books, 1981; S. 48/49: *New Scientist*, 1 December 2007; S. 54/55: *The New Yorker*, November 5, 2007; S. 57/58: http://www.livescience.com/environment/top10 emergingenvironment_technologies.html; S. 70/71: *Cosmetic Surgery Times*, 1 June 2006; S. 73/74: http://www.nrlc.org/news_and_Views/January07/nv010407part1.html; S. 76/77: *USA Today*, April 24 2007;S. 80/81: ©2005 American Institute of Biological Sciences; S. 84: *Bradbury Stories*, Perennial, 2005; S. 94/95: *Watching the English*, Hodder & Stoughton, 2005; S. 98/99: *The Guardian*, 19 June 2002; S. 104/105: *A Raisin in the Sun*, Vintage, 1994; S. 108/109: *National Geographic*, May 2007; S. 113/114: *Newsweek Special Edition*, December 2007–February 2008; S. 118: *New Scientist*, 23 June 2007; S. 126/127: http://www.britishempire.co.uk/article/gapyear.htm; S. 129: *The Observer*, October 21, 2007; S. 130: *The Guardian*, October 20, 2007; S. 135–137: *Small Island*, Review, 2004; S. 139/140: http://news.bbc.co.uk/go/pr/fr/-/2/hi/uk_news/6988521.stm; S. 143: http://www.openeurope.org.uk/media-centre/article.aspx?newsid=988; S. 152/153: *USA Today*, November 2002; S. 157/158: http://www.schwarzenegger.com; S. 161/162: *Newsweek*, 27 September 2001; S. 164/165: http://www.whitehouse.gov/news/releases/2001/09/20010920-8.html; S. 168/169: *The Guardian*, Tuesday, April 20, 2004; S. 172/173: *Newsweek Special Edition*, December 2007–February 2008

Wir bedanken uns herzlich bei den folgenden Unternehmen für die freundliche Unterstützung:

headline publishing group, Random House Group, Westbasin Municipal Water District, PennWell, Siemens and the City of Anaheim, Schwartz Center for the Performing Arts

EUROPEAN UNION